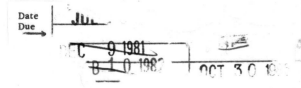

Creative
Salesmanship

Creative Salesmanship

Understanding Essentials

Second Edition

Kenneth B. Haas
Formerly Professor of Marketing
Hofstra University

John W. Ernest
Professor of Business Administration
Los Angeles City College

GLENCOE PRESS
A division of Benziger Bruce & Glencoe, Inc.
Beverly Hills

Collier Macmillan Publishers
London

Glencoe Press
A division of Benziger Bruce & Glencoe, Inc.
8701 Wilshire Boulevard
Beverly Hills, California 90211
Collier-Macmillan Canada, Ltd.

Library of Congress catalog card number: 73-7357

4 5 6 7 8 9 ACB 80 79 78 77 76

CONTENTS

PREFACE

Creative Salesmanship recognizes that today's salesman faces a skeptical, well-educated, and sophisticated buyer, and that the professional salesman must be far more than a mere purveyor of goods and services. To keep pace with scientific advances in industrial production and the marketing concept of distribution, a new kind of salesman is needed.

Many businesses desire sales representatives who have educational backgrounds in specialized fields, such as engineering, chemistry, physics, nuclear energy, or aeronautics. Nearly all businesses have a growing need for salespeople whose major studies have been in economics of distribution, social psychology, management, and creative thinking, with a well-rounded background in personal communication. It has been found that this kind of educational history best enables young people to move to positions of more responsibility. Surveys have shown that one out of three U.S. corporations is now headed by individuals whose backgrounds were in marketing and sales.

While *Creative Salesmanship* emphasizes the great changes that continue to take place in personal salesmanship, it does not entirely abandon those concepts and techniques of personal selling which have proven to be so effective in the past. An honest smile, good grooming, and a congenial attitude will always be assets for the salesman. In addition, today's salesman is expected to have more patience, more persistence, more energy, and more social awareness than ever before.

This textbook is divided into four parts depicting the important aspects of salesmanship. Part One, "Nature of Selling," defines salesmanship and the role of the salesman as a problem-solver.

Part Two, "Getting Ready to Sell," deals with the preparations a salesman must make in order to be more effective when before his clientele.

Part Three, "Basic Sales Techniques," brings the student face to face with the skills and methods used by professional salesmen. This is the heart of the course, and may be used along with role-playing situations and practice sales presentations.

Part Four, "Special Sales Situations," attempts to develop the many extraordinary facets of the salesman's job. Many new chapters have been added in this section, such as "Creative Industrial Selling," "Selling at Conventions and Trade Shows," "Introduction to Sales Management," and "Selling Your Personal Services." The latter may be considered the most important part of the sales course, because here the student is concerned with applying the principles of the course to obtaining a job and a career in the sales field.

Only the best of the end-of-chapter discussion materials from the first edition have been retained for this new edition. Many new projects, cases, and problems have been added, providing practical and interesting assignments for the salesmanship course.

The authors wish to express their thanks and appreciation to the many hundreds of companies that cooperated in furnishing material and providing interviews for this book. We would like to list all of them here but space limitations will not permit it.

Kenneth B. Haas
John W. Ernest

Creative
Salesmanship

PART

NATURE
OF
SELLING

CHAPTER 1

Nature and Significance of Salesmanship

Discuss salesmanship with someone who has had only casual contact with selling and marketing, and you will more than likely find him fairly critical of the field. A great many people have an inaccurate, stereotyped picture of the salesman because of the myths and legends connected with his occupation. For example, from the earliest days of the American nation, the figure of the snake oil salesman has been a colorful one. In a typical representation, Old Doctor Miracle rides into town on his garishly painted wagon with Chief Wild Coyote and his beautiful daughter, Minnetonka, at his side. The good Doctor mounts a platform and extols the wonders of his mysterious remedy. The gullible yokels gather round and plunk down their hard-earned dollars or gold dust for a dollop of the nostrum. Later, the Doctor whips his wagon out of town, and, at some dusty prairie crossroads, the three split the proceeds.

Colorful? Definitely. True? Well—

What happened to this picaresque, fast-talking salesman? According to *Fortune*, he has been "replaced by a new kind of salesman. He doesn't sell the product; he sells service and benefits. He knows the customer's business almost as well as his own. He is troubleshooter, marketing expert, problem-solver all in one." No doubt there were Doc Miracles, as, no doubt, there have been farmers' daughters; but the respectable profession of selling is something altogether different.

The modern salesman deals with a more sophisticated buyer, one who does not sign the order merely because he likes the salesman. The buyer's chief concern is: What's in it for me? For example, if you are selling furniture to Mrs. Smith, a housewife, her chief concern may be to satisfy her desire to enhance the attractiveness of her home. If you are dealing with a retailer, his chief concern is whether there will be a satisfactory profit in the transaction. The art of salesmanship has advanced far beyond the order-taking or back-slapping technique. Today's salesman must create wants and needs that never existed before. This type of selling requires imagination in developing new ideas and in persuading people to do things they have not contemplated. It creates desires in people that can be satisfied only by possession of the product or service. Our economy can prosper only when demand is created for both established and new lines of products that provide a higher standard of living to all Americans.

THE CREATIVE SALESMAN'S MANY ROLES

When the word "salesman" is mentioned, most people think of a retail store salesman whom they have patronized, or a door-to-door salesman from whom they recently purchased an article. However, few people have had the opportunity to see a professional salesman at work, for professional selling is carried on where it is observed and appreciated not by the general public but by wholesale and industrial buyers, retail buyers, plant superintendents and engineers, office managers, and purchasing agents. Professional salesmen are known by many names — company representatives, promotion men, account executives, and sales representatives. They may work inside a store or warehouse, or do considerable traveling to cover a territory. They may be known simply as order takers, or they may be called idea men, problem-solvers, business consultants or merchandise advisors. Obviously, today's salesman could be some or all of these things. Let's look at some of the fundamental roles played by the modern salesman.

The Salesman as a Communicator

Webster's New World dictionary defines communication as the process of "giving and receiving information, signals, or messages by talk, gestures, writing. . . ." Thus we see that communicating is a two-way street, involving not only the giving of information but also the receiving of information. The sales presentation is a process of communicating with the prospect or customer. The salesman must be an expert at composing and explaining the proposition to his prospect. He cannot afford to assume that his proposition (message) will be received effectively, so he must know how to evaluate how effectively his proposition (or message) has been received and understood. He does this through careful listening and skillful questioning.

Professional salesmen know that a sales presentation is not a monologue in which the salesman does all the talking. Rather, they consider the sales presentation as a friendly conversation between two people: one who has a problem, need, or want; the other who has the answer to that problem. A successful salesman once gave this advice to another salesman who asked the secret of his success: "When I sit down with a prospect I just let him talk, and very quickly he tells me how he wants to be sold."

The Salesman as a Problem-solver

Many people have come to regard the salesman as a high-pressure persuader whose sole aim is to manipulate the buyer to get him to buy something he does not want or need. This characterization describes only a few of the people engaged in sales work. It certainly is not typical of the modern professional salesman who considers himself an expert not only concerning his own products but also concerning the products of his competition. He realizes that the buyer has a problem which he wants to solve, and that it is his job to help the buyer solve his problem. In order to do this, the salesman has to realize the buyer's point of view and see things through the buyer's eyes. This understanding is known as *empathy* and, practically speaking, it means helping the buyer buy.

The salesman as a problem-solver recognizes that the buyer must make five decisions before the problem can be solved. These concern:

1. The need to be fulfilled.
2. The product to fulfill the need.
3. The source for the product.
4. The price to pay.
5. The time to buy.

Everything is dependent upon the first decision — the need. A *need* is defined as a lack of something, a feeling or state of inadequacy, a dissatisfaction with things as they are, or a desire to have something more or better.

In order to buy, the prospect must be aware of and acknowledge his need; otherwise, the sale will not proceed satisfactorily because there will be resistance throughout the sale on the part of the buyer. The creative salesman helps the buyer express his need. He tries to get the buyer to realize that he has a problem based upon this particular need, and that the product can fulfill that need. In some cases the buyer may not be aware of his need, which means that he may not realize he has a problem. The salesman must help him first to identify his need, then to establish the general problem, and finally to show how he has the product to help fulfill the need.

PROSPECT: I don't need any more insurance.

SALESMAN: Mr. Prospect, if your income was suddenly cut off tomorrow, would your present insurance supply your family with enough income to take care of their needs, say, at least five years into the future? Would it pay for your children's education through college? Could your wife and children continue to live in this lovely home?

PROSPECT: Well, I don't know. I thought I had enough insurance. What additional coverage should I have to provide my family with what they would need?

Often a buyer is aware of his problem but doesn't know how to go about solving it. A creative salesman simply rolls up his shirtsleeves and goes over the problem with the buyer, even though it has little to do with selling his product. For example, consider the case of the small grocery store owner who is complaining to a salesman.

GROCER: I don't understand it. I honestly think I have been buying right and pricing right in all of my departments, but I come out each month with an overall loss.

SALESMAN: Do you have a record-keeping system that tells you what costs and expenses there are in each department — grocery, delicatessen, and produce?

GROCER: No, I don't, and that's where the trouble lies. I just don't know how to devise one, and I don't feel I can afford a bookkeeper to do my accounts.

SALESMAN: I have a set of books in the car that I put together for a customer across town. Let me go out and get them. I bet we can devise a good system for your operation.

The last three buying decisions also involve problems which require the salesman's help. The buyer should choose the salesman's company as the source for the product if the salesman has done a thorough job establishing the need and explaining how his product can fill that need. In addition, the salesman must delineate any special services that his company provides, and make it clear that his company can provide these things more effectively than their competitors.

The two remaining decisions for the buyer are whether he can afford the product and whether it is the right time to buy. The insurance prospect in the previous example may be concerned about other financial commitments or priorities which demand his attention. Because the buyer has many needs and because many claims are made upon his funds, it is only natural that he should hesitate. Initially, the buyer exhibited high resistance when he stated that, as far as he was concerned, he didn't need any more insurance. However, the door was opened when he granted the salesman an interview, discussed and acknowledged a problem, and asked what should be done about it. The buyer is hesitant in most situations because he wants to be sure he is doing the right thing at the right time. The problem-solving salesman is well aware of the prospect's doubts and fears, and he feels that he is there to help the buyer overcome them. So, with tactful guidance and logical and emotional appeals he moves the buyer into making a decision. This problem-solving attitude truly identifies the creative salesman.

The Salesman as an Educator

Professional salesmen have learned the value of patience in the sales interview. They realize that, again and again, they must be ready to explain, to stress, to show the many new and complicated aspects of their sales proposition. Moreover, they have learned that this must be done skillfully, often step by step, making use of all of the modern audiovisual aids and other devices that can be brought into play. Like a skillful teacher who knows in advance the areas of difficulty and prepares for them, the creative salesman marshals all of the forces at his command to help him make things clear to his prospect. As an educator, he never takes for granted that the prospect understands everything, and he constantly evaluates how his presentation is going. He is always willing to retrace his steps and start over or to bring in some new method or technique to explain a misunderstood point.

The Salesman as a Human Relations Expert

The salesman is constantly involved with human behavior. He must always be aware of how his own personality is "meshing" with those of the people he meets, and he must understand the role personalities play in the process of making a buying decision. Consequently, the more a salesman knows and understands about customer psychology and buying behavior, the better his chance of developing his selling skills.

The salesman must have not only a genuine liking for dealing with and being with people, but he must also think, talk, and act in the prospect's interests. He must unselfishly attempt to render service for his customers if he wishes to build a clientele. He must constantly bear in mind that customers often remember the salesman and the way he treated them long after they have forgotten the product or service sold to them.

THE IMPORTANCE OF PRACTICE

The ability of the salesman to handle his varied roles is an art, and he must practice rigorously in order to perfect his skills. This is why it is important for the student to get up in front of his salesmanship class as much as possible and try his hand at short sales presentations. Also, part-time selling jobs will prove helpful in developing selling skills. Retail selling jobs are preferable since they are easy to obtain and are not as discouraging as specialty and house-to-house selling positions. Later, as the young salesman graduates to full-fledged professional sales jobs, he should constantly strive to make personal contact with prospects and customers in order to sharpen his selling skills. The champion swimmer spends long hours in the pool attempting to build his strength and perfect his skills, never completely satisfied with his performance, always striving for a better mark; the same is true with the superior salesman. Practice and determination are absolutely essential.

METHODS AND THE LAW OF AVERAGES

It should be stressed that there is no one "best way" to practice the art of salesmanship. Some successful salesmen exhibit a self-confident, aggressive, and flamboyant manner in presenting the sales proposition and closing the sale. Others sell with a quiet dignity, a seemingly humble attitude. Some use the *hard sell,* a method of constantly urging, pressing, and suggesting action to buy; while others use, with equal success, the *soft sell,* a method of holding back, letting the prospect do most of the talking and acting, but always showing a desire to be of service. High-pressure salesmanship is not the same as hard sell. High-pressure methods are often deceitful and devious. The product is misrepresented and the prospect misled. Some prefer showmanship, that is, highly dramatizing the proposition and all of its features and benefits, and attempting to make the performance so realistic that the prospect actually experiences the feeling of owning the product or service himself. Other salesmen achieve success through a logical, well-planned format, avoiding anything that smacks of the theatrical while using every interest-creating device they can to bring the sale to a successful close. The use of a particular approach or method of selling will depend upon the salesman's personality. It is up to the student to analyze himself, to come to an understanding of himself, and to adopt the type of selling with which he can best work. However, in the process of selecting his own technique he should also study those of successful salesmen in his own company and in the industry.

Regardless of how skillful or creative he is in the methods he chooses in his relationships with prospects and customers, the professional salesman realizes that he is not going to close all of the sales. He may not even close half of them. In some fields of selling—house-to-house, for example — a ten-to-one average is considered excellent. This means that the salesman should attempt to determine the average number of sales he makes per day or per number of calls, and then resolve to call on as great a number of people as he can in the time period allotted for a week. The more people he sees the greater are his chances for making sales. The law of averages is working for him. As one successful industrial salesman put it, "Every hour of my working day I will either be in front of a prospect or on the way to see one."

SALESMANSHIP DEFINED

"A sale," according to one dictionary, "is the transfer of title in goods, property, or a service from one person to another for a consideration."

A *salesperson* is the individual who brings about the transfer. This individual is also known as a company representative, sales engineer, account executive, commercial traveler, promotion man, contact man, missionary, detailer, commission man, rack man, broker, and by many other designations. Depending on the situation and the function performed, all of the names apply to selling.

A salesperson has also been defined as an individual so adept at understanding and handling people that he is able to persuade them to buy what he has to offer at a profit to himself, to his company, and to the buyer.

The salesman is the ambassador of goodwill for his company. In this capacity, he has been described as the custodian of the firm's customers.

Salesmanship is the ability to interpret product and service features in terms of benefits and advantages to the buyer and to persuade and motivate him to buy the right kind and quality of product or service.

Consider the case example that follows: try to apply our definition of salesmanship as you read through it.

A customer enters the housewares department of a large department store and walks up to the nearest salesperson.

SALESPERSON: Good morning. May I help you?

CUSTOMER: Yes, I'm looking for something in outdoor barbecue equipment. Something to heat the coals.

SALESPERSON: Yes, ma'am, you mean an automatic charcoal heat starter. Here they are, right on this table. We have several kinds. (Salesperson stands by while customer makes a selection.)

CUSTOMER: Oh dear. I guess it doesn't make much difference which one I take. Barbecuing outdoors is such an ordeal. I wish I could get my husband and children to accept more of my regular recipes.

SALESPERSON: It doesn't make any difference which one you take. All charcoal lighters work the same way.

CUSTOMER: OK. I'll take this one. (Hands the salesperson a charcoal lighter and a five-dollar bill.)

SALESPERSON: That will be $3.15 out of five. I'll have your change for you in just a minute.

In this case, would you say that a sale was made? Yes, a sale was certainly made. There was a transfer of title in the goods from one person (the store) to another person (the buyer) for a consideration. Can one say that salesmanship was used by the salesperson? It would seem doubtful when the definition for salesmanship is applied. No attempt was made by the salesman to interpret the product features in terms of benefits or to persuade or motivate the customer to buy. In fact, the customer appeared to be "presold" when she entered the store. If any persuading or motivating took place, it originated with the customer herself, not with the salesman.

Incidents such as the above occur every day in retail stores. Similar situations can be found in the industrial and wholesale fields. In such cases the salesperson is merely an order-taker. He is doing nothing that an advertisement or a display could not accomplish. In order to qualify as a professional salesman applying the principles of creative salesmanship, the salesman must:

1. Determine the needs or wants of the customer.
2. Present the product features to the customer in terms of benefits.
3. Help the customer find the solution to his or her problem.
4. Persuade or motivate the customer to take action.

A professional salesman would have handled this transaction differently. Suppose the customer has chosen the charcoal lighter she wants and is handing a five-dollar bill to the salesperson:

SALESPERSON: I was interested in your mentioning that outdoor barbecuing is an ordeal for you. Would you mind telling me why?

CUSTOMER: Well, you see, we don't have a large patio, so we barbecue our steaks, chicken, and hamburgers outside and then bring them in to the dining room. It's a lot of work. And then I have to clean the messy grill afterward.

SALESPERSON: Those barbecue grills are rather hard to clean, aren't they?

CUSTOMER: Yes, I have to clean it in the laundry sink in the garage.

SALESPERSON: I suppose your husband and children like that barbecue flavor you get by using a grill?

CUSTOMER: Yes, that is the problem.

SALESPERSON: Let me show you something that might solve that problem for you. (Takes customer over to an appliance display.) Here is Farberware's open-hearth broiler that gives you an outdoor barbecue system right inside, on your kitchen drain board or dining room table.

CUSTOMER: But won't it spatter and make the air greasy and smelly?

SALESPERSON: Not a bit. There is no smoke, no spatter, no steam with the Farberware open-hearth broiler. We can promise you that, because this stainless steel chassis is designed so that you get a perfect draft just as in a well-built fireplace.

CUSTOMER: It seems like a good idea. But I just can't believe there won't be any grease or odors inside the house.

SALESPERSON: That's exactly why you don't get grease or odors. The top of the broiler is made out of thin air. No walls, door, or roof. The air can circulate freely as well as quickly. So the air you cook in doesn't have time to get greasy or smelly.

CUSTOMER: But what about steam or smoke?

SALESPERSON: Since the air isn't boxed in, it can't get steamy. Food fats drip down through the heating element, past a zone of cool clean air, into the drip pan where they can't spatter, flame up, or smoke. And the beauty of it is, all the natural meat juices stay in.

CUSTOMER: It certainly sounds like the answer to my problem. But I imagine it's just as hard to keep clean as outdoor equipment.

SALESPERSON: That's the nicest part of it. It's very easy to clean. Everything comes apart into four pieces, like this. (Demonstrates by disassembling each part and laying the parts out in front of the customer.)

Did you notice how easy that was? Now all you do is just put the parts into sudsy water and you wash them clean in minutes. And you don't have to wash the heating element. It's self-cleaning.

CUSTOMER: How much is it?

SALESPERSON: You can have the large size with the rotisserie for $49.00. I would suggest the large size with the rotisserie. It's very light, so you could take it with you right now.

CUSTOMER: I'll take the large size.

Would you say that this salesperson practiced the art of salesmanship? She certainly did. And that's what salesmanship really is—an art, not a science. Every customer must be handled as an individual. Every customer feels that his or her problem is a special one. Consequently, the salesman must learn to treat each customer as if he or she is a very special person. The process of determining wants and needs of customers requires techniques that can be learned only through understanding and constant practice. Did you notice how the professional salesperson picked up the remark about outdoor barbecuing being an ordeal? The salesperson recognized this remark as the root of a problem and, with a question, got the customer to talk about her problem. After pinpointing the problem, the salesperson provided the answer and completed the sale.

The salesperson here used an intuitive approach to selling. This approach views the sales process as a series of separate and distinct situations in which the salesman is working with and trying to understand people and why they behave as they do. Another name for this point of view is *phenomenological*. It is the approach to be presented throughout this book.

POWER POINTS

The old-time salesman, portrayed in the myths and legends of the late 1800s and early 1900s, has all but disappeared today. In his place has appeared the creative salesman. This man assumes many roles, all necessary in our market-oriented business economy. First of all, he is a master of the art of communication. He realizes that a sale is not a one-way street where the salesman does all of the talking and the buyer all of the listening. Rather, it involves a conversation between two or more persons in which the salesman discusses, explains, illustrates, and listens. In fact, listening may occupy a greater part of the presentation in many cases.

The salesman is also a problem-solver. He feels a deep obligation to the buyer who comes to him as a person who has a problem. The salesman is the expert who has the resources at his disposal to solve that problem, much as a physician has the knowledge and the ability to analyze and diagnose the client's medical problem.

The salesman is also an educator who uses all of the methods and techniques of a skilled instructor to help his prospect understand the many facets of the sales proposition and how it can solve his problems.

The salesman is also mindful of his role in dealing with people. He is a human relations expert constantly endeavoring to learn more about the psychology of handling people and applying this knowledge to his daily work.

In handling his varied roles, the professional salesman is an artist who perfects his art by practice.

By examining the widely differing methods used by successful salesmen, the student will be helped in choosing an approach suitable to his own personality.

DISCUSSION QUESTIONS AND PROBLEMS

---

1. What has happened to the old-fashioned salesman?

2. How has salesmanship and selling changed in America in the last century?

3. How does the salesman fill the role of a communicator?

4. "Personal selling is the area of greatest learning and experience for executives on the way to the top." Is this statement true? Explain your answer.

5. How does the salesman fill the role of a problem-solver? Discuss several examples.

6. How does the salesman fill the role of an educator?

7. Define *salesmanship*.

8. What is *high-pressure* salesmanship? How can a salesman be aggressive without using high-pressure tactics?

9. Explain how the following individuals use salesmanship in their everyday contact with people:

a. Physician

b. Carpenter

c. Teacher

d. Lawyer

e. Store manager

f. Army captain

10. In this chapter it was stated that the salesman must be a human relations expert. Discuss at least ten ways in which the salesman can practice this art.

SELLING PROBLEMS AND PROJECTS

1. Jim Green Case

Liza's Music Company features the Fender line of guitars and amplifiers. A customer is looking at the Jazzmaster, the finest electric guitar that Fender makes. Salesman approaches the customer whom he recognizes as Jim Green, lead guitarist for a popular recording group called the Groovy Sounds.

SALESMAN: Good afternoon, sir. You're Jim Green of the Groovy Sounds, aren't you?

CUSTOMER: Why yes, I am!

SALESMAN: Well, I must tell you that I have admired your guitar work for some time! I have all your recordings.

CUSTOMER: Really! I'm glad to hear that!

SALESMAN: I have been anxiously awaiting your next release. It's been so long since your last album.

CUSTOMER: Yes, I know it has been a long time. We've been in the studio for months. I can't seem to get a clean sound from my guitar. The engineer says that my guitar sounds "fuzzy."

SALESMAN: If that is the case, it could very well be your pickups.

CUSTOMER: Oh, come on, now! Pickups are pickups!

SALESMAN: On most guitars, this is true. However, Fender has designed pickups to suit the individual requirements for every kind of guitarist. Now, let's take the guitar you were looking at just a moment ago. This is Fender's finest sounding electric. It's called the Jazzmaster. This guitar has the finest electrical pickups available on any guitar at any price. It is possible to turn an amplifier to its highest possible volume, without obtaining a single buzz of distortion.

CUSTOMER: Oh, sure! And I was born yesterday, too! You're joking! (Customer laughs in disbelief.)

SALESMAN: Not at all. In fact, if you will step over here to our sound room, I will show you that what I say, hard as it may be to believe, is all very true.

CUSTOMER: Well, all right. Show me. (Salesman directs customer to the sound room which is located in the rear of the store. In this room there are many kinds of amplifiers and guitar accessories.)

SALESMAN: You will notice that there are many kinds of amplifiers in this room. Some expensive, and some not so expensive. As you know, Mr. Green, generally speaking, the more expensive are usually better sounding because they have more expensive and better quality components than are found in the cheaper models. Therefore, to further demonstrate the superior quality of my product, I will plug this guitar cord into this Vibro-verb, an amplifier which costs around $275.

CUSTOMER: That's fine with me.

SALESMAN: I will now turn this amp to its highest possible volume. The guitar, as you can see, is flat out.

CUSTOMER: Yes, I see.

SALESMAN: (The salesman is quite a good guitarist, but not in the same class with Mr. Green. Yet even with the guitar flat out and the amp on its highest volume, he sounds remarkably clear and very precise. The customer is impressed by the salesman's playing ability, and regards it as equal or even superior to his own.) As you can see, there is not a single buzz of distortion. Here, see for yourself.

CUSTOMER: (Green plays the guitar and is utterly amazed at the improvement of technique he is able to attain on this model.) This guitar is fast as lightning.

SALESMAN: Well, let's not give all the credit to the guitar itself. I'd say the musician has a lot to do with it, too. And I must say that you are a very talented musician. You will notice, however, that the neck on this guitar is exceptionally slim. This promotes easier playing.

CUSTOMER: Yes, I see. And there is not the slightest bit of distortion when I play.

SALESMAN: Now you see what a difference pickups can make. Notice, too, the vibrato bar located at the . . .

CUSTOMER: Aw, don't give me that baloney about vibrato bars and what they can do. The fact is that they all detune the strings if you use them more than once during a song.

SALESMAN: You've heard of Arte Butkins, of course.

CUSTOMER: Uh-huh . . .

SALESMAN: With all the punishment he gives his vibrato bar, you'd expect his guitar to be constantly out of tune — correct?

CUSTOMER: Absolutely!

SALESMAN: Well, he uses this very same guitar. The reason why it does not go out of tune is because the Jazzmaster has a special floating bridge, a feature which is found only on the Jazzmaster. See for yourself. (Salesman hands the instrument to the customer.)

CUSTOMER: (Green pulls and pulls on the bar creating wild tremulate notes. Yet, no matter how hard he tries, he cannot detune the guitar.) This guitar won't detune. You're right again. Here, take — ooops. (Green drops the guitar on the hard floor and is embarrassed, thinking he has surely ruined the guitar.) Oh, I'm terribly sorry! I didn't mean to drop it.

SALESMAN: No need for apologies, Mr. Green. If you will pick up the guitar, you will see that there is not a single dent or scratch on the instrument. This is due to the fact that Fender guitars are made of tough maple, specially coated with Fender's exclusive hard-gloss paint. It resists chipping and scratches.

CUSTOMER: Whew! I thought I blew it there for a second. What are all these little dials and switches for? Decorations?

SALESMAN: With these various dials it is possible to create dozens of exciting tones. It provides the guitarist with greater versatility, because he can achieve a greater variety of sounds.

CUSTOMER: (Customer experiments and finds that there are a lot of tones to be found on the instrument.) Just how many sounds are possible on this guitar?

SALESMAN: I don't believe anyone has found them all yet. But I am sure that you will probably be able to find more than most have. With your ability and this guitar there is no telling just how far you may go.

CUSTOMER: I see. (Green nods, indicating approval.)

SALESMAN: When you take this guitar back to the studio with you, I'm sure you'll get that long-awaited album finished much faster than with your other instrument.

CUSTOMER: I'm sure you're right!

SALESMAN: Shall we step over to my desk and make the necessary arrangements?

CUSTOMER: All right.

SALESMAN: I'm sure that you will be happy with your purchase.

Questions:

1. Review carefully this sales presentation, underlining those statements or phrases which, in your judgment, constitute good selling procedure. Be prepared to defend your choices in a class discussion.

2. In your opinion, did the salesman determine the customer's wants or needs?

3. When did the salesman attempt to motivate the customer? Was he successful? Explain.

2.   Coffee Table Case

A customer enters the furniture department of a large department store with a newspaper in her hand and walks directly to the nearest salesman.

SALESMAN: Good morning. May I help you?

CUSTOMER: I would like to see these coffee tables for $19.95, which you advertised in the morning paper. (Shows the salesman the ad.)

SALESMAN: Yes, ma'am, they are right over here. (Leads customer over to a display where he stands nearby while she examines the tables. Finally, she picks one out.)

CUSTOMER: I'll take this one.

SALESMAN: Yes, ma'am. Will that be charge or cash?

Questions

1. How would you rate this salesman: (a) above average, (b) average, or (c) poor? State the reasons for your evaluation.

2. Since there is always room for improvement, rewrite this sales situation as you think it should have been conducted. Before beginning, refer back to the section in this chapter dealing with the definition of salesmanship.

CHAPTER 2

The Role of Selling in
Our Market-oriented Economy

Although the salesman is his company in the eyes of his customers and is responsible for creating and making sales, he does not work alone. His function is very important, but he is only a member of a vast and complex marketing group whose job is to see that goods are distributed from the point where they are produced to the place where they are to be used. The modern salesman must have an appreciation of all of the other employees and corporate functions that make it possible for him to perform effectively. The products and services he sells are planned and engineered to provide customer satisfaction. His company's management has expended a great deal of time and effort developing and marketing these products. A great deal of thought was given to how to deliver the product to the final customer. These channels of distribution were carefully selected. Wholesalers and retailers have to be familiarized with the nature and uses of the product and trained in the techniques of promoting and selling it. The salesman who has an understanding and appreciation of this vast marketing world, with its complicated marketing functions and institutions, will be more likely to achieve success in his career field.

MARKETING DEFINED

A great abundance of natural resources and practical application of advanced technology have enabled American industry to produce an excess of wealth. At the present time the American economy is producing goods and services valued at over one trillion dollars a year. This figure is known as the *gross national product,* or *GNP.*

The strength of the American economy is based upon the ability of industries to sell the goods and services they produce, and this aspect of the economy is known as *marketing. Marketing is the activity through which goods and services are made available to consumers.* Marketing means, simply, providing people with what they want and need at the best possible price and at a profit to both seller and buyer. Today, this function has taken on such increased importance that we refer to the American business structure as a *market-oriented* economy.

THE MARKETING CONCEPT

Intelligent and diligent efforts are required to maintain the kind of economic freedom upon which our economic well-being is based. It requires marketing, and all successful business organizations today stress marketing. This was not true a few years ago, and the rapid transition to the marketing concept has affected all of us in many ways.

In the past a manufacturer might have said, "This is what we make, now hit the road and sell it." Now he says, "What does our prospective customer need and how can we help him?" Instead of being product-oriented, industry is becoming consumer-oriented. "We don't sell equipment," says William Bader of IBM, "we sell solutions to problems."

The marketing concept is a philosophy or attitude that permeates a typical firm's entire organization. The company's objectives are formulated in terms of what the market needs or wants. The production, engineering, research and development, and finance divisions of the firm are all organized so that they will be broadly consumer- and market-oriented. While engaged in their day-to-day operations, these departments do not lose sight of the consumer. When decisions are made regarding the company's products and markets, these decisions are the results of the joint efforts of all the various divisions of the company. Each division, contributing directly to such decision-making, will naturally be concerned about the success of the company's marketing program.

The marketing division, rather than the production division, has become the all-important focal point of the company's operations. The sales department is a part of the marketing division, sharing in the promotional effort along with advertising, display, and sales promotion. The person in charge of marketing is assigned a broad range of duties and responsibilities, including sales, advertising, display, product planning, marketing research, pricing, and dealer relations. He is usually known as the vice-president in charge of marketing, director of marketing, or product manager.

MARKETING ACTIVITIES

The marketing process encompasses those activities concerned with determining consumer wants and needs, planning and producing products and services that will satisfy those wants and needs, distributing the products and services, and selling them to consumers. Marketing activities can be divided into three major groups: exchange, physical distribution, and facilitating.

Exchange activities include buying and selling. *Buying* consists of three activities; they are (1) the purchase of products by a business for use in manufacturing another product, (2) the purchase of goods by a commercial firm for resale, and (3) the purchase of goods by an ultimate consumer for his own use. *Selling* is the transfer of ownership of goods by the seller for a price paid by a buyer.

Physical distribution activities are concerned with moving, handling, and storing commodities between their original place of production and their final delivery to the consumer. Transportation and storage enable manufacturers to market more efficiently. Raw materials are shipped from farm, ocean, forest, and mine to the processor or manufacturer who then ships his finished products to wholesalers' warehouses for storage and final transfer to industrial customers or retailers. Physical distribution is important in making products available when and where they are wanted. Our mass production system depends upon mass transportation of finished products and raw materials by railroads, trucks, ships, planes, and so forth.

Facilitating activities help and support exchange and distribution. These activities include financing, insurance, market research, product planning and development, standardizing and grading, advertising, and sales promotion.

CHANNELS OF DISTRIBUTION

A *channel of distribution* is the method used by a producer or manufacturer to sell his goods. The distribution of products can be accomplished in one of two ways, direct or indirect.

Direct and Indirect Marketing

The simplest channel of distribution is that in which the producer sells his product directly to the user; it is called *direct marketing*. For example, a farmer sets up a roadside stand on a highway and sells fruits and vegetables, or he loads his produce on a truck and sells it directly to housewives in their homes.

Many industrial products are distributed by the direct method. For example, a company that bottles and sells soft drinks would probably order bottling equipment directly from the manufacturer of such equipment. Tire manufacturers often sell their tires directly to automobile manufacturers. Paper manufacturers often sell directly to printers and publishers. However, most commodities are not distributed by direct-marketing methods.

Indirect marketing is the type of distribution channel in which the salesman is more interested because he plays an important part in it. Approximately 75 percent of all products sold in this country pass through the hands of one or more people on their way from producer to consumer; these people are called *middlemen*.

Middlemen

There are two chief kinds of middlemen; they are (1) merchant middlemen and (2) agent middlemen.

Merchant middlemen may be either wholesalers (often called *jobbers*) or retailers. These middlemen own the product they sell.

Wholesalers buy products in large quantities from producers and sell them in smaller lots to retailers and institutions such as hotels, hospitals, schools, and commercial and industrial buyers. In the industrial products market, the wholesaler is usually referred to as an industrial distributor. Wholesale firms are independent firms that own their merchandise and are usually located near the retailers or industrialists who buy their products. They often offer credit, delivery services, and other assistance to their customers. Most wholesalers employ salesmen who make regular calls upon their customers.

There are several kinds of wholesalers. There are *general line* wholesalers who handle a complete line of merchandise in one general field. For example, a wholesale grocer may handle all kinds of food and other products from apples to soft drinks and a hardware wholesaler may sell everything from appliances to wrenches.

Specialty wholesalers handle only part of a general line, such as coffee, tea, spices, electrical hardware, or cotton fabrics. "Wagon" wholesalers, for instance, have regular routes and sell primarily to restaurants and delicatessens.

Cash-and-carry wholesalers have a stock of fast-moving staple items such as food or clothing. They require customers to call in person for their needs and to pay cash. *Drop shippers* keep no stock on hand, but take orders and arrange to have the goods shipped directly from the manufacturer to the wholesaler's customer.

Retailers, the most familiar merchant middlemen, own and operate their own businesses. Retailers buy most of their merchandise from wholesalers, although they may also buy directly from the producer. Normally, however, retailers stand between wholesaler and consumer.

There are three main kinds of retailers: chain, independent, and multi-independent. *Chain stores* are numerous, and familiar examples are Woolworth, A&P, Kresge, J. C. Penney, and Sears. This type of retail store consists of four or more stores with central ownership and management operating from a headquarters office. *Independent* retailers are those who own and operate a single store or establishment. Barber shops, hardware stores, furniture stores, restaurants, gift shops, and drugstores are examples. *Multi-independents* are retailers who operate from two to four stores, and many department stores fit into this group.

Agent middlemen do not assume ownership of the products in which they deal. In many instances they do not even take possession of them. The function of the agent middleman is to bring the buyer and seller together. They receive a fee or commission from the business they represent.

There are three common types of agent middlemen: commission merchants, brokers, and manufacturers' agents. Each of these agent middlemen employs salesmen who call upon prospective customers.

Commission merchants take goods on consignment from a supplier and sell them to buyers. When a commission merchant collects the money for the merchandise from the buyer, he deducts his fee and sends the money to the consignor or shipper. Commission merchants deal in many kinds of goods, usually agricultural in nature. They sell to wholesalers, retailers, and anyone else who wants to buy. Many commission merchants *auction* products to the highest bidder. Tobacco is a good example of this kind of transaction.

Brokers, like commission merchants, handle various products, such as grain, soybeans, cotton, fruits, and vegetables, for a fee. They may represent either the buyer or the seller, but the representation is usually temporary. Unlike commission merchants, they do not take physical possession of the product.

Manufacturers' agents are independent representatives who act for one or more clients. Like commission merchants and brokers, they are paid a fee for their services.

CHOOSING A CHANNEL OF DISTRIBUTION

The producer will choose his channel of distribution based on its efficiency in meeting his needs. He may choose to do any one or more of the following:

1. Distribute all his products directly to retailers, bypassing wholesalers.
2. Distribute all his products directly to consumers, bypassing wholesalers.
3. Distribute all his products through wholesalers, who sell them to retailers.
4. Distribute all his products through an agent who will distribute them to wholesalers, who, in turn, will sell them to retailers.
5. Use a combination of these channels.

Very few producers adhere to one channel of distribution. Also, the channel chosen may vary with the product. In short, there is considerable flexibility in our system of distribution.

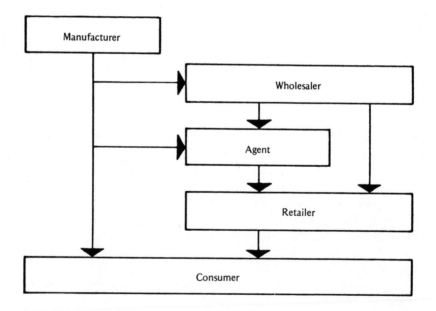

Figure 2-1. Channels of distribution through which a common household item might pass from producer to consumer

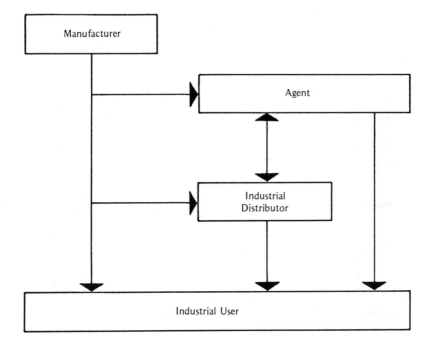

Figure 2-2. The usual channels of distribution for industrial goods

THE MARKETING REVOLUTION

The marketing revolution has been progressing for more than a century, but in the last forty years it has gained impetus. To understand what has happened in marketing, let us trace the history of a fictitious company, John Fuller, Inc.

One hundred and fifty years ago, on the banks of the Allegheny River, John Fuller founded his company. Actually, he set up his forge in what was then a very small city, and went to work. The surrounding land was rich; farmers began to clear the forest and build homesteads; river traffic began to grow. This was the first phase of his company's development. John Fuller had a location. He was open for business and was the only employee. Here is how he might have described his business: "I make and repair farm implements. I do a good job. I charge honest prices. People around here are beginning to know who I am and are starting to do business with me." Obviously, the enterprise was *owner-oriented.*

In the succeeding years, Fuller's business grew. He found that he sold much better by *going to* potential customers rather than waiting until they came into the shop. Fuller began to build a sales force. Here was how he spoke about the business at that stage: "I make things and they have to be sold. If I do a good job, people will come back to me, but they have to find out about me first. I hire people to help me make farm implements, and I hire people to sell them. If a man does not measure up to his job, if he does not sell enough, we will get someone else." At this stage the company was *manufacturing-oriented*.

The Fuller Company acquired more ground. The office and plant occupied separate buildings. The sales force expanded, and was headed by a sales manager. The sales function was recognized as vital to the company's well-being.

When John Fuller's son, John Junior, became more active in running the business, he talked about it this way: "We're a farm implement company. We make quality merchandise, and we think it's the best available. We have built a top-flight sales organization to sell what we make at a favorable price, and we will do everything within reason to support that sales organization and to keep it a strong one." At this point the company was *sales-oriented*.

It remained sales-oriented through the early decades of the twentieth century. There were changes, of course. Financing was needed for expansion, and the company was incorporated and began to sell stock. Ownership broadened and branches were established for national distribution. But, essentially, the company continued to make and sell a single line of high-quality products.

During the 1940s, a number of important changes affected the John Fuller Corporation. In World War II, Fuller converted to military production and made vital contributions to the war effort. The know-how acquired during this period made possible a wide expansion of plant facilities. The company grew and diversified into making products which were needed in many areas.

John Fuller III had this to say about the company: "Fuller makes products for a variety of consumers all over the world. We have to know what the consumer wants and reach him with it at the right time and the right price. To do this, we must coordinate a number of functions: selling, advertising, research, product planning, manufacturing, and finance." The company was *market-oriented*.

Today, rapid technological changes continue. Fuller Corporation has thousands of owners and is expanding internationally, not only in the established markets but in newly developing nations. It operates according to a philosophy that suits the times: "Our responsibility is to use all of our skills to serve our many owners, our millions of customers, and the society we live in. We can accomplish this by proceeding on the assumption that *every activity of the company, without exception, is designed to satisfy public need* — at a profit to our company." The company is now *consumer-oriented.*

Although the Fuller Company is fictitious, the story is by no means unreal or uncommon. It is the story of many businesses, much of whose success is based on marketing. Marketing is a dynamic, changing, growing movement. Its influence is present everywhere, its potential is vast. It is said that the consumer is king. That is why there is a market-oriented economy. Producers cannot afford to manufacture products without considering the consumer's wants and needs, regardless of the products' quality. The emphasis is on marketing and the modern approach to marketing involves two preliminary steps: market research and product planning.

MARKET RESEARCH AND PRODUCT PLANNING

A study and evaluation of present and potential markets and of company policies, methods, and performance related to these markets is known as *market research.* Some of the areas in which market research helps to provide vital information necessary for good marketing decisions are: package design, product type, pricing policies, distribution channel, plant or store location, salesmen's activities, and advertising and promotional methods.

Today's manufacturer relies on market research to help him with *product planning.* He asks his marketing director to determine in advance the potential sales volume for his kind of product, specific needs and preferences of buyers, and the price which can be charged. After obtaining this information, the manufacturer can tell the research and development department to design a new product that will meet these requirements.

Salesmen play a large part in market research. For example, their director may ask them to report on buyer reactions to prices, policies, and products; to report reasons for lost sales; to evaluate competition; to estimate future sales volume in their territories.

Market Research and Technology

Modern technology strengthens and extends human skills. Computers can reduce hours of human thought to an instantaneous calculation. Electronics project a salesman's sight and voice thousands of miles. He can travel thousands of miles in just a few hours.

Also, technology has enormously enhanced the power and effectiveness of the salesman's presentation. When in the presence of a prospect, a salesman can now actually demonstrate how a process takes place in an automated plant; give life to otherwise dry statistics and figures with animated charts; unfold to his prospect a theater in miniature that vividly reveals the benefits to be gained from his proposition. This technology has also increased the salesman's knowledge and skill to enable him to make the most concise and dramatic presentation possible. The salesman today is backed up by research which is very sophisticated and effective. Computers can build actual mathematical models of a market and predict its ups and downs, its twists and turns. The salesman is the benefactor of these unique developments, and he constantly *feeds back* ideas which make these developments even more effective. The creative salesman is constantly intrigued by new insights into the area of market research.

Advertising

Scientific marketing has also affected the development of *advertising.* As research has become increasingly important, so has advertising. Not only has advertising become more creative; it has also become highly sophisticated in the areas of advertising research and media selection. Today an advertising agency can turn out copy which has been tested and proven effective, and the agency can place this advertisement before the right prospect at the right time. The result for the salesman is an informed and preconditioned prospect, one who has been effectively introduced to the sales points on which the salesman builds.

There are many other aspects of scientific marketing, for example, packaging, transportation, finance. These functions, too, are designed to help the salesman to increase sales. His success is central to the entire business structure and the reason for its existence. So when a student chooses to become a salesman, this is the structure which will support him.

POWER POINTS

Because selling is the core of the distributive process, a producer's or manufacturer's success depends on the efficiency of his sales force. The salesman is often the only contact a buyer has with the producer, and therefore *the salesman is the company* from the buyer's viewpoint. The buyer's attitude toward the producer and the product often depends upon the personal qualifications of the salesman. Therefore, business organizations select their salesmen with great care, knowing that sales volume often depends as much on the salesman's personality, competence, and knowledge as on the quality of the product and the company he represents.

The modern salesman operates in an economy which is becoming consumer- or user-oriented, rather than producer- or manufacturer-oriented. He operates in an economy in which a company's chief executive officer is a marketing man who knows the importance of "mixing" all the departments to obtain greater sales volume. He understands the principles of total marketing activities, including how his company's products move through the channels of trade. He is well aware of the revolution taking place in marketing and in selling methods. He appreciates the value of market research, product planning, sales promotion, and technological advances which assist him to sell.

In the future, there will be a continuing need for salesmen, even in greater numbers, simply because people do not buy anything new until it is sold to them by salespeople. Today, sophisticated buyers and customers expect more from salespeople.

DISCUSSION QUESTIONS AND PROBLEMS

1. Define *marketing*.

2. "Salesmanship is the key which winds up the economy, for nothing happens until a sale is made." Is this statement true? Explain your answer.

3. Is the salesman as important a factor in our economic system as advertising? Why?

4. What is the meaning of *marketing concept?*

5. What are the three major groups of marketing activities? Give examples of each.

6. Define *channel of distribution.*

7. What are the methods of distribution and how do they operate?

8. What are the steps, or phases, in the marketing revolution which has taken place over the last century?

9. "The consumer is king." Do you agree with this statement? What does it mean in terms of modern selling?

10. How is modern technology and research affecting salesmen and marketing activities?

SELLING PROBLEMS AND PROJECTS

---

1. Wonderbago Motor Home Case

Gary Addison and Frank Conley had successfully operated an Oldsmobile dealership for the last few years. They had built their business on sound customer relations, good service, and a strong sales force. They had wisely reinvested their earnings, so that they were now ready to take on a new business venture in addition to their auto dealership. Arrangements were made to enter into a contract with the Wonderbago Co. and to open a dealership for recreational vehicles.

"It wasn't too hard to get it started," Addison said. "After spending ten years in the car business and working 13 to 14 hours a day, I suddenly realized that my family was growing up without me. So, on a camping trip with a friend who had a motor home, I discovered a new way to make even bigger money than we were making in the car business, and without the pressures, too."

After a year in their new venture both men were ready to sell out. They both felt they had had enough. Frank Conley explained why.

"We opened up on a small lot on Morningside Boulevard and put a couple of recreational vehicle units on it for display. Then we hired and trained three young salesmen. We had plenty of prospects come in, and they spent a good deal of time looking, but we couldn't get them interested in making a decision, even though our salesmen were willing to make attractive deals. Many of them didn't come back; and those that did, came back four or five times before they were willing to make a buying decision. All in all, we sold only 30 motor homes during the entire year.

"Our prospects gave us a bad time. They complained about not being able to drive those big units, and not having room to store them at their residence. Also, a lot of prospects complained about restrictive ordinances and diminishing availability of camping sites. It seems private and public parks usually have a minimum of a 90-day delay on their waiting list.

"We got a lot of 'static' from the customers who bought our motor homes. Our service department just couldn't seem to satisfy them. They expected a lot more than just mechanical service. We were asked to install cupboards, repair refrigerators, make body and interior alterations. What do they expect our mechanics to be—cabinetmakers and air-conditioning experts, too? I'll be glad to get out of this business. There may be money in it, but it isn't like the car business."

Questions

1. What is the main problem in this case (in answering this question, think about the consumer-oriented, marketing economy)? Is this new business like the car business?

2. What are some of the factors that Gary and Frank should have considered about their market when they entered this new business?

CHAPTER 3

Opportunities in Selling

In early America, there evolved four types of salesmen: the Yankee peddler, the credit investigator, the greeter, and the drummer.

The *Yankee peddler* carried a pack and sold largely to back-country settlers. Pins, needles, buttons, razors, knives, and other so-called notions were sold by these early salesmen. Later, as the interior road system was improved, the peddler used pack horses and specially built wagons on his rounds.

The *credit investigator* traveled to make financial inspections of customers, to call on old customers, to collect past-due accounts, and to iron out difficulties. His goodwill activities gradually made him a full-time salesman who sold from samples.

The *greeter* was sent by wholesalers and manufacturers to hotels to greet newly arrived buyers from small-town and crossroad stores, and to invite them to visit the wholesale house or the factory represented by the greeter.

The *drummer* went a step further than the greeter. The drummer went to the railroad station to meet customers, and arranged for entertainment and a trip to the wholesaler's warehouse or factory. These men were known as drummers because they tried to "drum up" trade for their companies. Little by little, drummers began to board trains before they reached the city; later, they went all the way to the buyers' places of business.

John H. Patterson, founder of the National Cash Register Company, was the first man to recognize the need of sales training for "outside" salesmen, as well as the need for stimulation and supervision of sales, sales quotas, high salaries, use of visuals, dramatizations, and standardized sales talks.

Later, retail selling made great progress, too. John Wanamaker, founder of a chain of department stores, was the first to introduce large sales volume and rapid turnover, liberal use of advertising, handsome fixtures and equipment, window displays, customer services, strict honesty, one price, and training of personnel.

From these beginnings, there developed our modern types of salesmen who may be classified by the customers to whom they sell and the services they offer. These salesmen include retail, wholesale, specialty, service, and several other classifications.

In the United States there are more than eight million people engaged in retail selling and approximately four and a half million engaged in "outside selling," or selling in which the salesman contacts the customer.

All kinds of selling are going on right now, all around us: the insurance man is selling security; a job applicant is trying to sell his personal services; the retail store owner is selling merchandise; and the instructor is trying to sell his course. Everyone who deals with people uses salesmanship: doctors, lawyers, clergymen, accountants, and practically any other person who works for a living.

TYPES OF SELLING

The first broad division of salesmanship is between tangible and intangible selling. Examples of tangibles and intangibles are:

TANGIBLES	INTANGIBLES
Autos	Advertising
Groceries	Computer services
Lumber	Insurance
Oil	Stocks
Typewriters	Travel

In general, tangibles are products; intangibles are services. Some people like to sell products, or tangibles; some like to sell services, or intangibles. Both areas are rewarding and both are worthwhile.

Specialty Selling of Tangibles

A *specialty* has been defined as "any article of relatively high price, of fairly durable nature, nonconsumable in use, irregular in time of purchase, and in practically every case, calling for the exercise of personal selection upon the part of the buyer."

This form of selling requires considerable creativity and presents many challenges because it is admittedly not easy to take a new product, whether it is an air conditioner, a vacuum cleaner, or a new computing machine, and sell it to people who are sometimes only barely aware of the need for it. When selling is that difficult, however, it also is generally associated with a higher salary, commission, bonus, or other reward. In the following sections we shall present some typical examples of specialty selling.

Specialty Selling of Accounting Machines

Specialty selling of accounting machines involves a wide range of duties and responsibilities.

Interviews. The first phase in this kind of selling is securing and conducting interviews. Prospective buyers must be selected carefully so that time will not be wasted on those who are unlikely to need accounting machines in the near future.

Conducting surveys. Unless the prospective buyer knows what he needs as a result of the advice of a consultant or a specialist, it is necessary for the salesman to study and survey his operations in order to recommend suitable equipment. This may be done by the salesman himself or by a specialist employed by his company.

Presenting and selling the proposition. After the needs are evaluated, the salesman can make a proposal. In guiding the prospective customer, the salesman has an opportunity to perform creative work. Explanation and demonstration are needed to aid in the solution of the prospective customer's problems.

Closing the sale. The process of closing the sale requires special techniques and these are discussed in Chapter 19.

Servicing customers. Accounting machines are so technical and complicated that it is not possible to operate them without instruction and practice. The salesman is expected to instruct the customer's personnel or refer them to his company's training department. As work is turned out on the machine, the salesman will review it with appropriate company executives until everybody is satisfied that the personnel are capable of operating the equipment with the desired results. Sometimes the salesman must lend a hand in recruiting and selecting the necessary personnel to operate the machine. He will always tell his customers about the latest equipment and methods, who is using the equipment in competitive industries, company publications which may be of help, and accessory services which are available.

Handling executive duties. The accounting machine salesman needs to utilize his time and talents in the most productive manner.

He must (1) schedule his work and use his time efficiently; (2) get acquainted with several key men in each business; (3) analyze territory opportunities; (4) learn manufacturing methods, products, and problems of prospects; (5) maintain a list of active prospects; (6) prepare call reports and other reports as needed; (7) keep in touch with former and competitive product users; (8) constantly study competitive products, the claims made for them and their limitations.

It will be noted that persuading and convincing prospects requires only a relatively small part of this salesman's time as well as skill. The bulk of his work involves preparing the survey, analyzing the prospect's needs, and, after the sale is made, making certain that the customer is satisfied with his purchase and is adequately serviced to get the most out of his machine.

Specialty Selling of Automobiles

In contrast to selling accounting machines, selling automobiles involves devoting a great proportion of time to persuading and convincing prospects. The automobile salesman's varied duties have been described as follows:[1]

Locating prospects. Obviously, the first task is to locate prospective customers who either are or may be interested in buying a new car. Some prospects will appear at a showroom; others will have to be discovered by diverse methods.

Evaluating the needs of prospects. Since the needs, tastes, and purchasing power of car buyers vary, it is necessary to learn something of the needs of prospects. Such matters as how much use and under what driving conditions the car will be operated are factors important to evaluating the needs of the buyer.

Recommending the model. Since manufacturers make many models, the salesman can recommend the one best suited. He can show the prospect the actual car, if he has it in stock, or he can use illustrations.

Explaining the recommendation. Once he has recommended a particular model, the salesman carefully explains and skillfully demonstrates why the recommended model fits the customer's needs.

Handling objections. Knowing the common objections made by prospects and devising effective ways of handling them are especially important in dealing with problems relating to competitive makes of cars.

1. Eugene J. Kelley and William Lazar, *Managerial Marketing: Perspective and Viewpoints.* (Homewood, Ill.: Richard D. Irwin, Inc., 1958), p. 392.

Asking for the order. At every interview the salesman must try to close a successful sale and he must take the first opportunity to ask for the order.

Handling the trade-in. Before making an offer for a trade-in, it is important to sell the new car thoroughly, or else the emphasis in the sale will shift quickly from the customer buying a new car to selling his old one.

Selling accessories. Suitable accessories should be mentioned and suggested to the buyer.

Routine duties. Routine duties include the data cards which are the heart of a salesman's operations. Information to be transmitted to the sales manager is recorded on these cards, and they must be filed properly to facilitate the follow-up of prospects. There are separate cards for (1) new prospects, (2) calls on prospects, and (3) summary of sales efforts.

Executive duties. A salesman is expected to manage his time and effort so as to facilitate and assure future business. To fill his job successfully he must (1) mail advertising to prospects before he calls on them; (2) build his prospect list from customers, friends, canvassing, and other sources; (3) set a daily objective of calls, demonstrations, and appraisals; (4) read company literature, industry trade papers, and competitive literature to obtain a broad knowledge of the field; (5) make a daily work plan each night for the next day's work; (6) attend sales meetings.

Building goodwill. When the salesman takes a sincere interest in seeing to it that the customer obtains the fullest measure of service that the dealer is capable of giving, he is not only doing a favor for the customer but for himself and his employers as well. It is desirable that the salesman be present when the service manager delivers and explains the service policy to the customer. He is also expected to remind the customer to get the service provided in the policy. By calling on the customer once a month, the salesman can assure himself that the customer will be satisfied with his purchase and will therefore recommend him to others.

Specialty Selling of Intangibles

When a prospective customer can see, touch, smell, taste, or test the article he contemplates buying, there is a greater possibility of the customer imagining himself as the owner and, of course, purchasing the item.

A different approach to selling is demanded of the salesman who sells such intangibles as advertising, life insurance, and investment securities. In the latter case, the salesman asks the prospect to exchange his money for a sheet of paper, such as a stock certificate, which may represent a share of ownership in a company a thousand miles away, making products used only in heavy industry. If the prospect could see the plant turning out the product or the orders flowing in from a large sales staff, it would seem more real to him. Without this opportunity, the prospective buyer of securities relies on the salesman to inform him about what is to be gained from investing in the company. Imaginative selling, therefore, requires the ability on the part of the salesman to paint a picture that will portray clearly to the prospect what he is buying. The salesman knows the prospect is buying not only a share in the company but also an opportunity to share in its profits and its growth.

Continuity and Nonrepeat Selling

Continuity selling means calling on a steady list of customers and offering a product or a service to them. A route milkman is an illustration of this kind of selling. A wholesaler's salesman who calls on the same accounts week after week is another example.

Nonrepeat selling involves such items as heavy machinery, building materials, and other products which ordinarily will not be purchased frequently. Some salesmen sell autos, appliances, and other specialty items on a onetime basis, while hoping that their selling will be on a continuity basis, at least in part.

CLASSIFICATION OF SALESPEOPLE

Classifying sales activities can be quite difficult because so many variables form the basis of classification. If we base our classification on the salesman's employer, we will recognize that some salesmen work for manufacturers, some for wholesalers, some for retailers. Other bases for classification are:

1. Type of product: Products can be tangible or intangible as discussed earlier in this chapter.
2. Degree of prospecting: There are inside salesmen who serve customers who come to the business premises, and there are outside salesmen who call on prospects and customers in the field.
3. Complexity of the sales job: Some sales jobs are extremely simple, requiring little or no training; while others are extremely technical, requiring a great amount of training and education.

4. Method of compensation: Salesmen may be paid on straight salary, or a commission basis, or on a combination of both.

5. Type of market: The salesman's job may require selling to wholesalers and retailers for resale purposes, selling to industrial buyers for processing and fabricating purposes, selling to purchasing agents, selling to professional people, selling to personal consumers, or selling to government agencies.

For the purposes of this discussion we shall analyze selling in terms of three broad markets and classify the various types of sales activities within each market as shown in Table 3-1.

Table 3-1. Classification of Selling Markets

CONSUMER SELLING	WHOLESALE SELLING	INDUSTRIAL SELLING
Retail store selling	Wholesaler's repre-	Manufacturer's
Personal direct selling (house-to-house, specialty selling)	sentative	representative
	Merchandising man	
	Promotional man	
Telepurchasing (catalogue and mail-order selling, telephone and television selling)		
Detail salesman		

Consumer Selling

The largest of the three markets is, of course, the consumer market, which is composed of approximately 220 million persons and is expected to rise to 275 million by 1985, an increase of 41 percent over 1965. Salesmen who work in this market see many prospects and customers, regardless of whether the salesmen work in a retail store or in the field. Consumers have many wants and needs; they also have the purchasing power, in the form of cash or credit, to purchase goods. They have a great deal of leisure time and varied buying patterns which must be studied and recognized if the salesman is to enjoy above-average success.

The woman is the predominant customer in this market. She owns or controls two-thirds of the personal wealth in this country. She spends over five billion dollars on her personal needs every year and is the decision-maker in the expenditure of more than $650 billion for family purposes. Other important submarkets that are recognized within the consumer goods market are the leisure market, the youth market and the senior citizen market, each of which has its own peculiar characteristics.

Salesmen in the consumer market may represent manufacturers who sell directly to consumers, or manufacturers or retailers who sell to consumers by mail or telephone. However, the largest group comprises retail store salespeople. We shall discuss the latter type of selling first.

Retail Store Salespeople

The professional retail salesperson considers himself both a problem-solver and a creative salesperson. He knows his stock and how to analyze the customer's needs. He knows how to introduce the right merchandise to fit those needs.

Retail selling is characterized by the fact that the customer contacts the salesman instead of the salesman going to the customer. Since many customers already know what they need or want when visiting the store, the salesman must be alert to recognize, as well as to help satisfy, the customer's needs and wants. The duties of the retail salesperson will vary, of course, according to the size and type of store and its policies. In general, however, the retail salesperson must:

- Approach and serve customers.
- Write up the sale in a sales book or operate a cash register.
- Wrap the merchandise (where such policies are followed).
- Make change.
- Arrange and replenish stock.
- Keep the stock clean and neat.
- Handle complaints and adjustments.

In some retail store situations, salespeople will be required to engage in outside selling. For example, automobile dealers require their salesmen to spend a definite proportion of their time outside the showroom. Sears salesmen who sell in the building materials, roofing, fencing, plumbing and kitchen-modernization departments spend a great deal of their time in contacting prospects in their homes or offices.

Such retail salesmen are much like the direct-selling, specialty salesmen described in the next section. They have the opportunity to use creative sales ability and earn a larger income than the typical inside retail salesperson. They follow leads, solicit new business, and persuade prospects to visit the store for demonstrations. This type of selling requires an amount of aggressiveness and hard work equal to that of the typical house-to-house salesman. Besides being interested in and liking people, this type of retail salesperson must possess a good imagination and stamina. In addition, he must be able to manage his working day, since he is responsible for his own time and amount of business produced.

Personal Direct Selling

House-to-house selling produces approximately 1 percent of the total retail sales in the United States every year. Many people think of house-to-house or direct-to-home selling as the most typical form of selling. In fact, this method of selling is relatively unimportant, as can be seen from the percent of sales volume mentioned above.

This form of direct selling is especially expensive because it involves intensive training and selling effort which must be backed up by an abundance of sales promotion and costly sales branch organizations throughout the country. Since this type of selling requires a great deal of prospecting and sales effort, it must command an income commensurate with the selling effort. Commissions for house-to-house salesmen selling such goods as cooking utensils, cosmetics, brushes, and vacuum cleaners range from 20 to 40 percent of sales. Some companies have built sizable businesses on the basis of this method of selling. The Fuller Brush Company, for example, has more than 7,000 full-time dealers. Avon Products, Inc., with more than 100,000 part-time saleswomen, has the largest sales volume of any cosmetics manufacturing firm in the United States.

Personal direct selling is also exemplified in the specialty salesman who may sell real estate, insurance, or stocks and bonds. He usually works on a commission basis and attempts to build his own clientele.

The retail routeman sells and delivers to individual customers. Most retail route selling is house-to-house, for example, laundry, newspapers, and milk routes. The retail routeman has many prospective buyers, but each account is small. His chief job is to retain his established clientele, find new accounts, and sell more to all accounts.

Telepurchasing

A resurgence of an old method of selling, known as *telepurchasing* (from the Greek *tel* meaning "far off"), is emerging again in retailing.[2] It may be thought of as "long-distance" buying in which the product is brought to the customer instead of the customer to the product. A large part of this new trend is simply a stepped-up use of

2. "Telepurchasing: Major Trend in Retailing," *Forbes,* October 15, 1967, pp. 56–59.

the old methods of catalogue, mail-order, and telephone selling. House-to-house selling itself may be thought of as a form of telepurchasing.

Some forms of long-distance buying are entirely new, such as the touch-tone telephone which is hooked up to a central computer, enabling shoppers to order a variety of items from their own homes. Another electronics development being considered for future use in selling is the picture phone, which, when integrated into a closed-circuit television, will bring this type of transaction closer to a direct-selling situation.

Probably the biggest area of telepurchasing today is catalogue and direct-mail sales, which in 1967 amounted to approximately $44 billion in the United States. These sales were generated by the expenditure of $2.5 billion for direct mail advertising, exceeding the amount spent on either television or magazine advertising.

In its earlier forms, catalogue selling meant using the mails to promote goods, which were displayed throughout the pages of large and elaborately printed catalogues, to rural consumers. The present trend is the modern catalogue store where the customer can order from a catalogue goods that the store itself does not carry. Often this store is a separate retail outlet located in a town or small city where the company has not established a complete store.

Catalogue selling accounts for a significant share of the total sales of many old and established retailers. Sears has increased its catalogue and telephone sales offices from 984 in 1960 to 2,507 in 1972, and is contemplating an even greater increase in these outlets in the years ahead. The J. C. Penney Company launched its catalogue sales operations in 1962, and in 1972 had approximately 1,080 catalogue desks in existing stores. Catalogue sales increases have also taken place among the thousands of small, independent mail-order retail firms that offer the consumer everything from food to housewares.

From this description of the various forms of telepurchasing, one might easily assume that we are dealing with an automated, nonpersonal type of selling that has little or no use for the art of salesmanship. But this is far from true, since the people who are responsible for planning these activities must constantly pay attention to the needs and wants of the consumers in the market. The people who prepare the sales-promotion literature in the catalogue and mail-order field appreciate and understand the principles of persuasion that salesmen everywhere must learn if they are to be successful. The success of a catalogue, a direct-mail brochure, or advertisement is based upon the effective use of selling principles. These sales promotion devices must be designed to attract attention and create interest and desire. In addition, they must win the confidence of the customer and, indeed, close the sale by inducing buying action. Although catalogues and electronic picture phones often cannot close a sale, a salesman present at the time can accomplish this goal if he or she is skilled in using salesmanship principles.

Wholesale Selling

Wholesale selling involves the sale of goods and services to middlemen, who, in turn, resell the goods to others for a profit. Examples are selling to retailers, to wholesalers, and to industrial and commercial firms. The goods sold to these latter firms become a part of a finished product or facilitate the production of finished goods; for example, electronic condensers sold to a potentiometer manufacturing firm or the sale of soaps to an industrial firm.

Wholesaler's Representative

The person who sells to retailers works for a wholesaler, jobber, or distributor of products, and may handle from 500 to 50,000 items. He is known as a *wholesaler's representative.* He literally sells from a catalogue, because he has too many items to memorize, and he usually represents more than one manufacturer. He may work for two or more competitive companies that sell the same kind and class of products.

The wholesaler's representative makes regular calls and becomes well known to his customers. Often he goes directly to his customer's "want" book, checks off the items that his company supplies, writes up the order, and asks for approval. At other times, he may spend hours with a customer, turning over page after page of his catalogue and price book. When the buyer sees something he needs, the wholesaler's representative enters the quantity, stock number, and price in his sales book on the appropriate order form.

For many years, wholesalers' representatives were considered order-takers because it was necessary for them to write as much business as possible in their short working days. These men would frequently see one or two hundred customers a week. It was hard work but it provided a good, stable income. Substantial changes, however, have taken place in this kind of selling, and today the salesman really sells a merchandising program. Whether it is a new drug or a different kind of cigarette, the salesman stresses the sales-promotion plan his company will employ to popularize the new product and gain consumer acceptance for it. Actually, he sells the sales promotion as well as the merits of the product itself.

The objective of this kind of selling is to communicate enthusiasm to the retailer and to make him feel the excitement of handling a new or improved product. The representative often gets a department store to stock his product and advertise it. Then he takes the advertisement to other stores as evidence that the product is everything he claims it to be. Salesmen who sold the first cash registers, refrigerators, television sets, vacuum cleaners, or typewriters often pioneered sales in this manner. Such men, and their activities, are a vital force in their industries. They are action-minded, that is, they plant new ideas and they stir retailers to do something about the merchandise which they sell.

Very few wholesale salesmen are the pressure kind. They are usually steady, reliable, friendly, always available. They must be well schooled in their field and in the needs of their customers, for an important part of their job is to keep customers posted on changes in prices, merchandising, new or special products, or special sales that the company is offering.

This is well-paid, secure selling, but it takes time to master its intricacies because the salesman has to learn about so many items. Many wholesale salesmen have worked in the warehouse, stockroom, shipping room, order room, and other departments of the company before traveling, and most have also had previous selling experience.

Generally, wholesale representatives do not travel extensively. Many of them, in fact, never leave their own city or, at most, county limits, although occasionally they may cover a state, especially in the West and Midwest.

The Merchandising Man

The *merchandising man* sells to retailers. His main responsibility is to develop a territory so that it produces the maximum volume of business for a product. Not all companies that employ merchandising men follow the same policy in fulfilling this objective. For example, one company may insist that the representative be held responsible for maximum sales volume. When he calls on retail accounts in his territory, he is directed to follow a program designed to get the dealer to buy and sell as large a volume as possible. A good example of such a program is the following procedure developed by a large food manufacturer:

1. Check stock. It is hardly possible to discuss buying without knowing what is needed; therefore, this first step is important. Food merchants are usually too busy to do this thoroughly. They welcome the salesman who checks their stock for them.

2. Discuss and take regular orders. Recommend and discuss the amount needed of the merchandise regularly carried.
3. Show the monthly special. Obtain the order for it.
4. Show other varieties. Try for an order for a product that the dealer is not carrying at the present time.
5. Discuss special sales. Make a determined effort to get company's goods on display or in dealer's advertising.
6. Service stock. Keep it clean and well organized. While this may be handled in connection with checking inventory, it may be best to defer this job to the end of the visit while following through the seventh step.
7. Build displays. Put up signs, promotional displays, and displays of merchandise.

To carry out their duties, these men may purchase stock from wholesalers, when necessary, at the regular wholesale price. They may also work with printers in preparing advertising for retailers. Besides performing sales-promotion duties, these men adjust complaints and credit or replace damaged merchandise. They keep the company informed about competitive activities in their territory, new products being tested, price changes, new or changed packages, and other merchandising activities. Merchandising men must also report their activities regularly and prepare expense reports and a schedule of planned calls for the next week.

Comparison of the selling operations of a variety of companies shows that success can be achieved through the use of widely differing approaches to the selling task. Generally, it is the role of sales management to determine these policies, while the job of the field men is to operate within the framework of his company's requirements.

The Promotional Man

The *promotional man* (also called a *missionary* or *pioneer*) usually sells for a company that is establishing its product for the first time in a new market. Promotional men work in every field, but most commonly in those which sell to department, variety, and specialty stores, as well as to drugstores and grocery stores. They make initial calls on jobbers, wholesalers, distributors, and dealers to familiarize them with the product. When a promotional man has established his product or service in one area, he moves on to another.

The promotional man may also cover the retail trade, selling and promoting the product by performing merchandising and display work much in the manner of the merchandising salesman. Since, in addition to selling, he offers advice on prices, problems, and services to distributors and dealers, he must be well informed about company policies and products. The promotional man should have teaching ability as well as selling and promotional skills, because jobbers, dealers, distributors, and other salesmen must learn from him how to sell the products. He must have initiative and imagination, and he must be able to make an appeal so attractive and convincing that buyers take his product.

So that he may coordinate his own promotion with magazine and newspaper advertising, the promotional salesman usually works closely with the company's advertising agency. Sometimes he works for the advertising agency directly, either for special campaigns or on a permanent basis.

Detail Salesman

There are two general kinds of detail salesmen: the straight detailer and the detailer and missionary.

Straight detailing is a routine kind of selling. The *straight detailer* will go into a grocery or drugstore which already stocks his merchandise and proceed to check the inventory. If, for example, custom calls for six bottles of Breck's shampoo on the shelf and there are only three, the detailer proceeds to the stockroom and replenishes the supply. He checks advertising displays and rearranges them when necessary. He also checks the amount of stock on hand to be sure it is adequate until his next visit.

He then reports to the buyer or manager and tells him of his findings. He tells the buyer what merchandise the store needs, what should be increased, what should be ordered, and finally he writes the order.

Both the drug and grocery detailer may also show the manager or buyer how the store can increase its sales by better displays, better advertising, where and when shelf space could be used to better advantage, and other operating suggestions.

The medical detailer is in a class by himself. He must be fully and accurately informed about his company's products and its claims. He must be able to converse intelligently with doctors, dentists, pharmacists, veterinarians, stockmen, cattlemen, and other specialists. He must know his company's background, policies, and services thoroughly, so that he can make concise, informative presentations.

The medical detailer usually receives thorough training before he tries to sell, and is closely supervised and observed during his initial selling period. After that experience, ordinarily he is responsible for his own time, his own calls, and his own success.

The *detailer and missionary salesman* is usually found in the pharmaceutical field. His work pattern is to call on from four to eight doctors each day with samples of his products and literature. This detailer must represent an ethical house with known ethical products, for doctors are skeptical about new products, new companies, and new developments.

Instead of selling to the doctor, this salesman "details": he introduces his company's products, and describes their properties and ingredients, capabilities and usages. He provides documentation from authorities and information on research; he explains who has used the products and with what results, how long the products have been on the market, and how they have been accepted by other physicians. Finally, he will leave free samples and ask the doctor if he would prescribe or recommend the product to his patients.

The pharmaceutical detailer then visits three to six drugstores during the same day, again introducing himself, his company, and his products. He suggests that it will benefit the druggist to be able to supply the new products he has introduced to local physicians.

This kind of detail salesman may establish a new product in a store that is already a customer of his company, a new product with a new account, or an established product with a new account. He may also turn the account over to a straight detailer when he has established it.

Industrial Selling

Manufacturer's Representative

The *manufacturer's representative* works directly for the manufacturer and is an employee of the company. He calls on wholesalers, dealers, and distributors.

The manufacturer's representative is in reality an industrial salesman. He is not only a salesman, but also a contact and promotion man, advertising supervisor, sales manager, complaint handler, adjuster, and goodwill ambassador. In short, he *is* the company more than any other type of salesman.

He must be a topflight man of considerable selling experience. He must be imaginative, aggressive, emotionally well-adjusted, able to manage his time, and capable of making fast decisions. He must know all about his products, their uses, and utility; company policies and prices; and the benefits his products will bring to prospects. He must be able to make intelligent presentations to a buyer about a new product, a dealership, or a franchise.

He must be well educated and know business operations so that he can offer advice and counsel to his buyers. He sometimes calls on established businesses, or he may develop his own outlets by setting up new distributorships and dealerships in new areas. If the product is already established, the manufacturer's representative will enlarge and increase the number of products handled as well as the sales volume.

This type of sales position demands a great deal of travel. The salesman may cover an area with a 500-mile radius, or a region, or the nation. He lives out of his suitcase more than other salesmen. The person who wants to be home with his family every night will not fit into this kind of selling.

He must be able to train others to sell his product on the retail level, hold meetings, give lectures, and teach salespeople how to overcome customer objections and how to close profitable sales. He must be able to inspire others to sell more.

Sometimes this salesman turns over his sales to the wholesaler, jobber, or distributor, since he receives credit at any level. He must keep his manufacturer informed at all times about every aspect of the product and territory, refer back customer complaints, offer suggestions related to advertising and sales promotion in general. He actually conducts his activities as though he owned the company in his territory.

Many of the best salesmen prefer this kind of selling, because it offers them an opportunity to earn bigger salaries as well as to be their own boss. Compensation may be on a base salary and commission basis, but more often will be a straight commission.

This kind of selling is for the man who wants to be his own boss, has the ability and willingness to perform the tasks required, and who wants to be paid in full for his planning, time, and effort.

THE PROMOTIONAL LADDER

The various levels of positions in selling are not always easy to classify and catalogue. The following descriptions and explanations of the typical levels of promotion may, however, be of help to the individual who is not familiar with them.

Retail Selling

Many young people are interested not only in money but also in obtaining a challenging job. Retailing offers this kind of challenge.

As far as salary is concerned in retail operations, the beginner must resign himself to starting at a rather low wage. Retail management, however, has stated that bright people can move up quickly from a beginner's salary in the large stores and retail chains. The beginner can be earning from $10,000 to $20,000 in ten years. In short, if he is intelligent and enjoys dealing with people, he can enter a field that is challenging and worthwhile.

Route of Advancement

In retail selling, advancement is from salesman to head of stock, department manager, assistant buyer, and buyer. The buyer in a large department store carries an important responsibility and may earn an income of from $6,000 to $30,000 a year, depending upon the type of merchandise and whether the firm practices unit buying (single department buying) or centralized buying (buying a single merchandise line for all the departments).

The position above buyer is the division merchandise manager, who is in charge of a group of buyers. He must coordinate their activities and transmit policies to them from top management.

The next position is the merchandise manager, who is in complete charge of all merchandising activities. Finally, there is the general manager, who is considered the top-ranking administrative officer of the firm.

Wholesale and Industrial Selling

The usual sales trainee in the industrial or wholesale firm has had little or no selling experience or related education; he is not familiar with the product or service. The training period may start in a company division or department connected with sales activities: receiving dock, shipping room, sales order desk, or telephone sales.

These beginning jobs are provided to familiarize the novice with the company products or services, its mode of operation, its policies and other details of value to a salesman. While they are learning on the job, beginners may take correspondence courses, receive on-the-job instruction, or attend formal sales instruction classes. The training period may also include a minimum of selling under supervision. Training may extend over a period of one month to four years, depending on the needs of the company.

Junior Salesman

Junior salesmen are those who have completed a training program. Salesmen who have had from one to three years of selling experience in another line or for another company are known as junior salesmen. The junior salesman is an active salesman; he starts selling immediately after his initial training, either alone or under supervision. If he starts as a junior salesman with considerable experience, he may receive shorter initial training and move ahead much faster than the un-experienced beginner.

Senior Salesman

The *senior salesman* may have had from two to twenty years of selling experience. He has come up from trainee and junior status and has obviously had much practical experience. He thoroughly knows his product, service, field, and industry. He knows how to handle ob-stacles, manage his time, use visuals, and give demonstrations. He is a qualified, able craftsman in his occupational group.

Sales Supervisor

The *sales supervisor* is a salesman who has been promoted to the supervision of a small number of other salespeople. In most compa-nies he also continues to sell. He may be responsible for the field train-ing of trainees and junior salesmen in his territory, as well as for supervision of senior salesmen. He is one of the middle-management group who stands between top sales management and the sales force. He maintains company policies; sustains and increases sales volume; travels with his salesmen; turns in various sales reports; coaches, boosts morale, and appraises the men who work for him.

Assistant Sales Manager

The position of *assistant sales manager* is often the same as that of sales supervisor. The assistant's duties, however, may include much more than supervision, since they often entail handling paper work, statistics, chart-making, study and analysis of sales reports, and many other details. He may also help the sales manager organize sales meet-ings and prepare material for them; recruit and screen prospective salesmen; handle complaints and claims of both salesmen and cus-tomers.

Product Sales Manager

Companies with many products find it profitable to place specific responsibility for a product or group of products on the shoulders of specialists in selling them; these men are known as *product sales man-agers*. In present-day management concepts, the product sales man-ager does not exercise authority over the field sales force but deals only with product policy, pricing, and promotion of their particular products. Some companies segregate their sales force on a product basis. At the head of each product division is an executive who is re-sponsible for managing the men who sell one line of the company's products.

Territorial Sales Manager

There can be a great many territorial sales managers in a large company and as many as three kinds of job levels. Each one has responsibility for a certain geographical area that may be called region, division, area, district, or territory; each is headed by a *territorial sales manager*.

In the case of the regional operation, for example, a large company may divide the nation into five major regions with a regional sales manager in charge of each. Each region may be divided into five to twelve territories, depending on the importance of the areas, with a territorial sales manager in charge of each. Under each territorial head, several districts would be in operation, each with a district sales manager.

The territorial sales managers have direct authority over their sales forces. In modern sales organizations they do most of the recruiting and selection of personnel. They are also directly concerned with the supervision, motivation, training, and education of the salespeople.

Sales Manager

The *sales manager* can be a supersalesman or a top-management director of marketing.

Usually the sales manager is in charge of the administration or management of an outside sales force and its activities. With larger companies, he may be in charge of a branch, district, territory, area, or region. In smaller companies, he may be in charge of the entire selling program. His duties are not the same in all organizations, but usually they include the recruiting, selection, hiring, and training of salesmen. The sales manager is also in charge of organizing them into a work force and appraising the results of their work. His responsibilities include the operation of the entire sales force under his jurisdiction and all duties assigned to him by his management.

General Sales Manager

The *general sales manager* has overall administrative responsibility for the sales staff. His role varies among companies, but he is usually given some responsibility for price and distribution policies of his company's product. This executive, often a company vice-president, is in charge of other kinds of sales managers and supervisors. His duties are to transmit company information to his sales managers and to see that policies are carried out. He assigns and delegates responsibilities and orders throughout the sales organization.

In addition to his selling functions, the general sales manager is in charge of all company service operations. He assigns territories, branches, areas, or regions; assigns quotas for each; and often estab-lishes selling prices. He conducts market studies, anticipates trends, and plans adjustments to changes. He keeps abreast of new develop-ments in operation, organization, and distribution methods. The posi-tion demands much paper work, interdepartmental conferences, sales meetings, field inspections, and morale building.

Chief Sales Executive

The chief sales executive (usually called *the marketing manager, director of marketing* or *vice-president of marketing*) focuses atten-tion on the total marketing concept rather than on selling alone. In brief, the chief marketing executive's activities include all responsi-bilities connected with the administration of the following four major areas: product policies, pricing policies, channels-of-distribution poli-cies, and promotional policies. He is in charge of the entire marketing program for his company.

Sources for Sales Managers

A recent American Management Association survey reveals that 95 percent of all first-line sales managers are selected from within their own company. It is estimated that replacement and expansion of sales forces will require 75 percent more first-line sales managers within the next few years. Moreover, a recent Dartnell Corporation survey reveals that approximately 50 percent of company presidents and board chairmen rose from the rank of salesman.

With only a few exceptions, the practice prevails of filling sales management positions with salesmen who have the highest sales records, regardless of their leadership or executive ability.

The rate of turnover of top-management personnel is greater than popularly supposed. The American Management Association survey states, "The average corporation president's job lasts five years. In the past, companies picked lawyers, bankers, engineers or accountants to head up businesses. Men with their backgrounds are finding it difficult to cope with current business conditions. . . . You have to be a marketing man with selling experience to compete in today's op-portunities for advancement."

A survey conducted by Victor Lazo of New York University re-veals that more than 60 percent of the directors added since 1950 have had marketing backgrounds. Furthermore, according to *Industrial Marketing* magazine, corporation presidents reported that if a vacancy were to occur on their present boards, 19.5 percent of the vacancies definitely would be filled by men who rose from the rank of salesman.

Preparation for Selling

Marketing men view the modern salesperson as a problem-solver. He has replaced the earlier concept of the salesperson as an order-taker, and the still earlier concept of the seller as a spellbinder who was able to influence people to buy things they did not need or want.

The modern salesperson must know something about his own behavior and thinking; he must also understand the emotions, perceptions, attitudes, and behavior patterns of the people with whom he transacts business. With this psychological insight, he is able to advance from the older concept of making people buy to the newer concept of helping people buy. As a result of this new approach, the modern salesperson finds that his activities are less a matter of personal persuasion than of intelligent, planned explanation.

In today's market the person who sells is responsible for possessing complete knowledge of the economic and social significance of the product or service he sells. He must study every feature of the item, in relation to its usefulness, from the buyer's point of view.

POWER POINTS

Salesmanship goes on around us all the time, and it takes many forms: the insurance man sells a security: a person applying for work tries to sell himself; the retailer sells merchandise; people try to sell others on the idea of doing what they want done.

Salespeople may be classified according to the customers to whom they sell and the services they offer. First, there is the familiar *behind-the-counter* selling, the kind done in retail stores. Then, there is *specialty* selling: the kind used in selling autos, insurance, office equipment, and manufactured products of a special nature.

Industrial salesmanship includes selling to industrial concerns, fabricators, and processors who buy machinery, raw materials, equipment, professional supplies, and miscellaneous items. This kind of selling requires technically trained experts and its nature varies with the kind of goods sold.

Salesmen who sell to *retailers* work for wholesalers, jobbers, or distributors. These salesmen make regular calls, check stocks, communicate enthusiasm, and avoid pressure. Others who sell to retailers are known as merchandising men, promoters, missionaries, or pioneers.

The *selling agent* and the *manufacturer's agent* sell manufactured consumer products to middlemen.

Detail salesmen are of two kinds: the *straight detailer* and the combination *detailer and missionary.* Straight detailing is a routine

kind of selling in which the salesman checks the inventory in a grocery or drugstore, suggests the purchase of whatever he believes is
needed, and writes up the order. The combination detailer and missionary is found in the drug field. He calls on medical doctors, drugstores, wholesalers, and hospitals, leaving samples with each. He does
little or no selling; he presents his name, his company name, his
products, and tells what his products will do.

Door-to-door salesmanship is another form of selling. Great skill
is required to approach customers in their homes and to effectively
make a sale.

Wholesale selling is another form which is limited to the sale of
merchandise in wholesale lots to dealers, jobbers, brokers, and other
bulk distributors.

Service salesmanship consists of retailing such items as cleaning
and dyeing, laundry, beauty treatments, auto, and jewelry repairs.

Self-service selling is exemplified by food markets where the customer chooses items displayed on counters and shelves. There is also
semi-self-service selling, a kind of merchandising in which displays
do the biggest part of selling, but with the aid of salespeople.

In addition to the normal requirements for salesmen, some companies train their men to *sell to buying groups.* These men often sell
programs of continuous supply and must not only know how to do
this, but also be adept in speaking before groups made up of expert
buyers.

The art of pursuasion enters into all selling activities. Persuasion
is employed by those who sell to manufacturers, wholesalers, dealers,
jobbers, door-to-door prospects, and retail customers. Today, many
businesses such as banks and public utilities, usually not thought of
as selling organizations, are insisting that new employees who meet
the public shall have salesmanship training. Also, doctors, dentists,
lawyers, teachers, and other professional personnel are realizing more
and more that selling skills may mean the difference between success
and failure in their professions.

Each kind of salesmanship requires emphasis on different things.
The industrial salesman is often an engineer who is able to offer
technical advice and help solve production problems. Salespeople
who sell to wholesalers and other dealers must understand the problems of these business people. Those who sell door to door and
behind the counter must know how to deal with the vagaries of the
retail customer. Basically, all salesmanship aims at convincing the
prospective buyer that he will benefit if he buys the product or service
offered to him.

DISCUSSION QUESTIONS AND PROBLEMS

1. Briefly describe the characteristics of the following kinds of early salesmen:

    a. Yankee peddler   c. Greeter

    b. Credit investigator   d. Drummer

2. How do the selling methods for tangibles differ from those used in selling intangibles?

3. "House-to-house selling is doomed to extinction as a selling method." Do you agree or disagree with this statement? Explain your position.

4. What basic, common requirements are necessary for success in all kinds of selling?

5. What makes a professional salesman?

6. From your viewpoint, what do you believe are the advantages and disadvantages of being a salesperson? Why?

7. Do large manufacturing or industrial firms have any right to expect salespeople who call on them to give technical advice to company engineers, research men, and production experts? Why?

8. What is meant by *telepurchasing?*

9. Is selling the perfect occupation for everybody? Elaborate on your answer.

10. From local newspapers, collect five advertisements which are concerned with selling merchandise. Discuss the effectiveness of these ads in relation to selling techniques which have been covered so far in the text.

SELLING PROBLEMS AND PROJECTS

1. **The Wilshore Company**

    "Do you need a teacher? Then I'm your man. Call me a specialist if you will, or just a plain salesman. In any case, I like to specialize in solving problems and in educating customers. The more problems I can solve, the more orders come my way. The more customers I can educate, the more customers like me. In a nutshell that's how I, Tom Byrnes, sell paper. And I claim that this kind of selling depends on one factor: You've got to be able to get inside whatever company you're dealing with and analyze its operation.

"Finding a problem is not difficult, however, and once you've found one it means you're already on second base. To get on first base and into the place of business where you can see the problem, you must gain the prospect's confidence in you as a salesman and in your company as a reliable concern. The customer must be completely convinced that he is talking to an expert from a reliable house. You can do this only by making his lot easier for him by taking over his problem in which you are an expert.

"After all, the buyer's job is purchasing, not solving problems. Let me give you an example of what I mean. One firm that we do business with had been oversold by another manufacturer. I happened to observe that the product he was using was twice as heavy as it needed to be and was costing him nearly twice as much money. It wasn't the buyer's job to question the product, for it was working fine; but when I showed him that he was purchasing more than double the protection he needed at more than the price of my product, he gave us his company's business. You see, I'm a troubleshooter and a teacher. It's surprising how many mistakes a buyer can make. Sometimes they're not really mistakes, because a buyer cannot keep informed of all the new developments. Again, that's where teaching enters the picture. That's my job: finding problems, solving problems, and educating the buyer.

"It takes only one or two examples of helpfulness to win the buyer's confidence completely, and I guess winning his confidence is the whole philosophy on which I operate. It sometimes takes years to develop this confidence and gain an account, but then it's our account."

Questions

1. Does this man sell to dealers, retailers, wholesalers, or manufacturers?

2. How does the sales technique of this man differ from that used in other kinds of selling?

3. Is it actually possible for a salesman to know more about the uses of a product than a well-informed purchaser?

4. How do the activities of this kind of salesman differ from those of an instructor or teacher? Do you believe a salesman is an educator, instructor, or teacher?

5. What other ways for winning confidence can you suggest in addition to the one mentioned in this case?

2. The Case of the Disgruntled Student

A distributive education supervisor received a letter from one of the students in a cooperative retail training program. The young man had recently been placed in training in a large branch department store and was disappointed in what he found.

Dear Supervisor:

A large percentage of the salespeople working for my store are over 50 years of age.

These people have no desire to better themselves, and are only interested in having a secure job, in which they try to do no more than the minimum required of them.

The attitude of these people is a real problem for the beginning salesperson, since it demoralizes those of us who are looking forward to a career in the retail business.

The older people fear that the young people can do a more efficient job, and they try to defend themselves by showing a certain aggressiveness toward the new employees.

Besides, they usually have their habits already firmly developed in regard to attention to the public, service, care of stock, and so forth. These habits are not always the best, but are passed on to the new employees.

Very truly yours,

Horace Goodwin

Horace Goodwin
Student trainee

Questions

1. In your opinion, do you think that this young man has sensed a genuine problem? Explain your reasons.

2. Assuming that the situation described in the young man's letter is correct, what do you suppose the store could do about it?

3. Should young people be critical of the organizations for which they first work?

CHAPTER 4

Selling as a Career

The Sales Manpower Foundation of the Sales Executives Club of New York has found that only 30 percent of the employers with which it has worked insist that a salesman have a college diploma. Of those companies requiring a degree, more than half do so because an engineering degree is necessary for the work.

However, the statistics do not tell the whole story. It is evident that college training *does* give a man an advantage in selling.

EDUCATION FOR SELLING

Regis P. Duel of New York State University recently conducted a massive research project to determine what sales managers thought was the best college-level preparation for a selling career. The greatest number of managers described a combination of liberal arts and marketing subjects as most useful.

An overwhelming percentage of sales managers said they were hiring and would continue to hire qualified two-year college graduates. They felt strongly that two-year colleges should offer specifically designed courses in selling and marketing. When asked to list in the order of importance those subjects which they considered to be desirable, they replied as follows:

1. Oral and written English.
2. Effective use of oral communications.
3. The fundamentals of salesmanship.
4. Basic psychology.

5. Business organization and management.
6. Consumer economics.
7. Sociology.
8. Marketing procedures and techniques.
9. Fundamentals of sales management.
10. Market research and its effective utilization.

Liberal Arts — General Education

Is a liberal arts or general education of any value to the potential salesman? The answer is undoubtedly yes. There are few jobs that use more general subjects than does salesmanship. Not all courses help, but many do. Among the major subjects taken by students who later succeeded in selling are anthropology, English, journalism, science, psychology, mathematics, marketing, sociology, and history.

As competition has increased and as marketing has grown more important, the stature of the salesman has increased. In his territory he *is* his company. He is closest to his customers; that is, he can sense their possible reactions before they occur. A liberal arts background can give him greater sensitivity to human behavior and social trends. If he can understand individual characteristics and differences and quickly assess the personality and character of a customer, he can gauge the selling situation accordingly and adjust his presentation to make it consistent with his judgment. Obviously a broader educational experience can be of value in accomplishing this ability.

Is it possible that it makes no difference what a student's major interest may be? That one course is as good as another for selling? Not quite. It means that the student should decide on his main interest, choose his subjects accordingly, and at the same time find out as much as he can about how they will apply to a selling career.

A part-time job in selling, for example, is an excellent way to acquire a "feel" for the work and to begin to use academic training. Then the student should talk to his family, teachers, and friends about choosing a career. It is also important to talk to people who are in selling.

He can also get information for selecting the right direction for a selling career if he works with high school and college guidance counselors in choosing the major which interests him most. The counselors can also point out how the student's courses will help him in his career.

The following is a brief discussion of some major subject areas and how they relate to selling.

Anthropology. A knowledge of human customs, relationships, and mores may be of tremendous value in certain kinds of selling.

Economics. An economics major would study such subjects as national income and national output, money and banking, economic history, price systems, distribution of wealth, federal regulation of commerce and industry, and comparative economic systems.

Business administration. In the marketing area, the business administration major is introduced to sales management, selling, market research, distribution, and other basic marketing topics. This information is useful not only in selling but also in sales supervision and sales management.

Science and engineering. This age of technology presents many opportunities for a career in sales. For instance, a mechanical engineer may start as a trainee, selling to industry and mill supply houses. As he acquires experience, he may find himself selling and servicing systems to assure proper operation of space vehicles and rockets. Beyond this, a salesman will find a technical background an asset in handling a great variety of items, from household appliances to factory equipment.

English. The English major acquires a great amount of information which will help him in a sales career. In modern business, selling is recognized as a form of communication. The man who, after listening to a prospect's problems, can describe a product's benefits is likely to be an effective salesman. He understands language and its uses, and he is aware of the impact of words on others.

As a man progresses in his sales career, he will find that the study of English has equipped him in another way. His reading of literature has made him familiar with human nature; it has given him an ability to know and to understand people, to judge character, personality, and to deal with the many types that exist. This helps in personal selling, of course; it is also of enormous use for the manager and trainer of other salesmen.

Many salesmen, in managing their territories, communicate in writing; and in sales management there is always the need for well-written booklets, newsletters, and bulletins. The ability to communicate effectively can help make a man a leader in marketing, whether he remains in selling or goes into related fields.

Social sciences. Sociology, psychology, and history can help a salesman. A sales career involves knowing people and how they respond. A student who understands people can motivate and stimulate them to buy. For example, many prospective customers set up defense mechanisms, and the salesman who is aware of this can deal with it. He can convince and persuade people because he has studied the persuasive techniques that induce them to buy. He knows something about guiding people into buying patterns.

COMPANY SALES TRAINING

Let's imagine that you have decided to become a salesman and that you have been employed by a large company. How does your employer train you?

Obviously, no business could long survive if it simply handed a man a suitcase of samples and told him to "hit the road." The employer has too much at stake. Undoubtedly, company training is necessary, and many programs, it is claimed, are equal to a four-year college course.

In many companies, sales training is a highly developed process. A wide variety of subjects, including psychology, education, communications, and selling skills, are emphasized; and, of course, the newcomer is given a thorough background in the business. His preparation for selling is often very broad because he must be familiar with all the ramifications of a modern business.

The sales trainee is taught how to best serve customers' wants and needs so that they will find it beneficial to buy from him. He may find himself participating in stimulating programs which broaden his outlook and experience. Sales trainees often attend classes at recognized universities in special courses designed to develop the whole man.

There are major professional associations devoted to sales training—for example, the National Society of Sales Training Executives and the American Society for Training and Development—in addition to many comprehensive company training programs. There are also consultants and advisory organizations whose training efforts complement those of the company itself.

The new salesman does not immediately start traveling, even after preparatory training ends. Ordinarily, he begins under the guidance of an older salesman, or a sales supervisor. In this way the beginner has a chance to ask questions, test himself, and discuss his job.

Continued Education

Education and counseling should continue even when a salesman has had substantial experience. Modern marketing organizations recognize the importance of continual guidance. Effective salesmen like to keep their skills sharp by using all the supervisory training they can obtain.

No longer is the salesman isolated when traveling. Only a few years ago his main and often only means of contact was by mail. But today's instant communications enable the salesman to call immediately upon the resources of his company to help him with on-the-spot decisions.

In many companies, salesmen can expect a lifetime of educational offerings, as can doctors, lawyers, accountants, and engineers. A good example is the Mobil Oil plan for graduate engineers who will sell Mobil products to industry. First, the sales trainee is indoctrinated for three months in a district sales office. This is followed by an intensive ten-week review of engineering fundamentals and sales-service techniques. The trainee continues his schooling until a territory becomes available. Then he tries out his skills under the watchful eye of his manager. After selling for one year, the trainee spends time in the purchasing department, remaining for three weeks with a purchasing agent.

He is then ready for a regular territorial assignment, although his training does not end. Actually, it continues throughout his career with Mobil. Regular courses are scheduled two years in advance for veteran salesmen, to keep them informed of technical changes, new product applications, and better selling techniques.

Most salesmen like the responsibility of making instant decisions, and their training enables them to handle it. However, when they need information or backing, a modern marketing organization, like Mobil's, is always ready to cooperate.

THE MODERN SALESMAN

Modern salesmen deal with prospective buyers who are better educated and more skeptical than those of the past. Also, today's buyers dislike too much talk and unsubstantiated claims. They want salesmen to be straightforward, employ controlled selling techniques, and, above all, to be able to prove what they claim.

Today's salesmen must be problem-solvers, motivators, and marketing experts, all in one. They must be able to cope with all kinds of people and be thoroughly conditioned and oriented toward persuading and motivating them. They should be able to deal with a prospect's skepticism and come away with an order.

Modern salesmanship includes procedures for orderly, planned, and purposeful ways of finding new customers, new markets, and retaining the goodwill of established customers.

Through the use of marketing research and advertising, modern salesmanship aims to create among users and consumers a maximum awareness of, and a desire for, established, innovative, and improved products and services. It also strives to provide efficient facilities through which these products and services can flow to users and consumers.

The technical age has caused a selling revolution, and a new kind of salesmanship is required. The Du Pont Company has described the new kind of salesman: "A Salesman of today must offer more than a good product; he must offer, as well, the technology to go with it. Unless he shows customers how to use the product profitably, he often makes no sales . . . [He] must be part scientist and sometimes part economist, sometimes part market or product-development specialist."

In addition, according to the Du Pont Company, this new kind of salesman must have a broad educational background, the ability to handle people and be liked, and a knowledge of the product and its application.

A modern salesman's occupation is also distinct in other ways. First, there is little supervision over his work activities. While he is studying his prospects, his competition and his market, and especially when he is talking to a prospective buyer, he works independently. Details of what happens, what he says and does, or what the prospect says usually remain unknown to his manager.

The salesman also operates alone, without the benefit of an audience. He does not work with other employees nor is his manager in evidence. He must sell by himself, he usually travels and lives by himself when away from home, and he must often direct his own efforts. Therefore, a salesman has to provide much of his own motivation and morale, since he is often unable to obtain either from fellow salesmen.

REWARDS OF A SELLING CAREER

Successful salespeople have jobs that are secure, full of opportunity for advancement, interesting, challenging, vitally useful, and well paid.

Security

Selling is one of the craft professions that can never be replaced by machines. Good salespeople have been, are now, and always will be in great demand. In our country the salesperson is important, for his efforts are necessary to sell our surplus and keep the wheels of industry turning.

The salesman helps industrial expansion and helps raise the national standard of living. In a vigorous, expanding economy, the salesperson will have work and security because the demand for good salespeople is always greater than the supply. For example, it has been stated that during this decade there will be a shortage of one million salespeople in the United States.

Employment Trends

The growing sophistication of business has placed greater, not less, emphasis on personal selling. The Klein Institute for Aptitude Testing, in New York City, surveyed 389 chief executive officers of corporations worth a million dollars or more. Here is what it found:

1. Seventy-nine percent of business leaders said the salesman's job is becoming more important.
2. Seventy-four percent employed more salesmen than in 1960.
3. Sixty-three percent increased the proportion of marketing budget allocated to personal selling since 1960.

For the past thirty years the number of workers in sales occupations has increased fairly rapidly. In some kinds of sales work, however, the rate of increase has been far greater than in others.

Among the large occupations which have had relatively rapid increases are real estate salesman, insurance agent, manufacturer's salesman, and wholesale salesman. The smaller sales occupations of demonstrator, stock and bond salesman, and house-to-house salesman have also increased rapidly. Among the slowest growing of all sales occupations during this same period has been retail sales worker, an occupation which nevertheless employs more people than all other sales occupations combined.

The main reason for the anticipated rise in employment is the prospect of increased sales resulting from continued population growth, business expansion, and rising income levels. Within retail stores, however, special circumstances have restricted employment growth in the recent past and will probably continue to do so.

Automation

According to sales authorities, it is hardly likely that automation will greatly affect the number of employed salesmen. This fact confirms the statement that in the 1970s we shall need one million more outside salesmen, or a total of five and a half million.

However, some major companies have some form of automatic inventory control, either punch cards or computer systems. In these companies, orders are placed automatically. Consolidated Industries, for example, reports that it has tied its sales computer to its customers' purchasing computer to handle the selling of industrial staples and shelf items.

Computers in the retail field maintain inventories, calculate turnover, and determine order sizes. In some instances they report items that should be discontinued. Routine orders are printed, and often mailed, automatically. Buyers see salesmen only when there is a change in the products, when a new product is being introduced, or in promotion situations.

The use of computers limits the salesman's ability to increase sales through his selling skills; computers do not react to persuasion and motivation. Even greater limitations to salesmanship may be on the horizon. One major food manufacturer has experimented with the idea of eliminating salesmen altogether. After a salesman has recorded his presentation on tape, the tape and sales materials are left for an unseen buyer to consider at leisure.

In some cases, according to a Dartnell survey, "The salesman will become more of a local manager in charge of administering marketing programs, locating new customers, service, and credit."

It should be noted that automation does not affect all industries; in many, its role is small. Automation by no means eliminates salesmen. It is still true that at least 10 percent of the nation's employed will be salespeople.

Opportunities for Advancement

Most people want their future jobs to grow. In addition to paying well along the way, selling offers one of the most rapid means of reaching the top. No job provides a more well-rounded experience with a company than selling.

Dartnell Corporation has reported that approximately 55 percent of the presidents of American corporations rose from the rank of salesman. The Sales-Marketing Executives Club of Chicago has reported that, of the 250 presidents of member companies, 38 percent came directly from sales, 6 percent came from sales and manufacturing, and 4 percent came from sales and finance. In other words, a total of 48 percent of the 250 company presidents came from the selling divisions of their businesses.

Normally, a salesperson may be promoted to a branch, district, or territorial managership. Advancement opportunities for salesmen, however, are not limited to the sales field. Work areas that often need the experience of a salesperson include: sales training, advertising, sales promotion, market research, credits and collections, and merchandising. Also, departments not related to selling, such as personnel, public and industrial relations and the like, often need workers who are good at dealing with people.

Although certain types of firms are not usually classified as sales organizations, many require that new employees have sales training because, in their jobs, such workers meet the public. Among such firms are banks, public utilities, brokerage businesses, hotels, transportation companies, and certain types of restaurants.

In the sales field, job openings and promotions are constantly available. The experienced salespeople in a firm may be transferred to other departments or territories, may be promoted or may retire; expanding business requires additional salespeople; new businesses demand sales forces.

For those who are suited to it, selling offers an opportunity limited only by the individual's own ability and ambition. Selling can be an open door to a lifework that can produce all that a person may reasonably ask, both in personal satisfaction and in an assured, substantial, ever-rising income.

Interesting, Challenging Work

Do you like the excitement of travel? Do you want to see new places, meet various kinds of people, inspect new markets — or would you rather work close to home? Do you want to be your own boss, or do you prefer direction and support? Are you fascinated by dealing directly with people — watching their mental and emotional processes, their buying habits, their behavior in the marketplace? Or would you rather work behind the scenes, preparing catalogues and brochures, answering correspondence, planning advertising campaigns? All this variety and more is offered by the selling field—variety in prices, products, prospects, services, dealers, competitors, forecasting, research, promotion.

If you want a job that is interesting, challenging, exciting—a job that promises personal satisfaction—selling is the job for you.

Usefulness

Everyone in the modern community is served and benefited by salespeople, because everyone regularly uses much of the great variety of merchandise and services that are sold. Consider any item in daily use—for instance, a new and improved form of food. A salesman sold it to the grocer, who, in turn, sold it to the consumer. Today the automobile is commonplace, for it has been widely sold by salesmen. The electric refrigerator, the television set, the vacuum cleaner—these and thousands of other items have been sold by salesmen, who have played an important part in our American way of life.

Economists tell us that, to maintain our present economy, we must sell $300 billion worth of merchandise each year at present price levels. This would require from ten to twelve million salespeople. The salesperson is indeed indispensable in our economic system. To stimulate purchases for more and better things, greatly stepped-up sales are required to balance the supply of and the demand for merchandise.

Financial Rewards

Salesmen are well paid. A great many are so well paid that their company treasurers and their sales managers have good reason to resent the size of the checks some of their salesmen receive.

Earnings of salesmen depend almost entirely on personal effort. Influence, nepotism, knowing the right people, all have little or no effect on his income. Successful salesmen clearly recognize that to earn more, they simply have to sell more. And there is rarely a ceiling on their income. The salesman is sure to be paid according to his effort and skill, because his contribution to his company's operations can be measured and he is usually paid according to his personal production.

Many salesmen earn $25,000 a year. Some are paid as much as $50,000 yearly, and a few earn $100,000 yearly. College graduates entering the sales field are often paid $675 to $900 a month as initial salary, plus cost of their training.

In addition to providing a means for advancement to a position in company management, a selling job is well compensated during the period of progress to an executive position. Although starting salaries are currently reported to be somewhat lower than those offered engineers and scientists, the opportunity for rapid salary increases is greater in sales than in other fields. At the end of ten years, outside salesmen usually are paid more than engineers and scientists who have held their jobs an equivalent length of time.

Salesmen work hard, often under difficult conditions, but there are financial compensations for their effort. The man with the largest income in his company, reports James R. Bingay of Mutual Life Insurance Company, is not the president, but a salesman. How much commission does a salesman earn from selling one million dollars worth of insurance? "It depends on the mix, or kinds of policies, but probably over $30,000 minimum."

There are a great many compensation plans for salesmen. Even within a particular company they may vary according to the product or service, the territory, and, sometimes, the individual man. These plans range from straight commission to salary. A good many salesmen choose straight commission, which simply means that you are paid for what you produce. For a good man, the earning possibilities are high under such an arrangement. Many other salesmen prefer a combination of base salary and incentive pay based on performance. Often this is adjusted as a man's experience grows and his production increases. He chooses to take less in base salary and more in percentage (the total being higher than if a large proportion of his compensation were fixed).

Family Life

A salesman does not necessarily need to have an unsatisfactory family life, but selling is not the right career choice for someone who wants regular hours and no overtime or extra hours' work. All good salesmen like travel and occasional trips away from home, but family life need not suffer as a result. Psychologists have commented negatively on the breach that occurs between a man and his family when the family is totally uninvolved in the man's work. Selling provides maximum opportunity for family participation and involvement. Since a salesman is really his own boss—keeping his own records, handling his own desk work—many have enlisted their wives, and even their children, as partners in the enterprise. The family provides the salesman with logistic support. They share in his successes and his disappointments; they are involved and therefore interested.

POWER POINTS

Students enter the selling field with various educational backgrounds. A liberal arts or general education curriculum usually includes some courses which help in the selling field, although a good background of specifically designed courses in selling and marketing is desirable. Certain technical and professional subjects — science, engineering, psychology, English, marketing—are especially helpful for specific kinds of selling. The salesman's training and education continue in various ways throughout his career, from the preliminary training program he invariably will receive when he first joins a firm through his efforts to keep informed about his product and related marketing developments.

There are tremendous rewards in selling: advancement, interesting and challenging work, financial benefits, security, steady employment, and usefulness.

Some of the most important, prominent, and useful people in a community are salespeople. Their education and experience enable them to be natural leaders of others. Their social status is high and increasing as technology advances.

Modern salesmen are educated to discuss facts, employ controlled selling techniques, and, above all, prove their claims. They can use procedures for orderly, planned, and purposeful ways of finding new customers and new markets and retaining the goodwill of old customers.

The most rewarding type of selling in the future is likely to be personal salesmanship. The so-called buying public has never been known to beat a path to a seller's door and to demand to buy something. The prospective buyer must be sold through personal salesmanship. True, advertising media can influence him, but the final decision comes through contact with salespeople.

Within the next decade there will be numerous new products to sell, each requiring personal salesmanship to gain public acceptance. Our rising standard of living means many more people will have leisure time and this will open many new, rich markets for creative salesmen. Millions of new suburbanites will want new appliances, new homes, new services, new pastimes.

Every study made of opportunities in the selling field has concluded that young people who aspire to executive positions in business would do well to have selling experience. These studies were concerned with *outside salesmen,* the men who sell to wholesale and retail channels of distribution as well as to industry. In marketing circles, outside salesmen represent what is known as an *elite group.* There are 300,000 executive positions that are vacated and filled each year, according to Executive Register of New York. Who fills most of these jobs? The elite group—salesmen! "No matter what position you ultimately hold in the marketing function, most people start out as salesmen," according to Dr. David J. Luck.[1] Based on a survey of 200 corporations, Dr. Luck notes that among the manufacturing and service firms which he polled, 92 percent of all college graduates for advanced marketing jobs began work as salesmen.

1. David J. Luck, "Careers in Selling: Facts Versus Campus Fallacy," *Sales/ Marketing Today,* March 1968, p. 8.

Obviously, management is well aware of the importance of the salesman's job, as evidenced by their response to questionnaires: "The salesman's role in our economy is of extreme importance." "Business profits do not come from making things, but from selling the things that business makes." "Salesmen are a company's most valuable asset, and a good one can not only get business, but can also save business when customers complain." "I believe that nothing can ever displace the personal touch of a good salesman." "When sales are made we can build plants, buy machinery, borrow money, hire experts to operate the business. But, sales are necessary, *first*."

DISCUSSION QUESTIONS AND PROBLEMS

1. What educational qualifications do sales managers seek when hiring new salesmen?
2. For a career in sales and marketing, what are the first five desirable college courses which sales managers want to see in job applicants' backgrounds?
3. What general liberal arts subjects have peripheral value for sales work?
4. What assistance can students expect from guidance counselors and placement officers?
5. What are the salient subjects included in a company's training program?
6. What are the primary rewards of a selling career?
7. What is the future importance of personal selling?
8. What are five qualities that a modern salesman should possess?
9. In what ways is a selling job distinctive?

SELLING PROBLEMS AND PROJECTS

1. Henry Weber Case

Henry Weber has been a successful field representative for thirty years. The other day he had this conversation with a friend.

"Do you know why I like to sell? First of all, I like security. The most secure job in the world is the job of the man who can sell. There never have been enough good salespeople.

"Second, I like to sell because of the money angle. Money — that's what everybody wants. There is no better-paid job in the world than selling.

"The next thing I like about selling is the chance for promotion. Do you know, Ken, that 50 percent or more of the presidents of American business concerns rose from the selling end of the business?

"I also like interesting, varied work with people. I like people and there is no job more interesting, more varied, more human, than selling.

"Finally, I like the feeling that I am doing something for my fellow men. There is no group in America doing more to keep factory workers in jobs, raise the scale of living, and promote the general welfare than the salesperson."

Obviously, Henry Weber is "sold" on this job and he is undoubtedly a success. In order to discuss the topic "Selling as a Career," consult a bibliography for source material in books, pamphlets, magazines, and reports. In addition to the ideas you find in these sources, develop your own ideas, opinions, and attitudes on the topic. Include them in your discussion.

Questions

1. What are the key points in this case that indicate why Henry Weber is successful?

2. Are there other claims about selling that Henry could have introduced in addition to the ones mentioned?

2. The Restaurant Story

Jack Salton had a roadside stand where he sold short-order food. His business thrived, so he decided to open a restaurant. To attract customers to his restaurant, Jack placed a large sign on the highway nearby, which advertised the good quality of his food.

Business increased. Jack ordered elaborate menus to be printed, and he doubled his food and supplies orders. He bought new, expensive kitchen equipment. The demand on his time was so great that he decided to bring his son into the business to help him, so he recalled him from college.

But then something happened. His son said, "Pop, haven't you been listening to the business news? If money stays 'tight,' there will be a slowdown in business. You'd better prepare for a big drop in sales." The father thought, "Well, my son has gone to college. He should know what he's talking about."

So Jack cut down on the kitchen help, he reduced his overhead as much as possible, and he took down the highway advertisement. His sales declined noticeably in a short time. He said to his son, "You were right. We are headed into a depression."

Questions

1. What is the significance of this story?

2. What is wrong with the son's advice?

3. Would a technical sales-marketing education have offered the son better criteria with which to judge the business situation?

PART

GETTING
READY
TO SELL

CHAPTER 5

Building
Personal Worth

Sam Gower and Bob Gellerman were just emerging from a sales meeting in which the company's top salesman, Bill Smith, had been presented with a check for $5,000 and a week's paid vacation in Bermuda for himself and his family.

"That lucky stiff," said Sam. "I don't see how he does it. I had his territory several years ago and couldn't do a thing with it. Why, his biggest account is a company I spent several years calling on. I knocked myself out trying to get their business, and Bill walks in and has it within two months."

"I don't know," added Bob. "Bill is a hard worker, and he seems to get off on the best foot with people when he first meets them."

"Yeah, yeah, so Bill has charm," replied Sam. "Why, he's only had a limited education. I graduated from college with a B.A. and honors. I know more about the product line than he does, but I don't get a chance to prove it. I say he's just plain lucky. He's a born salesman."

What is the difference between Sam Gower and Bill Smith? Why is it that some salesmen gain measurable successes in the presence of their prospects and achieve far above average sales and income than their fellow salesmen who possess the same educational backgrounds and product knowledge? Is it their manner, ability, or the idea that they are "naturals"?

George Cowan knows the answer. Mr. Cowan is the district sales manager for R&R Products. He has had the opportunity to observe closely the performance of his sales force, both in the field and in the office. One of his salesmen, Sam Rogers, has a B.A., a nice appearance and an excellent product background, but he doesn't get a chance to use these because he "turns his prospects off." His personality doesn't click for him when he is face to face with the prospect. Bill Smith, on the other hand, seems to possess those ingredients of personality that command respect and win the interest of his prospects. In this chapter we will attempt to explore the role that personality plays in sales work, and show that certain personality traits are the tools that the salesman must take with him on every call.

A personality consists of everything about a person which distinguishes him or her from another person, or which makes an impression on another person. A salesperson's personality is no different than that which makes anyone attractive to his friends and associates. Personality is the outward expression of an individual's personal worth; it is the qualities or traits which people like or dislike about a person.

Personal worth consists of our mental, social, and physical attributes. It is the sum of all the many and varied qualities and traits possessed by a person, and includes his attitudes toward his job and life in general, his enthusiasm, courage, dynamic drive, self-confidence, imagination, responsibility, and integrity.

Many sales executives believe that more than 50 percent of a salesperson's success stems from his sales-winning personality. They believe that prospects and customers forgive and forget honest mistakes, but they never forget a salesperson's personality. The salesperson's attitude toward his career and work environment is one of the most important aspects of his personality.

ATTITUDES

One's attitude toward his occupation can often determine his future success in it. In *The Salesman—Ambassador of Progress,* Donald Robinson identifies ten attitude traits which are essential to a selling career. Robinson says selling may be for you if:

- You value independence.
- You have ambition and drive.
- You are sensitive—and interested in the problems of other people as in your own.
- You are articulate, with enough command of language to communicate fluently and precisely.

- You have an analytical mind and enjoy solving problems.
- You are ethical and sincere. There is no place in selling for the confidence man.
- You are reliable and self-disciplined.
- You are enthusiastic.
- You are a good administrator who can draft and implement plans.

Do you have many, or all, of these personality attitudes? If so, you have every reason to believe that you can become a topflight salesperson. Here are other personal qualities which help salespeople.

Enthusiasm

Enthusiasm is defined as "a spirit which animates the whole body." When enthusiasm is added to a salesperson's knowledge and selling technique, it provides the spark so vital in creative selling.

There is an old maxim which holds that mediocre selling skills that are backed with genuine enthusiasm will produce more sales than a brilliant presentation that is delivered half-heartedly. Too often the missing ingredient in selling is enthusiasm.

Enthusiasm is usually the result of having confidence in one's ability and believing in what one is doing. The more a salesperson knows about himself and other people, his product or service, his buyers and his selling skills, the more enthusiastic he becomes.

Emerson said, "Nothing has ever been done without enthusiasm." It enables a salesperson to accomplish great things, for when he is enthusiastic, he creates a similar mood in others. Enthusiasm is *contagious*.

There is no doubt that enthusiasm is a powerful force in human relations and it can be developed by most people. However, when it is not natural with a person, he should not feign or pretend it. If he puts on an act and is insincere about his real feelings, if his enthusiasm does not arise from an honest belief, then it can do him more harm than good. But when a person's enthusiasm is honest and sincere, it can be a very powerful selling tool.

Cheerfulness is a part of enthusiasm and it, too, is contagious. A pleasant, positive manner always assures better relations with everyone with whom the salesperson deals. Of equal importance is the fact that a cheerful person always feels better himself. How would you evaluate your enthusiasm and cheerfulness?

Self-confidence

Elbert Hubbard once wrote: "The greatest mistake you can make in this life is to be continually fearing you will make one." A salesperson must keep his confidence constantly alive and view each new experience as a challenge to his ability. When he has the kind of confidence that refuses to be defeated by fear, he is on the road to achievement.

Overconfidence is, of course, undesirable, but it is generally conceded that it is better to have a bit too much confidence than too little. The right kind of self-confidence will cause others to feel confidence in a salesperson, and therefore make them more ready to listen and to be persuaded. Because salesmanship involves surmounting a constant series of obstacles, courage and confidence are primary requisites.

Dynamic Drive

Nearly all successful men and women have worked diligently in the face of great difficulties to attain what they have. These people never lost sight of their goals; they worked, they planned, and they persevered even when they were discouraged. They were ambitious, but their ambition was well directed. Another name for ambition is dynamic drive. When dynamic drive is intelligently applied, most formidable difficulties are overcome.

Dynamic drive may manifest itself in many ways. It includes the ambition to become an executive, a determination to increase one's income, a desire to become socially prominent, as well as the ambition to become a successful salesman.

Initiative is included in dynamic drive. A salesperson has initiative when he possesses the ability to act without being urged, to originate a new sales program for himself, and to do more than just an average job. Knowing when to use initiative requires a constant study of work one is doing and some thought as to more effective ways of selling than those which have long been acquired by habit or rote.

Individualism

Selling is really for the individualist. You need not be a conformist to be a successful salesperson. A salesperson is judged on his ability to produce, and it is frequently the unusual approach that produces best. Moreover, the salesman is self-motivated. He can sell to whom he wants, when he wants, what he wants.

The salesman's customers don't care what he thinks or how he lives. If he serves their needs, they are satisfied. Raymond Johnson of New York Insurance Company has pointed out that the salesman's real "boss" is his customer. As long as he serves this "boss," he remains independent.

Imagination

Imagination and initiative are first cousins. Imagination has to do with the constructive or creative part of the mind. It is of great importance in selling. Initiative puts creative imagination to work; otherwise imagination is little more than daydreaming. The information which a salesman gathers, the facts which he assimilates, are organized and made use of through initiative and imagination, and when used constructively, the results will be the best selling technique.

The salesperson should imagine himself in the buyer's place, thinking as the buyer would, contending with the buyer's problems, and making the decisions the buyer has to make. This process requires a better than average imagination and is cultivated only by the application of keen observation, by inquisitiveness, by attention to detail, and by a good memory.

Speech

The first words a salesman utters must influence the prospective buyer to like him as a person, and at the same time stir his curiosity enough to make him want to hear more. Many successful salespeople spend hours over opening statements. When a buyer says, "Sit down, I'd like to hear your story," the salesperson has reached his objective in creating a positive, favorable attitude.

It is practically impossible to outline definite forms of address that will serve to create the right attitude for all interviews. It is always advisable, however, to avoid commonplace opening lines and stereotyped phrases such as: "I thought I'd drop in to see if I can interest you in . . ." "My name is Jones, representing the Blank Company. We make a very good product and I'd like to tell you about it."

Entire textbooks are devoted to speech, rhetoric, grammar, and vocabulary. A pronouncing dictionary and a thesaurus can be quite helpful, but it is not always necessary to wade through Webster's or Roget's to learn how to say every word correctly. However, when the proper pronunciation or usage is in doubt, or when one wants to expand his vocabulary, both of these references can be of great value. The old lady who said, "Thank God, I ain't got no use for grammar!" may have suffered little loss from her scorn of good English, but the salesperson similarly uninhibited will find himself severely handicapped in the presence of many of his prospective buyers.

The salesman should avoid the many insipid phrases that are so common today. Don't offend your buyers with a flood of nonsense words and clichés from which you emerge to gasp and groan, "I mean . . . yuh know . . . I mean . . . like . . . yuh know." You hear these utterances every day on campus, in the classroom, on radio and television. Avoid them like poison. They can destroy an otherwise good sales technique.

Responsibility

A responsible person is one who does a thorough job. He has studied his territory and knows it like the palm of his hand. When he sets out on a trip he covers his territory intensively and thoroughly. He does not take advantage of the fact that he is his own boss, that he does not have to sign in at nine o'clock every morning. In short, he is a mature, reliable person.

Poise

To be well thought of by customers and prospects, to deserve appreciation, and to prove himself worthy of responsibility, a salesperson must have poise and self-confidence.

The salesman's greatest problem is not the occasional person who tries to "get his goat." Important buyers rarely indulge in that form of sport, and those who do are few in number. Sometimes it is done purposely to test a young salesperson's mettle. It is always a disturbing experience for the beginner and is apt to throw him off balance.

An old-time salesman tells of this experience: "On my first road trip I was greeted by a prospect with the shouted inquiry, "What the hell do you want?" The brusqueness of the man floored me. I could only stammer my sales talk. I repeated the call on the next trip and he flung the same question at me. I was ready for him this time. "All I want," I said, "is the same consideration you expect your salesmen to get from their buyers." That caught him off guard. He sputtered, but he asked me to sit down. I had learned one of the secrets of poise.

"The buyer who can upset your poise most quickly and effectively has no intention of doing so," says a sales manager. "He's the man who asks relevant questions you can't answer. If you happen to know the answers, you're all right. If you are as sure you can render a service as the buyer is sure of his position, you will not lose your poise."

Poise is more than self-confidence or self-assurance. It is these qualities, both of them, tempered with knowledge. The more a salesperson knows about himself, his product or service, and the skills of selling, the more certain is his poise.

Liking for Travel

Selling usually requires at least some travel. A sales territory or district can comprise as much as thousands of square miles or as little as several square blocks — or even several floors in one building. Since the salesman schedules his own time, he is freer to be a perceptive traveler and to absorb and enjoy the many pleasures of travel.

APPEARANCE

First impressions are important because buyers react much more favorably to energetic, well-groomed salespeople. The creative salesperson must give daily attention to maintaining his health so that he can have the energy he needs to work successfully. A proper balance of work, exercise, nutritious food, and relaxation will ensure general good health. This is especially true for the salesperson who has irregular hours, frequent changes of locale, or other occupational peculiarities which make regular and constant check of health extremely desirable.

Neatness and Apparel

We know that people respond favorably to the person who knows how to make a good entrance. A professional salesman, like a professional actor, should enter an office with calm resolution. He should make the impression that he has something worthwhile to do and that he is aware that his client's time is valuable.

The salesman sets the stage, creates the mood, and builds the attitude for a sales presentation. A poor start jeopardizes the entire proposal. When a salesman dresses slovenly and is inattentive, it is easy for his prospects to assume negative attitudes.

A salesman should dress neatly and attractively; his speech should be cheerful and enthusiastic. In this way, his prospects respond to him by adopting a positive attitude. The success of any salesman largely depends on how well he can sustain the enthusiastic attitudes of his prospects for his proposition. A cheerful greeting, a pleasant manner, and neat appearance, all serve to create the atmosphere and the attitudes that help to make buying easy for the prospect.

POWER POINTS

A creative salesperson combines facts and selling skills with the vital spark of a positive personality. Many sales managers say that over 50 percent of a salesman's success stems from a winning personality.

Good personal qualities mean the ability to get along with people and to be effective in dealing with them. A sales-winning personality is based on a neat, pleasant appearance, acceptable social manners, and mental ability. Personality is the combination of an individual's good and bad traits; it is a reflection of a person's life-style; it is the projection of the inner self.

A good selling personality is the great equalizer which makes up for many deficiencies in a salesman. It is the quality which helps attract new customers and hold old ones. It is often said that unless a salesman has more than average positive personal qualities, he will be no more than average in his ability to sell.

Among the personal qualities which often need strengthening are attitude, enthusiasm, courage, dynamic drive, appearance, speech, poise, self-confidence, imagination, and integrity.

The suggestions offered in this chapter should help a student toward a much greater appreciation of his personality and how to improve it. Many people do not take advantage of their best personal qualities because they have not learned to identify them. Ask yourself, "What can I do to become a stronger personality?" When you identify personality traits which need improvement, you will then be able to gradually seek ways to develop them.

To develop a winning sales personality, you must realize the need for improvement and have a strong desire to improve. Then you must make a systematic plan for development. You must work on the qualities and traits you want to develop and decide on new habits and practices which will improve your total personality.

No one is ever too old to acquire a better personality. In fact, psychologists tell us that our personal qualities and traits improve with age, but we must practice their development if we want them to become something of which we can be proud. Self-development is not easy, but the rewards to be gained are worth the effort involved.

DISCUSSION QUESTIONS AND PROBLEMS

1.   Reread the case example involving Sam Gower at the beginning of this chapter.

    a. What, in your opinion, is Sam's problem?

    b. What do you think Sam's sales manager should do about this problem?

2.   What is the meaning of personality?

3.   How may salespeople employ autosuggestion to improve their personalities?

4.   How does a salesman's appearance affect a prospect's attitude toward him?

5.   Why is enthusiasm an important quality for selling?

6.   How do the opening statements of an interview affect the buyer's attitude toward a salesman?

7.   Specifically, how would you start to enhance your personal worth?

8.   Why is *integrity* the one special character trait which every salesman must possess?

9.   What is the advantage of *individualism* to a salesman?

10.   Why is a salesman's *speech* important?

SELLING PROBLEMS AND PROJECTS

1.   Bob Lawrence Story

One of the authors of this book was a college freshman when he began his selling career. He was probably the most frightened salesman in his home town. The following are some interesting comments about how he solved his *fear* problem:

    I quickly learned that I had to overcome my fear or get out of selling. My greatest fear was reluctance to call.

    I needed something to help me get over my timidity about the first call on prospects; something that would enable me to go in and make a good presentation. I needed mental conditioning and some kind of self-motivation. I vaguely knew this, but I didn't know what to do about it.

Fortunately, I knew a brilliant salesman named Bob Lawrence, a man so expert that he could have sold anything to anybody. I discussed my fear with him. He helped me analyze my abilities and shortcomings. We reviewed my selling technique. When I use the word "technique," I am exaggerating, for I really had no technique worth mentioning. But I was ambitious to become a better salesman, and I was very happy to have Bob outline some rules for better selling.

Bob started candidly. He asked me if I was trying to "cop out," to make excuses for myself. Then Bob startled me again by saying, "What you need is a good swift kick, but you'll have to do the kicking yourself. You must develop the drive and ambition. You'll have to motivate yourself. Nobody can do it for you."

Bob had several suggestions concerning how I could overcome my hesitance to make calls.

These four rules changed my life as a salesman. They worked so well for me that I am sure they will benefit anyone who wants to conquer his reluctance to make calls.

Rule 1. Say to yourself: I am a great salesman. I am prepared to meet this prospect. I have something beneficial to offer this prospect. I'll like him as an individual. I'll make the sale and I'll make a friend.

Rule 2. Say to yourself: I'll put my best effort into this presentation, and I will succeed in doing it well.

Rule 3. Say to yourself: I have everything to gain and nothing to lose by trying; I will try hard to close every sale.

Rule 4. Say to yourself: I'll do it now.

Make up your mind to succeed. Follow these four rules and you will find that your fear of making calls will disappear and you'll be on your way to successful salesmanship. Bob's advice worked, too, because it was just good common sense, given at the right time.

Questions

1. Are timidity, fear, and reluctance to make calls common and normal for most beginning salesman? Explain.

2. What is the reason for reluctance to make a call and how may it be overcome?

3. How would the elimination of fear affect a salesman's total personality?

4. How would the four rules mentioned above affect a salesperson's attitude?

5. Do you believe that an application of these rules would enhance your personal worth? Explain.

2. Jim Otis Case

The district sales manager for Jim Otis' company asked him to come into the office. The manager explained to Jim that he was checking with all men below 85 percent of their quota to see what could be done to improve the situation. He then asked Jim why he sold only 65 percent of his quota. Jim's answer was:

"Well, in the first place, I've got a heck of a heavy quota for my territory. Whoever set this quota certainly didn't know the conditions. The fact that I ended up last year with 65 percent of quota should prove that it was wrong to give me the same quota this year.

"I don't know what more I can do. I'm working as hard as I can now. Why, it's a job just keeping the buyers we have. I'm lucky I haven't lost more business than I have, with my competition throwing their weight around. Most of my time is spent putting out fires and keeping buyers happy.

"My buyers all feel there isn't any money to be made in selling some of our items, and they just aren't interested in building their sales. Any good prospects I do find in my territory are all tied up with competitors. This is their territory, you know, with lots of promotion, big deals, and three—three, mind you—salesmen covering the same territory I do. Besides, with that aviation plant closing up and people moving to Georgia, business is just folding up and disappearing. The business just isn't there—not for us, anyway."

Questions

1. What is wrong with Jim's attitude? Discuss.

2. What other personal qualities, both good and bad, are revealed in this case?

3. Is it possible that Jim's position might be right? Explain.

CHAPTER 6

Using Product Knowledge

Everyone is familiar with the fact that seven-eighths of an iceberg is submerged and invisible. Seven-eighths of a salesperson's work may also be unseen, because it consists of preparation for meeting the prospective buyer. The preparatory activities are numerous, but among the more important are learning to know the product or service from A to Z, and using facts to build the salesperson's oral presentation.

There are four good reasons for knowing the facts about your product or service thoroughly: (1) to enjoy your work, (2) to overcome sales obstacles, (3) to develop self-confidence in selling, and (4) to make effective sales presentations.

KNOWING PRODUCT FACTS

No more impossible task exists than trying to explain to a prospective customer what you yourself do not understand. Salespeople without sufficient knowledge tend to talk in generalities, hoping to make a sale without preparation.

A salesperson who knows his product or service thoroughly is confident. If the opening remarks do not convince the customer that he will benefit from the sale, the informed salesperson is ready to elaborate, introducing new ideas. He can be patient and unhurried because he knows that he can eventually demonstrate the values and benefits of what he sells.

Knowledge is power. If a salesperson lacks knowledge, he may worry, and he may unintentionally convey his worry to the customer. The salesperson may be apprehensive that the customer will not buy;

he may anticipate that difficult objections will be raised; he may fear making a mistake; or he may dread competition. Most of his tensions are the result of insufficient preparation for the sale.

A salesperson should know his product or service thoroughly so that he will be equipped to overcome sales obstacles. He should anticipate the types of questions customers will ask. Although many of these questions are never voiced, the salesperson can be spared the embarrassment of not being able to answer.

Self-confidence is like money in the bank. A sale is based largely on confidence. The salesperson's confidence in himself is an important factor, and the customer's confidence in the product, the company, or the salesperson is equally important. Confidence produces confidence, and the natural result is a sale.

Complete knowledge of your products or services and of their advantages for the customer develops the personal quality of self-confidence which you yourself feel and others readily perceive.

As soon as the customer meets you, he can tell whether you have self-confidence. Self-confidence is a quality you can acquire by study or training. It can come to you as the result of your knowing all about your products or services and what they will do for the customer.

All through your presentation, keep clearly in mind that your facts are for customers who are really interested only in themselves. Your customer wants to hear facts about things that will contribute to him, his wants, his interests, his desires, and his gain.

If your facts do not appeal to your customer's basic interest in himself, you will not be a successful salesperson. Every customer you meet has this question he wants answered clearly and satisfactorily: "What's in it for me?"

Usually your prospect or customer will be interested in a money gain, which means added profits, or savings, or both. Some prospects are also motivated by safety, pride, competition, increased efficiency, dependability, outclassing competition, employee satisfaction. There are other buying motives, but chances are that the preceding are among the most important. The success of all your endeavor will depend on the direct-benefit facts you have for your prospect. When your proposition appeals to *his* interests, *his* desires, *show him a gain,* the chances are that he will buy.

PRODUCT BENEFITS

Today, no matter what is sold or to whom it is sold, the salesperson must have a complete awareness of such benefits as exclusives, values, advantages, and gains.

In general, benefits are of three kinds: (1) apparent benefits, (2) exclusive benefits, and (3) hidden benefits.

Apparent benefits are attributes anyone can see, such as the beauty of the product or the purpose for which it was made. These are the qualities that any salesperson can easily recognize and that require little explanation to the customer, yet they play an important part in closing successful sales.

Exclusive benefits are attributes that competitors do not possess; therefore, they give the salesperson a clear advantage and distinct selling point. Many products and services owe their popularity to the discovery of only one exclusive benefit.

Hidden benefits, in contrast to apparent benefits, are values not recognizable without explanation. Finding hidden benefits requires the kind of thinking that raises a salesperson above the mediocre and denotes creative status. It also lifts selling out of the humdrum and makes it a joy instead of a chore.

Hidden benefits add strength, character, and glamor to a sales talk. For example, when creative salespeople sell clothes, they really sell personal appearance and attractiveness. When they sell shoes, they sell foot comfort. When they sell television sets, they really sell the pleasure of entertainment, knowledge, and relaxation. When they sell furniture, they really sell a home that has comfort and refinement. When they sell toys, they really sell gifts that make children happy. When they sell books, they really sell education, ideas, emotions, knowledge and enjoyment.

Facts about products, merchandise, or services must be stated in terms of what appeals to, or benefits, customers. Customers are rarely interested in bare facts or technical information unless such facts furnish solutions to their buying problems or needs.

USING PRODUCT KNOWLEDGE

Professional salespeople sell benefits; average salespeople usually concentrate on features. People do not ordinarily buy features!

A *feature* is any marked peculiarity, anything especially prominent. Features include such things as quality, delivery, design, workmanship, and construction. A feature tells the prospect what went into the product.

A benefit, on the other hand, is whatever promotes welfare, advantage, or gain. A benefit explains why the proposition is important to the buyer and states the advantages of owning the product or using the service. A benefit tells the prospect what the product will do for him. Of benefits and features, which would most often persuade and motivate you to buy? The answer is easy: you would buy benefits. Since your customers respond to the same influences as you, they would also buy benefits rather than features.

THE HAMMER STORY

To learn the importance of selling benefits and knowing your merchandise thoroughly, read the famous Hammer Story as told by Dr. Paul W. Ivey. Doctor Ivey has effectively illustrated the necessity for knowing the facts about your proposition in the story which follows:[1]

> The first principle of salesmanship is to know your merchandise from A to Z, so that you can take the value out of your merchandise and paint a picture of it on the customer's mind.
>
> Many salesmen use glittering generalities instead of specific points of value, and then wonder why the customer does not buy.
>
> I will illustrate this principle by an experience I had in buying a hammer. No matter what you are selling—hats, shoes, automobiles, refrigerators, real estate, insurance, or what not—this hammer story will help you to sell more of your merchandise, provided you apply it. Think of your merchandise as I talk about this hammer.
>
> One day some years ago I wanted a hammer. I went into a hardware store, and this is about the way the salesman handled me:
>
> He put a hammer in my hand, and as I looked at it he said, "That is a mighty fine hammer. That is a real hammer. We sell a good many of those."
>
> I shook it up and down as though I were going to drive a nail, wondering whether I should buy it or one of some others displayed in the case.
>
> He looked at me, I looked at him; then we looked at each other.
>
> After a while he spruced up a little, thought he had better say something more, and said, "That is a mighty fine hammer. That's a real hammer. You can't go wrong on that hammer."
>
> Nothing registered in my mind—no value. But I absentmindedly shook the hammer, balancing it a little, and wondered if I had better ask to look at some of the others in the case.
>
> He looked at me, I looked at him, then we looked at each other.
>
> After a while he brought in his final, closing sales talk. He

1. From Paul W. Ivey, *Successful Salesmanship,* 2nd ed. (Englewood Cliffs, N.J.: Prentice-Hall, Inc., 1947). Reprinted with permission.

brought in his heavy artillery, the heaviest he had. Do you know what he said? He said, "That's a mighty fine hammer. That's a real hammer. You can't go wrong on that hammer."

I said to myself, "Ye Gods! Is that the way they are trying to sell merchandise in the United States of America, the greatest commercial nation in the world?"

I decided I would find out. So on my next business trip, I went into more than one hundred hardware stores in ten different states asking to look at hammers, and not one salesman told me much more about a hammer than was told to me in the first store.

If any of you want to have a little fun even now, just drop into half a dozen hardware stores and ask to look at hammers.

A short time after this experience, I went through a large mail-order house in Chicago. In those days they had no retail stores and did strictly a mail-order business.

The guide took a crowd of us around, showed us many interesting things and told us many illuminating facts. He also told us the gross sales. I marveled that a company could reach out with a long arm and pull in all those millions of dollars through a mail-order catalogue. Finally, a bright idea came to me and I said, "By the way, my friend, you have interested me very much; but at this particular time I am interested in one line of merchandise. What were your gross sales of hammers last year?"

"Hammers?"

"Yes, hammers."

I could see by the way he looked at me that he thought I was crazy. Now it is always a hard thing for me to know just what to do when a person thinks I am crazy; so I said, "I can see by the way you look at me that you think this ridiculous. Of course, I have never had the pleasure of meeting you before, and you have never met me, but, if you only knew it, you are looking at the greatest hammer expert in the United States."

Then he was sure that I was crazy.

Well, he did not know what to do with me, so he turned me over to another man. When you don't know what to do with anybody, turn him over to somebody else.

This other man, when he saw that I was a very inquisitive individual and wanted to know how the wheels ran in business, treated me in a wonderful way. He told me more interesting facts, showed me some more interesting things, and finally told me the gross sales of hammers.

"Do you sell that many hammers?" I asked.

"Yes," he replied.

"Would you mind letting me look at them?"

"Certainly not."

He brought out four. Ugh! They looked like old friends of mine.

I said, "You will pardon me, but they look like ordinary hammers. How in the world do you ever sell so many of them?" And he replied, "Maybe you will find the reason if you look in our catalogue."

I went to their catalogue, and the sales talk that I am now going to give you about a simple thing called a hammer, I read in that catalogue: and if you happen to have the latest edition of their catalogue, you will find an enlightening sales talk embodying several changes which they have made in recent editions:

First, "This hammer is full nickel-plated."

I said to myself, "I am sure some of those hammers I looked at must have been full nickel-plated."

You say, "Mr. Ivey, when you had those hammers in your hand, and looked at them, couldn't you tell whether they were full nickel-plated?"

To tell the truth, that fact never once impressed itself upon me. All I knew was that they were "mighty fine hammers; real hammers; I couldn't go wrong on them," whatever that means.

Second, "The handles are mahogany-finished."

"Oh," I said to myself, "some of those handles I looked at must have been mahogany-finished."

You say, "Mr. Ivey, when you had the handles in your hand, couldn't you see whether they were mahogany-finished?"

I suppose I knew it in a general sort of way, but here is a company that does not believe in glittering generalities. They believe in a bull's-eye hit. Take the value out of the merchandise and paint a picture of it on the customer's mind, so the latter will want it and pay the price for it.

Third, "This hammer is made of crucible cast steel!" Now an ordinary customer might not know what crucible cast steel is, but he feels it must be some steel. It is.

Fourth, "The faces and claws are tempered just right."

What comes into your mind as a practical person? That is a test of any salesmanship. I know what comes into your mind. You say, "If the faces and claws are tempered just right, I can pull a big spike with that hammer and the claws won't break." Certainly!

Have any of you ever owned a one-claw hammer? Why, as I recall it, I was nearly twelve years old before I knew that a hammer was supposed to have more than one claw. Ours was always broken off.

Fifth, "The claws are split to a fine point."

What comes into your mind?

I know. You say, "I can pull a very fine nail with that hammer." You bet you can. Have any of you ever tried to pull a very fine nail with the hammer at your home and had the nail slip right through the claws? Then you tried again and the same thing happened; then you tried once more and it happened again? (Then you paid your respects to the hammer!)

Here is a company that says, "You can pull the finest nails with our hammers." The don't say it in so many words; they leave it to your imagination.

Sixth, "The handles are made of selected, second-growth hickory."

Not one salesman told me that. Some salesmen did say to me, "That is a mighty fine hickory handle." How fine? Mighty fine. Ugh! I can't grasp that, quite. Mighty fine!

Another salesman said, "This is a real hickory handle." I thought it might be artificial hickory.

Here is a company that says "selected, second-growth." The customer feels that this is not an ordinary handle. They have been selecting the hickory for those hammers.

Second-growth! Now what goes through your mind? People who do not know what it is may say to themselves, "Well, I guess it must be very good or they wouldn't say so"; or they may even think, "They couldn't grow it good enough the first time so they grew it the second time."

Seventh, and final, "The handles are put in with iron wedges so that they will not come loose." Does that ring a bell?

Have any of you ever had the head of a hammer fly off? At one time I used to think it was one of the functions of a hammer for the head to fly off.

Do you see this hammer?

Full nickel-plated, mahogany-finished handle, made of crucible cast steel, faces and claws tempered just right, claws split to a fine point, handles made of selected second-growth hickory, put in with iron wedges so they will not come loose.

Do you see it?

Do you know what I have done? I have gone into a retail store and had a flesh-and-blood salesman put a real hammer in my hand, and I have looked at that hammer with my own eyes; yet I have seen less value in that real hammer when I held it in my hand than when I read about a hammer in a mail-order catalogue.

I take off my hat to any company a thousand or five hundred miles away that can make me see more value in a hammer when they put a cut of it on cheap paper with a description underneath than I can see when I actually have a real hammer in my hand in a retail store.

And that brings me to one of the most remarkable principles of merchandising and selling: nine people out of ten do not see what they look at. They cannot even see a hammer by looking at it. They only see what they are educated to see. Are you educating your customers to see the full value in your merchandise?

Do you think a person could come into a salesroom and look at an automobile and immediately see the style lines, the speed lines, the luxurious comfort, the staunch and reliable bumpers, the artistic instrument panel, the performance of the motor? Do you think customers can see anything by looking at it? Let us not deceive ourselves.

Take the dark glasses off the customer's eyes. Make the picture clear in the customer's mind by talking about specific, definite points of value.

Did you ever wonder why your competitor, with an inferior product, sometimes takes business away from you?

You may have better merchandise for the money than a competitor, but you lose out because your competitor makes the customer see more value in his merchandise.

This is proved by my study of hammers. Do you think that this mail-order house has more value in their hammers for the money than all the hammers I saw in a hundred different stores? Do you think they have? Not on your life. I know. I am an expert on hammers.

They have excellent value for the money, but there were hammers I saw in retail stores that had drop-forged steel, instead of crucible cast steel. I have seen better hammers for the money. Did they sell as well as the mail-order hammer? No. Why? They did not look as good in the customer's mind.

I have seen many a merchant put out of business, not because he did not have better goods, but because he did not know merchandise value himself and he could not make a customer see what he did not see himself. He was not a salesman.

Do you ever take it for granted that the customer sees the full value in your proposition?

When value is lower than the price, the customer loses interest.

When value is equal to the price, the customer feels that he is getting a fair deal.

But, when the salesman builds up value until it is higher than the price, then the customer feels that he is getting extra value— a bargain.

Be a creator of value.

Leave generalities for the order-taker.

Make the picture clear with specific facts.

In short, apply the "Hammer Story" to your merchandise, and you will increase your sales.

SELLING PRODUCT BENEFITS

It is wrong to sell only features, because they leave too much thinking to the customer and he will not or cannot think about them. You have to translate your product, service, and merchandise features into benefits if you want people to appreciate whatever you are selling. Benefits do not speak for themselves; you must sell them! Imagine yourself trying to sell a proposition on the basis of features such as these:

performance	service
reputation	price
components	design
colors	availability
taste	method of
smell	installation
sizes	packaging
exclusives	promotion
uses	laboratory
applications	tests
ruggedness	terms
delivery	workmanship

Personal benefits. Read the following list carefully and note how personal benefits do most of the thinking for the prospect, chiefly because they are not generalizations. They are specific and they have personal appeal.

time saved	economy in use
reduced costs	preservation of
prestige	beauty
better health	ease of operation
maximum comfort	reduced inventory
bigger savings	low operating cost
greater profits	simplicity
pride of possession	reduced upkeep
greater	increased safety
convenience	satisfied ambitions
uniform production	added protection
uniform accuracy	reduced waste
continuous output	self-improvement
leadership	ease and comfort
increased sales	long life
pride of	greater production
accomplishment	mental ease

Whenever you point out the personal applicability of benefits, you increase the possibility of concluding the sale successfully. Some personal benefits can be used even in selling to a professional buyer or businessman. For example:

"This is something that will speed up your work."

"This will reduce the number of complaints you have to handle."

"The workers who use this product will appreciate your giving them a better tool."

"This is a chance for your company to get out in front of competition."

"This gives you more of the advantages enjoyed by your competitors."

Dealer Benefits. Benefits for dealers always arouse the buying interest of this group. For example:

more consumer business	faster turnover
more retail business	higher markup
more repeat business	lower inventory
ease in selling	community leadership

Old Selling Habits

When selling benefits, one should guard against a natural tendency to continue to sell features because of the tendency to rely on established habits of selling. Most salespeople are probably trained to appreciate their product features. The more they know about the features, the more likely they are to sell them rather than benefits. The rule is: "Sell benefits, not features!"

Feature selling has other pitfalls. For example, features imply more for the money. They leave too much thinking to the buyer. You must translate your product, service, and merchandise features into benefits to the buyer. How about you? On thinking it over, would you actually sell benefits? Or would you really sell features while telling yourself that "benefits speak for themselves"? Do they? You cannot prove that benefits speak for themselves. You must speak for them.

Side Effects of Selling Benefits

A valuable side effect accrues to the salesman who deliberately and consciously sells benefits rather than mere product features. First, when benefits are sold, the salesman makes a more enthusiastic, interesting, and natural presentation. He will have a buoyant quality that can rarely be acquired in any other way.

Second, the salesman who sells benefits will no longer regard himself as a seeker of favors, but as one who offers them. Furthermore, with this viewpoint he will not call on prospects because he is directed to do so, but because he wants to.

Benefits Analysis

Before attempting to sell a new product or service, creative salespeople get the facts about each of its features. Then they make a list of the benefits offered by those features. Since all customers want benefits for their money, you should find out the benefits your merchandise or service possesses and concentrate on selling them.

The usual method of determining the benefit points of a product or a service is to list the important features. On the basis of the features, the salesman can easily determine the product benefits for the buyer.

Many salesmen prepare benefits-analysis forms that assist them in listing not only the features and exclusives of the product, but also the benefits and advantages the prospect will enjoy if he purchases it. These salesmen draw up a form like Table 6-1.

Table 6-1. Prospect Benefit Analysis

Product: Long-handled Shovel

PRODUCT FEATURES AND EXCLUSIVES	BENEFITS, ADVANTAGES, AND VALUES PROVIDED BY THE FEATURES AND EXCLUSIVES
1. Perfectly balanced handle and blade.	Means less strain on your back. Feels comfortable to handle.
2. Rigid lock-socket design.	Prevents the blade from coming loose.
3. Steel blade and straps are forged, high-carbon steel.	Prevents the blade from breaking off when and if you happen to catch the blade on a root or other object.
4. Back strap and all seams electrically welded.	Assures a longer life for your shovel. Assures greater strength because it has uniform welding throughout rather than common spot-welding.
5. Handles are made of selected northern ash.	Provides a strong, hard-to-break handle selected of the very best second-growth ash by men trained to choose the best wood.
6. Handles are sanded, polished and shaped.	For a comfortable grip. Splinter-proof.

How would the previous benefit analysis help a salesman make a sale? Let us study the following situation which shows how hardware salesman Harry Green closes a sale on shovels to a concrete building contractor. The benefit statements are in italics.

The scene takes place in the builders' hardware department of a retail store. The customer has removed a shovel from a display and is carefully examining it. Harry Green, a salesman who sells benefits rather than features, approaches.

SALESMAN: Good afternoon, sir. How does that feel?

CUSTOMER: Pretty good.

SALESMAN: We consider this one of our best shovels. The reason it's *so comfortable to handle* is because handle and blade are perfectly balanced. This means *less strain on the back* to the person who is using it. A pretty important point, wouldn't you say?

CUSTOMER: Yes, it would seem to. I'm a building contractor. I'll be needing a few of these for my men.

SALESMAN: Then it's pretty important to you that they have a shovel they can use *easily and comfortably in order to accomplish more work.* Of course, you are entitled to our *contractor's discount.* How many shovels would you want, sir?

CUSTOMER: I'll need six right now, but I'm not sure this is the one I want yet. It seems a little high-priced (looking at the price sticker on the handle).

SALESMAN: I'm sure you're interested in *buying something that costs less* over the long run, isn't that true? Lower-priced shovels often break or splinter, causing you to discard them sooner than a shovel of this type. This means you are buying shovels more often.

For instance, sir, consider the rigid lock-socket design of this shovel. This *prevents the blade from coming loose* and would be especially important to you when working in hard ground.

This shovel *will stand up to hard use.* Notice the steel blade construction with the holding straps. They are both forged with high-carbon steel. This *will prevent the blade from breaking off* when and if you happen to catch the blade on a root or hit a rock. All of this means *a longer life for your shovel.*

And notice the back straps and seams, sir. They're constructed for *greater strength and longer life* because they are electrically welded instead of just being spot-welded.

CUSTOMER: Those are good points. But our men have broken a lot of shovels, even some that have had extra strong blades and straps. They broke in the handle.

SALESMAN: I'm glad you brought that up. You are right to be concerned about the handle. The handle on this shovel is made of selected northern ash. The company that makes this shovel has skilled buyers who are trained to select only the best wood for the handles. This means *you get a strong handle.* I won't say you can't break it, but it will be *extremely hard to break.* Here, let me show you.

(Salesman places shovel on top of two tool chests, then stands on the handle. Next he sits down on the handle and lifts his feet off the ground for a second. Customer is visibly impressed.)

CUSTOMER: You sure made your point.

SALESMAN: But don't forget that even though this shovel is built for heavy-duty work, it is *still comfortable to use,* and it's *splinterproof.* That's because the handles are sanded, polished, and *especially shaped for the kind of heavy-duty work you and your crew will give them.* Did you say you needed six? We have about ten in stock right now, sir.

CUSTOMER: I'll take the ten. Also, I want to look at your axes and hammers.

Motivation Analysis of Benefits

Many salesmen use a motivation-analysis form to learn more about the prospect's basic reasons for buying their products or service. In the left-hand column, they list the benefits and values that they believe their proposition possesses. In the right-hand column, opposite each benefit, they explain why and how the benefit should assist in motivating people to buy. The form often used is shown in Table 6-2.

Table 6-2. Prospect Motivation Analysis

Product: Bentag Washing Machine

PRODUCT FEATURES	BUYING MOTIVES
1. Gyrofoam water action, sediment trap, roller water remover—all mean quick, easy, and thorough cleaning.	Physical comfort
2. Square, one-piece cast aluminum tub.	Utility-economy gain
3. Each part skillfully made, carefully fitted. This guarantees perfect performance throughout the life of the washer.	Happiness-utility gain
4. Reduces electrical cost. Uses less soap.	Economy gain
5. Bentag means quality in washers. More than three million owners enjoy satisfied use.	Imitation, pride-of-ownership gain

Simple analysis of the product can reveal many ways in which it satisfies the buying motives of the prospect. The preceding breakdown shows how the major features of a washing machine may be attuned to the buying motives of a qualified prospect.

Sources for Benefit Facts

The most obvious and practical source of product facts is the product or the service itself. The salesman should study it and, if possible, use it himself to become thoroughly familiar with it.

Second, in every sales organization there is a collection of product bulletins, advertising materials, catalogues, manuals, and information booklets that contain much of value to a salesman. It should be clear, however, that the salesman must study these publications thoroughly to receive anything from them, and he must then put his facts to productive use.

Other good sources are (1) fellow salesmen, (2) sales managers, (3) customers, (4) company executives, (5) library books, and (6) dealer publications.

What to look for. Several road signs serve to help the salesman who is seeking benefit facts. For example, he can examine his source materials with the following considerations in mind:

1. Concept of the product or service. What led to its creation? What is the history of its development?
2. What the product is made of. Are the materials new and different? Where are the materials obtained? How are they selected?
3. The finished product. Its appearance, quality, novelty, special or individual features, appeal, style, suitability, or intrinsic value.
4. Product uses. What will it do? How can it be used? Does it have convenience, ease and speed of operation, patent features, a good service record, and durability?
5. Price in relation to quality and competition.
6. Service and replacements.
7. How to care for the product.
8. Consumer recognition by consumer agencies.

Comparison with competition. To obtain a complete representation of a product or service, every aspect of it should be balanced point by point against competitive products or services. If a product has special benefits, values or advantages, the alert salesman gauges these in advance against competition. He gains this information through attention to competitive advertising, trade papers, personal examination of competing products, and continual alertness and watchfulness as he covers his territory.

Full-line Knowledge

Salesmen who work for wholesalers and other distributors, as well as many who sell for manufacturers, may handle so many lines that a thorough knowledge of each one is impossible. However, they should at least be able to explain why each one has been included in their list and why the buyer will benefit from its purchase.

It is natural for a salesman to try to boost his sales volume with the easy sellers and to neglect to push the slow items, even when the latter are the most profitable. But a professional salesman has enough pride to do a well-balanced job. He has considerable knowledge about his best-selling items and sufficient familiarity with the others to enable him to discuss them intelligently with buyers.

PLANNED ORAL PRESENTATIONS

One of the chief complaints of industrial buyers, as well as consumers, is that too many salespeople do not carefully prepare their sales presentations. Buyers like the kind of planned sales presentation which was made recently by a young salesman of industrial specialties who believed in organizing himself. For example, he knew the name of the buyer, the average production of the factory, the type of product that was manufactured, the approximate amount of supplies that were used, and other facts about the business.

When this salesman entered the buying office and introduced himself, there was a businesslike air about him which instantly appealed to the buyer. His sales presentation was complete, brief, and well constructed. He did not force himself upon the buyer, but let the facts speak for themselves. He asked the buyer to test the product before he asked for the order.

Of course, it required considerable time to prepare a sales talk of this kind, but that time was well spent. And it is so different from the presentation of the salesman who has that "happen-to-be-near-and-just-thought-I'd-drop-in" attitude that makes it so easy to turn him down.

Even George Jessel, known as one of the greatest extemporaneous speakers, admits that the most successful of the "extemporaneous" speeches he has made were very carefully prepared in advance. But

Mr. Jessel's art is so perfect that he makes his speeches appear extemporaneous, because he is able to give them an apparent freshness and spontaneity, even when they have been rigidly planned before he speaks.

The best trial lawyers carefully prepare each presentation in advance. Every point they expect to make is worked out, placed in its logical position, and rehearsed. Just like a professional salesman, the lawyer concludes by summarizing the points he has proved. Every outstanding lawyer is actually a professional salesman who tries to influence the judge and jury by proceeding through every step of the selling process.

A professional salesman emulates the professional speaker, the actor, or the lawyer by leaving nothing to chance. What can the ambitious salesman do to remove the chance of errors from his oral presentation? What is the best way of presenting a proposition? What words and phrases should be used? To what motives should he appeal and in what order should he appeal to them? How can he prove that the prospect will benefit if he buys? How can he avoid making "off-the-cuff" sales talks? He can perform all of these things by preparing a well-constructed, interesting sales presentation.

Planning Procedure

A prepared sales presentation requires a definite plan of procedure or action. However, it should not be inferred that a sales presentation should always be learned word for word. The ideas and the order of presentation should be learned, memorizing only a few distinctive words and phrases which are particularly descriptive or striking. These words and phrases may then serve as "memory hooks" on which to hang the entire sales presentation.

A *planned* sales presentation is the most useful kind to attempt. Many salesmen write their own presentations, occasionally reviewing their manuscripts so that they can express their benefit points in the best manner and in the most effective idea sequence. They do not memorize their presentations and repeat them verbatim, but they do constantly review and strengthen them. Turn back and read the Harry Green example on page 96 again, and notice how Harry memorized and used specific points from his benefit analysis.

Outlining the Presentation

A prepared, planned sales presentation is not transcribed, it is not wholly memorized, and it certainly is not impromptu. It should first be outlined in complete statements rather than in words or phrases. This forces the salesman to organize and clarify his ideas and eliminate useless, meaningless words.

When the outline is complete, it should be transferred to small note cards. The salesman rehearses the talk, referring to his notes when necessary. He should rehearse at least ten times, varying the wording each time. The value of this method is to train the salesman to think on his feet and to prevent him from giving a routine presentation.

Once the salesman is familiar with the material and has practiced it many times in varying ways, he replaces the complete statement outline with an outline of key words or phrases on a single card. After further speaking practice, he throws this card away. Thereafter, he develops and refines his technique, analyzing and judging the suitability of his examples and supporting materials.

A professional salesman gives to his sales talk the same amount of interest and practice that he gives to a sport he likes. He knows that good form is what matters, the same as it is in a sport, and that good form only *seems* effortless—it is achieved through hard work, planning and practice.

Standardized Sales Talks

Many successful sales managers insist that their salesmen be able to recite their presentations before they are permitted to sell.

These companies claim that through the combined experience of their best salesmen they have developed the most effective sales presentations. They insist that, unless other salesmen can develop something better, they should be willing, for their own good as well as for that of the company, to use the tested methods that obtain results.

There are three possible ways to use standardized sales talks. The first way is to give the salesman complete sales information and to allow him to organize and develop his own sales presentation. Second, specific sales presentations are given to the salesperson, but he is instructed to give them in his own way. Third, the salesman is given specific sales talks with instructions to memorize them completely and to deliver them verbatim.

The first method is effective when the salesman is exceptional and has the ability to organize facts and translate them into usable material. For certain salesmen, the second method is more desirable, provided they memorize the substance of the complete information.

For inexperienced salesmen, the third method may be the best. It concentrates the salesman's attention on what he is going to do and not on how he is going to do it. It gives him something definite to say. It keeps him away from generalities and ambiguous statements which might create confusion rather than a clear picture of values, advantages, and benefits.

The chief criticism of the memorized sales talk is that it creates a mechanical presentation. If this happens, it should be discarded, since there is nothing more ineffective than a salesman who parrots information. However, does memorizing a sales talk make the salesman mechanical? Many sales trainees and sales managers say, "No."

Some sales managers argue that although every word uttered by an actor is memorized, it does not necessarily make his performance mechanical. Why? Because the actor thinks out every idea as he goes along. He lives his part. He becomes, for the time being, the person he is portraying. Memorizing by an actor has one purpose: It acts as a guide to his thinking.

This is probably the best answer to the critic who says that memorizing anything produces a parrotlike delivery. Mechanical sales talks are not produced by memorizing, but by lack of thinking. There are many salesmen who have never memorized anything, but their presentation is nevertheless mechanical. They have merely developed through numerous repetitions a sales talk of their own, with no planning or logical development.

Every professional salesman has a prepared sales talk whether he develops it himself or someone develops it for him. What is needed is to produce the most effective sales talk possible, and it can be developed only when based on sound planning and organization.

Preparing for Buying Committees

More and more often, salesmen are finding it necessary to sell to a purchasing committee instead of to one buyer. This is particularly true in the food field, where committee buying now accounts for as much as 80 percent of sales volume and is soon expected to increase in the future.

The growth of large business units and the decline of small ones has caused this shift from traditional buying methods. The supermarket, stocking more than 8,000 different items of merchandise, is an example. The purchase of such a great variety and volume of merchandise could not be performed through a simple salesman-to-buyer relationship. The movement away from person-to-person selling has caused the men who sell major accounts to employ a more formal group-audience approach.

As in all good salesmanship, the group-audience approach requires adequate preparation by the sales representative. Before the meeting, the salesman may try to talk to each committee member to introduce his proposition, as well as to learn something about each individual's interests, attitudes, behavior pattern, experience, and education. He may attempt to discover their opinions of his product or service. If he cannot meet everyone on the committee, he may try to discover the strongest personality in the group and talk to him. He may also find it advantageous, when possible, to have an advance talk with the member who usually raises the most objections. This kind of salesman also studies a prospect's current purchases or use of competitive products or services. He tries to discover the strong and weak points of his competition and what complaints the prospect may have about the competing product or service.

An important part of the salesman's preparation should be to plan an agenda of the major points to be presented. This might be in the form of a schedule, showing the time limits for each part of the presentation.

Next, the salesman should prepare a specification sheet stating briefly the chief advantages, benefits, values, services, conditions, and other facts of interest to the committee. A copy of the specification sheet should be given to each member of the buying group at the start of the meeting.

Finally, a rehearsal is needed. This should be somewhat like a theatrical production, and it demands practice on the part of the salesman. If a mechanical product is being presented, a cast of characters may be needed in the presentation, corresponding to the make-up of the buying committee: engineers, finance men, accountants, and researchers. The sales representative's purpose is to have enough specialists on his team to satisfy the needs of the buying group and to make an effective presentation.

POWER POINTS

Sales of any consequence are said to be more *the result of preparation* than of selling techniques. Just as it is too late to begin to formulate a strategy for a battle when on the battlefield, so the preparatory planning of the presentation cannot be delayed until the salesman is facing the prospect. It must be done long in advance of the interview.

Product knowledge, which includes features, characteristics, specifications, performance, advantages, benefits, and competitive differences, are things the salesman must know perfectly and in detail. These things are his tools, and he must have them stored in his mind to be recalled *in toto* or individually.

To paraphrase Peter F. Drucker, well-known authority in modern management, the salesman has a specific tool: *Information.* He does not "handle" people; he motivates, guides, and organizes people to do their own thinking. The primary means of attaining these ends is oral communication.

DISCUSSION QUESTIONS AND PROBLEMS

1. Briefly explain the "iceberg" principle and why it is important to the salesman.

2. What are four good reasons for knowing the facts about your product?

3. How can a complete knowledge of his product increase a salesman's income?

4. If you were selling in a hardware store and a customer asked you if the mixing valve needed a volume regulator and you did not know, what would you say?

5. Can a salesman know too much about his product?

6. What is the right way to use facts in a sales presentation?

7. What information would you need about women's shoes before selling to customers? About men's shoes?

8. Should a salesman listen to people who find fault with his product? Explain.

9. What are the three kinds of product benefits? Describe each briefly.

10. What is a feature? A benefit?

11. What is a benefits analysis? How can it help the salesman?

12. What is a motivation analysis? How does it differ from a benefits analysis?

13. Where does the salesman get facts and product knowledge about the product he sells and the company he works for?

14. Bring an item to class that you have purchased recently. Prepare a benefits analysis on it. Be prepared to talk about its selling features and benefits before the entire class.

15. What is a standardized sales talk?

SELLING PROBLEMS AND PROJECTS

1. Hardware Sales Trainee Case

A young salesman for a wholesale hardware house was taught to sell by the company trainer. He was told to memorize many facts and features about the items in the company's line. One of his products was a sprayer used chiefly on farms and in certain industries. He was trained to say these words about the sprayer: "The tank has electric seams; operates on compressed air; has a brass pump with a two-stage pump lock; has high pressure; is guaranteed; and is the best on the market."

Choose the statement that best applies to this short, short story:

a. The young salesman did not furnish the kind of information which would persuade and motivate a prospect to buy.

b. He did well at recalling what he had learned about his product.

c. He should have repeated more of what his trainer told him.

d. The trainer did a bad job.

2. Biff Small Case

Biff Small sold television sets for the Monarch Manufacturing Company. His territory included western Kentucky and Tennessee. We begin with Biff showing a retailer his newest model, which has been set up in the retailer's store.

Biff points to the guarantee and Underwriters' Laboratory approval plate as he begins his demonstration.

BIFF: This set is designed to give your customers reliable, picture-perfect television. No fuzzy, out-of-focus pictures. (After he has made the set ready, he points to the solid-state circuit board, including rectifiers and a 19-inch television picture tube.) Notice the tubes and rectifiers that come with this television set. No skimping here. The cabinet is available in gum wood and walnut finish, and can be moved all over the room without having to change the wire and plug.

PROSPECT: What about the operating controls and the speaker? Many of these television sets give fuzzy, jumpy pictures.

BIFF: The operating controls in this set provide fine tuning, channel selector, contrast, volume control, on-off, picture horizontal hold, and brightness and vertical hold, all conveniently located for fast, simple station location.

PROSPECT: What is the retail selling price?

BIFF: You'll be surprised. You can sell it for only $199. You get a 33⅓ percent markup on it, too.

PROSPECT: I wonder if television sets will sell in this area. We're rather far from . . .

BIFF: These sets will pick up video casts from as far away as seventy-five miles. Your customers can get both Cincinnati and Louisville. We guarantee excellent reception.

PROSPECT: How about service?

BIFF: We will provide service for you until you have learned to do it yourself, or until your business grows sufficiently for you to hire a serviceman. We will drop-ship for you, connect, make necessary adjustments, and service each set for ninety days — until you are ready to install and service your own work.

PROSPECT: It is a good-looking job, but . . .

BIFF: Here, you try it out for yourself. Notice how simple it is to operate. Notice the clear image, the tone. This set will be in heavy demand when your customers hear about it.

Questions

1. Did this salesman appear to know his merchandise?
2. How did this salesman emphasize benefits to the dealer?
3. Why did this salesman ask the prospect to try out the set?
4. What suggestions can you offer to improve his presentation?

CHAPTER 7

Prospecting for Customers

Authorities in the field of selling have stated that "prospecting is the salesperson's search for those that are *needers* who can be changed into *wanters* and then into buyers."

NEED FOR PROSPECTING

Because of the inevitable mortality in prospect lists, it is constantly necessary for the salesman to discover and search for new buyers who will benefit by purchasing his product, service, or idea. Therefore, each salesman must recognize the need for a healthy ratio between active buyers and nonbuyers, as well as between prospects and nonprospects.

Successful salesmen never lose sight of the fact that their customers are their competitors' best prospects. They never assume that an account is their personal property or that they have an account tied up. Salesmen exercise constant vigilance about this point, because they realize not only that their competitors are trying to take away their customers, but also that there is frequent turnover among key buyers because of promotions, resignations, and so forth.

Despite the old rule that customers are the best prospects, the salesman who merely tries to keep his established accounts is overlooking the attrition rate among established customers. In many lines of business, customers leave at the rate of 20 percent each year, so that a man who takes over a territory with 600 customers and doesn't replenish the list will be down to approximately 300 at the end of three years. (See Figure 7-1.)

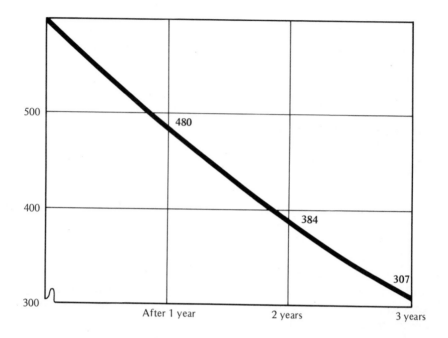

500   480

400   384

307

300

After 1 year   2 years   3 years

"Customer Mortality—Why Prospecting Pays." Reprinted with permission from *Salesweek*, published by Vision Management Publications and Sales-Marketing Executives International, Inc.

Figure 7-1. Customer Mortality—Why Prospecting Pays

Extensive-intensive Selling

The successful salesman, like a lawyer, realizes that the better he prepares his case, the greater are his chances of winning it. To increase his sales, the salesman must sell to more prospects and more to each customer.

Extensive selling increases sales by selling to more prospects. *Intensive selling* increases the unit of the sale; that is, instead of selling one or more items, the full line is sold.

In extensive selling, the salesman needs to have imagination, information and ideas, and to use both ingenuity and initiative to get new customers. Finding hidden prospects requires skill and patience. When model homes are shown in a new subdivision, only an alert salesperson can locate the real buyers. The beginning salesman may waste valuable time until he learns to distinguish the lookers from the real customers, but this experience develops his skill in identifying prospects and nonprospects.

In selling, one should never overlook any possibilities for new customers. Many gas-station attendants become annoyed when rush-hour customers casually say, "Oh yes, and check the battery, too." One attendant noticed that all his associates disliked this service, but he determined to make it a selling device. Whenever a car drove into his station, he asked the driver if he could check the battery. Most of them were happy to have it done. He would show them the hydrometer reading whenever the cells were low, and would then explain the unpleasant situation of a dead battery on an expressway, the trade-in value of the old battery, the guarantee on the new, and the security of a quick start on a cold day. As a result, he sold many batteries that would not otherwise have been sold. His ingenuity and initiative increased his sales.

Suppose a friend of yours gave you a list of 100 names and said, "Jim, these prospects need what you sell. They'll buy from you if you can prove yours is best." What would you do? You would start seeing the prospects and you would not stop until you had seen every one. In this chapter we are going to be that mythical friend and tell you where 100 or more prospects can be found.

First, however, you should make a complete study of the benefits that your product or service offers. When you know what your product will do for the people who might benefit if they bought it, you will be able to determine who might buy it. The young salesperson should understand at the start that a steadily maintained and up-to-date list of prospects is as important to his success as a steadily increasing volume of orders. This is true whether he is sent into new territory where his company has few or no customers or to an area where there are many. He must be prospect-minded as well as sales-minded.

Personal Advantages of Prospect Hunting

Prospect hunting has other advantages in addition to plugging holes caused by lost customers. In the first place, a salesperson must not only be able to present a convincing sales presentation; he must also learn to find new buyers by using his own initiative and imagination. In the second place, nothing boosts a salesperson's morale and self-confidence more than finding a prospect and turning him into a customer. A large order from an old buyer is always an accomplishment, but to open a new account, even if it is only a sample order, is a greater achievement.

SOURCES FOR CONSUMER PROSPECTS

Before setting out on his first trip, the salesperson is usually given a list of customers (unless the territory is new to his company, in which case he gets a list of prospects). He may be given a list of both, but he will be wise to build up his own prospect list, or add to the customer names given him. He will naturally be more interested in potential buyers he finds himself; his own list will be screened and will probably have more potential than a list prepared for him. Here are a variety of sources used by successful salesmen to build a prospect list:

Company files and records are usually replete with information about customers and prospects. Company officers and older sales-people possess great funds of information.

List houses, or organizations that make a business of selling assorted lists of all descriptions, are useful sources for prospects.

Organization membership lists may be obtained from chambers of commerce, service clubs, alumni associations, country clubs, and many other similar organizations. Such lists are valuable not only for the names they contain, but also because they reveal many things about the prospect's interests.

Lists of professional people such as doctors, lawyers, and other groups are of value when selling to the members of the professions.

Local tax lists are also valuable not only for the names and addresses they offer but also for their indication of the prospect's ability to buy.

Newspapers, trade journals, and *house organs* provide some of the best sources for new business with the information they offer on new products, new equipment, new applications, personnel changes, and other vital facts useful to the alert salesman. Many men make a practice of filing away such lists on the principle that something of little value today may later supply a lead for new business.

Telephone directories in every city contain a classified section from which salesmen can select prospects engaged in the various lines of business that could benefit from their product or service.

Advertising leads from the salesperson's home office, classified advertisements for customers, sales letters, and direct mail advertisements are also valuable prospect finders.

News items in local papers are rich sources of prospect information. Every day there are news stories of incidents which reveal the needs of potential customers. For example, an accident in a local factory reveals the need for insurance or safety shoes; the organization of a new bowling league indicates prospects for athletic supplies, uniforms, shoes, and other items; or damage to the roof of a house by a fallen tree may result in the homeowner's need for new roofing materials and insurance. Local papers also identify potential buyers of various products and services in their reporting of weddings, births, and such events as the opening of factories or restaurants.

Consider the *businesses* in your community or territory. What are the employees' needs and how can your products fill these needs? Workers, as well as management and owners, can be contacted through their unions or by direct canvassing. When a salesperson makes his proposition known to any organization or person, he helps to increase sales volume.

METHODS FOR FINDING PROSPECTS

Creative salesmen have developed definite methods for finding good prospects. All of these methods employ techniques for dealing with people. Some of the common methods are the endless chain, referral, the center of influence, sales-associate method, group prospecting, trade shows and exhibits, cold canvassing, creeping-vine technique, and personal observation.

Endless Chain

The endless chain method of prospecting is based upon the idea that everyone on whom the salesman calls is a source for prospects. For example, the insurance salesman calls upon Mr. Smith, who purchases a basic home-protection policy. Just as he is getting ready to leave, the salesman presents the new policyholder with a handsome little address book, saying, "I'm sure that you may have some friends, neighbors, or business associates who would be interested in the same service I have rendered for you, Mr. Smith. I would be more than happy to contact them if you want to jot their names down in my address book."

Professional salesmen attempt to get prospect names regardless of whether they succeed in selling their product or service. If they use this technique with finesse, it results in an endless array of prospects. In fact, the salesman may never run out of people to see, as is shown in Figure 7-2. Can you count the number of prospects obtained by calling on Mr. Smith?

Present customers or users of a product or service are often the most valuable sources of prospects that a salesman can have. In selling some product lines, more than 50 percent of new sales are obtained through these sources. The endless chain guarantees that new prospects are available to the salesman.

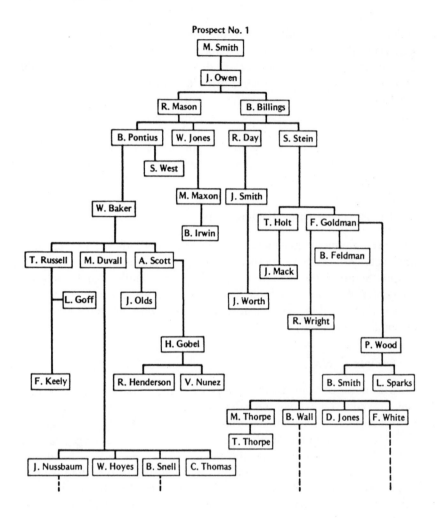

Fig. 7-2. How the endless chain method creates prospects

Referral

The endless chain technique supplies names and addresses; the referral method goes a step further. Customers can pave the way for a sales interview with their friends or associates by telephoning them, by writing a letter of introduction, or by providing an exchange of business cards or even a personal introduction.

The value of an introduction is that the prospect to whom the salesman is referred will usually listen to the salesman's proposition, because he respects his relationship with his friend or associate. If the salesman can demonstrate that he is able to fulfill the referral's need, there is a good chance of making the sale.

The telephone introduction is usually the most effective, since it is used when the caller is enthusiastic about the salesman's product or service. Often the caller takes the role of the salesman himself over the telephone, stressing the advantages of the product and attempting to overcome any reluctance or resistance from the person on the other end of the line.

The personal introduction is also an excellent type of referred lead, and is often used when the referral is within convenient access of the original customer. The card of introduction is widely used by all types of field salesmen. The salesman must be careful, however, not to spoil the chance for additional sales by giving the referral the feeling that someone else is making up his mind for him. For example:

SALESMAN: Good afternoon, Mr. Chase. I've just been talking with Mr. Goodman. Here's his card. He was telling me you need new typewriters in your office, so I thought I'd see if we could arrange a demonstration of our new standard office machine.

MR. CHASE: Goodman said that? What does he know about my setup? I think you're wasting your time, Mr. Salesman.

The letter of introduction is usually the most difficult type of introduction to obtain. Most businessmen are too busy to take the time to write an introductory letter. The solution to this situation is to offer to compose the letter on the client's stationery for his signature—with his approval, of course.

Center of Influence Method

Often the salesman is friendly with influential people in the community who are willing to refer prospects to him. Such people may be prominent business leaders, clergymen, educators, union officials, or attorneys. They may supply all the information a salesperson needs. They may even make appointments and recommend the salesperson and his proposition to the prospect. Salesmen offering genuine benefits should not be timid about asking customers or friends for the names of new prospects.

Because of their broad general contacts in many areas, bankers are one of the best sources or *centers of influence*. They have a real interest in promoting more business, and when a salesman shows them how his proposition will benefit the banks customers, they are usually willing to help.

Prominent accountants, attorneys, and consultants in various specialized fields are all worthy of consideration as client sources because of the respect in which they are held by their clients. When a salesman convinces them of the merits of his product or service, they are often happy to furnish names of potential users.

The ability to use influential people is important. The preferred method is a letter of introduction, but a telephone call by this person is also effective for making introductions, and even for appointments. The advantage is that influential people have prestige which the prospect transfers to the salesman, responding to him as if he were as important as the influential person. This is called third-party influence, and is one of the strongest testimonials a salesman can have.

Some salesmen claim that it is best to go to the center of influence with a previously prepared prospect list. These salesmen say, "When you ask a busy banker, broker, lawyer, or businessman to suggest who might need your proposition, you ask too much. His mind is on his own problems." But when a salesman presents a list of people or companies who look like possible prospects, the center will usually know most on the list personally, or at least know of them. The salesman does not ask for introductions to everyone on the list, just the few whom the center says he knows rather well. A letter of introduction or a phone call to those on the final list is usually agreed to by the center.

Sales-associate Method

In the sales-associate method the salesman engages people in various occupations or organizations to search out leads for him. Consequently, this method is also known as the *bird dog* or the *spotter* method. It is commonly used in specialties such as life insurance, homeowner's insurance, major appliance, and home-improvement programs. Sales associates are not permitted to do any selling; they merely pave the way for the salesman to call. They are usually people such as postmen, movers, real estate agents, meter readers, deliverymen, P.T.A. officials — anyone who can furnish information about new developments and new prospects in the community. These sales associates are commonly paid a commission or fee on all leads which they furnish or on all leads which result in a sale.

Some companies will employ *junior salesmen* to make door-to-door or office-to-office calls to qualify prospects and make appointments for the senior salesman. As in the case of sales associates or bird dogs, the junior salesman makes no attempt to complete the sale, but only paves the way for the senior salesman.

Group Prospecting

In group prospecting, the salesman conducts or associates in programs that attract a large number of people from which he derives his leads. An example of this method is the dinner or party plan used by direct-selling companies in which the salesman finds a housewife who, in return for a small gift or the prestige involved, will lend her home for a demonstration of the products offered.

Trade Shows and Exhibits

Many consumer and industrial goods firms set up exhibit booths in trade shows or conventions and staff these booths with salesmen. People who attend these shows are usually interested in the products on display and thus provide the salesman with a chance to meet many new prospects. Often, contests are held and product samples are available. Inquiry cards are usually filled out by people visiting the booth and can be used to measure the effectiveness of the display and the effort of the salesman. However, the main use of the inquiry card is in follow-up appointments to show and demonstrate the product or service in the prospect's home or office.

Cold Canvassing

The Victor Adding Machines' house magazine is entitled *Walk and Talk*, a name that aptly describes much of the daily activity of the salesmen in the Victor organization.

When a Victor salesman canvasses for his line of products, he literally walks and talks. He covers his territory block by block. He goes into every store, office, or factory in search of prospects who can and may buy. Having found them, he talks with them, educates them on the value of a Victor product, and persuades them to own one. Since the law of averages is working for the salesman in such cases, a certain number of sales will likely result. This type of prospecting is called *cold canvassing*.

Not only must the cold canvasser have the courage and the will to put forth the effort required for this type of prospecting, but he also needs a systematic approach. One of the most difficult and discouraging types of selling is house-to-house. Consider the example of a stainless-steel cookware salesman using a systematic approach in cold-canvass prospecting:

> SALESMAN (at the door): Good morning. I'm Jack Cramer with Kitchen Kraft. Kitchen Kraft has just opened a new branch office in your area and we want to acquaint you with our location. May I present you with this booklet? It's filled with ideas.
>
> HOUSEWIFE: Thank you.
>
> SALESMAN: Do you have a set of waterless cookware?
>
> HOUSEWIFE: No, I don't. I'm not sure I know what it is.
>
> SALESMAN: We love to show off our new cookware. May I make an appointment for twenty minutes to show it to you tomorrow morning?

Creeping-vine Prospecting

Creeping-vine prospecting is not a mysterious kind of prospecting. It simply means that the salesman (1) places himself in his customer's shoes concerning general problems and attitudes; (2) estimates the kind or class of business and marshals answers to problems likely to be related to it; (3) prepares the sales talk and plans its presentation in a way that will interest the prospect. This kind of prospecting is also known as *back-door* prospecting and *progressive* prospecting.

Creeping-vine prospecting also means starting on a fact-finding tour before seeing the person with authority to buy. It is natural for the salesman to seek facts and related information from people who work for or with the prospective buyer. These people can tell the salesman what the problems are, what future purchasing plans may be, whether a change of supply sources is contemplated, and which other personnel might influence the buyer's decisions.

If a salesman were selling an industrial product, he might start his creeping-vine prospecting with the engineer. He could ask questions of anyone and everyone he sees, including the custodian or elevator operator. If the engineer is out, the salesman could see a mechanic, a serviceman, the doorman, the manager's secretary, the buyer's assistant, the plant superintendent, foreman, workmen, clerks, or receptionist.

Creeping-vine prospecting should not be used to undermine the authority or prestige of the buyer or purchasing agent. The salesman should not sneak around and surreptitiously gather his facts. If he finds that his fact-finding activities may cause ill-feeling in a certain situation, he should discontinue pursuing this method.

Questions to Ask

Through asking questions and listening to these people, the salesman may gain a complete picture of the buying situation and at the same time deliver a short sales talk to each one. He can arouse their interest by assuring them that they are the real buyers, regardless of their actual titles, because they are the people who will be directly concerned with his product or service.

When the real buyer is not available, the salesman must not withdraw from action. That is the time to ask the assistant buyer a few questions, to give a demonstration, to offer solutions to problems, and to mention benefits and exclusives to be gained if the product or service is purchased.

When preparing a creeping-vine approach, the salesman should plan to solve problems by preparing answers beforehand. A buyer does not order if he feels that he will have to justify his decision later by explaining and selling it to others.

The questions to ask when making this type of sales approach will vary according to the type of business, but the salesman should find out if the firm has a product similar to the one he is recommending, what condition it is in, who bought it and why. He should learn who the buyer is and whether others also have authority in this area. He should obtain as much specific information as possible in order to make a sales presentation designed to appeal to the specific firm.

After obtaining this information, the salesman is ready to ask the buyer for an interview. He knows what benefits, values, and advantages will interest his prospect. Because of his questioning and back-door selling, he has acquired allies and well-wishers and should be on his way to a successful sale.

Personal Observation

Personal observation is simply a method of keeping your eyes and ears open—being on the alert to recognize a good lead. While it may not warrant a separate heading as a sales method, noticing things that are happening around you is an important skill that can be developed by constant training and practice.

Observation in the field will provide the best leads for a canvasser. A salesman for lubricants says that much of his success came from looking for smokestacks when he visited a new area: Smoke meant machinery and machinery needs lubricating. A salesman for a domestic oil burner outstripped all other members of the sales force. He toured residential districts and noted the ash cans outside large houses and apartments: Coal ashes gave him his leads. One young fellow who sold office supplies built up a good clientele by systematically working the big office buildings in his city, beginning at the top and working down.

Specialty Prospecting

The Toledo Scale Company has defined and described its ideas of what constitutes good prospecting or canvassing. Canvassing, states the Toledo Scale Company, "is the systematic coverage of territories to find the most likely customers in each community, and preselling them on our products and service whenever possible."

The Toledo Scale Company trains its salesmen to pursue the following course when seeking new business through canvassing for new prospects:[1]

1. Spend some time canvassing each day. Usually the more good prospects you have, the more business you'll get.

2. Make your friends prospect-conscious. Keep them on the alert for new business.

3. Keep records of your good prospects. List their names and addresses, type and size of business, kinds of present equipment, names of buyers, dates and results of your contacts with them.

4. Call back on satisfied customers. A happy customer usually is so proud of his new machine that he shows it off to his business friends, neighbors, and customers. He's your assistant salesman and presells other people. A friendly call-back is a good way to get the names of these new prospects, and to pyramid the sale of another machine to the already satisfied customer. Add these names to your mailing list, too.

5. Watch for new business, moves, remodeling. Canvassing the territory, items in the newspapers, and tips from your friends will help.

6. Get route lists for your territory from the local newspaper. Such lists give store names by streets, the addresses, and frequently show the managers' names. Sometimes the lists are free; otherwise, the cost is small.

1. Sales Training Manual, Toledo Scale Company.

7. Get reverse telephone lists from the local telephone company. These can be rented at relatively low cost and show stores and industries by streets, the addresses, and types of business, and often include the managers' names. The Yellow Pages of the telephone directory is a good source of prospects by type of business.

8. Get acquainted and attend local meat, grocery, and other dealer associations.

9. Presell by mailing appropriate literature a day or two before you plan to call.

10. And, once you get a prospect, keep him active.

Prospect Cards

Prospect cards may contain a record of all sales and calls, particular problems, names of individuals the salesman contacts, names for a mailing list and many other details. A prospect file should be made from these cards, and each card should show the following information: company name, address, telephone number; name of buyer and his position; names and positions of others who might influence the sale; credit clearance; competitors' products bought by prospects; data of special interest about the buyer; space for listing calls and progress notes.

PLANNED SALES STRATEGY

When seeking new customers, make sure you have fully explored your own territory. Have you tackled the big accounts? They are the real challenge, calling for persistence, perseverance and self-confidence, plus *planned sales strategy*. The extra preparations, presentations, and planning required to sell a substantial account will give you better organization of your selling preliminaries, plus the confidence that comes from being thoroughly familiar with every phase of it.

QUALIFYING PROSPECTS

Value of Qualifying

One of the keys to successful selling is carefully qualifying the prospect. Failure to qualify prospects is reported to be the chief reason why salesmen make 65 percent of their sales calls on the wrong person.

Qualifying means that the salesman determines whether or not the prospect has certain attributes, qualities, or genuine interests which indicate that he may benefit if he buys the proposition. To determine if the prospect has the qualities necessary to make him worthy of a salesman's effort, answers to these questions are required:

- Does the prospect *need* the product or service?
- Has he the ability to *pay*?
- Has he the *authority* to buy?
- Is he readily *accessible*?
- Does he have a sympathetic *attitude*?
- What is his business *history*?
- What is his *reputation* as a buyer?
- Is he a *one-source* buyer?

In addition to saving otherwise wasted effort and increasing sales, the salesmen who qualify prospects have a fund of information which enables them to visualize how their propositions can be of *maximum benefit* to the prospect. While qualifying entails considerable preparation, it is an infinitely better method than the drop-in call when the salesman merely hopes the law of averages will bring him a sale.

The salesman who prepares himself in these ways receives the kind of welcome never accorded to the salesman who drops in to pass the time of day. The prospect recognizes that the professional salesman is there to serve him, not simply to meet him.

Basis for Qualifying

To turn a prospect into a customer, the salesman must have in mind eight criteria about each prospect. If a prospect meets these criteria, the salesman can actively pursue the account, knowing that he will probably acquire a customer.

The most important of these qualifying factors is the customer's *need* for the product. A need may be known or unknown, latent or felt, realized or unrealized. It is the job of the salesman to discover the need, and if it is not yet a realized need, to call the need to the prospect's attention.

Ability to pay for the product or service is the second qualification. It may be necessary to eliminate customers who do not possess sufficient income, purchasing power or credit standing. This does not mean that some people should be eliminated because they appear to lack buying power. It does mean that people who cannot pay under any conditions, or who are slow payers, do not ordinarily qualify as prospects. It is an obvious waste of time to seek business from someone who will be refused by the credit office.

Authority to buy is the third qualification. Salesmen can afford to deal only with those responsible for purchasing—for example, husband and wife, business partners, or proper company officials. It has already been mentioned that a salesman can sometimes influence those who influence the individuals with authority to buy.

Accessibility is the fourth qualification and it means: Can the prospect be readily interviewed? Is he within easy or economical travel distance? Is he located in a convenient place for a sales call? Is he usually available for an interview. Obviously, unless the prospect is accessible, he cannot qualify.

A *sympathetic attitude* on the part of the buyer is the fifth qualification. When a buyer is favorably inclined toward the salesman, his company, and his product, he will frequently qualify regardless of his need. Similarity in background, education, and temperament is helpful in establishing a cordial relationship between salesman and prospect.

An investigation of the *business history* of a prospect to determine if he is a progressive businessman is the sixth qualification. It is valuable for a salesman to know if a buyer is interested in increasing his business and whether or not he is a good merchandiser.

Qualifying prospects according to their *reputations as price* or *quality buyers* is the seventh criterion. Neither should be taken for granted, for the salesman may make the mistake of emphasizing price to a quality buyer and quality to a price buyer.

Occasionally, the salesman qualifies a prospect by determining in advance if the prospect is accustomed to purchase from *one source of supply*. If so, he may not attempt to sell the prospect. On the other hand, the salesman may feel he is justified in making a much greater effort to obtain the account because of its probable permanence.

Every salesman will find it necessary to work out his own system for gathering prospect information. What will be effective for one salesman may be ineffective for another. However, every salesman should have a systematic method of finding and cataloguing information on the buyer and on his business needs.

Qualifying will vary with the individual service offered and with the method of selling in that business. If a prospect has good qualifications, then the salesman has a guide to determine in advance whether a prospect is an immediate prospect, a future prospect, or an indefinite future prospect.

It is a good idea, now and then, to review prospect lists, discarding accounts which are unlikely to be active and applying an "aging formula" for accounts one has brought in. This means to develop a checklist for qualifying prospects for one's own business and then scoring them on the checklist.

POWER POINTS

Prospecting for new customers is necessary because of the high mortality rate of buyers, competition, changing product and economic conditions, and growing sophistication of prospects. *Extensive* prospecting increases sales by selling to more prospects, finding hidden prospects and searching for *needers* who can be changed into *wanters* and then into *buyers*. *Prospect* files benefit salesmen by helping them to keep track of good and excellent prospects as well as poor prospects; they save his time and energy; they help him to sell more to more buyers.

There are many novel methods or techniques of prospecting. Most of them are good only for the salesmen who use them in particular situations and with certain prospects. With these cautions in mind, the following are some of the methods for prospecting:

Cold-canvass prospecting means that the salesman depends on walking and talking and the law of averages. This is a difficult method of prospecting, for it requires determination to walk into unknown places, meet equally unknown people, and start selling without much previous analysis or survey of their needs. Nevertheless, it is a common method and for some situations it is good.

The *endless-chain* method is based on the idea that everybody on whom the salesman calls is a source for prospects. Customers suggest friends, relatives, and associates who might be good prospects.

The *referral* method is a slight variation of the endless-chain technique. Users pave the way for an interview with friends, relatives, or acquaintances by telephoning, writing a letter of introduction, or by a personal introduction.

Centers of influence are respected and well-known individuals in a community who are willing to refer prospects to their salesmen friends. These persons may be bankers, educators, clergymen, businessmen, attorneys, union officials, and those in similar positions.

Prospect sources for business and industrial salesmen include company files, list houses, membership and professional lists, news media, periodicals, trade journals, house organs, telephone directories, sales associations, and advertising leads.

Creeping-vine prospecting, also known as *back-door* or *progressive* prospecting, is one in which the salesman seeks information from persons other than the prospect, but who know the prospect. The salesman asks employees about problems, present suppliers, future buying plans, personnel influence on the buyer. In short, he tries to find out all he can about the prospect by asking others in the organization about him and his job.

Specialty prospecting involves combining several forms of prospecting. It includes some cold canvassing done each day; keeping good prospect records; training salesmen in the use of prospect sources; encouraging salesmen to use their eyes and ears as they cover their territory; attending trade association meetings; giving salesmen literature to mail to prospects.

Public-contact prospecting means that salesmen engage in civic work and belong to social and professional organizations. In this way, they get to know prominent people in the community. From these people they get suggestions and recommendations about prospective buyers.

Qualification of prospects is a necessity. The factors useful for qualifying are: need, ability to pay, authority to buy, accessibility, sympathetic attitude, business history, reputation as price or quality buyer and as one-source buyer.

Good prospect qualities help the salesman determine in advance whether a prospect is an immediate, a near future, or an indefinite future buyer. It is a good idea to evaluate prospects frequently, and to review prospect lists and apply an "aging formula" so that the salesman does not waste his time on inactive accounts.

DISCUSSION QUESTIONS AND PROBLEMS

1. Why is prospecting a constant necessity?
2. Why is extensive prospecting important?
3. How do prospect lists benefit salesmen?
4. What is cold-canvass prospecting?
5. What is the endless-chain method?
6. What is the referral method?
7. What is the center of influence method?
8. What is group prospecting?
9. What is creeping-vine prospecting?

10. What is specialty prospecting?

11. What information should be entered on prospect cards?

12. What is the personal observation method?

13. Bill Strong was angry and upset. He had just lost a sale. "I made a good presentation—too good to waste on the guy. He didn't have enough money to buy a toothpick."

    a. What did Bill do wrong?

    b. What basic rule about prospecting did he break?

14. What are the basic factors for qualifying prospects?

15. Referring to the situation on page 113 of this chapter, rewrite the introduction as a professional salesman would handle it.

SELLING PROBLEMS AND PROJECTS

---

1. The Prospect-to-prospect Method

You have just completed an interview with a prospect who seemed at first to be a "natural." You did your best and the prospect seems as much impressed with you as you are with yourself. Then comes the surprise! "You have a wonderful idea, Mr. Brown, but we cannot buy right now. You have a lot of good ideas we'd like to apply to this business, but we just can't afford them."

Although you do not quit at once, you conclude that he is an honest man and that you have won his confidence and made a friend if not a sale.

Questions

1. How could this situation be used to get more new prospective buyers?

2. Do you believe the proper response from the salesman would gain him any new prospects? Explain.

2. Aging the Prospect File

Jim House is a very successful salesman who has built up a large and regular volume of business in his territory. He believes in an occasional housecleaning of prospect files. Jim says: "If I don't get some business from each of my prospects in a two-year period, I stop calling. Here's the way I see it. If they don't think of me when they need my company's services after I've been calling on them for two years, they must have given the business to someone else—so I quit calling."

Sam Smith sells a service to banks. He covers his territory three times a year, which means he sees his prospects about every four months. Here's what he says about aging a file: "No matter how big the order might be, if I don't get it in the third or fourth time around, I scratch the prospect from my list and use the time to call on a new prospect. In my business I figure that they know *me* by the fourth call, know my *product*, and I know all I need to know about *them*. If they don't buy by this time, then I'm the wrong man, or some other salesman is getting the business, or they just don't like me."

Questions

1. Is there a formula for aging an inventory of prospects?

2. The salesmen in this project are quite definite in their actions. Do you agree with them? Explain.

3. Should salesmen ever give up on inactive prospects? Explain.

CHAPTER 8

The
Preapproach

An important part of a salesman's preparation for a meeting with a prospective buyer is known as the *preapproach*. What kind of person is he calling on? What are the prospect's problems? What are his needs and wants? How should he be studied and analyzed before he is interviewed? These are some of the activities to be discussed in this chapter.

PREAPPROACH DEFINED

Topflight salespeople often accumulate more information about their prospective customers than would be found in an FBI file. For example, it might not be important to anyone else, but the knowledge that Mr. Abbott, purchasing agent for the Steel Corporation of America, likes baseball, has a son on the Washington crew, is allergic to onions, dislikes cigarette smokers, and collects wood carvings is invaluable to the salesman. While calling on Mr. Abbott, the salesman will be careful not to offend him by smoking, and he might inquire about the son in college, mention a wood carving he has seen written up in a magazine, or comment on a recent ball game.

Knowledge of these personality facets indicates to Mr. Abbott that the salesman is alert, friendly, and considerate. He is then inclined to be more receptive to the salesman's presentation. If it is not possible to get an order on the first call, the way is paved for a return visit when the salesman will be cordially received and a sale may be made.

KNOWING THE PROSPECT IN ADVANCE

Salesmen should really appreciate the advantage of understanding the buyer and knowing his needs *before* the interview. Too often it is only at the end of a presentation that the salesman has a good grasp of the buyer's needs, and then it may be too late. Salesmen have often been heard to complain, "If I could have another crack at Brown, I'm positive I could sell to him."

The solution to this problem is to profile the buyer before coming face to face with him; to do the planning before, not after, the presentation. Furthermore, the salesman should reveal to the prospect early in his presentation that he knows something about his problems and needs and that a solution will be offered. This approach will provide hope and arouse interest in the prospect's mind early in the interview.

Business Data

To complete a working profile, the salesperson should know at least some of the following business data about his prospect:

1. His specific need for the product or service.
2. Whether he is a retailer or wholesaler.
3. His personality, including temperament.
4. The reasons he should buy, including any peculiar motives he may have.
5. The approximate volume of his business, including the kind and class of merchandise he handles.
6. His merchandising methods, including the peculiarities of his clientele.
7. His financial standing and credit rating.
8. His present suppliers, including the reason he is or is not buying from their salesmen.
9. His typical objections, including possible methods of shunting the salesman aside.
10. His family relationships.

Personal Data

A professional salesman might like to have even more information about a prospect. He might, for example, like to have answers to the following rather personal questions in addition to those above:

1. What is the prospect's general attitude toward the salesman, his product, and his company?

2. Does he buy on the basis of impulse or logic, friendship or reciprocity?

3. What are his hobbies? Does he play golf, bridge, checkers, chess, tennis, croquet, cribbage, pinochle, or poker? Is he interested in boating, swimming, bowling, motoring, gardening, painting, boxing, wrestling, or the like?

4. What kind of a home does he have? Does he have a wife and does she help or hinder him? Does he have children? How many and what sexes? What are they interested in? Are they in grade school, high school, or college?

5. Where did he go to school? In which state was he born? To what fraternal organizations and clubs does he belong?

Possessing this kind of detailed information places the salesman in a better position to understand the prospect. Much of it may never be used, but the salesman has the facts, if needs them, to close a successful sale. It has been said that if a salesman can base the first five minutes of his presentation on the above knowledge of the buyer, he will have advanced at least halfway through the job of closing a successful sale.

You cannot expect to obtain all this information before your initial interview, but by keeping alert from call to call, you will always discover more interesting details about your prospect.

Credit Information

When special information is needed about the finances of a customer for specialty items, such as life insurance, automobiles, stocks and bonds, or real estate, it is possible to obtain credit ratings from credit associations and banks. Large firms usually have departments that obtain such information and it is available for their salespeople.

Preparation for Selling to Professional Buyers

Selling to professional buyers requires salesmen who possess poise, urbanity, technical information, and great selling skill. Therefore, this kind of selling requires such skillful preparation that it is said to result in the ideal sales call.

Professional buyers have their own ideas of how salesmen should sell and they have suggested the ingredients that should be used in the creation of an ideal sales call, as well as the order in which they should be mixed. For example, Harry T. Flynn describes the ideal sales call in the following words.[1]

1. Whenever feasible, the salesman should telephone in advance to make an appointment.

2. When the salesman arrives at the buyer's office, he should be able, briefly but thoroughly, to describe his product and its purpose. If possible, a sample of his product should be shown at this time.

3. The salesman should state briefly the need his new product is going to fill for the consumer.

4. The salesman should be prepared to tell the buyer what the new product might replace in the buyer's present inventory.

5. The salesman should be able to give the buyer a price comparison between his own product and that of competitors. While pricing is not always a determining factor in completing a sale, it helps if the price is a realistic one.

6. The salesman should be prepared to give a brief description of his company's promotion plans for the product. He should be ready to sketch the upcoming advertising campaign and have samples of art work or proofs of ads which will be used in the promotion effort.

All the information the salesman expects a buyer to utilize should be briefly stated in writing so that the buyer can digest it after the sales call.

The content of the sales presentation could also be based on the value analysis used by many industrial purchasing agents.

The *purchasing value analysis* involves a careful analysis of each purchased item, in search of the answers to the following questions:

1. Does the item's use contribute value to the end product?

2. Is its cost proportionate to its usefulness?

3. Does it need all its features?

4. Is there anything better for the intended use?

5. Can a usable substitute be made by a lower-cost method?

6. Can a standard item be found to do the job?

7. Is it made with the use of proper tooling?

8. Do material, labor, overhead, and profit charges total the purchase price or reasonably approximate it?

1. Harry T. Flynn. Adapted from McCall's Supermarket Buyer's Pocket Letter, McCall's, 230 Park Avenue, New York, N.Y. 10017.

9. Will another dependable supplier provide it for a lower price?

10. Is anyone else buying it for a lower price?

Value analysis assures purchasing agents that they buy on the basis of the cost-in-use of products. Salesmen of industrial products in particular would be wise to correlate their thinking, research and development, and selling techniques with the purchasing value analysis.

The questions in the *purchaser's value analysis* could be studied and analyzed by the salesman, who would then prepare specific answers prior to his presentation. This would certainly be a more realistic and accurate way to answer the purchasing agent's unspoken query, "What's in it for us?" It would be more convincing and dynamic than the customary sales talk.

FINAL PREPARATION FOR MEETING THE PROSPECT

Having acquired and prepared all possible advance information, the professional salesman successfully sells to the prospect *in his own mind* long before he calls on him. Selling to the prospect "in his own mind" means that the salesman rehearses his presentation before he actually sees the prospect. He makes definite decisions as to the sales strategy he will use.

Physical Preparation for the Sales Call

In addition to his notebook containing his planned route for the day and data about the people to be interviewed, the salesman may have other materials. It is best to assemble these things the night before to assure a prompt and orderly departure with the self-confidence that can only come from knowing that the preparation is complete in every respect from attitude and planned route, planned presentation, and personality data.

Samples, brochures, product and other visual aids should be packed so that their sequence in the actual sales talk is orderly. This prevents fumbling and stumbling which distracts from the power of the presentation and loses the attention of the prospect.

Among the many decisions the salesman makes is whether to leave his sales portfolio in his car or to keep it out of sight during the first few minutes of the interview. Some salesmen believe that the new prospect may be annoyed if confronted with a pile of selling accessories. The prospect may mentally defend himself by offering excuses and alibis to avoid being sold.

Seeing is believing, and the sample case or briefcase should be bulging with visual aids which have the *convincers* needed to close sales. It may be possible to sell without visual aids, but if they are available, the salesman has them for those situations where they may tip the scales in favor of him, his product, or his service.

If *testimonials* are to be used, they should be arranged in the most effective sequence, with the significant sentence and paragraphs underscored. It is the rare prospect who will read even one testimonial letter in full, much less a series of them.

A written testimonial may never be needed, but occasionally a prospective buyer is convinced by written testimony if it is presented to him on the spot. Information sent later from the home office is never as effective as proof presented immediately.

If *catalogues* or other publications are used as part of the presentation, the appropriate pages or sections should be marked to avoid fumbling and backtracking.

As preparation for this kind of presentation, it is advisable to study local business conditions through newspapers, calls at banks, and other sources of local information. These sources will provide facts useful in localizing a sales talk and fitting it to a customer's particular needs.

A good first impression should be of concern to the salesman.

Planning for Interview Time

Before a salesman interviews a prospect, he should make an appointment by telephone or mail. If he has an appointment, he should be on time. It is a good idea to make appointments flexible within a half hour, offering both the salesman and the client some leeway. However, even a good excuse for being late cannot entirely erase the salesman's apparent disregard for the prospect's time.

Sometimes a prospect will meet a salesman in a reception area instead of inviting him into his office. He does this to find out if the salesman really has anything of interest to offer him. The salesman must therefore quickly present the benefits of his product or service.

"Too Busy" Problem

If the prospect says he is too busy to talk, the salesman must ask for a firm appointment. Some salesmen give up as soon as a buyer says he is busy or shows impatience. The salesman who quits so quickly is not a salesman, he is a peddler.

At the other extreme is the salesman who barges ahead every time, continuing with his sales talk in spite of apparent signs of dissatisfaction from the prospect. This person's determination must be admired, but he cannot be called a salesman, either. Through lack of experience and perception, he antagonizes many buyers.

How should a salesman get around the claim that a prospect is too busy to see him? The best way is to arrange an appointment by telephone. Some salesmen are reluctant to state their business by telephone, but if they believe in what they have to offer, it should be natural for them to ask for an interview.

When a personal call is made, only the salesman can decide if the prospect really is too busy to see him or if he is only trying to avoid him. If the salesman is in doubt, he can offer to return at a more convenient time, leaving literature for the prospect to peruse. If the prospect really is not busy, this is the salesman's opportunity to interest him.

"Gate" Selling

The rule is that a salesman should never sell "over the gate." Many sales managers warn their salesmen against talking to any prospect over the "gate," or office railing, in hallways, or in any place other than the buyer's office.

When such a situation is unavoidable, the salesman should try to win the prospect's interest so that he will be invited to sit down to talk with him. The salesman will never gain the prospect's full attention and neither will be at ease discussing business in a hallway or reception room.

PREPARATION OF SURVEYS

The sale of some products is helped greatly by the use of a survey. The word "survey" means "to look over." In other words, instead of merely trying to sell a product, the salesman looks over the prospect's needs so that he may recommend the best product to satisfy those needs. The survey is a part of the problem-solving approach.

The survey offers the following advantages to the salesman:

1. Since the prospect is getting professional advice without charge, the product is raised out of the price-competition class. This very often eliminates competition.
2. The salesman can ask for help and advice from his manager, his fellow salesmen, or his home office, before he makes his final recommendation.
3. He can make an attractive, graphic, and poignant presentation as a result of his survey.
4. Such tailor-made surveys offer the smoothest, easiest possible kind of presentation.

5. Prospects and customers often like the survey idea and generally appreciate the efforts of the salesmen who use them.

Surveys vary in length and complexity. A survey may consist of only a few minutes' conversation to ascertain a few simple things. On the other hand, it might consist of a lengthy study of the needs in many different departments over a period of time.

The results of a short and simple survey might be communicated verbally or explained by a simple design or sketch. The results of a long, detailed survey should be given to the prospect as a neatly typed, prepared presentation folio. Such a presentation folio, complete with all the necessary supporting data and illustrations, serves not only to impress the prospect with the thoroughness with which the survey was prepared, but also carries a fairly complete sales story in cases where the prospect must convince other members of his own organization of the desirability of the proposition.

Naturally, the amount of time and effort spent by the salesman on a survey should be governed by the sales potential of the prospect. Obviously, it would not pay a salesman to spend several days of his valuable time on a prospect whose orders would never amount to more than fifty dollars each year. However, a salesman can afford to spend considerable time on a very small order if that order could lead to a great many other orders in a sizable account.

TERRITORY INFORMATION

In addition to preapproach information about individual and group prospects and prospect groups, salesmen need to know certain facts about their territories. They must keep informed about all developments and trends within their territory, such as changes in income, population shifts, business failures and successes, and many other factors which effect potential sales. They must find if their territories have any hidden or neglected markets, and they must keep abreast of general conditions. They must analyze and study the nature of these territories; terrain, transportation facilities, mores and customs, economic composition, nature of the population, and any other factors which might affect them and their sales potential.

THE RECORDING SYSTEM

Although it is possible for a salesman to recall many details about each customer, it is wise for him to draw up a memorandum of the individual characteristics of buyers with whom he deals regularly or hopes to do so. In this way he will record the correct information and can avoid making mistakes. For instance, he will not ask Mr. Abbott about his daughter at Vassar, and compliment Mr. Klein on the fact that his alma mater, Michigan State, seems destined for the Rose Bowl, when in fact Mr. Abbott has a son at Penn State and Mr. Klein attended Ohio State.

After the salesman has determined the kind of data he wants to record, his next step is to set up a recording system. It has been found that those data are best recorded on 3- by 5-inch or 5- by 7-inch cards. The 3- by 5-inch cards are handiest for daily use, because they can be carried easily in the salesman's pocket. After interviews, the salesman jots down the prospect's name, address, date, product sold, and any other pertinent information.

For office files, printed 5- by 7-inch cards, or sheets, are often used. These cards contain more complete details and are set up to suit the needs of the salesman and his company.

Record cards are extremely valuable. The salesman should study them the night before the sales calls. For example, let's assume a salesman is planning interviews with Messrs. Johnson, Black, Brown, Smith, and Jones. The cards are removed from the file and reviewed with the following ideas in mind:

1. *To help the salesman recall his last visit.* When pertinent details have been recorded, a glance at Johnson's card will remind the salesman that he had promised an order on the next trip. Black's card will remind the salesman that he wants a sample. Brown's card will warn against pressing him too hard for an order until next fall. Each card is read as preparation for next day's calls. Each card contains a short history of past dealings with prospects, and it is possible, therefore, to figure out what may happen on the next call.

2. *To help the salesman visualize his prospect.* The family doctor rarely diagnoses his patient's ills without checking his case history. Salesmen, too, should hesitate about trusting their memories. It is too much to expect them to memorize correctly the complete record of each customer and prospect on whom they call. A review of each prospect record will bring into sharp focus the people to be seen the next day. It will reveal exactly what they like and dislike, whether they are affable or reticent, whether they have families, hobbies, or civic interests. Briefly, the records will show what kind of person each prospect is. That knowledge will offer hints as to how to handle the prospect, enable the salesman to set the tone of his approach and to determine the best way to start the interview.

3. *To remind the salesman about the prospect's buying habits.* Salesmen who handle several lines want their buyers to purchase as much from them as they can sell. This is the way to increase volume.

Therefore, the salesman will check his cards to determine the progress he has already made. If a salesman has six lines, or products, he will have a different problem with each buyer on his list. Usually, not more than one or two of these will be handling the same group of products. A review of the records will pinpoint the area where the salesman is weak and will help him think of possible solutions before he calls on the buyer.

4. *To help the salesman determine a course of action.* Each visit a salesman makes should have a purpose. The purpose may be to sell to the prospect for the first time, It may be to sell more of the established lines to regular buyers, or to sell new items and lines. Unless the salesman has a purpose in mind before meeting with the prospective buyer, he will waste his prospect's time and his own. Therefore, he should plan his upcoming calls on the content of his prospect records. This kind of study and planning gives purpose and direction to his day's work, and, naturally, boosts his sales volume.

Sample prospect and call report forms are illustrated in Figures 8-1 and 8-2. Report cards for many salesmen can be adapted from these examples.

PROSPECT REPORT

□ NEW PROSPECT □ CUSTOMER PROSPECT □ CALL BACK NO.

PROSPECT _____

ADDRESS _____ PHONE NO. _____

KEY PERSONNEL

NAME	POSITION

ORDER	PRODUCT	PRICE	STOCK ON HAND

Today's Call: _____

Figure 8-1. Simple Prospect Report

SALESMAN'S CALL REPORT							
DATE	BRANCH	CUSTOMER CODE	TERRITORY	CALL	SALE	STATE	

SOLD TO   PURCHASE ORDER NO.

Company Name

Street Address

City & State

F.O.B. _____ Terms _____

Quantity	Unit of Sale	Code	Description	Price	Amount

☐ Buyer Out
☐ Service Call   MAILING LIST CHANGES AND COMPLAINTS
☐ Dealer   ARE TO BE DESCRIBED FULLY BELOW

Figure 8-2. Salesman's Call Report

ADVERTISING AS A PREAPPROACH METHOD

In many businesses some preapproach work is done through company advertising. Some preapproach advertising is national in scope, while some is regionally directed. It is all aimed at conditioning the mind of the prospect and making him do some thinking before the salesman calls. This process is a kind of preapproach which makes it easier for a salesman to tell his story.

Preapproach through advertising creates interest and often creates desire in a prospect. Salesmen think of this method as an introduction —a third-party influence that makes it easier for them to start an interview. The direct mail and telephone method of introduction can be practiced by small sales organizations or single salesmen just as easily as by huge concerns.

Mail and telephone preapproach activities help many salesmen, especially those who will not or cannot make cold-canvass calls. These people are often very successful when the groundwork is laid by a direct mailing or telephone call. At least some prospects will have read the mailing, and nothing can surpass a phone call for gathering certain information and starting a sale.

CALLING ON THE PROSPECT

When calling on a new prospect the salesman will probably be met by a secretary, switchboard operator, office boy, or receptionist. This person will ask him whom he wants to see and the reason for the call. Sometimes the receptionist will tell the salesman that another person does the purchasing or that several people are involved in it. If the salesman is alert, he will acquire information that might have taken him some time to discover.

The receptionist's job may include protecting the prospect from peddlers and order-takers who needlessly take up his time. The salesman should prepare to sell this person one idea: that he has such constructive benefits to offer that Mr. Prospect cannot afford *not* to hear him.

Frequency of Calls

How often should calls be made on a prospective buyer? A prospect's time is worth money, and so is the salesman's. If the prospect knows little or nothing of the salesman's firm, it might be argued that he cannot make too many calls; but calling for the sake of calling rarely gets the salesman anywhere. This is particularly true of the salesman who says, "I happened to be passing, and just dropped in."

Numerous tales are told of aggressive salesmen who have tried to take dramatic advantage of the prospect who does not want to see a salesman. Typical among them is: "My time is worth ten dollars a minute." This was the message relayed to a salesman by a certain prospect. The salesman promptly produced a twenty-dollar bill and asked for two minutes of the prospect's time. The stories usually have a successful ending and the salesman's money is returned to him.

Persistent Effort

A recent survey revealed that 80 percent of all sales are made after the fifth call. It also revealed that 48 percent of salesmen calling on unsold prospects make one call and quit; 25 percent make two calls and quit; 10 percent keep calling and make 80 percent of the sales. These figures indicate the value of systematic, methodical, purposeful, and patient follow-up of prospects.

POWER POINTS

A college student was the envy of the rest of his classmates. At final exams he came into the classroom smiling cheerfully and apparently unworried about a passing grade. He amazed everyone very much. So one day he was stopped and asked, "What makes you so sure of yourself, Bill? How do you know what the prof's going to ask?" His reply was one to remember: "Fellows," he said, "I pass or fail exams the night before when I prepare for them. I watch what the professor emphasizes and make a list of questions he likes to ask. I think of the topics he has stressed, then I study those topics. On exam day it's only a matter of drawing on my preparation. I'm confident because my preparation is thorough and I'm happy because I'm confident."

Salesmen long ago found that gauging a situation and a prospect is the keystone of their success. When they prepare the night before, they can face prospects in the morning full of confidence because they have equipped themselves to do their best.

The *preapproach* is an important part of getting ready to meet the buyer. Besides the standard comments related to the importance and techniques of the preapproach, there are many more or less novel methods which are good for certain salesmen and for certain prospect situations.

The preapproach involves learning all one can about a prospect: collecting, analyzing, and using facts for preparing the presentation to the prospect. All of these activities are the presale planning part of preparation to meet the prospect.

Profiling the prospect is one of the segments of the preapproach. This means, first, learning everything about the prospect's personality that is available; second, collecting and analyzing all available business data. When data have been collected, a *record sheet* is used to bolster the salesman's memory.

Selling to professional buyers requires salesmen who are urbane, poised, technically trained, and who have great selling skill. Professional buyers have their own ideas about how salesmen should sell, and their *ideal sales call* employs certain ingredients, mixed in a certain order.

Professional buyers also like salesmen to base their presentations on the *purchasing value analysis,* or cost-in-use of products. There are ten questions to be answered in this analysis and the answers become the basis for a professional sales presentation.

Physical preparation for a sales talk should include the review of the salesman's book containing his planned route for the day and data about the people to be interviewed. Other items should be prepared in advance, including samples, brochures, product, and other visual aids. These should be packed in orderly sequence so that they accompany the oral presentation, thereby preventing fumbling. Testimonials, catalogs, and miscellaneous sales aids should also be readied for appropriate use by the salesman.

Planning for interview time includes, when possible, an appointment by telephone or mail. The interview should not be at the "gate" or reception area, but in the prospect's office. "Gate selling" is rarely productive.

Surveys help the sale of some items. This means that the salesman looks over the prospect's needs so that he can recommend the best product to satisfy those needs. The survey is part of the problem-solving approach. It may consist of only a few minutes' conversation to learn a few simple things, or it might require many hours of preparation.

Territory information is concerned with searching for trends and developments in relation to income, population shifts, business failures and successes, customs, mores, and any other factors that might affect potential sales.

DISCUSSION QUESTIONS AND PROBLEMS

1.   What is the meaning of *preapproach?*
2.   Why is profiling the buyer important?
3.   What should a salesman know about a prospect's personality?
4.   What should a salesman know about a prospect's business?
5.   Why is it important to keep a record sheet or card for each prospect?
6.   What are the advantages of a survey approach?
7.   What preparation might be required to sell to a professional buyer through the medium of the ideal sales call?
8.   What would you do to prepare to meet the prospect?

9. When a prospect says he is too busy, what should a salesman do?

10. Why should a salesman avoid selling "over the gate"?

11. Salesmen who make 12 or 15 calls each day are not always able to do detailed planning as suggested in this chapter. What method do you suggest they use? What would you do under such conditions?

SELLING PROBLEMS AND PROJECTS

---

1. Harvey Salt Case

My name is Harvey Salt. I sell air-conditioning units for offices and, occasionally, for entire buildings. I analyze the problems involved and prepare a written report concerning the situation, what my product will do, the price, the time to install, and other information.

If, after I submit my report, the prospect shows any unwillingness to have me carry out my recommendations or indicates a lack of confidence, I discontinue pursuing the sale. I feel that a prospect has a right to choose the person with whom he may do business, and I reserve the same privilege for myself. I find that a client-salesman relationship develops only when there is mutual confidence and liking.

After he has my recommendations and he knows what he can buy with the amount he is willing to spend, it's up to him. If he wants the product, I'll arrange the details and close the sale.

Questions

1. Does this salesman reveal too much independence? Explain your answer.

2. Can this method be used by all salesmen? Explain.

3. Can a salesman leave a purchase up to the buyer? Explain.

2. Bronson Brothers Department Store Case

Many retail department stores limit their buying hours (and thereby inconvenience) and often discourage salesmen who wish to present their products. The reason behind this store regulation is that buyers must have sufficient time to perform a multitude of other duties. Often a buyer is forced to see so many salesmen during the day that he does not have time to plan advertising, check invoices, work on markdowns, tabulate sales reports, and attend to many other merchandising duties.

Guidelines for salesmen are usually issued by department stores. A typical guideline would be:

"Salesmen should strive to time their visits so that they interfere as little as possible with the other duties a buyer must perform. The best time for a salesman to call upon a buyer is between 9 and 11 A.M. Do not arrive before 9 A.M."

Question

1. Do you believe that there may be exceptions to the 9 to 11 regulation? Why?

Busy Periods

In one large department store the busiest selling hour is at noon, because the store is located near a large factory and those who work there like to shop during their lunch hour. At that time the buyers like to be on the selling floor getting consumer reactions. Each department store has its own special busy periods, especially Saturdays, when all buyers are too busy to see salesmen.

Questions

2. Why should a salesman study individual stores so that he can determine their busy periods?

3. Would it ever be advisable to attempt to sell to a department store buyer on Saturday?

Staff Meetings

Most department stores also advise against salesmen calling late in the afternoon. At that time the buyer must work with his sales staff, checking daily sales reports. It is a great inconvenience to all concerned, including the buyer, if he must sandwich in reports between salesmen's interviews or if he must discuss the day's sales with his staff in a salesman's presence.

Where an out-of-town salesman is concerned, it is to everyone's advantage if the salesman telephones the buyer when he arrives in town. The buyer can then make a definite appointment with the salesman, and avoid missing him during his trip.

Questions

4. How many hours during a day are available for selling department store buyers?

5. Are evening, holiday, and Sunday contacts advisable?

CHAPTER 9

Developing Sales Presentations

The successful salesman spends more time in the preparation of his sales talk, or *presentation*, than he does in the presence of his customer or prospect. He knows that to compete with his rivals and to deal successfully with sophisticated, knowledgeable buyers, he must make careful preparation.

Before he begins his preparation, the salesman should organize his approach carefully. He should rehearse what he is going to say and know what he is going to say. He should select effective, influential words for his presentation.

The salesman should write out his presentation. In this way he is able to weigh the value of his words and the visual sales aids he will undoubtedly use. Writing out the presentation will also help to determine whether it can be improved so that the quickest, clearest, and most appealing picture will be formed in the prospect's mind. The successful salesperson always has his sales talk ready before he is face to face with the buyer. When the person who sells needs a word or a visual aid, he needs it immediately.

People have been known to buy things after merely reading advertisements, or after hearing a very sketchy presentation given by a poorly prepared salesman. However, these cases are exceptions, for very few things are purchased in that way, and the really good salesman follows a carefully thought-out plan—a plan which moves in an orderly way to the climax of a sale, which is a successful close. The good salesman knows that a good plan increases his percentage of signed orders, and that a good plan is made long in advance of the interview.

TYPES OF SALES PRESENTATIONS

A well-prepared sales presentation requires a definite plan of procedure or action. The salesman should learn distinctive words and particularly descriptive phrases, which may then serve as points on which to construct the entire sales presentation. Many salesmen write their own presentations, occasionally reviewing their manuscripts so that they can express their benefit points in the best manner and in the most effective sequence. They do not memorize their presentations and repeat them verbatim, but they do constantly review and strengthen them.

Standardized Sales Talks

Many successful sales managers, however, insist that their salesmen be able to recite a standardized sales talk before they are permitted to sell. These companies claim that through the combined experience of their best salesmen they have developed the most effective sales presentations. They insist that unless other salesmen can develop something better, they should be willing, for their own good as well as that of the company, to use the tested methods that obtain results.

There are three possible ways to use standardized sales talks. The first way is to give the salesman complete sales information and to allow him to organize and develop his own sales presentation. Second, specific sales talks are given to the salesperson, but he is instructed to present them in his own way. Third, the salesman is given specific sales talks with instructions to memorize them completely and to deliver them verbatim. The latter is known as the canned sales talk.

The first method is effective when the salesman is experienced, and has the ability to organize facts and translate them into usable material. For certain salesmen, the second method is more desirable, provided they acquire the substance of the complete information. For inexperienced salesmen, the third method may be the best. It concentrates the salesman's attention on what he is going to do and not on how he is going to do it. It gives him something definite to say. It keeps him away from generalities and ambiguous statements which might create confusion rather than a clear picture of a product's values, advantages, and benefits.

The chief criticism of the memorized sales talk is that it sounds mechanical. If this happens, it should be discarded, for there is nothing more ineffective than a presentation that sounds like a recording. Some sales managers argue that although every word uttered by an actor is memorized, it does not necessarily make his performance mechanical. Why? Because the actor thinks out every idea as he goes along. He lives his part. He becomes, for the time being, the person he is portraying. An actor's memorization of a part has one purpose: it acts as a guide to his thinking.

This is probably the best answer to the critic who says that memorizing anything produces a flat, colorless delivery. Mechanical sales talks are not produced by memorizing but by lack of thinking. There are many mechanical salesmen who have never memorized anything. They have merely become mechanical through numerous repetitions of a sales talk which has no appeal or logical development.

Every professional salesman has a prepared sales talk whether he has developed it himself or it has been developed for him. What is needed is to produce the most effective sales talk possible, and it can be developed only when based on sound planning and organization.

Planned Outline Sales Presentation

A prepared, planned sales presentation is not packaged, it is not wholly memorized, and it certainly is not impromptu. It should first be outlined in complete statements rather than in words or phrases. This forces the salesman to organize and clarify his ideas and eliminate useless, meaningless words.

When the outline is complete, then it should be transferred to small note cards. The salesman then rehearses the talk, referring to his notes when necessary. He should rehearse at least ten times, varying the wording each time. The value of this method is to train the salesman to think on his feet and to prevent him from giving a routine presentation.

Once the salesman is familiar with the material and has practiced it many times in varying ways, he replaces the complete statement with an outline of key words or phrases on a single card. After more speaking practice, he throws this card away. Thereafter, he develops and refines his technique, analyzing and judging the suitability of his examples and supporting materials.

A professional salesman gives to his sales talk the same amount of interest and practice that he gives to a sport he likes. He knows that good form is the test here, the same as it is in a sport, and that good form only *seems* effortless—it is achieved through hard work, planning, and practice.

Presentation Formulas

Four formulas have been advanced to help the salesman in his efforts to develop a selling presentation which will motivate people to buy: (1) the stimulus-response formula, (2) the need-satisfaction formula, (3) AIDA formula, and (4) the idea sequence.

Each formula has its adherents, and a selling presentation may be developed from any one of the formulas, depending upon the circumstances. Consciously or unconsciously, the presentation methods employed by most salesmen are usually guided by one or more of these formulas.

Stimulus-response Formula

Based on the psychological principle that for every sensory stimulus there is an appropriate response, the *stimulus-response* theory is probably the simplest of the three approaches.

The application of this principle to motivation and selling means that the salesman must have certain things to say and do (stimuli), so that the prospect will act (response). Obviously, it is believed that if a salesman uses the appropriate stimuli, the prospect will be motivated to buy.

This selling concept means that the sales communicator is enabled to: (1) transfer his specific knowledge to the prospect, (2) ask questions and listen to comments and feedback revealing the effect of his presentation, and (3) adjust his continuing presentation to fit the needs of the situation. This is the process by which a salesman presents his information, asks questions, listens in order to keep himself informed of the success of his communication, and then adjusts it to suit a particular prospect, customer or situation.

An example of how this principle is applied in a sales talk may be seen in the following direct-to-home sales situation:

SALESMAN: Good morning, madam. I'm your Amway representative. We make products for household use. May I present you with this little gift from Amway?

PROSPECT: Thank you. I don't think I need anything right now.

SALESMAN: Here's our new cleaning compound. It is twice as powerful as the type you buy in the supermarkets, but extremely safe and gentle to your skin.

PROSPECT: It wouldn't chafe or burn the skin?

SALESMAN: No, madam. It could even be swallowed by a small child without any chance of injury.

PROSPECT: Mmmm— Well, I might as well try some.

The stimulus-response formula is useful when the selling situation is simple, when the selling price is low, and when little time can be spent with a customer. Its weakness is that a stimulus which motivates and influences one customer may not motivate and influence another.

This means not only that the salesman loses sales but also that he cannot analyze the reason for his success or failure. Since the salesman who uses this approach may be working in the dark, he is not likely to improve his selling skills as the result of his experience.

Need-satisfaction Formula

When it is assumed that prospects buy to satisfy needs, it follows that to make a sale we must uncover the prospect's psychological and social needs and motives. We then match our proposition's features and benefits with the prospect's needs and motives and reveal how we can satisfy his needs and solve his problems. Obviously, the need-satisfaction formula is a prospect-oriented approach, while the stimulus-response and AIDA theories are usually salesman-oriented.

Since the need-satisfaction formula begins with the discovery of a prospect's motives and needs, the salesman cannot talk about his product or service until he knows what those motives and needs are. The application of the need-satisfaction approach requires greater skill and maturity than do other methods, for the salesman must be able to dominate the sales situation through motivating, questioning, and listening, rather than merely through a sales talk.

When a sale is complex, the need-satisfaction approach is preferable. It may be more time-consuming, as some salesmen claim, but it may actually save selling time. It can be used advantageously in all selling above the canvassing level.

One use of the need-satisfaction theory is in the *programmed presentation*. This type of presentation is based upon a detailed and comprehensive analysis of the prospect's needs from which is prepared a complete written or illustrated presentation. The programmed presentation is used chiefly in the life insurance field, in office equipment, engineering and management consulting, and printing and advertising.

Four steps are usually taken in completing a programmed presentation: (1) getting permission to make the survey, (2) gathering and analyzing the facts and information, (3) preparing the program or proposal, and (4) presenting the program.

Before the salesman can get started on the development of a program, he must convince the prospect of the importance and desirability of gathering data, some of which may be personal. Although many prospects will hesitate or balk at this, the salesman can point out that it is a routine procedure agreed to by many others. He can produce case histories of other prospects who have realized substantial savings or gains from such surveys. He can also build prestige for his proposal by calling on the expert assistance of engineers and systems analysts.

Gathering the data may consist of no more than asking a few questions and writing the answers down on a scratch pad, or it may involve the use of a questionnaire which provides a complete record of all of the information the salesman needs in order to draw up an effective proposal. Where complex and expensive machinery, equipment, or installations are involved, the survey many require the services of technicians or engineers.

After the facts have been analyzed carefully, a written proposal or program is prepared for presentation to the prospect. The proposal normally includes a statement of the prospect's problem or need, followed by a description of how the salesman's company expects to solve the problem or meet the need. Also included is a statement of the cost of the salesman's solution.

Finally, the salesman must attempt to present his proposal in the most effective manner possible. He may be trying to persuade a single prospect such as a purchasing agent, company official, or art director. On the other hand, his target may be a committee of people, all of whom are involved in the purchasing decision. The salesman will want to dramatize his proposal by bringing in such visual aids as charts, diagrams, demonstration models, slide films, and motion pictures. If possible, copies of his presentation should be handed out to all members present. Above all, the salesman must not forget to attempt to ask for the order.

The advantages of the program type of presentation include:

- Getting at the real needs and problems of the prospect.
- Offering the opportunity to present a professional and personalized presentation.
- Allowing the salesman time to gather and analyze all of the facts and to prepare a written solution to the prospect's problems.
- Eliminating wasted time: The first sales interview concentrates on getting permission to make the survey; the second interview presents the salesman's recommendations.

The disadvantages are as follows:

- The survey is time-consuming and often expensive.
- The prospect may object to the survey on the grounds that the salesman is prejudiced and incapable of being objective.
- The buyer may be suspicious of the survey presentation because of previous experiences in which he had been misled or duped.

AIDA Formula

This formula is easily remembered by the acronym AIDA, standing for *Attention, Interest, Desire, Action.* The thought behind this formula is that all prospects should be treated alike and that successful sales are made by taking prospects through the successive mental stages of attention, interest, desire, action, and, perhaps, satisfaction.

Those who oppose this method believe that it approaches the motivation process from the salesman's point of view rather than the prospect's. They believe that the application of the formula tends to make the salesman feel that he is an engineer, who, with a standard operating procedure, can motivate a prospect to make a purchase. Opponents of this selling formula also point out that a prospect does not necessarily experience the mental steps of a sale in logical sequence and that the steps are not of equal importance in motivating and selling.

Nevertheless, this method has value when salesmen are too inexperienced to develop a presentation based on a prospect's individual motives and needs. It is also believed to have value when prospects have motives and needs similar to those of the salesman. The basic reason for the wide acceptance of the selling formula, however, is that it provides a logical framework within which ideas about selling techniques may be presented.

Idea-sequence Formula

At first glance the *idea-sequence formula* may be mistaken for the selling formula, or AIDA. However, the idea-sequence formula is more than that. It is a step-by-step plan for the complete development of a sales presentation. It includes every element leading to a successful sale, including the important preparatory activities. The formula then takes the prospect through the logical *starting* elements of a sale and then through the *telling, explaining, proving* and *successful sale.* In other words, the selling process is divided into phases: *Start, Tell, Explain, Prove,* and *Successful Sale.*

For further understanding, this is the way the Idea Sequence Formula appears in a schematic drawing.

The *idea sequence* is a device for assisting a salesman to better organize his thinking. When using the idea sequence, the salesman has a plan which will help him to close more successful sales. He will have written on paper his carefully planned ideas on how to *start* a sale which will win for the salesman favorable attention from the prospect; how to create real buying interest by *telling* and *showing* the prospect what can be done for him in terms of benefits; how to *explain* away obstacles and tell why the prospect will receive the benefits; how to *prove* through demonstrations, success stories, and other sales aids that the prospect will receive the benefits; how to *summarize* the sale and obtain the order.

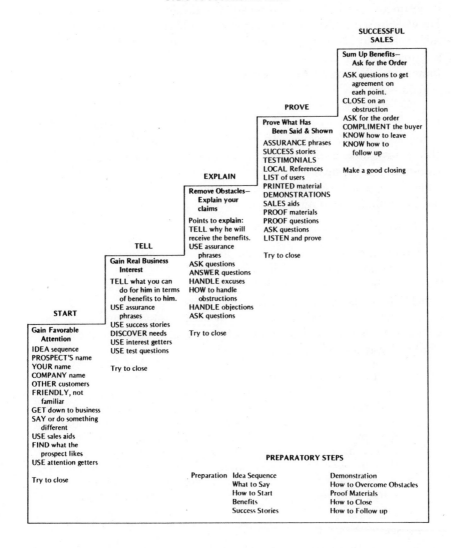

Figure 9-1. Idea sequence for successful sales

Starting a Successful Sale

How to start a successful sale is always an interesting dilemma to the novice salesman. Perhaps the best way is to realize that there are two aspects to a sales presentation: one is oral, one is visual. This makes the start doubly important.

The first visual contact that the prospect has is the salesman himself. He sees the appearance of the salesman. He sees his manner and deportment. He notes his businesslike attitude and facial expression. He likes to see salesmen who "get down to business" quickly. He likes salesmen who show respect. Prospects also watch gestures: how the salesman uses his hands, his body movements, his posture. When these things are pleasing to the prospect, they help the salesman get off to a good start.

The start may require only ten seconds. For example, Salesman (smiling): "Good morning, Mr. Black, I'm John Jones of the Ashville Manufacturing Company." In this brief moment the salesman can obtain favorable attention by pronouncing the prospect's name *correctly,* giving his own name *clearly,* mentioning the name of his *company,* having a businesslike attitude and appearance, being *friendly* but not familiar, getting down to business *quickly.*

Telling—To Create Interest and Conviction

Creating interest and conviction in the mind of the prospect seems to revolve around one simple rule: Find the key selling factors and then use them. Salesmen look for the *key factors* which are usually benefits that make things click in the prospect's mind.

A *professional* example of how to create interest and gain conviction is revealed by a manufacturer's salesman calling on a dealer. The dealer is already a satisfied buyer.

> SALESMAN (smiling): Good morning, Mr. Black. I'm John Jones of the Ashville Manufacturing Company. I appreciate your willingness to see me, and to *save your time,* I'll get right down to business. I have here an interesting *booklet* about a new product that we have just brought out. Because of what others have told me, I am sure it will *save you time* and thereby *save you money.* Many of my customers tell me that it has brought them *many new customers;* yes, and made those same customers *enthusiastic boosters.* Doesn't that sound interesting?
>
> PROSPECT: Yes.
>
> SALESMAN (opening book): This is how it works.

Note how the salesman started his sale. He greeted his prospect by name, told who he was, and gave the name of his company. He followed his opening remark with an assurance phrase that contained the benefit, "To *save you time,* I'll get right down to business." Then he introduced the new product and *told* the prospect *what* he could do for him in terms of these benefits: "Save you money . . . many new customers . . . customers enthusiastic boosters." Further, he didn't give the benefits as blunt statements but introduced them smoothly as being the opinions of disinterested third persons. He also checked his prospect for his real business interest with the question, "Doesn't that sound interesting?"

If you want to obtain your prospect's real interest, fast, tell him clearly and positively about the benefits he will enjoy if he buys your product or service. "Benefits" is the key which will open almost all closed minds.

The prospect will be interested only in what the proposition will do for him. So, professional salesmen talk in terms of *his* interests, *his* desires, *his* gain, because they know that these are the chief buying motives for most people.

What Is a Feature?

The dictionary defines a *feature* as "any marked peculiarity; anything especially prominent; trait; characteristic. . . ."

Assuming that you are preparing yourself to sell, you have already decided on a product or service in which you have belief or faith. You are in the process of analyzing your proposition's *key selling points.* The features of your proposition are outstanding, for you see these things quite clearly:

Performance
Reputation
Component materials
Colors
Taste
Smell
Sizes
Exclusives
Uses and applications
Method of handling
Ruggedness

Delivery
Price
Service
Design
Availability
Installation method
Packaging
Promotion
Laboratory tests
Terms
Workmanship

The salesman should not stop with picking out the *features* of a product. He should go on from the features and convert them into benefits. People do not really buy features, they buy benefits. The dictionary defines a benefit as "Whatever promotes welfare, advantage, profit. . . ." and that's what people buy.

Features only imply and suggest benefits. They leave too much thinking to the buyer and he will not or cannot think. The salesman must translate his product or service features into benefits to the prospective buyer. Benefits do not speak for themselves. The salesman must do the speaking for them.

Think of a product which you might like to sell. What are some of the common benefits? Are they to be found among the following?

Time saved	Simplified work
Increased sales	Reduced upkeep
Reduced costs	Greater safety
Prestige	Satisfied ambition
Better health	Greater convenience
Leadership	Uniform production
Pride of accomplishment	Uniform accuracy
Economy in use	Continuous output
Preserved beauty	Added protection
Maximum comfort	Reduced waste
Bigger savings	Self-improvement

Personal benefits may also need consideration when the salesman is preparing to sell a businessman. For example: "This is something that will speed up *your work*." "This will reduce the number of complaints that *you* have to handle." "The men who use this product will appreciate *your* giving them a tool that is easier to use." "This is a chance for *your* company to get out in front of competition." "This gives *you* more of the tools used by your competitors."

Never make your prospect think up the reasons why he should buy your product—*tell him*. And don't forget that all the time you are talking about your proposition he is asking himself, "What's in it for me?"

Let us take the example of a salesman calling on a prospect he knows quite well—one who owns a fairly large dealership. The salesman wants to interest him in a specialty item.

SALESMAN (smiling): Hello, Joe.

PROSPECT: Hello, Jack. How are things these days?

SALESMAN: Great. Can I have a few minutes? I've got something you'll be interested in—an item that, believe it or not, will really *put some profit in your pocket.*

Note that this salesman *started* his sale by approaching and greeting his old friend. Then he moved right to the *telling* phase and used an assurance phrase, "believe it or not," to introduce the benefit, "put some profit in your pocket." The plan is to *tell* your prospect *what* you can do for him and then proceed to explain *why* you can do it. Ask yourself this question before you call on a prospect: "Why should I ask this prospect to buy this product *now?*" In other words, learn the self-interest appeal that he will react to.

For example, these are the benefits that would interest almost all dealers:

More consumer business	Faster turnover
More retail business	Higher mark-up
More repeat business	Lower inventory
Easy to sell	Community leadership

Check the effectiveness of your opening statements and when you find those that fit you and those that your prospects should spark on, use and reuse them to get all your sales off to a winning start. You can find all the basic benefits by analyzing your product benefits to fit all kinds of prospects. But benefits must be built into his trade.

A word of caution: In telling of definite benefits which others have received through the use of your products, don't ever make the blunt statement that you can deliver these same benefits in equal or greater amounts. Never say, "You can increase your sales 20 percent by stocking this line." Rather say, "Others tell us that they are able to increase their sales 20 percent or more." And then be ready to produce *proof* to back up your statement.

Using Assurances

Using assurances to introduce benefits eliminates the possibility of making blunt statements which may offend or irritate the prospect, such as, "I can increase your sales and make more money for you." Let's observe how a good salesman works with assurance words and phrases.

SALESMAN (after he has approached and introduced himself): Mr. Prospect, *I am sure that you are like most dealers* in that you want to increase sales, get more repeat business, and make a good profit. *Now, I don't want to make any wild-eyed claims and if you question my next statement it won't surprise me,* but I have a proposition that is helping hundreds of our dealers get more business, more repeat business, and make additional profits every month. If I can prove this to you, you would be interested, wouldn't you? (Note use of three assurance phrases.)

Demonstrations to Prove Claims

There is no doubt that the most effective, most convincing, and most powerful proof of a salesman's claims can be obtained through demonstrations. Demonstrations will do these things:

1. Show and prove the value of a product.
2. Demonstrate usability and benefits.
3. Instill in the prospect a desire to purchase.
4. Provide full knowledge of product usage.

What can be demonstrated? Almost anything and everything. Nearly all products lend themselves to proof by demonstration regardless of their size, nature, or value. The following examples will serve to illustrate this point. Only a little imagination and ingenuity on the salesman's part will show how many other products can be used to offer proof and assurances through demonstrations.

Prospect Participation to Prove

When the prospect participates in a presentation, he is receiving the strongest kind of proof material, because it brings home to him full realization of how he can get the same benefits.

A self-demonstration brings him right into the picture. He actually experiences the benefits when he participates in the demonstration, and he also experiences a feeling of *ownership* which often helps the salesman to close a successful sale. This technique also obtains the prospect's undivided attention, and prevents distractions and interruptions. It appeals to the prospect's primary senses of sight, touch, taste, hearing, and smell.

Summary and Successful Sale

The preparation of a summary and successful close is the part of the idea sequence which always excites a salesman's enthusiastic interest. According to many authorities, the close is said to be the most important part of the selling process; it means the difference between crossing home plate and being stranded on third base. The summary and close is believed to be the climax of the sale and if a salesman fails to close—he fails period.

However, if the salesman has made a favorable impression at the *start;* stimulated the prospect's attention and interest by *telling* about the benefits; *explained* why the prospect, too, can reap the benefits, and nailed down the benefits with *proof* materials—why shouldn't he close a successful sale?

Closing Signals

Prospect reactions to the presentation are probably the first closing signal, or tip-off, that a salesman can detect. Few people bother to conceal their likes or dislikes, and their feelings, their facial expressions, and their reactions tell the salesman to stop or continue.

Other signals which reveal the prospect's state of mind are shown in the following:

- Attention while the salesman presents and demonstrates.
- Agreement with whatever the salesman says or does.
- Operating questions about the product.
- Storing questions: What to do; How to do it.
- Service questions.
- Interest in terms.
- Interest in a particular feature or item.
- Interest in guarantee or warranty.

Closing Methods

One who is preparing to be a salesman should know that he must be a master of a variety of closing methods so that he will be ready for any kind of prospect or selling situation that may arise.

As soon as the professional salesman has identified *buying signals,* he starts to summarize the important benefits, values, advantages, and exclusives. The summary is a way of making as sure as possible that when the salesman asks for the order, the prospect will say yes. It is the salesman's way of being sure that the prospect remembers and understands all the reasons why he should say yes. Also, the prospect may be confused and a summary helps to clarify the situation.

So, the prospect should be given a quick, clear review of the benefits that seemed to interest him most. The salesman talks in terms of "you" and "yours." He watches the prospect and notes how he reacts as each benefit is mentioned. Does he show approval? Does he seem to understand? If the salesman is not sure, the prospect should be asked a question such as the following: "Have I made that perfectly clear?" "So, doesn't it seem logical that this should get you new customers?" This method helps the salesman uncover any obstacles, or fears, which may be in the back of the prospect's mind and gives the salesman a chance to overcome them. When the salesman obtains agreement on every point why shouldn't the prospect buy? It would be the natural thing to do.

POWER POINTS

From the salesman's viewpoint, any means of communication can be used in selling. The communication medium may be his speech, personal appearance, manners, letters, printed materials, telephone, or visual aids. In short, any means which a salesman may use to appeal to any one of the five senses is part of the selling process.

Sales of any consequence are said to be more the result of preparation than of selling techniques. The buyer's office or a prospect's home is not the place to begin planning a sales presentation. Planning must be done long in advance of a selling interview.

Knowledge of the features, characteristics, specifications, performance, advantages, exclusives, values, and benefits of his proposition, as well as of competitive differences, is the salesman's ammunition. He must have sufficient and varied knowledge of his product, knowledge that he can use selectively or totally, when he needs it.

Preparation to sell includes putting all of the elements of the selling process into a plan which will work for the individual salesman and in a particular situation. The plan which appears to be best suited to the needs of most salesmen is the *idea sequence,* which is expressed in the words Start, Tell, Explain, Prove, and Successful Sale. Within these phases of the selling process are included a majority of all the attitudes, skills, and appreciations needed to enable a salesman to sell with pleasure and profit to himself and to his organization.

The successful salesman is like a good actor. When the curtain goes up the actor must give his best performance or he will be forced to leave the stage. Salesmen, too, must put on a good performance, chiefly by keeping the prospect's interests in the foreground from first to last. Otherwise the salesman will be forced to leave the selling interview because he did not put on a good performance.

The professional salesman will reveal selling points one at a time, giving the prospect frequent opportunities to think through and digest each point. By asking questions to gain agreement on each sales point, the salesman can smoothly come to the phase of the sale known as the *trial close,* or he can use one of the question techniques.

The professional salesman associates every new key point with ideas already explained or known to the prospect, because he knows that it is very difficult for anyone to grasp an entirely new concept or idea. The demonstration affords a wonderful opportunity to relate the new with what the prospect already knows, because he can understand the sales presentation and actually experience the benefits.

The professional salesman uses simple words that paint pictures of satisfaction in the prospect's mind, because he knows that clear language carries the most conviction.

The successful salesman reaches the prospect's understanding through a combination of oral and visual persuasion, with emphasis on the latter. He knows that the visual sense is the most important, and, whenever possible, he uses all of the visual sales aids which apply to his proposition.

Finally, the successful salesman makes his presentations as short as possible. He does not hurry, but he covers every essential detail. He eliminates information that does not help him motivate and persuade the prospective purchaser to buy, but he is careful to include motivators and persuaders that are essential for closing successful sales. Finally, he never forgets to *ask for the order!*

DISCUSSION QUESTIONS AND PROBLEMS

1. Why do successful salesmen plan their sales talks?

2. What are the advantages and disadvantages of standardized sales talks?

3. What are the advantages and disadvantages of the stimulus-response formula?

4. What is the main advantage of using the need-satisfaction approach in developing a sales presentation? The main disadvantage?

5. The programmed presentation is related to the role of the salesman as a problem-solver. Discuss.

6. What are the advantages and disadvantages of the AIDA formula?

7. What might a good salesman do to start a successful sale?

8. What might be involved in the *telling* phase of a sale?

9. Why should benefits be emphasized in a sale?

10. How would you use assurances in your selling process?

SELLING PROBLEMS AND PROJECTS

---

1. Art Clung Case

Art Clung was a young salesman who found it very difficult to keep his prospects interested throughout his sales talk. He asked several older salesmen how they accomplished this feat. In almost every case they replied that they kept the prospect in the picture.

Question

1. What did these experienced salesmen mean?

2. Jim Scrip Case

Jim Scrip says, "I'm no different from other salesmen who want to earn an honest dollar. My whole sales talk is based on an organized interview, and I organize it so as to aim first at getting attention, then interest, then desire, and finally a successful close. I keep my sales talk running right down the track."

"This method has worked for me," claims Jim Scrip, "but I know salesmen who either would not or could not use it. The reason for others not using my method is that they believe in leaving intentional pauses in their sales talk so that the prospect will feel impelled to ask questions to satisfy his curiosity."

Question

1. Which method is more likely to be the most effective?

3. Charlie Farrell Case

Charlie Farrell carried a card that he said he looked at before he went in to every interview. The card had these words written on it:

Establish the need.

Meet the need.

Relate need to prospect.

Show benefits.

Ask for the order.

Question

1. According to this card, what selling formula does Charlie Farrell use? Explain.

4. Tom Byrnes Case

Tom Byrnes is a very successful salesman of intangibles. Tom closes his presentation forcefully. He says, "It can never be emphasized too strongly that a salesman never hurts himself when he bluntly asks for the order; he can't lose when he asks the prospect to buy."

Question

1. Is there any truth in this statement? Can every sales presentation be ended this way?

PART

THREE

BASIC SALES TECHNIQUES

CHAPTER 10

Starting
Successful Sales

The first five minutes of a presentation are the most critical and probably will determine the final outcome of the sales talk. Instructors of salesmen point out that, during these five minutes, the salesman is on trial to win the prospect's approval for the continuance of the interview. Because it is natural to expect resistance on the part of every buyer, gaining the opportunity to continue the interview is the first hurdle to be cleared. It is also maintained that the salesman will not receive a brush-off if he is successful during the first five minutes.

FIRST FIVE MINUTES

The first five minutes of the sales interview is referred to as the *approach*. During this time, the salesman starts conditioning the buyer and establishes the fact that he has something to say that the buyer wants to hear. Surely the first five minutes is not the time to exhibit weakness or stumbling in speech or manner, nor is it the time to launch into an unorganized sales talk.

Because of the vital importance of these opening minutes, the professional salesperson makes definite plans for his approach. He knows what he intends to say and do to arouse the buyer's interest; he begins his presentation clearly and concisely, and makes it appealing enough to gain favorable attention and to establish empathy.

How to Establish Empathy

Empathy is the capacity to understand the feelings of others. The salesman with empathy has the ability to put himself in the position of others and to see things as they do. Empathy is not charm or exuberance, nor is it sympathy or pity. Empathy can be acquired by anyone. The salesman who appreciates and understands the prospect's concern about a buying problem can deal more effectively with this prospect and can quickly establish communication with him.

To create empathy between himself and his prospective buyers, the modern salesman deliberately tries to create an atmosphere of friendliness. He does not wait for friendliness to be shown by the buyer. Also, the salesman is earnest about his job and the other person's problems. He reveals enthusiasm for his proposition. He stimulates sufficient curiosity so that the prospect is willing to buy rather than to be sold. Above all else, he has developed the capacity of empathy.

The empathetic salesman is always aware that he should never center attention on himself or his company. He knows that the buyer is interested in only one thing: How he can be helped? In other words, the buyer wants to know what he is going to gain from his purchase. It is the salesperson's function, especially during the first five minutes, to establish empathy with the buyer by telling him, showing him, and proving to him that the salesman understands the prospect's problems. The salesperson unmistakably reveals that, to him, selling means solving problems and benefiting the buyer.

The salesperson's first job is to convince the prospective buyer that what he has to say is worth the prospect's time and attention. His opening statements should make the buyer feel that his search for a wanted product or service is at an end, or that he is going to benefit in some way.

Sales resistance is said to go up in direct proportion to the apparent sales effort employed. Therefore, to make the customer believe that he is selling himself, the salesman must see his proposition as the buyer sees it. The seller cannot think as an outsider and force his views on the buyer. Such an attitude places the buyer on guard against being sold. The seller will then have a difficult time convincing his buyer of the benefits to be gained from his goods or services, no matter how closely they may relate to his needs. A salesperson is truly empathetic when he is able to put himself in the buyer's place by identifying himself and his product with his buyer's needs, wants, and motives.

Making People Feel Important

The start of a successful sale often begins with the simple act of making the prospect feel important. This ability has great advantages to the salesperson and it makes transactions much more pleasant for both parties. Psychologists know the desire for recognition is a basic human need. Complimenting a prospect is one of the most useful tools a salesman has. *Compliments* make people feel better and more important. However, unless a compliment is sincere, there is danger in its use. Obvious flattery warns the prospect that he is being "buttered up" or "kidded" and he may resent it.

A compliment must be subtle. It should create a feeling of commendation without causing the prospect to wonder, "What's this character after?" If it is recognized, it is clumsy. Subtle compliments are the most effective kind.

BEGINNING THE PRESENTATION

It is practically impossible to outline forms of address that will serve in all situations. It is always advisable, however, to avoid uninspired, commonplace expressions and stereotyped phrases in getting the sales interview started.

Every successful salesperson avoids trite expressions, because he knows that he cannot open a successful sale until he has:

- Captured favorable attention
- Won favorable interest
- Created confidence

A professional opening to a successful sale may require only sixty seconds, if the salesman has properly prepared himself. For example, the following opening statements have been highly successful when used to sell a product to a new prospect:

> SALESMAN (smiling): Good morning, Mr. Prospect. I'm Joe Brown of the Pocono Process Company. I know you're a very busy man, Mr. Prospect, and I appreciate the time you have given me. So to save your time, I'll get right down to business. Here is an interesting sample of a product that we have just brought out, and, from what other customers have told me, I'm sure it will save you time and money. Here's the way it works.

Note the technique Joe Brown employed to make a fast, favorable impression and actually start toward a successful sale. (Several of the following points are mentioned in the idea-sequence formula discussion in Chapter 10.)

1. Pronounced the prospect's name correctly.
2. Gave his name clearly.

3. Gave the name of his company.

4. Complimented the prospect.

5. Had a businesslike appearance and attitude.

6. Demonstrated—showed something.

7. Showed friendliness but not familiarity.

8. Asked questions.

9. Listened.

10. Got down to business quickly.

This salesman's opening presentation centered around three factors: he sought to gain empathy with his prospect; he emphasized that the prospect would receive benefits; and he recognized the buyer's importance. When a prospect's attention and interest are obtained in this way, he will listen to the salesman. This kind of opening statement can be adapted to almost any product or service to obtain favorable attention at the start of a sale.

Recognition

Running through the salesman's speech in the foregoing example is the principle of making the prospect feel important. There is a sales advantage in making people feel important. Praise is a form of recognition, and the start of a sale is an excellent place to use that selling device. The good salesman offers praise to his prospect whenever he can honestly do so. Praise builds up the prospect's ego; it makes him feel important; it recognizes his position as an individual who deserves attention.

Prospect's Needs

Early in the presentation, the alert salesman will tell his prospect how he will benefit from his products or services. He emphasizes benefits throughout the sales presentation, because he realizes that a prospect is interested only in what a salesman can do for him. Some professional salesmen start an interview by saying, "Everyone knows how busy you are, Mr. Brown, and it is nice of you to give me the time I asked for. You will be interested in this product, because. . . ." Obviously, this is a far better approach than "I just happened to be in this neighborhood and thought I'd drop in." It offers the prospect recognition while starting the presentation from the "need" and "problem-solving" aspects.

Businesslike Approach

Relatively few prospects like discussions about the weather, base-ball, or politics. Both the prospect and the salesman know that the call is about selling and buying, and any other topics are mere time-wasters. Comments about topics not related to the prospect's interests do not command favorable buying attention or arouse interest.

Too often the salesman starts talking about the size of his company, how fast it has grown, or how much he wants to sell his product, without pointing out specific advantages for the prospect.

Prospects are never interested in such vague generalizations as, "This is a nice piece of goods," "This is a good seller," or "Mine is one of the largest and strongest companies." The salesman should describe a specific benefit to the prospect or suggest the solution to a specific problem. All prospects are primarily self-interested, and the approach which answers this query will command attention. For example:

SALESMAN: Mr. Jones, my name is Don Stevens. I'm with the XYZ Company. I imagine that like all businessmen you are trying to find some way of increasing your sales. Am I right?

PROSPECT: You bet you are.

This is a good approach because the salesman endeavored to do three things:

1. He planted an idea.
2. He translated the idea into a benefit.
3. He got a response from the prospect.

In an industrial sales situation, the presentation might begin in this way:

SALESMAN: Mr. Williams, how would you like to cut your milling costs by approximately 25 percent?

PROSPECT: Fine, but how?

SALESMAN: Our new chemical milling process can achieve that savings for you.

In specialty selling to a consumer, the salesman might use this approach:

SALESMAN: Mrs. Bosworth, I imagine that like most women you are interested in keeping your hands soft and young-looking, aren't you?

PROSPECT: Naturally, but what has that to do with water softeners?

SALESMAN: Just this, Mrs. Bosworth. Your present hard water system requires the use of substantial amounts of detergents which are harsh to the skin. Isn't that right?

PROSPECT: I hadn't thought about it that way.

SALESMAN: By softening the water in your home, you reduce the need for detergents and protect your hands. Of course, this is only one of many benefits. May I step in and show you how you can live better with all of the other advantages soft water brings you? It will take only a few moments.

Pedestal Questions

Pedestal questions are closely related to the compliment. By asking the prospect questions on subjects of interest to him, the salesman "puts him on a pedestal." The prospect is flattered to discover that the salesman is interested in listening to his ideas and opinions. This kind of conversation also frequently discloses to the salesman information useful to him in the interview. Pedestal questions might be phrased like these:

"How long have you been in this business?"

"How did you come to choose this fine location?"

"How do you attract so much business?"

"Where did you get your idea for inventory control?"

"How do you maintain such high morale in your sales force?"

"How do you keep your trucks so clean?"

"What do you think about this product?"

"What do you think is the most important part of selling?"

"What do you think business will be like next year?"

Showing deference to a prospect is another way to place him on a pedestal. For example, many people like to pretend that they are very busy. The salesman might start an interview by saying something like: "Everyone knows how busy you are, Mr. Black, and it's mighty nice of you to give me the time I asked for."

Skillfully avoiding an argument wins people to the salesman's side. By not arguing one shows that others have a right to their opinion. People do not argue with facts, such as testimonials or success stories, but they will fight hard to support their own opinions. Arguing puts prospects on the defensive and arouses resentment.

Pronouncing a *prospect's name* correctly and distinctly is important in selling. The one thing a person really owns is his name, and he feels complimented when people remember it.

"Something New" Technique

When possible, good salesmen use the *something new* technique because it has a strong sales appeal. The "something new" might be a product or service to be introduced, or it might be an exclusive feature. This selling device gains attention. It permits the salesman to maneuver and explain while adding interest to the presentation.

Here is an example of this technique.

> SALESMAN: Last year, Mr. Purchasing Agent, your firm spent $200 with our firm. I thought you would like to see an itemized statement of these repairs, so I brought one along. You can save $160 or more of that amount this year and every year from now on if you use my product. Are you interested?

Attention Getters

Where does a salesman find a good attention getter? This question is easily answered: the best of all attention getters is the product itself. A close examination of any product or service will reveal features and benefits that attract attention. If a salesman studies a list of the benefits, values, advantages, or exclusives of his proposal, he will be able to develop a presentation linking a buyer's interest to the product.

Consider a steel product as an example. Features related to size, shape, color, and finish can be presented visually to gain attention. If the article is portable, it can be shown to the prospect.

Almost any marketable item has characteristics that can be presented as attention getters. A professional salesman constantly seeks attention getters related to his products to aid in demonstrating benefit points.

For example, there was the salesman who attracted attention quickly by bouncing electric light bulbs on the desks of purchasers to prove that they were strong and durable. Another salesman carried a gasoline blowtorch to demonstrate the virtues of his flameproof fabrics.

Demonstrating

Showing the product at the start of a sales interview transfers attention from the salesman to the product itself and to the prospect.

If a necktie salesman, calling at offices, told his prospects that he would like to show them the merchandise in his case, they would all probably say they were not interested. However, if the same salesman entered offices with several neckties hanging over his arm, attention would switch immediately from the salesman to the neckties; and if he held them out to buyers, they would probably take them in their hands for closer inspection. In this way, *no* attention would have been transformed into *active* attention.

Showing something concrete to the prospect such as the product, a sample, a model, or the material of which the product is made will usually attract the prospect's favorable attention when the saleman's oral presentation will not.

Prospect Participation

It is good practice to get something solid into the prospect's hands as soon as possible after the presentation is started. The product may be placed in front of the prospect, or the salesman may hand him a sample, a book, or model, or a piece of advertising matter. When an interview is opened in this manner, the salesman attracts the prospect's attention and participation, and can lead smoothly into the sales presentation. When a prospect participates in a presentation, his attention and interest are secured. Interruptions by other matters will then be less likely to terminate the interview prematurely.

QUESTIONING AND LISTENING

Asking questions and listening attentively to the answers is a useful technique in stimulating a cordial relationship between salesperson and prospect. For instance:

> SALESMAN: Mr. Prospect, I have told you how others are stepping up sales, making more money, and building a following of satisfied customers by selling our products. Frankly, I do not know all I should about your particular kind of business. Would you be good enough to tell me about it so I can decide whether or not our product can give you the increase in sales that others are getting?

The salesman must listen to the prospect's response, guiding the conversation in the direction he wishes by asking further questions. Salesmen often talk too much; it is better to ask questions and listen.

Intelligent use of questions can promote friendliness, increase the prospect's understanding of and interest in a product, and obtain his participation in the selling process.

Listening attentively is one of a salesman's most important functions. Salesmen are often told that in selling it is important to talk well;
however, it is just as important to know how to listen well. A salesman
can often listen his way to a sale when he cannot talk his way to one.

Successful salespeople talk to prospects in terms of benefits for
them and ask questions to gain agreement. Then, they:

Listen, to show courteous attention.

Listen, to learn the prospect's needs.

Listen, in order to learn what to say.

A university professor once asked a student, "Why don't you join
in the discussions?" And the student replied, "I learn more by listening. Anything I would say I already know."

Discovering Needs and Problems

The value and effectiveness of planned questions in starting an
interview is shown by a recent study of the sales force of a large company. The survey revealed that a majority of its salesmen started their
presentations by telling their prospective buyers what their product is
designed to do. A smaller group in the same company launched their
presentations with questions concerning the prospect's needs and
problems. The second group consistently averaged more than 50 percent higher in ratio of successful sales to calls than the first group.

The following are some examples of planned questions which
might be used to start sales interviews:

"Would you be interested in cutting down your losses by 25
percent?"

"This is our new product. An improvement over our previous one,
isn't it?"

"How would you like to give yourself a raise in pay?"

"Would you be interested in cutting down your losses?"

"Do you have customers who would appreciate a product like
this?"

"You are interested in saving money, aren't you?"

"Would you be interested in stepping up the number of satisfied
customers, Mr. Prospect?"

"Have you ever heard of a glass bottle which won't break when
dropped on a cement floor?"

"We're calling on dealers to offer a free checkup. May I see your installation, Mr. Prospect?"

"Would you be interested in making $100 extra this month?"

"Do you have time to learn how to cut down on your operating expenses?"

"Will you try this out, Mr. Jones?"

These are attention-getting questions. Have you noticed how each one promises a benefit to the prospect?

The Listening Technique

In Washington, D.C., there is a men's store known as Raleigh Haberdashery. There is a salesman in the store who uses the question-listening technique with customers who want to buy a suit. He greets the customer, then asks about his needs and tastes: the size, color, style, and fabric he would prefer in a suit. The salesman brings out a coat and places it on a hanger, turning it to show both front and back. He says nothing, but he watches the customer. If he thinks the man is interested, he removes the coat from the hanger and holds it for the man to slip into. As the customer views himself in the mirror, the salesman calls the customer's attention to the fit, weave, color, or pattern.

The advantage of this method is that the customer is not bombarded with words and he has no feeling of being pressured; confidence is built. The customer is able to "think" himself into buying. The demonstration has lent considerable effect to the selling technique.

In any sales presentation it is worthless to generalize. In less than two minutes the Raleigh salesman asks enough "need" questions so that he knows what the customer wants. He directs a few well-chosen words to specific benefit points, demonstrates, receives the customer's attention, and goes on to conclude the transaction.

Another example of the need-satisfaction technique is revealed by a prospect who went into an automobile showroom intending to buy if his needs were met. He did not realize that he had any specific needs or desires in a car beyond the need for transportation.

The salesman greeted the prospect with a smile and began his usual sales presentation about the virtues of the car's appearance. He talked at length about several body features in which the prospect was not interested and emphasized things that were definitely not wanted. The prospect listened with growing displeasure while the salesman talked and talked. Even though the prospect really wanted a car, he left without buying one. Why? Specific needs were not established through questions and listening.

A few days later the prospect walked into another auto showroom. A salesman approached him and asked what he would like to see. Learning that the prospect was actually interested in purchasing a car, he asked what kind of performance was expected; if it was to be used to transport a large family; if it was to be used to call on customers; if economy was a factor; what color was preferred; which accessories wanted. The salesman asked many more questions regarding the needs and wants of his prospect and listened carefully to the answers. He then showed and demonstrated a car best suited to the needs of this prospect.

The man bought the car because it satisfied his needs as well as his wants and desires. This salesman sold by satisfying needs. He uncovered the needs by asking questions and listening.

Clarity of Expression

Clarity of expression is important in presenting benefit points to a prospect. Benefits must be outlined clearly; hazy ideas and vague generalities are to be avoided.

Your prospect must understand everything you tell him. If you know what you want to say, there is power in your words. If you have not carefully planned your presentations, it is apt to contain generalities and lame clichés.

Express the benefits and proof points in a conversational way. Simple language is the most forceful of all.

The product-minded salesman often makes the mistake of using technical language to describe the product to a nontechnical prospect. The salesman must avoid using technical terms that have no meaning for the prospect and tend to confuse him.

Understatements are more effective than overstatements because they are more believable. Exaggerations breed misgivings, understatements build confidence. A good rule is to speak cautiously.

The following points are worth keeping in mind when you want clarity in your presentation:

1. Keep your prospect's interests constantly in the foreground.
2. Introduce selling points one at a time, allowing time for the prospect to consider them.
3. Associate every new point with ideas already familiar to the prospect. It is difficult to grasp anything entirely new. The demonstration affords an opportunity to associate the new with what is already known.
4. Use simple words. Clear language carries the most conviction.

5. Reach the prospect's understanding through his eyes: use demonstrations, printed articles, copies of letters, photos of jobs, and other visual aids.

6. Make your presentation as brief as possible—but don't hurry. Cover every essential detail. Leave out information that doesn't help sell.

7. Guard against trade expressions that mean little or nothing to the average prospect and which mislead salespeople into believing they are delivering a strong sales statement. For example, a salesman might say, "This is a nice product," and consider that he has presented benefits to the prospect. Another salesman might say, "Our floor enamel wears a long time on any surface, is easy to apply, fast drying, with great covering ability and high gloss." Which approach conveys a better picture of the product to the prospect?

HOW TO REASSURE PROSPECTS

It would be fine if prospects would believe everything salesmen told them, but prospects have had too many experiences with exaggeration, resulting in disappointment or loss of money and time. Since most prospects fear being misled, the salesman must reassure them.

A salesman might say, for example: "Mr. Prospect, I realize that this may sound unbelievable, but Dick Jones of the ABC Company said to me yesterday, 'We've increased our sales more than 27 percent since we put in your product. We haven't had a single complaint!'"

In effect, the salesman is telling the prospect, "I realize that you do not know me and are afraid that I might mislead you; so I'll tell you what others, who would have no interest in misleading anyone, have had to say about my product." In using the assuring statement "I realize that this may sound unbelievable," the salesman is trying to quiet the buyer's fears and open his mind for further selling.

When you make an unusual claim, no matter how true it is, it is wise to preface it with an assurance. Admit that "it sounds too good to be true." For example:

"This may sound unbelievable, but . . ."
"If you question this I won't be surprised . . ."
"From what others have told me . . ."

The Importance of the Receptionist

At the start of a sale, the prospect's receptionist may be of utmost importance to the salesman, because she can help him get in to see the client, or she can prevent his seeing the client. The manner in which the receptionist announces the salesman can either block his way or smooth his path.

If she says: "There is a man out here selling something. You don't want to see him today, do you?" the answer is pretty sure to be, "Too busy now, try later." On the other hand if she says: "There is a gentleman out here who says he can save you time and money. Shall I send him in?" she is assisting the salesman to secure an interview. Therefore, it pays to be very courteous to this person, for she can ruin a sale before it actually starts. Often the prospect asks the receptionist what kind of person the salesman appears to be. If the buyer is not available, she can advise the salesman to see another person, or suggest a better time to see him. Since she can be of help, it is important to treat her with courtesy and respect.

The salesman can help the receptionist by properly introducing himself: "Please tell Mr. Prospect that Mr. Jones of the Blank Company is here to see him." If a letter has been sent or if the salesman has a firm appointment, she should be informed of it.

The reasons behind an introductory approach worded in this manner are fourfold: (1) The salesman infers that he is expected; (2) he reveals no fear of stating his business; (3) he makes sure that he is not mistaken for another salesman; (4) the name of his company may be well known and, therefore, lends prestige to the call. This kind of introduction increases the salesman's chance of obtaining an interview.

It is advisable to discuss the purpose of the call with the receptionist so that she will be able to outline the salesman's errand if the prospect asks her, "Why does he want to see me?" Sending in a business card to a prospect usually does not have much value, but a card clipped to a pamphlet or brochure can be helpful.

If the prospect is not in or is busy, the salesman should ask the receptionist to suggest a time when he might return. He should also leave a business card with a message written on it or clipped to advertising material.

The salesman should always thank the receptionist when he is admitted for an interview and when he leaves. A courteous salesman is favorably remembered.

CONTROLLED TELLING TECHNIQUE

Did you ever watch a sports event on television and become irritated at the announcer because he talked too much?

Sports announcers and salesmen have at least one thing in common—both must be careful not to talk too much. An excellent sales presentation is worthless if the prospect is not allowed time to consider the information and ask questions about it.

Controlled telling means a two-way discussion between the salesman and the prospect; that is, it is a dialogue. This kind of selling is managed so that both salesman and prospect ask questions and listen. When the prospect is encouraged to express his ideas and opinions, the salesman has a more relaxed and receptive buyer.

Ben Franklin, who was considered to be something special as a salesman, frequently stressed the importance of questioning and listening as a method of steering conversation in the direction he wished. This old skill is as valued today as it ever was.

Controlled telling is the most desirable kind of selling. "The man who converses well," said Cato the Elder, "may change his world." Likewise, controlled telling can change a salesman's world, for it can help him make friends, obtain customers, increase sales volume, and advance on the job. In order to accomplish these things, the salesman must know how to control a conversation.

At one time, the so-called *pitch* was considered the most important part of a sales presentation. Today, it has been replaced in importance by the ability to listen constructively.

Why do some salesmen think they are not selling if they are not constantly talking? If you observed these people, you will find that when they talk too much, it is for one of two reasons: (1) they lack sensitivity for the prospect's feelings; (2) they don't understand the nature of the selling process. They are afraid that if they stop talking, the prospect's interest may be lost and the deal will fall through.

Listening is the keynote of controlled telling. Listening helps the salesman find out what is actually on the minds of his prospects and customers. An industrial salesman does not talk about performance if the prospect is interested in imitating a competitor. He listens for possible buying motives. Does the prospect reveal motives of fear, curiosity, envy, rivalry, pride, or monetary gain? To discover buying motives, the professional salesman listens.

Conversational Art

Imagine a powerful automobile capable of traveling at 150 miles an hour, but also imagine that it has a solid steel windshield. With a car like that you could get places in a hurry, but you could never tell where you were going.

All of us have met salesmen like that high-powered car—plenty of ability and courage but handicapped by a lack of vision.

Salesmen like that forget an important fact: One of the greatest compliments that can be paid another person is to ask him questions and then listen attentively to his replies.

When salesmen question and listen, they are learning whether their presentation was understood, how it affected the prospect, and what else must be done to get the order.

Verbal Clues

Studying a person's use of words is helpful in learning about his attitudes and behavior.

For example, a word or a group of words used repeatedly by a prospect can give clues about his attitude or point of view. What a person is thinking about can often be determined by listening for and counting the number of times an idea is mentioned.

Metaphors, similes, and analogies used by a prospect reflect his thinking as well as his attitudes. Repetition of expressions such as "a penny saved is a penny earned," "security is a thing called money," "money in the bank" or "the good word is save your money" might mean that the prospect has had financial reverses or that he is a careful buyer and spender.

Adjectives used by the individual to express approval or disapproval can be revealing. Some prospects use words such as practical, functional, profitable, useful, or feasible to indicate approval. Things they do not like are described as unworkable, stupid, useless, or tiresome.

Prospects who judge everything on the basis of size and power use words such as overwhelming, strong, powerful, gigantic. Things they dislike are often said to be weak, tiny, or insignificant. Those prospects who have artistic interests usually employ terms such as beautiful, gay, colorful, charming.

A discomfort-relief quotient, or emotional barometer, has been devised by Doctors Mowrer and Dollard. This device is employed to compare the number of words a person uses to express discomfort, annoyance, boredom, ill health; with the number of words he uses to express comfort, relief, fun, or satisfaction. If within a few minutes a prospect has used no optimistic comfortable words, but has called the weather "terrible," the new headlines "deplorable," the traffic tie-up "dreadful," his associates "crumbs," he does not need to add that he is "sore" at the world.

The number of favorable self-references in a prospect's statements usually indicate an attitude of high esteem toward others.

Verb tenses may provide clues to a person's attitude toward the past as compared with his attitude toward the present and the future.

A preference for passive expressions such as "I found myself lost in speculation" instead of "I was thinking about it" may reflect a feeling of hopelessness, while active statements reveal a sense of strength.

A passive, discouraged attitude is unmistakably revealed by the following:

"But we've always done it this way."

"We tried it once and it didn't work."

"They didn't do it that way where I came from."

What's the use of working too hard."

"It's O.K., but they would never let me do it."

"It's not in the budget."

An experienced salesman once said that he could judge a prospective customer from his hesitations even more than from his direct answers. For example, ask a prospect "How's business?" If it's good, he will not hesitate to say so; a throat clearing may indicate that all is not good. Pauses may indicate tension or anxiety.

Clues such as these can aid salespeople to gain a better understanding of the people with whom they transact business.

The prospect's questions may be revealing about his problems. When the prospect asks questions regarding the performance of a product, whether it is economical to operate or how much service is provided, he is voicing positive buying clues. Such questions prove that the prospect is thinking about the proposition in terms of his needs and requirements, and indicate that he may be ready to buy.

The questions asked by the prospect furnish clues that will alert the listening salesman to methods of successfully closing the sale. The following are examples of such questions:

"Is this the latest you have?"

"May I see it again?"

"Is this the best price you can offer?"

"I wonder if this is a good buy."

"How safe is it?"

"Is this more effective than what I'm now using?"

"How much research has been done on it?"

"Are there any precautions I should know about?"

"How about chemical reaction?"

"How else can it be used?"

Anxiety, tension, or pressure can spoil a sale. A modern salesman rarely hurries through his presentation. He gives his prospect time to express his feelings and opinions about the points being presented. This can be accomplished by the salesman asking questions of his prospect.

Modern salesmen plan and organize so that they can (1) ascertain a prospect's feelings and attitudes, (2) ask control questions to discover needs, and (3) guide a two-way discussion toward a successful conclusion.

POWER POINTS

Professional salesmen always analyze their successful sales and look for the power points that brought those sales to a successful conclusion.

Other important points include: use of techniques that attract attention; assurances that develop interest; uncovering needs and problems; asking questions and listening to stimulate buying action and increase understanding. Use and revise the ideas, words, and plans that get results. When you discover the power of these methods for yourself in your daily selling, you will continue to use them.

To increase sales success, here are ideas that need emphasis:

- Be sure to know the benefit factors and be sure they are accurate. Statements which cannot be proved should never be made.
- Include the prospect in the presentation by asking his opinion and listening to his answers.
- Sell personal and business benefits: People do not buy products or services; they buy gain, profits, comfort, satisfaction, values, and advantages.
- A good presentation aims directly at the buyer's interests and desires. The prospect does not want to be bored with technical terminology unless it can be directly related to his own interests.
- Benefit factors should be pictured as well as described and explained. Every point should be visualized. Models, exhibits, photos, charts, and the like should be freely used. An appeal should be made to the senses of sight and hearing.
- Oral presentations should be simple. Clear, concise words should be used. The presentation should be made slowly, allowing time for the buyer to ask questions and clarify his understanding.

- Presentations should be tied in with stories of successful use of the product. The prospect should be told about the prestige accounts that have purchased the products, the satisfied users who have expressed favorable opinions. The salesman should be prepared to substantiate his success stories with written testimonials.

Naturally, there can be no sale without a desire for the product or services. Interest is the basis for desire, so it is necessary for the salesperson to arouse the interest of the prospective buyer.

The salesperson, too, must be interesting throughout the entire interview. Unless the salesperson can arouse and stimulate interest in himself as well as in his proposal, a successful sale is not likely to result.

DISCUSSION QUESTIONS AND PROBLEMS

---

1. How would you know when a prospective buyer is really interested in your proposal?

2. What are three things which help to gain favorable attention?

3. What was the keynote of the attitude of Joe Brown toward his prospect on page 164? Did he establish empathy and recognition?

4. Why is it important for a salesperson to ask questions and be a good listener?

5. What are six important factors in starting successful sales? Why are they important?

6. What are several successful ways of getting attention and how may they be used to increase sales?

7. "The first few minutes in a buyer's presence may be vital to some salespeople, but my selling is different because I call on only a few people whom I know well or have met before." Comment.

8. What effective openings or methods can you suggest to make your first five minutes original and to create in the buyer's mind a desire to hear you through?

9. Explain how call-backs and repeat calls on old customers affect the beginning of a salesman's presentation. Should he employ different methods in such presentations?

10. What sales aid can be used effectively to arouse a prospect's interest to the point where he will give you all the time you want to tell your story?

SELLING PROBLEMS AND PROJECTS

---

1.   Pocono Process Company Case

Sam Smiles sells specialty equipment and is now making his first call of the day. This is the way he starts his sales presentation:

> SAM (smiling): Good morning, Mr. Prospect. I'm Sam Smiles of the Pocono Process Company. I know you're a busy man, Mr. Prospect, and I appreciate the time you have given me. So to save your time, I'll get right down to business. Here is a sample of a product we've just brought out, and from what other customers have told me, I'm sure it will save you time and money. Here's the way it works. Isn't that interesting?

Questions

1.   In what ways has Sam Smiles made his interview client-oriented?
2.   What would you do to improve this method of starting a sale?

2.   Thirty Seconds to Open

Let's take a look at several salesmen as they open a sales call. Observe how each of them begins and then criticize and comment on each approach.

   a. "Mr. Henry, I'm Jim MacDonald, and I'd like to tell you how you can save 20 percent on your operation over a year's time. Would you tell me what your monthly costs are?"

   b. "I see from the plaque on your wall that you are a golfer, Mr. Henry. I try to get a few rounds in myself when I can. Where do you usually play?"

   c. "Mr. Henry, I sell life insurance. I'd like to talk with you a few minutes about your future planning. Now, I've found that few people look forward to this topic of conversation, and yet, when they have talked about it, it's one of the most satisfying feelings they have."

   d. "I'm here, Mr. Henry, because several of our customers have been able to save up to 20 percent on maintenance costs by using our plan. You may be able to do the same thing."

e. "Mr. Henry, if I told you that I have a plan that will enable you to relax and do anything you want after age 55, what would you say?"

f. "I think I have something to show you, Mr. Henry, but first I'd like to ask you a few questions."

g. "That was an interesting story in the papers about your new installation. Some of the people I've talked to have had some interesting tales to tell, good and bad, when they got their installations into operation. I wonder what your experience has been this month?"

All of these seven different openings have been used one way or another by many salesmen. Think about those you like and those you do not like, and explain the reasons for your feelings toward each one.

3.   Alpha Clampit Reminiscences

Alpha Clampit was in a reminiscent mood one day when he told me something I've never forgotten. This is what he said:

"Unless you can attract and hold a buyer's attention, you won't get to first base. You might as well leave. You've got to get 100 percent undivided attention all through the sale if you expect to conclude it successfully.

"There are said to be three kinds of inattention. The first is that of the fellow who merely pretends that he is listening. He acts the part; he nods, he smiles, he says, 'Yes, yes, it's all OK,' but you are rather sure that he is not really listening. You are pretty sure that you are not getting through to him. The second kind of inattention is overt. The prospect is blunt; he simply refuses to listen. You talk and he goes on reading his mail, signing his letters, yawning, looking out the window, answering the phone. The third kind of inattention is displayed by the harried person who can't pay attention, even when he wants to. He has too many things on his mind—business worries, a fight with his wife before he left home for his office, trouble with the union, an idea that he may have a serious illness."

Question

1. How would you attract the attention of the three buyers described by Mr. Clampit?

CHAPTER 11

Arousing and
Stimulating Interest

Why one salesman is not as interesting as another is not easy to summarize. However, the interesting, effective salesman begins his presentation skillfully and plans each successive point. He displays both enthusiasm and knowledge of his subject, and makes use of interest-drawing techniques, based on benefits and advantages. He believes in what he is selling, and structures his presentation carefully.

THE IMPORTANCE OF EMPATHY

As discussed earlier, the salesman with empathy appreciates the feelings of his prospects or customers. Since empathy means the capacity for participating in another person's feelings and ideas, the salesman with empathy finds it effortless to match his presentation to the personalities of the people on whom he calls. He does not use force or pressure. He understands the other person's problems, conflicts, and attitudes, and therefore easily arouses their interest.

A salesman with too much empathy, however, can find himself in trouble. It may be difficult for him to control the interview sufficiently to close the sale if he identifies too completely with the prospective buyer.

If the buyer is not empathic, he might regard the salesman as an intruder. If he is able to see the sales situation from the salesman's point of view, he is exhibiting empathy, and a productive relationship will result.

PRINCIPLE OF HOMEOSTASIS*

The principle of homeostasis is based on the supposition that it is natural for people to resist ideas presented by salesmen, for thought and action patterns are not readily changed. Usually, the prospective buyer is more or less satisfied with what he has or has not, and a sale will not take place until his complacency is disturbed.

The salesman must realize that the prospect may resent efforts to disturb his habitual manner of thinking or acting. It is the salesman's responsibility to stimulate a prospect's interest so that he will realize his need for the suggested idea, product, or service. When the prospect's need is latent, or unrecognized, the salesman's job is to make the prospect dissatisfied with his current status and encourage him to improve it.

Concentrating on Needs

While it is true that people do not want to have their complacency disturbed, the majority will be interested when told what this product can do for them. If homeostasis did not exist, there would be no need for salesmen, only for order-takers.

Whether a need is latent or active, recognized or unrecognized, the chief activity of a salesman is to stimulate interest and arouse a desire to buy. To accomplish this feat, the salesman must be able to find the need, and demonstrate how the proposal will satisfy it.

The need-satisfaction principle assumes that prospects buy to satisfy needs. It follows, then, that to make a sale the salesman must uncover the prospects' needs and reveal how his products or services will satisfy them. In other words, this is a prospect-customer–oriented approach, rather than a company-salesman–oriented one.

Uncovering Problems and Needs

After obtaining the prospect's favorable attention and naming general benefits prefaced by assurances, the salesman's next move is to find a way in which these benefits can be applied to the prospect's problems or needs. He is ready to pass from the general to the specific, but to do this he must know as much as possible about his prospect's problems or needs, both realized and unrealized.

*Homeostasis is a word coined by Walter B. Cannon, a psychologist at Harvard University. Of Greek derivation, the word comes from *homeo* meaning same and *stasis* meaning stand still.

Surveys of a prospect's problems before the interview will help to uncover many needs. Another way to discover unrealized needs is through conversation, which is usually initiated by asking questions and listening. The salesman may say, "Mr. Prospect, I have told you how others are stepping up sales, making more money, and building satisfied customers by selling our product, but, frankly, I don't know a great deal about your particular trade here in Centertown. Would you be good enough to tell me about it, so that I can decide whether or not our product can give you the increase in sales that others are getting?"

STARTING TO AROUSE INTEREST

Ordinarily, a prospect is interested only when convinced that he will gain a benefit. Prospects rarely offer reasons why they should buy a product; this is the saleman's job. While he talks, the salesman must realize that the prospect is saying to himself, "What's in it for me?"

Here is how a professional salesman who sells to manufacturers might introduce the benefits to be gained from his proposition:

> SALESMAN (smiling): Good morning, Mr. Cartwright. I'm Jack Smith of the American Box Company. I appreciate your seeing me and to save your time, I'll get right down to business. I have an interesting little booklet on a new product that we have just brought out. Because of what others in your line of business have told me, I'm sure it will save you time and thereby save you money. Many of my clients tell me that it has brought them many new customers; yes, and made those same customers enthusiastic boosters. Doesn't that sound interesting?
>
> PROSPECT: Yes.
>
> SALESMAN (opening booklet): This is how it works.

Note how this salesman started his sale. He greeted his prospect by name, told who he was and the name of his company. He followed with an assurance phrase that carried the benefit, "to save your time, I'll get right down to business." Then he introduced the new product and told the prospect what he could do for him in terms of these benefits: "save you time"—"save you money"—a "lot of new customers"—"customers enthusiastic boosters." He did not give the benefits in his own statements but attributed them to others. Finally, he checked his prospect for his real business interest by asking, "Doesn't that sound interesting?"

The plan is to tell the prospect what can be done for him and then to explain how it can be done. Salespeople should ask themselves before they call on a prospect, "Why should I ask this prospect to buy this product now?"

An example of how to employ the same approach to create dealer interest is revealed by a manufacturer's salesman calling on a dealer who is already a satisfied buyer. The salesman follows the same form as in the previous example: greets the prospect by name, introduces himself and his company, assures the prospect that he will quickly state his business. But because he is calling on a dealer instead of a manufacturer, he emphasizes different benefit points.

> SALESMAN (continuing): I'm sure this new product will increase your turnover, bring in new business, and raise your profit. Many of my customers tell me that it has not only brought them many new customers; it has also made those same customers enthusiastic boosters. This is how it works.

Note especially how this salesman mentioned three benefits that will interest practically all dealers:

- More consumer business
- More repeat business
- Faster turnover

When prospective customers are asked what they like best about salesmen, they invariably mention the very things mentioned in the above approach. For example:

- He pronounced the prospect's name correctly.
- He gave his name clearly.
- He gave the name of his company.
- He complimented the prospect.
- He had a businesslike appearance and attitude.
- He demonstrated his product.
- He showed friendliness but not familiarity.
- He asked questions.
- He listened.
- He got down to business quickly.

Assurance to Arouse Interest

The use of assurances helps to introduce benefits and reassure the buyer. They make a concession to the buyer's possible doubts by admitting that the salesman's claims may be difficult to believe.

The following are examples of assurances which salesmen use to preface benefits when they attempt to stimulate interest:

"If I hadn't seen it myself, I doubt if I would have believed it . . ."

"This may sound like just another sales talk, but . . ."

"Many of our customers were skeptical when I first told them about this, but . . ."

This is a practical example of how assurances are used to stimulate interest:

SALESMAN (after he has introduced himself): Mr. Prospect, I am sure that you want to increase sales, get more repeat business and make a good profit. Now I don't want to make any wild claims, and if you question my next statement it won't surprise me, but we have a product that is helping hundreds of our customers get more new business, more repeat business and make additional profits every month. If I can prove this to you, you would be interested, wouldn't you?

Problem Solving and Ideas

There are probably no prospects or customers who would not be interested in new ideas about their businesses, or who would not welcome help in solving some of their vexing problems. In many situations, no one is better equipped to do these things than the salesman.

For example, a wholesale salesman once asked, "How can I eliminate monotony from my business? I call on the same customers each week, fifty-two weeks a year. It becomes very much the same story on each call. Once in a while we have new products or new deals on old products; but, for the most part, it is a case of taking orders and copying down items from the grocer's 'want book.'"

Most of the monotony will be eliminated if this salesman suggests items that the prospect may have overlooked, and if he tries to have one new idea to present on each call. Successful salesmen know that merchants are eager for profit-producing ideas if they are tactfully suggested. Every merchant has problems needing solutions. A professional salesman identifies these problems and tactfully offers his suggestions and ideas for solving them.

A salesman might properly ask where he might get the ideas and the suggestions. The answer is from trade magazines and merchandising books. What magazines or books? The answer is the same ones the prospect receives. But the prospect is usually too busy operating his store or his plant or his service to read all the periodicals available to him.

Customers

Interest can be aroused sometimes by placing prospects or customers under obligation to the salesman, perhaps by the salesman disclosing information of value to the prospect.

In selling to lumbermen, for example, a salesman might offer information regarding permits that have been issued for the erection of new buildings. After the salesman shows tangible interest in the prospect's business, he feels under obligation to show interest in the salesman's presentation.

Tactful Minimizing

In convincing a prospect, the salesperson may tend to minimize any weakness in his product or service and to build up the outstanding qualities. However, a sincere and honest approach builds confidence in the salesman and his proposition. It is always advisable to tell the truth. It is ethical to minimize, but not to deny poor quality. For example:

A jewelry salesman is confronted by a young couple who plan to buy a modest engagement ring and wish to select a stone. The salesman displays a nicely cut fifty-nine-point diamond, sparkling and clear. The young man hesitantly inquires about the price. The young lady asks pointedly, "Is the stone perfect?"

The salesman, dealing first with the question of price, answers promptly that the value of cut diamonds increases with every point. The price he asks is fair on the current diamond market—a fact which he explains satisfactorily. Knowing that many people are more concerned with show rather than true quality, preferring, for the same price, a larger stone with a slightly yellow cast and some flaws, he explains the difference in the appearance of this small but beautifully cut blue-white stone.

The young lady appreciates these facts but is persistent in asking whether *her* diamond, even though fairly small, is perfect. The salesman has an answer for this. He says truthfully that this stone is commercially perfect. He explains that to most laymen, "perfect" means just that. The young people are satisfied. They feel that they are getting quality and beauty at a fair market price, and they are happy with their purchase.

To the discerning buyer, however, the salesman's device belittling the bad points and magnifying the good points of the stone would be sufficient. Some people would prefer to own a smaller, perfect stone rather than a larger one with any flaw, even an unnoticeable one. It is the salesperson's job to judge the individual buyer and proceed accordingly. The honest salesperson tells his customer the facts.

Success Stories

The term "success story" has the same meaning as testimonial. People like to hear success stories. In them, the motives of gain and imitation are especially prominent. For example, the salesman can tell a prospect a success story about another customer who is making more profits selling the salesman's merchandise. The businessman will probably apply the idea to himself by thinking, "I can do what he is doing and make more money, too." Many prospective buyers are imitators of other businessmen.

If a salesman is selling fire insurance, he may appeal to the fear motive by telling a story about a man who suffered a heavy loss because he postponed buying protection; however, it might be more effective to relate a success story about a client who had money in his pocket because he had purchased adequate fire insurance. If the salesman is selling a trust-company service, he may tell a success story of an estate left in excellent condition because of his firm's competence. If he is selling real estate as a speculation, he may tell a success story of someone who made big profits by buying property similar to the kind the salesman is selling.

In each of these cases, the customer becomes the central figure in an imaginary playlet of his own creation. His interest is in himself as the chief actor in the scene. If the customer is the star, the salesman is the producer, having supplied the script, properties, and audience. Also, by using the success story to bring in a disinterested third party to offer testimony, the salesman can avoid making blunt factual statements, which are often discounted by the prospect.

Another advantage of the success-story method of giving sales information is that stories are more easily remembered than mere statements of fact. Success stories, or testimonials, are to the listener what pictures are to the reader. Just as illustrated books and newspapers are more interesting than solid printed matter, so a sales presentation filled with anecdotes holds the prospect's attention, arouses his interest, and impresses itself on his memory.

The novice salesman might be unaware of the importance of telling an interesting success story and might too often bore the customer with lengthy statements of fact. The professional salesman never misses an opportunity to tell a success story, because he knows that it is an excellent method for stimulating interest.

THE VALUE OF QUESTIONS

It has been said that there is only one reliable way to determine what a customer wants, and that is to have the prospect tell the salesman. This may be done by asking the prospect questions; for example,

"What do you have in mind?" or, "How would you like to stop your worries?" When the prospect answers, the salesman can decide on the appeals which will most effectively influence him to buy.

Asking questions and listening is also a good method of stimulating interest in unrealized and latent needs. Uncovering hidden motives and unrealized needs calls for expert selling.

The salesman can say, "Mr. Prospect, I have told you how others are stepping up sales, making more money, and building satisfied customers by selling our products. Frankly, I do not know a great deal about your particular kind of business. Would you be good enough to tell me about it, so that I can decide whether or not our product can give you the increase in sales that others are getting?"

Then the salesman listens, guiding the conversation by asking intelligent questions and showing interest in the prospect's comments.

Many of the better salesmen ask questions to induce the prospect to agree with them. They do this to check the prospect's understanding and his interest, and to obtain the prospect's active participation in the selling process and "yes" answers as the sale progresses. These salesmen may say, for example:

"Does that check with your experience?"
"Have I made that clear?"
"How does that look to you?"

A skillful salesman does not ask questions as if he were the prosecuting attorney with the prospect on the witness stand. He invites dialogue by posing a question when conversation lags or when a point needs clarification. Until two-way communication is established, the salesman has not really begun to influence the prospect to buy.

There are other advantages to this approach. For example, the salesman flatters his prospect when he asks him questions, because he indicates that the prospect is an authority. In other words, when a prospect is questioned, he is encouraged to talk, and to him this means that the salesman is interested in him and his problems.

Timing and Questions

Timing the pace of a presentation and asking questions about the key points in it are important.

For example, a salesman may talk to a prospect and not be heard because the latter has his mind on another topic or because he has not had time to consider a previous statement. The salesman should delay each point in his preparation until he is sure the prospect understands what has already been said. If the prospect fails to grasp each point as it is made, he may not have a desire to buy because he will not know how the proposal will benefit him. The best way for a salesman to determine if he is communicating with the prospect is to ask questions and listen to the answers, or answer questions from the prospect.

Questions and their answers can also serve as a timing guide to indicate to the salesman whether his presentation is too fast or too slow. He can then adjust his timing of key points to a pace that will be perceived and understood by the prospect.

Listening is a part of the question technique. Successful salesmen not only ask questions and listen; they also listen when they do not ask questions. They listen for complaints, objections, references to competition, gossip, stories, and the like, so they may receive clues to the prospect's wants, needs, and desires.

Questions to Check Belief

Questions help the salesman discover if benefit claims are believed, since some claims sound exaggerated even when they are not. There are buyers who silently answer every point made by the salesman with the comment, "Yes, if it is true."

Most prospects will not say that they do not believe a salesman. They will not be that frank. Therefore, it is advisable for the salesman to check on the acceptance of his claims with such questions as, "That sounds reasonable, doesn't it?"

Statements as Questions

Many statements can be changed into questions. For instance, instead of saying that blue and chrome go well together, the salesman might ask, "Don't you think that the blue and chrome go well together?" By being asked such questions, the prospect is brought into active participation in the presentation. Often he will add other comments and suggestions, and sometimes proceed to "sell" the salesman.

Control over a prospect's decisions is always desirable, and one way to achieve this is to use statements as questions. Statements are often more effective when they are phrased as questions, particularly when the questions call for a "yes" answer.

Questions for a Wandering Mind

For any one of many reasons a prospect's mind may wander. The alert salesman will know when the thought thread is broken, because he will sense, or see, that the prospect is not mentally following him.

When the salesman loses the prospect's attention and interest, he must act promptly to regain them. He might call the prospect's attention to a new feature or benefit, and then ask a question about it.

For example, "Did I make it entirely clear to you, Mr. Jones, that this product will save you 27 percent each month on your operation?" or, "Incidentally, have you noticed this unique feature on our new model?"

Such questions are useful for bringing a wandering mind back to the subject. However, it is better to prevent the occurrence of wandering minds than to have to bring them back to the topic. The prospect's attention can be held by the same means used to recapture it: by asking questions to obtain agreement as each benefit point or feature is explained.

Questions to Obtain Agreement

Many salesmen ask questions to induce the prospect to agree with them on every point they make. They do this to encourage empathy, to check the prospect's understanding and interest, to promote his active participation in the selling process, and to obtain affirmative answers as the sale progresses. These salesmen may ask such questions as, "Does that check with your experience?" "Have I made that clear?" "Doesn't that sound interesting?" or, "How does that look to you?" Questions such as these assist the salesman in closing successful sales.

Negative Questions

Although the salesman wants his prospects to talk while he listens, he must do everything possible to avoid questions which may create a negative atmosphere.

Prospects may indicate a negative attitude when they think they are going to be asked to part with money. They'll say "Business is lousy," "I have no need for your product," or "We have stopped buying for a while." These negative statements are natural responses when the prospect's real need is not discovered through proper questioning.

When the salesman realizes that the wrong questions will bring negative replies, he will carefully avoid such questions as:

"Things picking up much?"
"That's simple enough, isn't it?"
"Could you afford this?"

Negative questions will start the prospect talking, but the salesman will probably listen to the prospect talk himself out of buying. Negative questions ask for "No" answers.

Suggested Response Questions

When salesmen ask suggested response questions, they are employing a technique that requires practice before use. These are questions intended to gratify the prospects ego and cause him to react favorably to the salesman. For example, "Doesn't that check with your experience, Mr. Brown?"

The following will serve to offer additional examples of how to suggest the response the salesman wants:

1. To suggest friendly attitude and common interests to a prospect:

   "You were in business with your brother for a few years, weren't you?"

2. To refer to a person who is a satisfied user of the salesman's product or service:

   "You know Bill Brown, the owner of Bill's Pharmacy, don't you? He's a good manager, isn't he?"

3. To suggest the prospect's response after the salesman replies to an objection:

   "When you evaluate the savings this product offers, as well as the service, the price is relatively unimportant, isn't it?"

4. To use a trial close, suggesting that the prospect buy:

   "Mr. Jones, you seem to approve everything about this item. When would you like to have it delivered—this week, or would next week be soon enough?"

5. To suggest that quality is more important than price:

   "But you realize, don't you, Mr. Black, that this is a quality product?"

6. To build buyer confidence:

   "Mr. Jones, I'm glad you had enough confidence in our product to examine it. I just want to ask you one question. What success have you had with it?"

Retriever Questions

Retriever questions are those which are formed by rephrasing statements made by the prospect. They bring him back into the conversation and may be used at any time during the interview.

Retriever questions are used when a prospect's eyes go blank, when he has a bored or faraway look or when he yawns, showing that the salesman has lost his attention and interest. If the prospect does not listen, it is the salesman's fault because the salesman should control the interview. Here is an example of a retriever question:

> SALESMAN: Would you like to see a chart that shows successive reductions in cost? Note that the reductions were observed in a situation similar to yours after my product was added to the manufacturing process. Isn't that important to you?

In this example, the salesman has regained the prospect's attention by asking a question, tying it in with the prospect's own interest while offering proof of statements.

Easy Manner

In addition to listening, the salesman will want to have a relaxed manner, a friendly smile, a thoughtful expression, and a pleasant tone of voice. The use of these simple devices can smooth out questions and not only make them acceptable, but induce the prospect to disclose his needs.

POWER POINTS

Why people buy certain products is relatively easy to understand when it is understood that they are seeking the answer to the question, "What's in it for me?" When prospects ask that question, they want to know *how* and *why* they will benefit if they buy. The most successful salespeople never forget that a prospect is not interested in them, their company, or their product or service. They know that prospective customers are interested only in what the salesman can do for *him.* Unless the proposition appeals to the prospect's interest, unless it satisfies *his* desires, unless it shows *him* a gain, *he* will not buy.

Usually a prospect will be interested only in a money gain, which means added profits or savings, or both. Some prospects are also interested in safety, pride, competition, increased efficiency, comfort, dependability, or employee satisfaction. There are other reasons for buying, but the chances are that these are the most important. The success of all selling activity will depend on the direct, selfish appeal the proposition has for the prospect. When the proposition appeals to *his* interests, satisfies *his* desires, shows *him* a gain, *he* will surely buy.

It is also valuable to know that people do not buy things. They buy status, prestige, safety, security, satisfaction, enjoyment, recognition, solutions to their problems, profits, values, savings, and advantages. To repeat: People do not buy products, features, and services; they buy what products, features, and services will *do* for them. One of the basic jobs of the salesperson is to translate product features into prospect benefits.

It is well to note that not all the benefits of a particular proposition are of equal interest to various prospects. One prospect may be interested only in economy of performance; another may be interested in safety; another, in increasing his status in the community. Therefore, a salesperson needs to discern a prospect's individual needs and decide which of these his proposition can satisfy.

During the presentation, searching questions about benefits should be asked. Questions that appeal to the other person's self-interest evoke the best answers, but the salesperson must also be interested. He should take care in asking questions; too many may not obtain the desired response. There are times when silence is more rewarding than another question. In every situation, the value of the answer depends upon the quality of the salesman's attention.

A salesperson's questions must spring from honest inquiry, not from attempts at flattery or obvious efforts to manipulate the prospect's thinking. Questions that deal with a prospect's feelings are more revealing than those dealing with facts.

DISCUSSION QUESTIONS AND PROBLEMS

---

1.   Explain the principle of homeostasis.

2.   Why is it important for a salesman to emphasize buyer benefits in his presentation?

3.   What is said to be the unspoken question of all prospective buyers?

4.   Explain how features are translated into benefits.

5.   What is meant by predicting needs and how could a salesman perform this activity?

6.   How may buying motives be used to stimulate interest in the mind of a buyer?

7.   What are the advantages of relating success stories? Give examples of this device in use.

8.   Explain how and why placing a prospect under obligation often assists salesmen to stimulate interest in the sales proposal.

9. Explain why assurance words and phrases can be used to increase a prospect's interest and desire. Provide five examples of assurance phrases and tell why they were chosen.

10. Explain and give examples to show how listening and questioning on the part of a salesman can help to create buying interest.

11. Explain how a salesman can help solve problems and bring new ideas to customers. Why will such activities help both salesman and customer?

12. Explain in detail why you believe one salesman sells more than another. Base your explanation on everything you have studied up to this point.

13. From the presentation viewpoint, what value do you see in outlining features and benefits a step at a time followed by questions, rather than subjecting the buyer to a nonstop presentation?

14. In relation to timing and questions, answer the following questions:

    a. Do you believe that a salesman should ever leave a prospective customer without trying to close?

    b. What are some of the manifestations that would indicate that the salesman has lost his prospect's attention?

    c. You were told in this chapter to check on the prospect's understanding of each sales point. How does this advice relate to the selling formula, or standard sales presentation?

SELLING PROBLEMS AND PROJECTS

1. The Bill Anderson Case

While reading this case, note the features that the customer wants in a truck and the way the salesman describes his product to meet his customer's wants. This dialogue is not intended to represent a complete sale; it merely shows portions of a sales talk to illustrate the points we have discussed previously.

    Short is calling on Bill Anderson, a general contractor. Short knows that Bill has been awarded a state highway construction contract. Short has just entered Anderson's office.

    SHORT: Congratulations, Bill. I just heard you were awarded that Rock Valley cutoff job.

    BILL: Yeah, I was afraid Wilson's bid might be under ours.

SHORT: Well, it was pretty close. I noticed there was very little difference in your bids. It looks like a good job. If you don't have too much trouble with your equipment, you should make some money on it.

BILL: Yeah, it ought to be a profitable job, but you never know what'll happen.

SHORT: Well, as you know, Bill, anticipating breakdowns often means the difference in the amount of profit in any job. When do you plan on starting?

BILL: Well, we're going to move some of our equipment over right away.

SHORT: That's a big job, Bill, and you'll have to hustle to meet the September first deadline.

BILL: Yes, it looks like I'll have to move in eight road gangs and all my local equipment.

SHORT: In view of that deadline and the size of the job, isn't there a possibility that you might get into trouble with some of the old equipment you have here?

BILL: Oh, I don't know. We take good care of our equipment. Most of it's still in good running condition.

SHORT: No doubt it is, Bill. You do take good care of your equipment. But aren't a couple of those old bulldozers nearly worn out?

BILL: Well, I have some that are getting pretty old.

SHORT: It could cost you plenty in time and money if those babies broke down! I'd like to fix you up with a couple of new models to help you make more money on this job.

Question

1.   What is the significance of the remarks Short makes in the opening conversation?

We have seen how Short approached his customer. Now he continues with the sale:

SHORT: . . . I'd like to fix you up with a couple of our new models to help you make more money on this job.

BILL: That's darned nice of you, Paul, but I've always used Pixies, and they've been very satisfactory. If I do replace those two, I'll probably get Pixies again.

SHORT: Pixies are good scrapers, Bill, but this new model of ours has some improvements that I think you'll be interested in.

BILL: How did they improve that thing?

SHORT: They have improved many things, to give you better operation and at a lower cost than other bulldozers.

BILL: What did they improve to do this?

Questions

2. What is this customer interested in?

3. How does Bill indicate this interest?

4. Do you think Short planned this sales approach? Why?

We have seen how Short found Anderson's interests and encouraged him to ask for information. As we interrupted, Bill was saying:

BILL: What did they improve to do this?

SHORT: Let's take the starting system. That's always been a headache to you, and you've got some cold weather coming up soon.

Short opens his briefcase and takes out a folder with cutaway drawings, which he shows to Anderson, as he begins to talk about the starting system. Short fully describes the operation of the new gasoline-conversion starting system.

SHORT: . . . and another advantage, Bill, is that the pistons and cylinders are warmed with gasoline heat at an idling speed. Then, when you switch it to diesel, it's ready to go. With our system it's impossible to have half-burned fuel forming carbon around the rings. Do you agree that this is an improvement over other starting systems?

BILL: Yes, I can see where it might be.

SHORT: Bill, in addition to saving you money in repair costs, this starting system saves you plenty of time, too. It's as simple as starting your car. All you have to do is climb up and step on the starter. No other operations are needed. The time you can save, plus what you can save on repairs in both time and money, add up to a real improvement that will be valuable to you. Do you agree, Bill?

BILL: It sounds like it might eliminate some of our troubles, especially in cold weather.

Questions

5. What is the value of the folder in Short's presentation?

6. How does Short follow up on Bill's two interests?

We have seen how Short found Bill's interests and how he explained the sales features of the starting system in terms of those two buying interests.

BILL: It sounds like it might eliminate some of our troubles, especially in cold weather.

SHORT: You bet it will, Bill. And it'll make your operators happier, too.

BILL: You mentioned several other improvements. What are they?

SHORT: Take the drawbar arrangement, for example . . .

Short opens a folder with a cutaway drawing and explains the advantages of the new model's drawbar arrangement over that of the Pixie. After giving Bill a full explanation, Short says:

SHORT: So you see, Bill, this gives you the proper balance between weight and power. This means you can move more dirt in a shorter time with less fuel cost. That's important to you, isn't it?

BILL: It certainly is.

SHORT: And you can see how this drawbar arrangement will make this possible, can't you, Bill?

BILL: Yeah, that makes sense.

Questions

7. How does Short appeal to buying interests when he tells about the new drawbar arrangement?

8. How does Short end his appeal to the benefits and advantages of the new model drawbar?

SHORT: You really have to operate this new model to appreciate these two advantages I've explained. I know you want to get started on this job, and time is short. I'd like to bring one out for a demonstration this afternoon or tomorrow. Which would be better for you, Bill?

BILL: Better make it in the morning. I'm busy this afternoon.

SHORT: OK. See you about nine o'clock tomorrow morning.

Questions

9. Why was it helpful for Short to plan his call before seeing Bill?

10. Why was it important for Short to know his customer's buying interests?

11. What is your reaction to this selling method?

CHAPTER 12

Analyzing and Guiding Buyer Behavior

Human beings are complex. They cannot be labeled or classified; they cannot even be accurately analyzed. However, having gained sufficient basic knowledge of human behavior, a salesman can often predict the way people will act in his presence. Salesmen deal personally and continuously with human beings, each of whom must be persuaded and motivated to act upon a sales proposal. This process requires skillful manipulation of the prospect's mind and emotions, in addition to the presentation of goods and services. Salesmanship is not solely a matter of selling *things*, it is also a matter of understanding people; it requires "people knowledge" as well as product knowledge.

REASONS FOR "PEOPLE" PROBLEMS

There are a number of common problems leading to difficulties and obstructions between salesman and prospect; these problems are known as *people problems*. Here are some typical examples.

Bad attitudes. Bad attitudes may exist because the prospect dislikes the salesman. This dislike may be caused by the salesman's manner of talking, his behavior, his mood, his attitude, or his manners; or he may remind the prospect of someone he does not like.

Buying habits. A prospect may be in the habit of paying a certain price, using a certain brand or quality of product, or wearing a particular style or color. Many prospects do not like to change their habits, but it is part of a salesman's job to jolt such prospects out of their complacency.

Prejudices. Prejudice may be based on bias, misinformation, or misjudgment of the salesman, his proposition, or his company. From the moment the salesman starts his presentation he may need to work toward overcoming the prospect's prejudices.

Alibis. Alibis, excuses, and delays arise because the salesman has not obtained the prospect's real buying interest. The answer to the question "What do you do when the prospect says 'No'?" is "What did you do *before* the prospect said 'No'?"

Honest reasons. Prospects have the right to reject a salesman's claims. They may be fearful of poor quality and high price. They may be fearful of getting something less than they are paying for. These fears may not prevent a sale, but they often reveal that the prospect wants more and better solutions for his problems.

Defense mechanism. A defense mechanism is a device—a way of behaving—that a person uses unconsciously to protect himself against ego-involving frustrations. Actually, it is not so much the frustration he defends himself against as the anxiety that stems from frustration. The common view is that defense mechanisms may be regarded as defenses against anxiety. For example, a person may conveniently forget about things that make him feel uncomfortable or anxious. He can forget to make a decision to buy wall-to-wall carpeting because spending $4,000 for carpeting means foregoing $4,000 of profit for his firm. Or a person can find himself refusing to accept delivery of an article because, he says, he "forgot" he had ordered it. Behavior of this type is called *repression.*

There are a number of other defense mechanisms besides repression. The following list gives you an idea how these mechanisms operate. We sometimes ascribe motives for our own frustration to someone else (projection); we identify ourselves with people who have the qualities we admire (identification); we bawl out someone, a salesman, for example, because we have had an unpleasant experience with our superior (displaced aggression); we explain our behavior by concealing the real motive and saying that some other motive has made us do what we did (rationalization); we shrug off frustration in one area of our lives by turning to a satisfying type of behavior in another area (compensation).

Advantages of Defense Mechanisms

Almost everybody uses defense mechanisms some of the time. Actually, moderate use of these mechanisms is a harmless and convenient way to dispose of conflicts. When defense mechanisms make a person feel better and make others more comfortable, as they often

do, their value in reducing tension and letting one get on with important problems more than offsets the trivial self-deceptions they entail.
However, when a salesman encounters people who use their defense
mechanisms on him, he is not likely to appreciate their value nor
enjoy the experience. He is more likely to become anxious and frus-
trated himself, unless he understands the behavior of such people and
knows how to counsel them.

HANDLING DEFENSE MECHANISMS

There are many ways to handle problems of the type discussed above.
The following points might be considered as a general pattern:

1. *Take time to listen.* Whenever a prospect evidences behavior
cues such as *repression, projection, displaced aggression, rationalization,* or *compensatory behavior,* it is worthwhile to give him your time
whenever possible. This effort will rarely prove to be a waste of time.
It will help him clarify his thinking and establish better communication.

2. *Be attentive.* If the prospect launches into a violent tirade, it
is best to let it flow uninterrupted until it is exhausted. A salesman
should make every effort to understand what he says and to sympa-
thize. In other words, be empathetic and attentive.

3. *Provide proper verbal reaction.* As the buyer talks, the salesman should listen attentively, occasionally acknowledging that he is
following the comments. If the buyer pauses momentarily, the salesman should nod his head indicating understanding until speech starts
again. In the field of psychology, this is known as the nondirective
counseling technique.

If the buyer becomes unreasonable, the salesman should restate
what has just been said, putting it in the form of a question. Examples
of such questions are: "Do you actually believe that our products are
of poor quality?" or, "Do you believe our products are not produced
under quality control?"

4. *Do not probe for additional facts.* There is a difference between willingness to listen and intrusion to get more information. In
nondirected counseling, there can be no inquisitiveness.

5. *Do not evaluate what has been said.* Refrain from passing
judgment upon statements heard from a buyer. In no case should you
give a buyer advice about his emotional problems, even if he
requests it.

6. *Do not lose faith in the ability of the buyer to solve his own
problems.* As the buyer talks, you are witnessing a human phenom-
enon. He is really talking things over with himself. If you refrain

from injecting yourself into *his* conversation, the chances are fairly good that the buyer will work things out for himself, to your benefit.

7.   *Relax.* When dealing with problem people, you cannot afford to grow tense. Tenseness brings anxiety, anxiety stimulates fear, and fear causes nervousness and often failure. Fear and anxiety are easily communicated to the prospect, causing him to react with obstacles to prevent buying. Obstacles are the last thing a salesman needs. His real need all through a sale is agreement, assistance, and consent.

Counselor's Technique

- Talk less and listen more.
- Make few or no suggestions.
- Give little advice.
- Never judge the buyer's ideas.
- Give the buyer nothing to fight against.
- Relax emotionally and physically.

PREDICTING THE BEHAVIOR OF CUSTOMERS AND PROSPECTS

How may a salesperson learn to observe, analyze, and manage the various behavior traits revealed by his prospects and customers? A successful starting point is to accept and use six basic principles:

1.   People cannot be categorized; categorizing is the most common error made in judging people.

2.   First impressions of prospects and customers are unreliable, and the salesman cannot depend on their accuracy.

3.   The use of psychology in the marketplace can be learned only through *practice* and *application.*

4.   People are much more alike than they are unalike; therefore, problem people are in the minority.

5.   There are profound psychological antagonisms which divide people more absolutely than differences of creed, race, or income.

6.   When prospects are qualified and the proposition properly presented, few obstructions to a successful sale will arise.

All salesmen, either consciously or unconsciously, attempt to classify or categorize their prospects and to adapt their approaches to fit each individual. The salesman observes the prospect's outstanding behavior characteristic and focuses the greater part of his attention on it. He then generalizes his impression of the prospect from the single outstanding trait. For example, the salesman says, "This prospect is a jovial fellow," or, "He's the biggest grouch I ever met," implying in each case that this is the prospect's predominant characteristic. Classifying is a poor way to evaluate people.

COMMON BEHAVIOR TRAITS

The behavior of people is indicated by common traits which are seen or heard. The following discussion of these traits should help in studying behavior in the marketplace.

Anger	Over-sociability
Skepticism	Vacillation
Indifference	Irritability
Reticence	Impulsiveness
Hesitation	Affability
Procrastination	Thoughtfulness
Disorganization	Insincerity
Self-importance	Fearfulness
Timidity	

The Angry Customer

The person whose overt behavior is revealed by anger is touchy, cranky, cross, mean, and easily provoked. He has an inflammable temper or a disposition which can be incensed on slight provocation; he is excitable, unreasonable, impatient, irritable. He is usually difficult to please or satisfy, and has fixed notions and standards.

This person is not really a good thinker, although he believes he is. His responses are largely impulsive and emotional. Quite often he likes to bluster and argue for the pleasure he gets from it. He may like to annoy and dismay a salesman whom he believes is vulnerable to abuse.

Ill health, either emotional or physical, may be the cause of irascibility. Bad attitudes, habits, prejudices, aggressions, projection, and certain defense mechanisms may contribute to this person's behavior.

It is advisable to study each prospect as an individual and then formulate a process for dealing with him. We cannot succeed if we argue with a person whose irascibility dominates his behavior. We can usually succeed if we remain calm, ask questions, and listen. In this way the prospect's inner drives and feelings may be made apparent, and the salesman can then learn how and where to focus his presentation.

Although there may be a natural inclination on the salesman's part to get tough in return, he cannot reciprocate in kind and still close a sale. This is the time for the salesman to remain friendly and poised. A good presentation, tailored to suit this individual's basic needs and desires, plus quiet self-control, will tend to calm the prospect down until he acts rationally.

The Skeptical Customer

The person whose chief behavior characteristic is that of skepticism is one who doubts that anything is certain. He is distrustful, suspicious, and dubious. He believes the salesman cannot possibly be truthful.

The skeptic's critical or incredulous attitude leads him to doubt, disbelieve, and inquire into everything said or shown by a salesman.

This individual is probably a skeptic because of past disillusionment. No matter what he is told, he criticizes and discounts it. It is difficult to pin him down to what he thinks he wants. He ordinarily does not reveal his reactions to the presentation and perhaps avoids the issues of the sale.

Once his confidence is gained, however, this person usually becomes a regular buyer.

The technique for handling the skeptic may start with sympathy on the salesman's part. The prospect's doubts may be removed through a conservative, sincere, and simple presentation. Understating and overproving will count here because this man will realize that testimonials and proof of benefits mean more than unproved oral claims.

Another technique for handling skepticism is to build up areas of agreement on minor points in the presentation, while at the same time building confidence in the proposition. The more he can find to agree with, the more confidence the skeptic will have in what the salesman says. Any questions or criticisms should be met with assurance, because the salesman knows that the product or service offered is right. The prospect's skepticism can be neutralized when the salesman remains sincere, honest, and helpful.

The Indifferent Customer

The indifferent customer is unconcerned, uncurious, aloof, detached, not feeling or showing interest in the salesman's presentation.

The indifferent prospect handles his job or business well enough, but apparently has no interest or initiative for anything. The salesman's ideas may be sound, but this detached prospect hardly seems to think it is worth the effort to act on anything suggested to him. He is probably emotionally and mentally inert.

Often this indifference is assumed for no one can really be indifferent to suggestions that can benefit him. The salesman's job is to give this man his best presentation and watch for clues related to his motivations. Just as there are hidden values in products, so there are hidden motives and interests in seemingly indifferent buyers. When they are discovered, they can be appealed to with the proper benefit facts.

Sometimes these individuals have to be shaken out of their indifference. They must be shown the losses and dangers they are facing through their indifference and inertia. While this procedure is dangerous for use with most prospects, the salesman must consider that he may not close the sale anyway, and therefore he has nothing to lose even if he makes this prospect angry.

The Reticent Customer

Reticence is a trait which indicates that the prospect is inclined to remain silent or uncommunicative.

The reticent prospect refuses to commit himself. He often reveals a poker face and tries to leave the salesman in the dark as to his reactions. Actually, this trait is often found in an individual who is either shy, timid, and retiring, or a capable executive who is really paying strict attention and sharply analyzing everything the salesman says.

When a stone wall of silence is encountered, it may be breached by asking questions and listening for the answers. Every time a benefit fact is mentioned, the prospect should be asked a question to obtain his agreement; for example, "Isn't that interesting?" "How does that sound to you?" "You agree with that, don't you?" Reticent individuals like questions, because it permits them to air their views to an interested, receptive listener. To give them a start, they may be asked why they refuse to talk. Ordinarily, when they do begin to talk, they convince themselves that they need to make the purchase.

The Hesitant Customer

The hesitant customer vacillates, wavers, falters, shows irresolution, or uncertainty. He is somewhat different from the procrastinator, because he has a reason for his hesitation. He may hesitate because he wants to talk to a partner or his boss, or because he is afraid of making a mistake. Many hesitant buyers think of themselves as careful shoppers and want to see several items and talk to several salesmen before they buy. They may have been previously sold on a single product benefit by a competitor who gave a good demonstration; or they may have received better demonstrations on everything except one point, which still concerns them.

These prospects may hesitate because they have not been convinced; they want to compare and judge relative merits. They really want the salesman to banish their doubts and prove that his proposition is the best, planning to obtain approval of the order later if their questions are adequately answered. The salesman could say, for example, "Let us approve this order while I am here, Mr. Jones. Then if we find that everything is all right, we can arrange for delivery."

This method is effective if the salesman is fairly sure that the prospect really wants the product or service, but is not sure of the opinion of others. The salesman should try to get the order signed before he leaves and while the prospect's interest is warm, or loss of a sale may result.

Another method which can be used when the prospect hesitates is to show him that it is costing more to be without the product than to buy and use it. Whenever the prospect hesitates to make the investment even though he knows he needs the product, the salesman can use this technique:

SALESMAN: Of course, Mr. Jones, you want to be sure it is a good investment for you. But you and I agree that you need this product. Isn't that right?

JONES: Yes, I could use it.

SALESMAN: And we have agreed that this product could increase your business by 25 percent. You cannot afford to throw that amount of money away, can you? Well, it is actually going to cost you more to do without this product than it would to buy and use it. Getting 25 percent more business is certainly profitable for you. So let's go ahead and complete the deal. Right?

The Procrastinating Customer

The individual who is dominated by this trait is one who puts things off from day to day; who defers and postpones; who puts off decisions again and again.

Usually, the procrastinating prospect agrees with the salesman that something should be done, and he may sometimes offer little or no objection during the presentation, but he rarely acts. He may say he is sold, or he may encouragingly tell the salesman to come back on his next trip.

Sometimes the person with this trait is termed "mentally soft." It is not that he has any difficulty with the process of arriving at decisions; the difficulty lies in his distaste for making any decision at all.

He does not often question what is said by the salesman—he simply does not have the courage to say "Yes" or "No." Possibly all his life this man has had someone to make decisions for him, or he may have suffered loss as a result of previous unfortunate decisions which he made without adequate evidence.

To handle a procrastinator, the salesman will usually need to use dynamic selling. The salesman must provide answers as to why he should buy now.

This prospect could be offered a desirable proposition and told that the opportunity may be withdrawn within a short time. The salesman might tell him that many people are inclined to delay making a decision, and then add, "I know that you are a man with the courage of your convictions. You don't dillydally, you act." It usually requires extra pressure to push the man having this trait toward decisive action.

If the prospect admits that the proposition is a good buy, but that he still wants to wait, the salesman might bring out his pencil and sales book and ask if he can write up the order for later delivery.

When the prospect admits that the proposition is a good buy, he really wants to purchase but he hesitates to act, every effort should be made to help him make up his mind by supplying him with adequate reasons for buying at once. In any event, the alert salesman will not congratulate himself when the prospect tells him he will think it over, for the chances are that the prospect will not recall the benefits after the salesman leaves.

Rationalization is also used by the procrastinating prospect. When he rationalizes, he may be evading the salesman's questions, so that when he says he will think it over he is really showing that he is too lazy to think. He may say that he is not interested, when he is really trying to conceal his procrastination. The salesman will usually need to do something startling to shock the rationalizer out of his attitude.

The Disorganized Customer

A prospect who has not systematized or planned his activities and who believes that he is too busy to settle down and regulate his buying affairs is disorganized.

There are prospects who sometimes actually are too busy to interview a salesman; there are others who delude themselves into believing that they are too busy. The latter may often be identified because his desk is piled high with accumulated correspondence and memos which should have been disposed of weeks before. He frequently has two or three telephones on his desk, a secretary who constantly interrupts, and vitamins in a top desk drawer. He is always in a hurry and constantly interrupts salesmen while they are making their presentations. This person has difficulty concentrating on one thing at a time for more than one or two minutes.

Obviously, a sale cannot be consummated if the prospect does not listen attentively. A desire to buy cannot be aroused if the prospect's mind is far away. The salesman could start by commenting on how busy the prospect is, how burdened with responsibility, and how much he accomplishes. This prospect will often listen to a little praise and he likes condolences about how hard he works. The salesman could remark that he knows that the prospect's time is valuable and that time will be saved if he will give a few uninterrupted minutes so that the proposition may be explained quickly.

This prospect should be shown that his ability is respected. The salesman should place strong emphasis on the prospect's need for the product or service and stress the importance of making a decision now.

The disorganized individual will often pay attention if he is encouraged to discuss or comment on a topic. He may respond favorably to an adventure story, a joke, or a question. If these devices do not accomplish the desired result, it might be advisable to arrange a future appointment. Usually the salesman is in a better position if he does not try to pressure the prospect who is disorganized.

Another method for handling the prospect whose attention wanders is for the salesman to stop talking when he observes that the prospect is not listening, for the silence may bring back the prospect's attention. The salesman might also try lowering his voice or speeding up his delivery, and from then on attempt to tell a more interesting story and make a better explanation.

Long interruptions may occur with this kind of prospect. At this point, the salesman might use the time to bring his sales strategy up to date and to formulate a possible closing technique. When the interview is resumed, the salesman should summarize what was said before the interruption and then proceed with his presentation. If interruptions are too frequent, another interview should be arranged for a more propitious time.

The Self-important Customer

A prospect who has an exaggerated estimate of his own merit is self-important. The self-important individual believes that he is superior and important because of the implied consequences of his buying decisions.

Such a prospect is often patronizing in manner, making salesmen feel that he is doing them a favor when he grants an interview. Sometimes this prospect is domineering and tries to show that he knows all the answers and that the salesman cannot conceivably give him any information.

A reasonable approach to use with this kind of person is to cater to his ego. First, the salesman should show respect for this individual. The salesman should appear to accept him as an important person, while keeping in mind that what is really important is a successful sale.

Second, the salesman should pretend that this prospect's time is valuable by acting alert and businesslike in his presence. The prospect might be complimented on his vast knowledge and understanding; he might be asked for advice on a minor matter, or even to do a small favor for the salesman. Finally, he should be induced to prove his importance by making a brisk decision to buy what is being offered.

The *bluffer* is closely related to the self-important prospect. The bluffer is essentially an uninformed person who feels that he must disguise his ignorance by pretending to be more knowledgeable than he actually is.

Dealing with this trait requires dignity on the salesman's part so that he will not be completely dominated by the prospect. He should present to the prospect a set of cold facts, which ordinarily penetrates the coating of bluster and leads to an understanding. The bluffer's pretense should never be challenged. The salesman can afford to let this person try to impress him and let him think he is a successful bluffer: what really counts for the salesman is obtaining the order.

The Timid Customer

When a person's behavior is hampered by timidity, he lacks courage and self-confidence. He may be fearful, apprehensive, uncertain, timorous. He shrinks from any action or activity which requires independence or self-assertiveness.

Many salesmen consider an individual who is unassertive, retiring, quiet, courteous, and shy to be a "sitting duck" for a high-pressure sales talk. This prospect conveys the impression that he is a weak person, so that many salesmen mistakenly offer a hard, fast sales presentation.

It is possible that this person's behavior has developed from past experiences of having been misled, and consequently he finds it difficult to place confidence in what any salesman says. Another reason may be his lack of self-assurance when meeting people. Many capable and brilliant people in responsible positions are sensitive, shy, and embarrassed when they meet strangers. Also, signing the order requires a decision, and the timid individual may fear to take the step.

The correct approach in handling this prospect is to build his confidence in himself and in the salesman. Loud, pushy sales talks are especially disagreeable to this buyer and a direct approach may cause him to react negatively. This person cannot be regarded as an "easy mark" simply because he is slow to decide. He wants to study every angle of the proposition, for he feels that he cannot afford to make an error in judgment. Patience is needed to win this sensitive prospect over to the salesman's side. He should be shown testimonials and hear success stories from satisfied users. He will also respond favorably to other kinds of proof material, such as graphs, charts, tabulations and demonstrations of the product.

The Overly Sociable Customer

Over-sociability means that a person is friendly, affable, and inclined to like companionship with others. He likes to converse and chat. He may chat about everything except the product or service being suggested, but the salesman should not delude himself into believing that talking with this kind of prospect cements a beautiful friendship. Usually, the prospect is simply amusing himself—and wasting the salesman's time—for he likes the sound of his own voice and the feeling of superiority which he acquires from voicing his opinions.

The method for dealing with this behavior trait is to use the prospect's remarks to lead his thinking into the desired channel. This may be done by interjecting something like, "A while ago you said that . . ." When the prospect stops for breath or reaches a place that indicates a pause, the salesperson might say, "You mentioned something a moment ago that seems to me to have an important bearing on your present problem."

Strict attention should be given to what this prospect says, and the salesman should ask frequent questions and listen to the answers. Somewhere in the prospect's chatter the alert salesman will find a place to interject suggestions, as explained previously. The salesman cannot often make a direct sales talk to this person nor can he force this prospect to listen to him.

If possible, the salesman should try to use a presentation based on his idea sequence, with many questions in it designed to obtain affirmative answers. In this way, the presentation may seem to spring spontaneously from the prospect's own thinking, so that he may talk himself into buying what is offered. If the salesman cannot obtain control of the interview within a brief time, and if he cannot pin the prospect down to a discussion of his proposition, it may be advisable to leave and try again at a later date.

The Vacillating Customer

This trait means that the person wavers in mind, will, feeling, conduct and purpose. He is changeable and irresolute.

The prospect who is fickle, changeable, and unreliable decides to do something and then quickly undoes it. He agrees one minute and disagrees the next. One day he likes people, the next day he dislikes them.

The basis for vacillation may be that the prospect simply lacks the power or authority to make a decision. He may have a fear of making a decision and standing by it, or he may not have been fully convinced of the proposition's merit.

To handle this man, the salesman must first qualify him. Has he the authority to make the decision? Has he the power to sign the order? If he is the buyer, the salesman must use patience and try to sell him on the need for his proposition. He should be given a quantity of facts and information, while the salesman emphasizes every benefit point in the presentation. As each sales point is made, the prospect should be asked if it is clear, if he understands it and if he believes it. In this way, agreement is obtained for each benefit point and when the time comes to ask for the order, the agreements usually add up to a successful sale.

Finally, it should be explained that the prospect is not merely being sold something; he is really being helped to work out a problem. His contribution to the solution to his problem is making a decision and sticking to it.

The Irritable Customer

Irritability suggests a person who is easily provoked and displeased; momentarily impatient and outraged; easily exasperated and nettled; sometimes roiled and peevish. This prospect is inclined to anger, easily excited, rather impatient, unduly sensitive to small irritants.

Such behavior directed against the salesman may have been prompted because the prospect has a complaint against the salesman's company, or because of personal problems, or because he may enjoy heckling salesmen in order to make himself feel more important, or because of ill health.

The salesman must answer sarcasm and heckling with courtesy and patience. He can often shame this individual into decency and perhaps win him with kindness, but he cannot arouse interest and desire by losing his temper or retaliating in kind.

The irritated prospect has also been described as a grouch or a crank. He should be listened to with respect, offered sympathy, and helped in solving his problems. He can then be sold the salesman's idea by making it his idea. Offers of help in correcting whatever bothers him are effective, especially if the salesman's company is at fault. Another part of the formula for handling him is to leave his presence as soon as possible, keeping in mind that he may be friendly tomorrow.

The Impulsive Customer

The impulsive person acts without deliberation, under stress of emotion or spirit of the moment, unconsciously or as if by instinct.

Impulsive people move fast, talk fast, think fast, and give the impression that they are always a step ahead of the salesman. Usually they are difficult to manage because it requires considerable selling skill to get them to sit still and listen. These men are proud of their habit of making decisions quickly. The salesman's problem is that it is just as easy for them to decide quickly against the salesman as for him.

Many times these men take chances, almost like gamblers. They often do something without reflection because it has momentary appeal. They may regret it later, but this does not worry them. These individuals will often insist on helping to sell themselves and they should be allowed to do so. Usually they are loyal customers, since they must defend their choice and judgment to others and to themselves and they do not want to be proven wrong.

The best way to deal with the impulsive prospect is to make the offering as attractive as possible. They want not only quick, concise presentations, but also case histories of successful use of the product. These men can be rushed more than some buyers, but timing is very important when presenting to them. After summarizing the benefits, and before the close is attempted, the salesman may pretend to retreat a bit and state that he wants the prospect to be sure he is doing the right thing, because he is making an important decision and the salesman does not want to rush him.

The Affable Customer

The affable person is one who is easy to speak to, courteous and amiable in response to the salesman's approach, mild and gracious in bearing and appearance. If this is a prospect's true basic behavior, all is well and a sale should be easy. Unfortunately, these people do not always respond as expected.

Affability may be possessed by a person who is completely agreeable and who has no apparent resistance, objections, or problems. He may be agreeable to the salesman's proposition, commenting favorably through the presentation, and say "Yes" to everything the salesman proposes up to the point of closing, when he says "No."

The basic skill of the affable prospect, more often than not, is to squeeze every possible bit of information out of the salesman without spending any money. This prospect is always friendly, always happy to see a salesman, and always tells him he is giving the proposition every consideration. Meanwhile, he tries to pick the salesman's brains in every way possible, ranging from technical data to merchandising ideas. He invites him to come back the next time, but rarely buys.

One way to deal with this behavior trait is to establish an issue, which could be an objection or a point of disagreement, then close on settlement of the issue through answering it or reaching an agreement.

Another procedure for dealing with affability is to use the method proposed for handling procrastinators. The salesman might tell the prospect that his friendly spirit is appreciated, and that he realizes that the prospect understands the value of the information and help he has received. The sales proposal should be presented constructively, with the hint that there are many people who show a friendly spirit, but do not conclude by placing an order. He might be placed in a position in which he either has to buy or admit, by inference, that he has been putting on an act. However, his agreeable attitude should not induce the salesman to leave with the expectation of a future order.

The Thoughtful Customer

The prospect who is attentive and who also reflects, reasons, deliberates, considers, and thinks before he purchases is showing thoughtfulness.

This prospect has trained himself to think logically and to employ reasoning before he buys. He is deliberate, slow to reach a decision, and cheerful in considering all the facts before he decides. He is shrewd, moves slowly, and cannot be rushed into buying.

Usually he is a quality buyer and is not inclined to worry about price. He is sincere in manner and action, and deliberation is not a pose to impress salesmen. He is essentially a careful person who is willing to make a decision, but dislikes making a mistake.

When dealing with this prospect, the salesman must be thorough in his presentation and let the prospect know that it is a pleasure to deal with a man who takes his time to reach the right decision. He should be told that because of his analytical ability, he will appreciate what the salesman is trying to do. He should be offered evidence, figures, facts, and visual proof. He cannot be pressured into buying, but his thinking can be guided and helped toward arriving at answers and solutions for his problems. The salesman's attitude should be one of patience.

If the salesman is not sure that this customer is ready to buy, he should ask a test question such as, "Have I made that perfectly clear?" or, "Does it not seem logical that this should solve your problems?" This method helps the salesman to discover any obstacles which may be in the prospect's mind and gives him a chance to overcome them. When the salesman has obtained agreement on every point, there is no reason why the prospect should not buy. The only requirement at this stage of the sale is for the salesman to ask for the order.

The Insincere Customer

All prospects do not possess unblemished moral characters. All do not conform to recognized standards of morality or business conduct. Some prospects distort the subject at hand in the hope of gaining an advantage of some kind.

Some prospects are deceptive in that they want to shop around, but do not want to admit it. They want to make a comparison between the features and benefits of the salesman's product and competing products, and for that reason use execuses and pretexts in the hope of obtaining lower prices.

This kind of buyer is a questioner and can skillfully disparage a salesman's claims. He is able to present his ideas in an adroit manner, with the intent of obtaining a concession of one kind or another from the salesman.

This individual should be treated courteously and his remarks met with facts and proof. Eventually he should tire of his tactics and listen to the presentation. If the prospect's behavior has not rattled the salesman too far, he can conclude quickly and ask for the order. Such "sharpness" and unethical tactics usually wear thin in the face of a salesman's enthusiasm and sound product knowledge.

The Fearful Customer

The fearful customer is apprehensive, afraid, timorous, and worried. *Apprehensive* implies good reasons for fear and is, therefore, a state of mind. *Afraid* may or may not imply good reasons for fear, but it usually suggests weakness. There are fearful prospects who stall and try to avoid making a decision. They offer excuses that are not the real reason for their fear. However, delays and excuses tend to follow certain patterns and it does not take long to become familiar with most of them. For example, a fearful prospect will sometimes say that he has to consult his partner, his boss, or his wife. Actually, he may really want to buy and can easily obtain immediate permission if he wishes. Often he hesitates because the salesman has not made him want the item strongly.

The salesman needs to find out the prospect's real reasons for hesitating in purchasing, so he *qualifies* him. If he *qualifies* on the following points, he is probably a good prospective customer:

- He has a need for my product (or service).
- My product will fill that need.
- My company is reliable.
- My price is right.
- He can pay for the item.
- He should buy now.

If the salesman knows that these are the facts and becomes convinced that the prospect is fearful, he will need to introduce an exclusive feature to increase his interest. Therefore, the salesman will give him another convincing benefit fact and then ask for the order again. He may say, "Mr. Jones, I have shown you many benefits, advantages, and features about this product that I believe you want. It is true that you obtain some of these benefits from other products, but here is something you can find only with mine, and it is so exclusive that no other product has it."

Professional salesmen know the impact of an exclusive feature and they don't discuss it until last, because they realize that it gives their proposition a boost and often clinches the sale when they are dealing with a fearful prospect.

POWER POINTS

All of the people problems that have just been mentioned can be handled so that they work for the salesman instead of against him. For example, prior to the interview the experienced salesman makes a thorough study of his prospective customer; he analyzes his needs, and studies his personality, his interests, his plans, his problems, and his behavior. In this way he is able to present interesting benefit points and avoid confusion and pointless arguments which so often enter into the presentation of an untrained salesman.

Salesmen who have analyzed the obstacles which they have encountered in the past find that a new one seldom occurs. Sometimes obstacles may be expressed in a different way, but basically they are recurrences of ones they have heard before. Further analysis reveals that whenever a prospect objects to something, he is inclined to defend his objection. Having committed himself to a negative attitude, the prospect's pride prevents him from changing his opinions and he will continue to defend his behavior to the end.

Reasoning from that premise, one of the major efforts of a salesman must be to anticipate objections, alibis, delays, excuses, and defense mechanisms. The right idea planted in a buyer's mind is the most effective antidote to the objections and other obstructions which all salesmen dread.

When interesting benefit factors are worked into a strong, convincing presentation, a prospect usually will be too interested to raise barriers to further progress. He will be too concerned about the benefits he can obtain to raise impediments. This skillful selling will give the salesman a new eagerness for his job, and he will no longer be fearful of defense mechanisms and other obstructive behavior patterns.

The salesman must proceed slowly with his presentation until he gathers enough clues to judge his prospect's behavior pattern. If a certain buyer were not too self-assured, for instance, he might be receptive to success stories, testimonials, or survey materials; an overconfident person, on the other hand, might resent this approach.

Should the salesman use his standard presentation on the buyer or should he dwell on only a few high points? The best answer seems to be that the same planned presentation cannot be used with every prospect, since each prospect has his own traits, behavior patterns, and needs. It is better to start the sale with a brief statement of the proposition and to mention only outstanding benefits as they seem to apply to the individual buyer's needs.

DISCUSSION QUESTIONS AND PROBLEMS

1. What are the six main reasons for people problems?

2. What is meant by a *defense mechanism?*

3. How can the salesman recognize a defense mechanism in a prospect?

4. What are the techniques recommended for handling defense mechanisms?

5. "All salesmen, either consciously or unconsciously, attempt to classify their prospects." Explain this statement.

6. What are the dangers or pitfalls in attempting to classify a prospect?

7. What are the six basic principles that a salesman should remember in learning how to manage people?

8. What are the common buyer traits as seen by a salesmen? How are each best handled by the salesman?

SELLING PROBLEMS AND PROJECTS

---

1.   The Topeka Wholesale Hardware Company Case

The buyer for a wholesale house regarded the salesman thoughtfully for a moment and said, "Joe, you are welcome to come into this office as often as you care to, but I will never buy anything from that company you represent!" Joe smiled and said, "Well, Mr. Smith, I'm glad that you let me come in to see you. Naturally, I'm sorry you don't regard my company favorably, because I make my living selling their products. If you don't want to talk business or learn about our products when I call on you, that's okay with me. But you should know that if I call on you, I'm going to try to get your business."

For many months Joe called on this company as faithfully as he did any of his regular customers. The manager would occasionally listen to his story, nod his head and say, "It's too bad you don't work for a good outfit." Or, he would listen to part of it and say, "There's no use of your trying to sell me that stuff," and switch the conversation to the weather, sports or local gossip.

After about six months of apparently getting no place, Joe walked in one day and the manager said, "Well, Joe, we need a carload of material and I'm going to give you the order. We'll show those people in your office that you're doing a good job in this territory."

Questions

1. What psychological principles are involved in this case?

2. How would you have handled this buyer?

3. Do you believe Joe could have succeeded in winning an earlier favorable reaction if he had pressed the prospect to buy?

4. What other sales strategies can you suggest for situations of this kind?

5. Does selling to wholesalers involve any behavior traits that do not apply to selling on other levels? Why?

2. Charlie Caprice Case

Suppose you walk in on a prospect (in this case, Charlie Caprice) without an appointment. You tell him who you are and the name of the company you represent. In reply the prospect snorts, "Not interested. Good-bye." What is your best comeback:

    a. Ask him why he's not interested?

    b. Ask him when he might be interested?

    c. Try to convince him that if he listens he might become interested?

    d. Attempt to make an appointment to see him later?

Explain.

CHAPTER 13

Motivating and Persuading Prospective Customers

Motivation provides the impulses and inducements that stimulate people to action. To a salesman, motivation means creating interest and arousing a desire in the mind of the buyer for whatever is being sold.

How buying behavior is motivated is a difficult but interesting subject. It is important to the salesman because he cannot be a professional unless he understands what makes people behave as they do in the marketplace. According to Crissey and Cash, "It is safe to say that success in selling depends largely upon a knowledge of customers' and prospects' motivation . . . the reasons why they behave the way they do."[1]

It is important to know that people have, generally speaking, the same basic motives for buying, and that each person wants to satisfy a want or need. Some of these motivations are dormant or unrealized, and an important part of the salesman's job is to make the prospect conscious of them so that they will become active and arouse him to buy.

MOTIVATING BEHAVIOR

With the exception of simple reflex activity, all human behavior is motivated; that is, it is directed toward the accomplishment of a *goal*, usually a reward or incentive, that will satisfy a particular need. The motives, or stimulus conditions, that direct our behavior may be classified as *biological, psychological,* and *social drives.* The word

1. W. J. E. Crissey and H. C. Cash, "Motivation In Selling," *The Psychology of Selling* (New York: Personal Development, Inc., 1957), p. 9.

drive refers to any condition of the organism which creates internal tensions and thus impels it to activity.

The salesman is primarily concerned with *psychological* and *social drives*. Among the most important of these are the need for security; the need for liking and esteem; the need for recognition, approval, and prestige; and the need for new experience.

Most of our drives are said to be acquired as the result of past experience. They may result from a learning process in which *symbolic rewards* or punishments are important in producing behavior. We may be motivated by acquired fears and the desire to *avoid* certain experiences, as well as by the desire to achieve rewards and incentives. Often our behavior is directed by acquired, learned motives of which we are not even aware.

Table 13-1. Rational and Emotional Buying Motives

RATIONAL	EMOTIONAL
1. Economy in purchase	1. Pride in appearance
2. Economy in use	2. Pride of ownership
3. Efficient performance	3. Desire to feel important
4. Increased profits	4. Desire for recognition
5. Durability	5. Desire to imitate
6. Accurate performance	6. Love of family
7. Labor-saving	7. Romance
8. Time-saving	8. Comfort
9. Simplicity in construction	9. Desire for adventure
10. Simplicity in operation	10. Desire for variety
11. Ease of repair	11. Health
12. Ease of installation	12. Safety
13. Space-saving	13. Fear
14. Increased production	14. Desire to build or create
15. Purity	15. Desire for security
16. Availability	16. Desire for companionship
17. Complete servicing	17. Convenience
18. Low maintenance cost	18. Amusement and pleasure
19. Good workmanship and materials	19. Desire to be different
20. Thoroughly researched and tested	20. Curiosity

Buying motives are both *rational* and *emotional* in nature. Rational buying motives are based upon reasoning things out objectively or thinking things through. Emotional buying motives are based upon emotional response. Table 13-1 provides examples of these two types of motives. Notice that the rational motives include economy in purchase and use, efficient performance, durability, increased profits. The prospect generally rationalizes or plans these things. Emotional motives include pride in appearance, desire to feel important, love of family, desire for comfort. These describe feelings.

The industrial buyer generally attempts to purchase on a rational, objective basis, while the household buyer tends to place emphasis on subjective, emotional factors. Even a supposedly rational buyer, however, may be influenced more by emotion than by reason. People show inertia when forced to think, and even a small amount of deliberation and decision-making is distasteful to them, particularly when they can make an easy response based on emotion.

While the professional salesperson appeals to the customer's reason to a certain extent, he does not expect decisions grounded only in reason. He knows that appeals to the emotional or subconscious mind often motivate the customer toward deciding in his favor.

Needs and Problem Solving

Throughout the preceding chapters, it was stated that among the most important psychological and social drives are *needs* of various kinds. The salesman, therefore, should be capable of determining a prospect's buying needs and problems, and be able to satisfy and solve them. A prospect's need may be known or unknown, latent or felt. It is the salesman's job to discover the need, and if it is not realized by the prospect, to call it to his attention. A felt need varies in intensity with different people, but any real prospect has a need of some kind; otherwise, he cannot qualify as a prospective purchaser.

Wishes and Needs

While a sharp distinction cannot be made between an individual's wishes and needs, there is no doubt that they exist. The difficulty in recognizing them arises from the fact that they are not always specific in nature. Some of the wishes and needs are latent and some are active; some are not realized and some are vividly felt by prospective buyers.

Wishes and needs arise from many complex sources, such as habit, custom, conformity, or individuality. The demand for a new automobile, for example, might be caused by a genuine *need* for transportation, but it may also be caused by the wish to keep up with one's neighbors or to be the first person in the neighborhood to own a new car. In most cases, there is an overlapping of many causes, so that it is difficult to isolate the principal one.

Needs and Motives

The prospective buyer of any product is an individual who has: (1) a need for the product or service and (2) the means to pay for it.

Since every sale presupposes a buyer who wants something, it is logical to begin the study of motivation by investigating what causes a person to become a buyer. If the prospect's need is active, he is aware of the need and will probably attempt to satisfy it. A dormant need, on the other hand, will not be felt by the prospect until it is brought to his attention, usually by advertising or by a salesman.

A salesman is concerned with both kinds of prospective buyers. When the need is active, the prospect usually, but not always, lets the salesman know of his requirement. When the need is dormant, the salesman must make the prospect aware of the need and let him know how his product can satisfy it.

The needs of people are expressed through different motivating factors. Sometimes one motive alone is sufficiently compelling to cause a purchase, but more often the decision to buy is caused by a combination of motives. Salespeople know that the prospect, of his own volition, will rarely state the basic motive that will cause him to buy. However, he may express his motives by his reactions to the presentation, by asking questions, by handling the product, or by other similar clues. The salesman must determine from such hints what buying motives are most important to the prospect in order to find the most effective method of inducing buying action.

PSYCHOLOGICAL MECHANICS OF MOTIVATION

Four theories have been advanced to aid the salesman in his efforts to motivate people to buy: (1) the AIDA theory; (2) the stimulus-response theory; (3) the need-satisfaction theory; and (4) the idea-sequence theory. These are discussed in Chapter 9.

Each theory has its adherents, and the selling approach may be based on any one of them, depending on the particular circumstances. The motivation methods employed by most salesmen are usually guided by one or more of these theories.

Cybernetics, as it relates to sales communication, is one aspect of the stimulus-response theory. The meaning of cybernetics is "steersman" or "governor."[2] In addition to being a mechanism for personal development, cybernetics helps us to understand the stimulus-response theory more thoroughly.

The selling concept of cybernetics means that the sales communicator is enabled to (1) transfer his knowledge to the prospect; (2) ask questions and listen to the feedback revealing the effect of his presentation; (3) adjust his continuing presentation to fit the needs of the situation. It has been pointed out that man is not a machine, but that he has a "machine"—the subconscious mind—and he uses it. The subconscious mind is a mechanism consisting of the entire nervous system, including the brain. Since man is capable of storing or memorizing information, the prospect's mind may be said to work with the data that salesmen feed into it in the form of perceptions, interpretations, beliefs, understandings, thoughts, and attitudes.

Through his planned presentation, the salesman feeds this data into the prospect's storehouse of knowledge. If sound information is fed into the prospect's nervous system, it will be processed and used in solving related problems. Thus, according to some psychologists, whatever is fed into the prospect's nervous system will automatically bring an appropriate response when the proper sensory stimulus is set in motion by the salesman.

The stimulus-response and cybernetic theory is useful when the selling situation is simple, when the selling price is low and when little time can be spent with a customer. Its weakness is that a stimulus which motivates and influences one customer may not motivate and influence another. This means that not only does the salesman lose sales but also that he cannot analyze the reason for his success or failure. Since the salesman who uses this approach may be working in the dark, he is not likely to improve his selling skills as the result of his experience.

PROSPECT MOTIVES

The prospect is not motivated by the salesman, by his company or by the product or service being offered, but only by what the salesman's proposition will do for him. Unless the proposition appeals to *his* interests, unless it satisfies *his* desires and shows *him* a gain, he will not buy!

2. Norbert Weiner, *The Human Use of Human Beings* (New York: Doubleday & Company, 1965).

The prospect may not be influenced by a pure monetary consideration in all instances, for there are other important buying motives—practically all selling involves more than one. The prospect must be motivated by a *gain* of some kind that will satisfy his own interests. Salesmen spend more time planning appeals to motives of gain than they do on any other phase of their sales presentation.

Very few prospects will announce what motives prompt them to buy. When a prospect does make a direct statement, such as, "My present trucks cost too much to operate," it is probable that the salesman should appeal to the *economy gain* motive. However, the real reason the buyer is considering new trucks may be because his competition is buying them. The salesman, therefore, should touch upon the benefits of his proposition in such a way as to appeal to the prospect's fear of loss of business as well as to the more obvious economy gain motive. The salesman can see if the prospect reacts more favorably to some appeals than to others. He then concentrates on those motives by showing how his proposition will fit the prospect's need.

A useful way to learn what motivates prospects is for the salesman to determine his own buying motives. For example, he may ask himself, "Why did I really buy that sport jacket or that auto?" Was it to imitate someone, for pride of possession, or to gain something? Was it rational or was it emotional?

Plainly, motives for buying are mixed; they overlap; they are combined. But it is certain that a buyer never makes a purchase unless he believes he will *gain something* in some way. The most frequently cited motives include gain, pride, imitation, fear, pleasure-comfort, curiosity, rivalry, and envy.

The Motive of Gain

A great many sales are decided within the first two minutes of the interview. Unless the salesman can successfully appeal to the motive of gain within that time, the prospect will usually decide that neither the salesman nor his proposition are of any interest to him. All motivation carries a promise of gain. In general, all personal marketing can be reduced to this one phrase: The planned and constant promise of *gain*.

There are four kinds of *gain:* money, economy, happiness, and utility.

Profit

Quite naturally, many salesmen appeal to the prospect's desire for savings and profits, for this is the motive that causes the most favorable responses from buyers.

In appealing to the profit motive, the salesman emphasizes not only price and financial gain, but also high quality, performance, economy, and savings. To make his attempts to motivate more effective, he offers proof for everything he claims. The salesman's discussion could be so illuminating and so authoritative that the sale might be consummated solely on one point—how the customer would gain from using the salesman's proposition. Both profit and the economy motives are important in industrial and commercial buying decisions.

Economy

The economy motive, properly handled, can be used to overcome the prospect's objection to the price of the new product, as well as to give him additional reasons for deciding to buy. For example, manufacturers, thinking in terms of profit and loss over a long period, often replace machinery and equipment in excellent condition with newer equipment that, because of improvement in design, will perform the same tasks more efficiently and more economically. This is done because within a reasonable period the new equipment will pay for itself and will result in a net saving. For example:

SALESMAN: Mr. Prospect, I know you are interested in cutting costs wherever you can, without having to lower the fine quality work that you give your customers, isn't that right?

PROSPECT: Certainly is.

SALESMAN: And lower costs mean that you can lower bids on printing to your prospects and customers. Lower bids mean more jobs for your plant, and more jobs in your plant mean more contribution to overhead as well as more dollar profit. Doesn't that make sense?

PROSPECT: Yes, it does. But how will a new Harris-Jones offset press accomplish all this?

SALESMAN: Because you can turn out twice the amount of work on a new H-J press than is now being turned out on your present equipment. The key to it is your high wage costs. Let me show you the figures and I'll prove this to you.

PROSPECT: I hope you can. This may be the proposition I've been looking for.

Satisfaction

Appeals to the prospect's desire for profit should be matched, whenever possible, with an explanation of satisfaction to be gained from a product. A store manager who is worried about operating costs, for instance, is interested not only in saving money, but also in obtaining peace of mind. The industrial buyer is interested in added profits, or savings, or both, but he may also be vitally interested in the dependability of the product. He may be looking for safety features which will reduce accident rates and insurance rates. He may also be interested in satisfying his employees so that they will take greater pride in their work.

Happiness, contentment, and peace of mind are also motives in the consumer goods market. Listen to the following sales interview between a roofing salesman and his prospect:

SALESMAN: A new roof on that house would certainly put your mind at rest.

PROSPECT: Oh, I don't know. Why do you say that?

SALESMAN: Have you noticed any ceiling leaks yet?

PROSPECT: No, I haven't.

SALESMAN: But if you let that roof go any longer, you will begin to experience leaks. Notice the deterioration on the shingles all along the ridge line. Also look at the bare spots next to the hip where the bedroom juts out. Those are trouble spots that could cause damage and inconvenience when winter comes.

PROSPECT: Why couldn't I get by with just a patch-up job?

SALESMAN: You could get by, maybe. But wouldn't you rather have the feeling of comfort and security that a new, well-installed roof will provide? Why put up with an annoying leak or two and perhaps even a complete repatching and painting job because you waited too long?

Notice how this salesman established the general problem and attempted to create dissatisfaction with the existing situation. As soon as the prospect was aware of his problem, the salesman attempted to motivate him by pointing out what he would gain by following the salesman's advice and the satisfaction from the new roof.

Utility

Any new product is presumed to have utility not possessed by previous products of its kind. A prospect who owns an old product, therefore, stands to gain utility if he buys a new one. This applies when a new product is offered in place of an old product of a different form, and also when a new and improved product is offered in the same form.

By pointing out added utility in his product, the salesman not only appeals to an important buying motive but also justifies the price. Further, when he is recommending the replacement of an old product, he must emphasize the gain in utility over the product now being used, if the prospect is to justify the expenditure required to make the purchase.

The Motive of Pride

There are four basic methods for appealing to the customer's pride: (1) offering praise; (2) referring to the prospect's opinions; (3) asking the prospect questions about himself; and (4) appealing to his pride of possession. These motives are just as important as *gain* to many people.

Praise

Praise is something we all like. Anything distinctive about the prospect or his possessions should be praised. For example, outstanding features of the prospect's store, office, or factory provide good points for praise, and the salesman should single these items out. Offering praise enables the salesman to meet the prospect on common ground and to produce the first agreement in the interview, as well as to bolster the prospect's ego. An appeal to pride is not flattery and it is effective only when it is honest. Flattery is an imitation of genuine praise and its hollowness is often detected.

Seeking Opinions

The following statements illustrate one of the effective methods of complimenting the prospect: "That was a very interesting point you brought up." "I am very much interested in getting your viewpoint." "You certainly hit the nail on the head when you said that." "Very few people understand the situation as you have just described it." The prospect usually reciprocates with a high regard for the salesman who employs this technique because he feels that the salesman understands him and, of course, everyone likes to be understood.

Questions

A different way of appealing to the prospect's pride is to ask him questions about things he has done or in which he is interested. The purpose of these questions is to prepare him to accept the proposition and to establish an environment of friendliness and agreement for a successful sale. Such questions are presented in Chapter 12.

Pride of Possession

Pride of possession takes two general forms. One is the *sense of achievement* that an individual may derive from possessing something.

The object may be the realization of an ambition that the prospect has had, or it may be so valuable to the owner that it is a source of great pride to him. Many people like to feel that they have the best that is made, the most expensive item, the brand that means highest quality all over the world. The salesman should recognize that many people seek status through the possession of such items, and should, consequently, appeal to their pride of possession.

The second general form is what is known as *keeping-up-with-the-Joneses*. For many people, having what their friends and neighbors have is very important. First, the salesman must realize that pride of possession comes from the qualities that can be seen and immediately appreciated by the prospect, as well as by his neighbors and friends. The salesman must enable the prospect to anticipate exactly how he will feel when he has possession of the product. He does this by the adroit use of descriptive phrases which result in an imaginative response in the mind of the prospect.

When the salesman says, "You can see how the distinctive beauty of this refrigerator will improve the modern appearance of your kitchen," the prospect visualizes her pride and satisfaction in having the impressive new refrigerator in her kitchen in place of the old refrigerator which reveals its age all too clearly.

When the salesman says, "You may buy this turret lathe with the confidence that its features offer you the last word in performance and economy, and you can be sure that there is nothing finer available," the prospect should feel confident that he will receive features that competitive products do not possess.

Other Motives

Imitation

Imitation as a motive for buying is very obvious to anyone. All of us do it. If a salesman tells a truck operator about the advantages of Blank trucks, he could include in his presentation a statement such as: "John Smith was telling me some time ago that he would use no other trucks because he had proved the superiority of Blank trucks by actual road tests similar to the ones I have described to you." The salesman then goes on with other portions of his presentation.

The advantage of this method is that the appeal to follow what others have done or are doing is made in a subtle way, and the prospect is not aware that he is not making an independent decision, his pride is not hurt, and he does not realize that he is an imitator.

Imitation is extremely important in the consumer goods market. In fact, the fashion industry bases its success upon this motive. A *fashion* is any style which is popularly accepted and purchased by several successive groups of people over a reasonably long period of time. A *style* may be adopted by an elite group of people who seek distinction. The style catches on among the taste-makers in various social strata, and finally is taken up among the masses of people, the emulators. The teen-age market is especially sensitive to the imitation motive. For example:

SALESLADY: May I help you?

TEEN-AGE PROSPECT: Gosh, I hope so. I'm looking for those sweater dresses that come in those weird colors.

SALESLADY: Surely. On this rack are some of our most popular designs. Here's a shapely wool chenille in lemon that would look well with your complexion.

PROSPECT: Gee, it's sure bright. I don't know. It's so different from what I've been wearing. I wonder if I could wear it.

SALESLADY: I'm sure you could. These cables and stripes are extremely popular right now. My daughter wore one like this to her sorority dance, and the fellows flipped. Her boy friend wants her to get a frosty blue, also.

PROSPECT: Well, maybe it would be okay.

SALESLADY: Here's a design that's popular with the Grossmont College girls. It's a size eight. Like the many other girls who wear these, you have just the figure for it. I'll show you to the dressing room.

Fear

At first glance, the motive of fear may appear to be a negative factor which might prevent a sale. However, *fear* can be a positive factor in selling. An astonishing number of articles are sold on the basis of the fear motive: dental and medical services; automobile, casualty, and fire insurance; paints; cosmetics; insecticides; automobiles with seat belts; lubricants; dry cleaners; and hundreds of other items.

Protection is another aspect of the fear motive and it is a powerful reason for buying, since it embraces protection of health, property, loved ones, or anything that the prospect may value. Life insurance, burglar alarms, safes, seat belts, and similar products and services are purchased solely for the reason that they protect and provide security. Consider the example below of how a salesman uses the fear motive in selling automobile tires.

SALESMAN: I imagine, like thousands of others, Mr. Smith, you spend a great deal on auto insurance, most of it designed to protect you against lawsuits from injury to others.

PROSPECT: Yes, I do. It seems like quite a bit.

SALESMAN: Driving these freeways like you do in rainy weather could mean a serious accident and injury to yourself and others if you don't get those smooth tires replaced. I'd like to spare you that anxiety by putting on a set of Guardian treads, now.

Pleasure / Physical Comfort

Anything that saves time and gives a person more leisure makes a strong appeal to the pleasure motive. Household electrical appliances are good examples.

Everyone likes to be comfortable, to eat good food, to lie back in an easy chair, to have ease of mind, and to have the conveniences of modern living. If a salesman can show a prospect how a product will make his routine easier and help him gain these pleasures, he can often motivate him to buy.

Curiosity

A salesman can utilize the curiosity appeal in numerous ways. To obtain an interview, he may disclose some facts that make the prospect want to learn more; for example, "Mr. Buyer, I am sure you will be interested in our new gear assembly which will increase your profits."

Two motives are appealed to in this example: profit and curiosity. The prospect wants to make more money, of course, but he is also curious to know more about the new gear assembly.

Intriguing phrases may also be used to motivate. The salesman might refer to "our new development," "our success plan," "our profit-making scheme," "our plan for reducing operating costs," or he might say, "Mr. Prospect, I have a message for you from twenty other satisfied users."

It is often possible to motivate curiosity by asking questions which induce a reply, such as: "Mr. Businessman, when you buy you are interested in just one thing, getting the most for your money. If I could show you proof that you could make a considerable saving by using our products, you would be interested, wouldn't you?"

Rivalry

Nearly everyone has a desire to surpass others. This reason for buying may not be as strong as pride or gain, but some people are motivated by rivalry, especially when they are stimulated by the proper appeal.

Suppose two merchants were competitors, one of them more aggressive than the other. If a salesman offered the latter a product or service that he could show would increase profits or attract a high-income clientele, he could probably stimulate this merchant's spirit of rivalry.

Envy

Envy is a trait which varies with different people and is not as universal as the motives of pride and gain. With a prospect in whom the trait is strongly developed, envy can be a powerful inducement to action.

The salesman usually thinks of envy as the reflection of the prospect's discontent because a competitor possesses what he would like for himself. Most salesmen know competitors who may be envied for their success. If they happen to be his customers, he has the foundation on which to build a sales talk which will give the prospect a reason for attempting to gratify his envious attitude.

COMBINED MOTIVATING APPEALS

Ordinarily, salesmen must try appeals to several motives before they find the *primary* motivating forces which impel, invite, and urge a prospect to buy. It is a rare sale which is motivated by only one factor. Nearly always there is a complex of motives and appeals. The trick is to find the chief benefits which supply the motivating force.

How a combination of motivating appeals may be used is revealed in the following example. The salesman relates the experience himself:

SALESMAN: "My sales manager first appealed to my motive of gain but without success, because I did not feel that I had the ability to sell something which people did not want. He then appealed to my pride without success, so he reversed his approach and risked injuring my pride by ridiculing my low earnings and my lazy work habits. This depressed me, but did not change my attitude.

"Then he appealed to the motives of imitation and envy by naming other salesmen who were earning enough money in six months to spend the remainder of the year vacationing in Florida. That did it! I envied men who were no smarter than I, but who were able to take a six-month vacation. I became discontented with myself. I found myself wishing that I could do what they were doing. A further appeal to pride in my own ability lifted my morale to a new high and I decided that I would really try to sell."

All motives aided in the decision, but it is possible that envy of the other salesmen's prosperity was the chief motivating force, supplemented by the motives of gain, pride, imitation, and rivalry.

The following example illustrates how five different motivators were used to stimulate buying action in retailers. The first four motives were appealed to once, and the fifth received four different appeals:

SALESMAN: "Joe, you are losing money every day with your present setup *(profit)*. Pete Jones on Beech Street, whose location is no better than yours, is outselling you two to one *(rivalry, imitation)*.

"Now, Pete is not a better businessman than you are—probably not as good *(pride)*—but he is using our sales promotion plan to move his products and he is making more money than he did with his old setup *(profit)*.

"You could use some more money, Joe, couldn't you? *(profit)*. And probably you are making plans for expanding your business. That's going to make you some money, isn't it *(satisfaction)*? Why not make your business produce it *(curiosity)*?

"Let me show you the modern merchandising plan that has made more profit for other dealers *(curiosity, profit)*."

POWER POINTS

The process of motivating and persuading prospective customers is important for gaining favorable decisions. However, there is more to this process than has been presented in this chapter. A salesperson also needs to know something about analyzing and guiding the behavior of problem people; the principles of counseling people who are difficult to handle; how to predict buyer behavior; and understand common behavior traits as observed by salespeople. These appreciations, skills, and understandings were presented in Chapter 12.

DISCUSSION QUESTIONS AND PROBLEMS

---

1. What do you understand by the word "motivation" as it is used in this chapter?

2. From the salesman's viewpoint, what is the significance of understanding and using buying motives?

3.   What is the relation between buying motives and buying appeals that are used in personal selling?

4.   What buying motives would you appeal to in each case if you were selling the following items?

a. Life insurance.   e. Cadillac cars.
b. Reducing pills.   f. Filter-tipped cigarettes.
c. Winter coats.   g. Rebuilt auto tires.
d. Wheelbarrows.   h. Fur coats.

5.   Name five logical and five emotional reasons for buying.

6.   In your opinion, what social class and what intimate group influences might motivate an individual's buying behavior?

7.   What do you consider to be some of the characteristics of good appeals? How might the effect of various appeals be tested?

8.   Under what conditions may a negative form of presentation be effective?

9.   Briefly explain how you would appeal to the following buying motives:

a. Gain.   e. Pleasure and physical comfort.
b. Pride.   f. Curiosity.
c. Imitation.   g. Rivalry.
d. Fear.   h. Envy.

10. If your file records and advice from older salesmen indicated three different buying motivations for one of your customers, how could you use such information?

11. "No two persons are likely to have identical motives for buying a particular product or service." Do you agree or disagree? Give examples or reasons to support your position.

12. "Very few people respond to logical, reasoning appeals. People buy on the influence of prejudice, emotions, and habit more than on good sense." Do you agree with this statement? Explain your answer.

SELLING PROBLEMS AND PROJECTS

1.   Assignment

Clip advertisements from magazines and newspapers illustrating each of the seven major motives for buying goods. Paste each ad in your notebook and write a brief discourse explaining how the advertisement appeals to that particular motive.

2. A Look at Buying Motives

What are the probable buying motives in each of the following cases?

a. Mr. Johnson, a traveling salesman, purchases a Cadillac.
b. Mary Jones enrolls in an evening class in college.
c. William Alvarez buys a piece of land.
d. Dr. Clark purchases an expensive set of office furniture.
e. Barbara White buys a ticket to a football game.
f. Mrs. Green purchases expensive carpeting.
g. Mr. Larkin purchases an annuity insurance policy.
h. Mr. Brooks purchases a secondhand car.
i. Jim Russo buys a ticket for the sideshow.
j. Mrs. Lane purchases an evening gown for her daughter.

3. The Mortgage Insurance Case

A salesman, seeing that he was getting nowhere in outlining the advantages of life insurance to a farmer, changed his tactics by appealing to the individual's immediate problem—a $3,000 mortgage—and presented a life insurance policy as a solution.

"How much interest are you paying on the mortgage?" asked the salesman.

"Six and a half percent," replied the farmer.

"Would you be willing to pay me 2½ percent additional if I agree to cancel the mortgage and give your wife clear title to the farm in the event of your death?"

The farmer immediately agreed.

Question

What buying motive did this salesman use?

4. Fred Gorley Case

Fred Gorley is calling on an old customer, who has placed a regular standard order with him for many years. The customer is friendly and likes to talk. He is conservative and considers new ideas for a long time before acting on them.

Fred was sure he could pick up a standard order on this call. However, he had something new to tell this customer. In three months his company was bringing out a new product, one that this customer would need. Gorley hopes to sell him on the idea. He can take orders on it now.

At the moment, Gorley is in the middle of a sales contest based on total volume for the month. He has a good chance of winning it if he can write up some big sales in the next few days.

Gorley thinks the call will be routine. The old customer indicates that he will buy the standard order. He is not too busy, so Gorley has time to talk with him for several minutes. Of the four choices below, which course should Fred Gorley take?

a. He should make a maximum effort to double his usual sales volume to the customer on this call.

b. He should talk about the new product that is coming on the market.

c. He should tell a few interesting anecdotes and make it a pleasant occasion.

d. He should leave as soon as possible and hurry on to another call which should help boost his volume.

5.   Who Buys Life Insurance?

Phil Garcia has been discouraged this last week. He called on nine prospects and made only one sale—a $5,000 ordinary life policy. Next week he has appointments with seven prospects, and he's worried. Something isn't working right, but what? Phil decides to drop in and talk it over with his sales manager, Bob Green.

"What's the matter, Phil?" said Mr. Green, as Phil took a seat in his office. "You look a little downhearted."

"Nobody wants to buy life insurance," said Phil. "I had nine prospects last week, all of whom could afford to buy but none did, even though I outlined the features of our best policies."

"That's not true. People are buying life insurance," said Bob Green. "They're buying it every day. Our company sells over one billion dollars worth of insurance every year. Think about it, Phil. Generally speaking, why do men buy life insurance?"

Bob Green then asked Phil to go over some of the prospects he would be calling on next week.

Prospect No. 1 is a rising young executive with a new and growing company. He is twenty-five and unmarried, and enjoys some very risky hobbies among which are auto racing and surfing.

Prospect No. 2 is in his middle forties and is investment-minded. He has considerable holdings of securities that are worth more than he paid for them.

Prospect No. 3 is a young married man with two young children. He is a valued employee with a plastics manufacturing firm and has reason to believe that his income will steadily rise over the next 15 years.

Prospect No. 4 is the part owner of a successful restaurant business and father of three teen-age children. Recently, this man lost his partner in an automobile accident and is involved in trying to straighten out the affairs of his partner's widow.

Prospect No. 5 is very impressed with his own importance. He is a very wealthy man, married, no children, but possesses little life insurance.

Question

1. What do you think are the main motives why each of these five prospects would buy life insurance? How do you think Phil should handle each of the prospects?

CHAPTER 14

Proving, Demonstrating, and Dramatizing Claims

THE NEED TO PROVE CLAIMS

The salesman must be ready to substantiate every claim and suggestion that he makes. The transition from the claim-suggestion phase to the proof phase usually entails an overlapping and blending of one into the other. It is an easy transition to make, provided the salesman uses the proper techniques, materials, and devices. Proving a claim usually combines both oral and visual presentations.

Sales are consummated every day without actual proof that the buyer will receive benefits, values, or advantages. This may be due to the buyer's genuine need for the product or service; because of his earlier acceptance of the proposition; or because of his confidence in the salesman and the company he represents. However, even when the salesman assures his prospect that the benefits claimed will be forthcoming, it is only the salesman's word that is presented as proof. Something more is usually necessary to verify a salesman's statements and thereby to bring about conviction, belief, and buying action.

Selling to industrial users is not only more competitive than other kinds of selling; it also requires more presentation skill and many more factual proofs, usually in the form of sales aids. The industrial salesman calls on mining companies and oil producers, manufacturing and processing industries, the transportation industry, power and public service companies, construction firms, and many specialized industries.

How does a salesman approach those who purchase for these concerns? What must he do to close sales? David Seltz states, "Unlike the consumer sale, the industrial sale is always made on the basis of cold, hard facts, concretely proved by test, research, experiment, and experience rather than through appeals to emotions. Another difference exists in the amount of time necessary to complete the industrial sale as compared with that needed to sell the average consumer product."[1]

The industrial sale is not often made in minutes; therefore, the industrial salesman must make thorough advance preparation. This preparation will include sales aids, materials, and devices to help him present his proposition swiftly and dramatically. Many companies spend millions of dollars on these sales aids.

It may be assumed that any prospect is normally skeptical and cautious and his mind is often closed to the salesman's presentation. A good salesman, nevertheless, can quiet many of his fears through the use of the *suggestion selling technique* described in Chapter 20, as well as through the use of *proof materials*. A salesman's proof materials may be divided into two broad categories: oral proof and visual proof.

ORAL PROOF

Evidence is an oral presentation of facts which aims at producing conviction and bringing about favorable action.

Facts are more impressive than hearsay, and when many facts are presented in a positive fashion, they bring conviction to a prospect. A salesman's method of presenting his facts should be as effective as possible, because an alleged fact stated positively is often more convincing than a known fact stated weakly.

One kind of oral evidence is known as *user proof*. When a salesman is representing a well-known and reputable company, he can offer evidence of the reliability of his proposition by referring to the reliability of his company. If the salesman is representing the distributor of a dependable and recognized manufacturer, he can also bring in its trustworthy name to help establish confidence and conviction.

Another kind of evidence is *authoritative proof*. It is furnished to the salesman by a person or organization recognized as an authority. Evidence drawn from the expression of the sales representative is known as *personal proof*. This evidence is drawn from the experience of the salesman and is usually satisfactory for use with customers whom he has been serving for several years and who have faith in his personal assurances.

1. David Seltz, *Successful Industrial Selling* (Englewood Cliffs, N.J.: Prentice-Hall, 1958), p. 5.

Simple Words

The oral presentation of benefits and proof of claims must be carefully planned and skillfully made to arouse conviction and the desire to buy. One of the rules for making a clear presentation is to avoid technical words and phrases. It is difficult for a prospect to pay attention to someone whom he cannot understand. On the other hand, if every word uttered produces a clear-cut picture of the idea in the customer's mind, he will listen because he is interested.

Technical terms scattered throughout sales talks may produce confusion and cause a lack of interest. For example, some salesmen who sell to small garage owners may say: "Precise unfluctuating gas flow eliminates oxidized and carbonized welds; has large gas channels and eliminates restriction of second stage diaphragm, having relief valve and compound springs." Do such technical terms arouse the interest of small garage owners? The answer is obvious: Technical terminology should be used sparingly and then only when the prospect has sufficient experience or education to understand what is being said.

Avoid Generalities

A generality is a vague and indefinite statement. To say that a car is a "good" car is to state a generality and proves nothing. The descriptive word "good" might apply to the entire car, or the engine, or its appearance. To be convincing, the presentation must make clear statements about specific features and benefits.

For example, "This engine is dependable, powerful, economical." This specific statement enables the prospect to visualize the engine very clearly. One salesman says: "That is nice upholstery in this car." Another says: "Just sit in the rear seat and feel the luxurious comfort that has been built into this car."

It is not strange that buyers are skeptical about generalizations. They may even believe that salesmen mean well, but the buyer is interested only in a clear-cut picture of benefits such as economy and profits. Buyers want facts and the proof that they will receive the specific benefits if they buy. Generalities do not offer convincing proof.

Using Questions to Prove

Successful salespeople know that it is easier to prove, convince, and gain understanding if the prospect or customer will participate in the sales talk. Therefore, salesmen often ask questions during their

presentations. Questions, properly used, are useful tools. Salespeople cannot look into their prospect's mind, but they can discover his misgivings when they induce him to talk, and can then offer proper proof. Inducing a prospect to answer questions, however, requires both tact and good judgment. Questions have to be properly phrased. Their purpose is to make the prospect want to disclose the information that the salesman desires.

Salesmen can use test questions not only to offer proof, but also to find out where they stand in an interview, especially when they encounter a reticent prospect. For example, test questions can be used to discover:

- If the prospect is listening.
- If the prospect is interested.
- If the prospect's reaction is favorable or unfavorable.
- If the salesman's presentation is clear.
- If enough proof has been offered to support claims.

Examples of Test Questions

The following are examples of test questions used by successful salespeople to determine where they stand in an interview:

"Have I made that perfectly clear?"
"Does this check with your experience, Mr. Brown?"
"Isn't that just good common sense?"
"You have had that experience, haven't you?"

Oral Success Stories

During the presentation, the prospect can be given added proof and assurance by citing the successful experiences of satisfied customers. These experiences are known as oral success stories, or testimony. They are powerful proof materials, because they tell of someone similar to the prospect who has used the product or service, likes it and has benefited from its use. Success stories can be even more effective when the prospect goes with the salesman to visit a satisfied customer and hears about the benefits at first hand.

There are right and wrong ways to use success stories. To obtain the best results, the following points should be included:

Tell where it happened. The salesman may start by saying, "All over my territory," but he should be very sure that he can also give specific individual and company names.

Tell when it happened. He must be definite as to time: was it last month, last week, or yesterday?

Tell who knows it happened, and will back him up. For an unbiased witness, the salesman should choose somebody in similar circumstances to the prospect or someone known to be favorable to him. If the user is not known to the prospect, the salesman must be sure to explain who he is. For example:

SALESMAN: It is happening all over my territory.

PROSPECT: Well, just where?

SALESMAN: Well, take Elgin. You know John Ore at 228 Main?

PROSPECT: Yes, I know him.

SALESMAN: Do you think he is a smart businessman?

PROSPECT: Sure, John does a swell job.

SALESMAN: Well, only last Tuesday, John said to me, "Bill, I never had anything work better for me than this device!" So I asked him to put it down in writing. Look what he says.

The salesman started with a general claim and supported it with a definite example. He inquired how his prospect felt about John Ore. If the prospect's reaction had been unfavorable, the salesman should have shifted to another testifier. He was definite about his location and date. He also had a written statement and he could have suggested a telephone call to John Ore.

Telephone Calls

Closely related to the oral success story is the telephone call which can link the prospect at his place of business with a satisfied user. Quite often the value of a telephone call is worth more than the cost, if the testifier represents a prestige account that is substantial.

VISUAL PROOF

Many prospects insist that a salesman offer proof which is more substantial than word-of-mouth claims. The prospect may insist on being *shown* valid, reliable proof before he will commit himself to a purchase. He may want a demonstration; he may want to test the product; he may want written testimony; he may want visual sales aids. When these materials are skillfully used in their proper place, they can be the most substantial way of revealing to the prospect what benefits he will receive when he buys.

"Constant use of visual aids is the key to volume sales and profits." This statement expresses briefly what salesmen learn through costly experience. Since the prospect possesses five senses, each of which helps him select and comprehend messages, it is wise to appeal to as many of those senses as possible when communicating with him.

Advantages of Visual Proof

Demonstrations and visual aids enable salesmen to understand their claims while proving them. If salesmen had a true appreciation of the value of visual sales aids, they would use them more often. Visual sales aids help salesmen in these ways:

By simplifying the features and benefits related to a product or service. The proper visual aid will enable a prospect to understand more quickly by eliminating nonessentials and spotlighting benefits of real importance.

By obtaining and holding the prospect's attention. Only the most gifted salesmen can hold the attention of prospects for more than a few minutes. Visual aids keep prospects alert and interested.

By using additional sensory organs to assist the prospect in the assimilation of facts. Without sales aids, the salesman can only tell his story, depending entirely on the prospect's sense of hearing to carry the message to his brain. When sales aids are added, the prospect is stimulated not only by what he hears, but also by what he sees and feels and sometimes smells and tastes.

By creating more vivid impressions. Sales aids properly used can dramatize a presentation, get across the important points vividly and leave the prospect with permanent impressions.

Attention of the prospect is attracted more easily and quickly when visual aids are employed. Also, what prospects see is more believable to them than what they hear. A salesman cannot gain a prospect's understanding until he first obtains his attention, and a sale can start only after attention has been gained.

The relative attention-attracting power of each of the five senses is shown in the following tabulation. The salesman should note that sight has about seven times the attention-attracting power of all other senses combined.

SENSE	PERCENT
Sight	87.0
Hearing	7.0
Smell	3.5
Touch	1.5
Taste	1.0
Total	100.0

Retention. What prospects see attracts their attention. But how much do they retain after they have seen a visualization and listened to the oral part of a sales presentation? Here are research findings on this topic published recently by Sales-Marketing Executives, International:

People retain

10 percent of what they hear.

35 percent of what they see.

65 percent of what they see *and* hear.

Therefore, for the best results, oral appeals should be combined with visual; a skillful combination of the two will produce more successful sales than either method used alone.

HOW TO SHOW AND DEMONSTRATE

The easiest, quickest, and most effective method for a salesman to communicate claims and prove assertions is to demonstrate the product itself. This is true for five reasons:

1. Seeing a demonstration of a product is more convincing than hearing about it.
2. A demonstration is easy to remember.
3. Demonstrations translate abstract ideas into concrete form.
4. Demonstrations paint pictures quickly, and save time.
5. Demonstrations produce strong impressions: because many people are "eye-minded," they tend to learn more quickly through sight than through hearing.

Product Demonstration

Because it is often necessary to demonstrate a product or service, the salesman must train himself to demonstrate the item effectively. It is therefore important that the salesperson carefully determine how to show the product most favorably. If it is a food, it must be served at proper temperature; if a household appliance, it must be cleaned, well serviced, smooth-running.

Before the salesman demonstrates, he must decide what he wants to prove. The professional salesman does not emphasize economy if his customer wants speed. He first demonstrates speed, and then goes on to the other attributes: economy, safety, performance, construction features, or beauty in terms of the product or service he is selling.

As he demonstrates, the salesman makes sure his prospect is grasping what he is saying and doing by asking questions. Sometimes a failure results because the prospect does not understand. The presentation may be too fast and the salesman gets far ahead of the prospect's understanding. The salesman should emulate the teacher who explained his success in teaching this way:

"I tell them what I am going to show;
Then I show it;
Then I tell them what I've shown.
Then I ask questions and listen."

The effective salesperson uses the same principle. He tells his prospect what he is going to demonstrate. Then he demonstrates. Then he tells the prospect what he has demonstrated. Finally, so the prospect will never forget it, the salesman hands him the product and lets him repeat what he has just seen. Then he asks questions and listens.

The salesman should not ask the prospect to perform tasks beyond his capability; it is important not to confuse or embarrass him. A failure during a salesman's demonstration will ruin a sale, but it is also important that mistakes do not take place when the prospect is repeating the demonstration.

Dramatic Demonstration

In a dramatic demonstration, the salesperson shows exactly how his product works. He places floor polish on a board, or auto cleaner and polish on an automobile. He takes out spots with a clothes cleaner. He kills flies with insect spray. He heats lubricating grease to prove its tenacity and body; he stretches a fabric; puts rugs and furniture into a demonstration room; shows a washing machine washing clothes; holds a necktie against his shirt; shows how an automobile operates; has a floor lamp connected for actual use; cleans a rug with his vacuum cleaner.

Nearly all products lend themselves to proof by demonstration, regardless of their size, nature, or value. The following examples will serve to illustrate this point.

Tire　Show a cross section to prove the superiority of construction.

Vacuum cleaner　Demonstrate how it will easily pick up sand, lint, cotton, and other debris.

Necktie　Place it against a shirt, or hold it against the customer's suit, to prove its attractiveness when worn.

Aluminum utensils   Boil water or cook something to show their practical uses.

Electric dishwasher   Show it in actual operation.

Aluminum siding   Build a model to prove the merit of the materials which may otherwise be too abstract and difficult to visualize easily.

Life insurance   Show a sample or facsimile policy.

Hosiery   Stretch to prove its tensile strength.

Furniture   Make a room setting to suit the customer's idea of comfort and taste. Show the construction of an upholstered model.

Prospect Participation

Another way of proving the superior advantages of a proposition is to induce the prospect to participate in the demonstration. Have him test the product. When he handles, sees, smells, hears, and perhaps tastes it, he will find it difficult to remain unconvinced about its benefits.

When the prospect or customer participates in a demonstration, he is receiving the strongest kind of proof material. A self-demonstration brings him into the picture. The salesman is talking about him, his business, his worries, and showing him solutions to his problems. The prospect actually experiences the benefits when he participates in the demonstration.

Prospects can be induced to participate in many demonstrations; in fact, the possibilities are almost unlimited. The following are only a few examples.

Clothing   Have the customer try it on to prove its fit, style, comfort, and wearability.

Automobile   Have the customer drive it to prove its acceleration, flexibility, comfort, control, and speed.

Aluminum kitchen utensils   Have the customer cook in a utensil to prove its benefits to her.

Shoes   Have the customer try them on to experience their style and comfort.

Food products, beverages   Have the customer taste them to prove their delicious flavor.

Furniture   Have the customer sit in a chair, feel the high-polish finish of a desk, lie on a mattress, to prove their comfort or quality.

Book   Open to certain pages and have the customer see the pictures or read to prove that it is worthwhile.

Perfume   Have the customer smell and try to prove its distinctive quality.

Typewriter   Encourage the prospect to type something to prove its light touch and efficient operation.

Tools   Let the customer handle and operate them to prove their merit.

Musical instruments   Have the customer play them to prove their tone and pitch.

When the prospect participates in the demonstration, when he tries it out himself, he experiences the advantage of using the product or service. His participation conveys to him a feeling that the salesman is there to help him, not just to sell him something. While he is participating, the prospect may make a comment or suggestion indicating that he feels that he is solving his own problem and that he appreciates and believes in the promised benefits. This is the appropriate time to try to close the sale.

Competitive Demonstrations

Demonstrations that compete against other products or companies should be avoided. If a customer insists on a competitive test, he should select the competing product and an impartial person to conduct the test.

A better way to show improvement and superiority and thereby interest a prospect in a product or service is to compare its operation or uses with his previous or present product or service.

Demonstrations are so important in selling that they cannot be overemphasized. It is not only profitable to demonstrate; it is also easier for a salesman to demonstrate than to explain to a sales manager why he did not obtain the order.

VISUAL SALES AIDS

A visual aid is any visible device or material that assists salesmen to transmit and communicate facts, knowledge, understanding, appreciation, and skills to a prospective customer. According to this definition, there are many visual aids with merit, including:

blackboard	motion pictures
catalogues	photographs
demonstration kits	paper and pencil
display windows	portfolios
direct view slides	transviewers

exhibits
flash and flip cards
graphs
table viewers
manuals and booklets
maps
mock-ups
models

presentation books
samples
sand tables
scrapbooks
sound slide and strip films
specimens and models
success stories
turnover charts

Advantages of Visual Aids

After using visual sales aids over a reasonable period of time, salesmen have offered laudatory testimony about them. These salesmen stated that visual aids:

Enabled them to understate and overprove.

Helped them to avoid blunt or contradictory statements.

Never irritated prospects.

Helped to close more successful sales.

Furnished a track on which to run sales talks.

Anticipated the prospect's objections.

Made presentations more interesting and thereby encouraged the prospect to listen to the whole story.

Often gave the prospect an opportunity to participate in a demonstration.

Revealed product uses, values, benefits, and features in a way that the prospect did not expect to see.

Helped focus the prospect's attention on the sales points.

Told a complete story about each benefit, feature, value, advantage, or exclusive.

In their advertising, Williams and Myers, Chicago photoprinters, say, "A well-organized sales portfolio or presentation, with a few words and many pictures, may present in five minutes what the most swift-tongued salesman could not successfully prove in half an hour. A picture never mumbles, never forgets, never confuses. Present it visually and in a flash the prospect has received and perceived the idea."

Use of Visual Sales Aids

Visual sales aids, including the product itself, are used to prove oral claims, as well as to enhance, amplify, and clarify the entire sales

The value of visual aids has been so widely accepted, in
, that no salesman or prospective salesman needs to be
t "see power is sales power." However, many salesmen,
nced that visual aids are useful, use them less frequently
ively than they might. Too many adopt a "Yes, but"
attitude: "Yes, but I haven't the money to buy materials." "Yes, but
the company doesn't furnish them and I'm no artist or mechanic."
"Yes, but where do I find the things and what do I need?" "Yes, but
I wouldn't know how to use them anyway."

Two key points should be kept in mind: good sales aids need not
be costly, since some of the best are improvised; artistic and mechanical skill is much less important than common sense in choosing
sales aids and being alert to opportunities for using them.

METHODOLOGY FOR USING SALES AIDS

Relating Oral and Visual Proof

When offering proof of claims, the salesman should make his oral
presentation first, then introduce the related visual material. To illustrate how this is done, the salesman could be saying: "Mr. Black,
when I came in here, I said that hundreds of dealers who handle our
products are increasing their sales, making higher profits, and enjoying
a faster turnover. I am now going to prove to you that what I have
said is true, and that our products can do the same for you." The salesman then proceeds to offer his proof in the form of a demonstration,
written testimony, exhibits, charts, photos, or other sales aids.

Presentation Outline

While a presentation is being made, visual aids arranged in sequence serve as an outline for the salesman to follow. An outline
enables the prospect to remember facts and figures. It also helps
the salesman remember his strategy, and frees his mind to concentrate
on his presentation while allowing him to watch for opportunities to
close the sales successfully.

Quantity of Aids

The presentation of visual materials, or sales aids, should never
become more important than the person who is conducting the interview. This may happen if several visual aids are in evidence at
one time. To avoid losing control of the interview, the salesman should
offer for the prospect's attention only one item at a time, and then only
to prove a specific point made in the oral presentation. When the

proof material has emphasized the benefit point, it should be removed from the prospect's sight. Otherwise, the prospect may object to the clutter on his desk, or he may become confused by the amount of material confronting him and be unable to make a decision.

Timing

There is no predetermined point at which visual aids should be introduced into an interview. Professional salesmen meld them into their presentations, especially during explanations and as a help in dealing with obstructions. Sales aids should be used sparingly, and only when specifically required to influence a prospect's wavering judgment.

Good timing indicates that visible proof is necessary to confirm oral statements, but only after the salesman has explained briefly the importance of the facts, features, or benefits that he intends to prove. He should not talk while the prospect is looking at the visuals, because it is difficult to look and listen at the same time.

For example, suppose the salesman observes that the prospect is not agreeing with his claim that the product will provide a solution to his problem. The salesman's procedure might be this: "Mr. Black, I understand perfectly why you believe that your problem is different from others. Actually, I am glad you brought that up because it offers me the chance to prove that we can help you. I have with me some user experience reports, from many different sources, but I want to show you just one that I selected when you told me over the phone that you could see me this morning."

At this point, the salesman extracts a specific letter from his carefully indexed file of success stories. He handles it with respect and as something of value, while he directs Mr. Black's attention to the exact paragraph containing the proof of practical benefits.

Handling Visual Aids

All demonstration and testimonial material has greater impact if it is handled impressively by the salesman and is carefully framed, mounted, or otherwise arranged so that the prospect is impressed with its quality. People judge the value and worth of the things the salesman shows them by the value *he* places on them.

Portfolio Management

Since the salesman cannot always provide himself with full-sized products for demonstration, he should provide himself with a portfolio, a binder, or a folder in which to keep testimonial letters, photostats, photographs of the product or service in use, lists of satisfied customers, specification sheets, brochures, survey charts, graphs, and many other items that help to prove his claims.

Competition. No success letter or other evidence of value should be placed in a salesman's kit which could be used equally well by a competitor. Such material is usually colorless, uninviting, or unconvincing.

Cross-indexing. When the salesman must carry with him a quantity of testimonials and similar material, it requires careful indexing. The form of the indexing will depend on the character and diversity of the salesman's line, but in general the best system is a simple cross-index.

One general heading might be "Demonstration Materials." This heading might include photographs, company advertising, newspaper and magazine tear sheets and clippings. A second heading could be "Testimonials," which might include letters from satisfied customers, photostats of repeat orders, and charts and graphs summarizing experiences of satisfaction. Cross-indexing also includes an analysis of all these materials under subject headings like "Names of Customers" and "Applications of Product," as well as others, depending on the character of the line and the salesman's job requirements.

Preserving materials. There are several ways to keep proof materials fresh, clean, and attractive so that the buyer will receive a good impression. Proof materials are often kept in a common three-ring binder with separator tabs on division pages. To preserve typed or printed materials in spotless condition, many salesmen use ready-made clear acetate envelopes which can be purchased already punched for three-ring binders, or in large sheets for large items.

Portfolio size. Portfolios of visual materials should not be so bulky that they cause the prospect to fear a lengthy interview. In all situations, it is wise to keep sales aids on the floor beside the salesman's feet with only one item on the prospect's desk at any one time.

Filing. Following the interview, it is good practice to restore every item of proof material to its proper niche. This should not be done in the prospect's office, but in the reception room, or in the salesman's car as he reviews his plans for his next call.

Dramatization. In order to dramatize proof materials, the salesman must display enthusiasm and conviction in his bearing, facial expression, and tone of voice.

Picture Books

Closely related to the *portfolio* is the "picture book." As the name implies, this book is composed of photographs. It is not difficult or expensive to build up a picture book. One successful salesman carried a small camera on his travels, photographed installations made by his company, then placed his pictures in a loose-leaf binder. He also acquired suitable photos from other sources, as well as tear sheets from periodicals, and included both in the picture book with his photographs. These visuals presented the merits of his proposition more vividly than a mere oral presentation. Many salesmen in many lines use photographic materials to advantage in proving claims and illustrating benefits.

Written Testimony

Written testimony is synonymous with written success stories and letters. The best testimony bears a recent date and describes as specifically as possible the experiences for which success is claimed. The testimonial letter which the salesman likes best and which the prospect respects most is one that meets the newspaper requirements of *who, what, why, when, where,* and *how.* With few exceptions, a prospect is far more interested in the experiences of a competitor a mile or a few miles away than of an unknown firm a thousand miles distant. For this reason, a salesman might have his portfolio cross-indexed to include one heading for "Industries" and another for "Location."

When the customer does not have time to write a testimonial, the salesman might ask for his letterhead, type the testimony, and have him sign it. It might also be profitable to make a scrapbook of testimonials, accompanying each one with a picture of the satisfied user and the company name to give it authenticity.

Route books, or order books, have been successfully used by salesmen as testimonial proof. It is convincing to many prospective customers to see actual orders and the names of those who have already purchased. In addition, the route book can show what and how the salesman sells, what service is provided, how deliveries are made, and supply other details of interest to an undecided prospect.

Maps, charts, graphs, and similar materials can illustrate increased production, savings, or increased turnover for which the salesman's product or service is responsible. Visual materials of this kind should be small, simply constructed, and readily understandable.

Scrapbooks

Closely related to portfolios, the *scrapbook* most often contains material related to the general prestige of the salesman's organization. It may be made up of tear sheets of his company's national advertising in trade papers, general magazines, newspapers, and the company's annual report. Some salesmen have reproductions made of letters received from their customers. With these they attach photographs of the customer and his office, store, building, or other items of interest.

Pencil Selling

The simplest and easiest form of visual proof for the salesman to prepare and use requires only a piece of paper and a pencil. Every benefit topic of a sales talk may be jotted down on a sheet of paper in outline form. When the salesman has completed his presentation, the prospect has before him a written outline of benefit points. This device is often helpful in proving claims.

Presentation Books

Closely related to picture books, scrapbooks, and portfolios, the presentation book consists of professionally prepared graphic materials and illustrations.

Maps, Charts, Graphs

Maps, improvised or professionally made, are indispensable in selling many products.

Charts are used chiefly to analyze a problem or situation. They show proper sequence and relationship. Flow charts, for example, can be used to show each division of a business and its breakdown into individual or functional departments.

Table charts are indispensable in many selling situations. They are effective, for example, in presenting a breakdown of financial statements. They may also be used for comparisons and for listing advantages or disadvantages of a business organization.

"Strip-tease" charts are specially successful in focusing attention on one point at a time in developing a sales talk. Each important point on a chart is covered with a thin strip of paper that can be removed as the sales presentation unfolds.

Process charts are adaptable to many kinds of selling. They may illustrate the complete production process of a product or they may depict the channels of distribution for various kinds of merchandise.

Graphs are especially useful for making comparisons and contrasts or for presenting complicated facts to prospects and customers. A long column of figures or statistics appears impressive, but is usually skipped over by a prospect. A graph of the same figures may make the prospect stop, look, and think.

Flash cards are small, compact cards which are shown briefly to the prospect. The message contained on the cards must be brief and to the point to be effective. Flash cards may be used to summarize, to review, or to repeat the sales talk, or to emphasize and highlight important points.

Posters

Posters have been defined as "visual combinations of bold design, color and message ... intended to attract and hold the attention of the prospect or customer just long enough to implant a significant idea in his mind."[2] For effective use, posters must be simple, since they are used to transmit an idea or an image at one glance. Posters can utilize graphs, charts, pictures, cartoons, or almost any item that will help to present facts or emphasize a selling point.

Sales Manuals

A *sales manual* is a book or binder containing complete information related to a certain product, service, or line of merchandise. Some manuals may contain information on a number of products. A manual should contain all possible information pertaining to a specific product, service, object, device, or type of merchandise. A manual will enable the salesman to talk intelligently about his products or services; answer customer's questions concerning the products or services offered; give suggestions on how to use and care for the product; and help the salesman to display and prove more effectively.

Easel Portfolio

The *easel portfolio* is usually placed on the buyer's desk, although it may be used with a floor easel. In either case, the demonstration is developed page by page. The pages are arranged to appeal to the prospect's point of view.

The easel portfolio serves two purposes: first, it helps the salesman to keep on the track and bring out salient facts in the proper sequence; second, it helps to dramatize the presentation and arouse interest. This sales aid is useful to salesmen who sell to business executives, dealers, purchasing men, and others who sit at a desk when buying. It is effective in building up interest in a specialty or technical product to engineers and purchasing agents who do not care for emotional appeals.

Company Advertising

According to David Seltz, advertising by industrial companies has a twofold purpose: first, to educate the company's most logical

2. Walter Arno Wittich and Charles F. Schuller, *Audio-Visual Materials* (New York: Harper & Brothers, 1957), p. 127.

market in the use and benefits of its products; second, to stimulate inquiries from prospects interested in learning how the company's products might be of use to them.[3] In addition, some large companies buy space in popular publications to assist their public relations departments. Salesmen can use these advertisements in several ways.

First, advertisements help the salesman obtain prospects. Second, advertisements often assist the salesman to emphasize his company's status, reputation, and policies. A prospect may feel that a company large enough to advertise would be a good one with which to do business.

Third, advertising may be used to show product and service features, benefits, values, and advantages. Fourth, advertising can help a salesman when it indicates to a prospect that the company is interested in his industry. For example, a steel company might run an advertisement showing the use of steel sheets in the manufacture of lockers, thereby boosting that particular industry. Also, the customer's plant might be photographed and used in an advertisement by the vendor's company.

Catalogues

Catalogues may consist of from one to several hundred pages presenting the various products of the company in an informative and appealing manner. Catalogues are often sent to prospects in advance of the salesman's call and can, therefore, serve as an entry for the salesman. They can also serve as a conversation piece when the salesman says, "By the way, have you seen our latest catalogue?" or "What do you think of the new product shown in our electric appliance catalogue?" They may also be used as a presentation manual.

Business Cards

A salesman's *business card* can be an important sales aid, for it is the first contact the prospect has with the salesman and, through him, his company. It may be the first impression the prospect receives of the salesman and it may also be the most lasting. Business cards contain the name and address and telephone number of the caller; they may also contain messages, illustrations, or symbols related to the salesman, his company, his sales proposal and other imprints designed to attract and impress potential buyers. Business cards left with the buyer serve as constant *reminders* of whom he may call for certain products and services.

3. Seltz, *Successful Industrial Selling*, p. 29.

Guarantees and Warranties

Printed *guarantee* and *warranty* forms may be used as sales aids. The simple fact that a product is guaranteed or warrantied to perform according to specifications may attract attention, arouse interest and stimulate conviction in the buyer.

Visual Devices

Blackboard

There are times when a salesman may want to use a portable blackboard to emphasize important points about a product or sales problem. The blackboard is a good tool for emphasizing the key points of a sales talk. A portable blackboard can be used to advantage in presenting proof materials.

Films for Selling

There are certain products and services that can best be sold by showing films. A salesman may find it desirable to have a room arranged for projecting films or have a portable projector for field presentations. Films for selling include motion pictures, sound slides, strips, motion slides, and slides. Each of these film types is useful for offering proof in certain kinds of creative selling.

Motion pictures may be in black and white or color, silent or sound. For selling intangibles, the motion picture is a valuable selling aid. For selling appliances or other products that have motion, the moving picture has great value. For appealing to emotions, creating appreciation and encouraging understanding, the motion picture is an effective device. The motion picture is not so effective for portraying facts, skills, knowledge, and for proving a point. It also is more expensive and difficult to acquire, transport, and use than other selling devices.

The portable *sound-slide projector* is light and easy to carry. Sound-slide film is valuable for selling certain products. Most important, it helps to picture products or services to a prospect.

Also, sound-slide projectors and film are easy to transport, use, and acquire. Pictures can be shown in sequence with a sound recording or as strip film without the recording.

A *strip film* is a continuous strip of film consisting of individual frames or pictures arranged in sequence, usually with explanatory titles. Each strip may contain from ten to more than a hundred pictures with suitable copy. For most sales use, the silent strip film is best because it permits questions, answers, and discussion. For many items, it offers excellent proof of values. It is easy to transport and use. It is the most economical of all film media.

The *motion slide film* combines the values of the motion picture with the strip film. Where motion is needed, it gives motion; where motion is not needed, or where motion is not good, the picture is frozen until motion is again required. For certain kinds of products or services, this dual feature is a valuable aid in proving benefits.

Slides are convenient, inexpensive, and versatile. They are portable and effective in demonstrating particular points in a presentation.

For illustrating details that sell better when enlarged, such as work sheets, charts, graphs, pictures, maps, operational sheets, and sales checks, an *overhead projector* is best. However, all materials to be projected must first be transferred to transparencies. Transparencies are inexpensive and may be made by professionals or by the salesman. Intricate details requiring draftsmanship in art work should be done by trained experts. For spot work, the salesman can prepare the transparency by writing on it with a china marker or grease pencil.

The transviewer is a variation of the overhead projector. It uses the same kind of transparencies and gives a brilliantly lighted background for dramatic effect. This is an effective, easily used device.

Direct-view slides can add the potency of full color, three-dimensional sight selling to a sales talk. This is the modern selling version of the stereoscope. It is useful for showing products, services, installations, manufacturing processes and other selling factors. It is pocket-sized, and uses film to show objects and designs in relief or three dimensions.

The *table viewer* uses ordinary 2- by 2-inch slides and operates by electricity. It is small: only 9 by 12 inches. The slides are dropped into a chamber where they are automatically inserted for project and restacked in their original order. This device is a creative selling tool for salesmen of all types of products and services.

Presentation Board

The *presentation board*—also known as the felt board, flannel board, or slap-on board, as well as by several trade names—is a simple but effective device for controlled disclosures. With this modern version of a blackboard, a salesman can build up his story visually at the same rate as his accompanying sales talk. This is done by emphasizing the main sales points with a series of pictures, designs, or symbols made of stiff cardboard. Flock or sandpaper is then glued to the back of each unit. The board itself is wood covered with a felt material to which flock or sandpaper adheres when pressed against it.

Transparency Portfolio

The *transparency portfolio* illustrates the working parts of the product that are illustrated on separate transparent sheets. As each sheet is placed in position, another part of the product is added. The item is completed while the prospect watches and listens to the explanation.

Used most often by salesmen of industrial products, the transparency portfolio is excellent for showing the construction of a product or demonstrating an engineering principle.

Plant Trips

Plant trips may be one of the best selling aids a salesman can use. He might talk about a product, service, or production process at great length, and yet fail to get his story across even when he uses all other available visuals.

When other methods appear to be inadequate, a trip through the plant, mill, or factory will give prospects a firsthand view of the things the salesman wants them to know about his product or process of manufacture.

When such a trip is considered, plans should be prepared regarding what prospects are to see and why. They will then know, before the start, what they should look for and where they will find it. Likewise, there should be a discussion with the prospect after the trip, to review what has been learned and to answer questions.

Trips by salesmen through the plants of customers are also valuable because salesmen learn how the products are made. Such knowledge helps them to sell more.

Recordings

Wire, tape, and disc recordings are not visual aids, but they are aids to sales presentations. They can be used to present speeches, skits, or any staged situation where sound alone can transmit a message to a prospect. It should be noted, however, that recordings rank lowest of all the sales aids in effectiveness.

Recordings may be used to reveal the wrong and right way to start questions or to conduct a conversation. The start of an actual sales talk can be recorded up to a certain point, when it is stopped and the salesman continues the conversation with the prospect. Recordings may also be used to convey personalized messages from individuals in top management who are unable to meet prospects. They may also be used to entertain prospects and customers.

Sales Trailer

One of the most useful sales devices for manufacturers of furniture, durable goods, machinery, and certain appliances is the *sales trailer*. It is not only a good visual device; it also reduces sales costs by allowing the salesman to make more calls more efficiently, since the salesman brings a showroom to the buyer who does not have the time to go to it.

These rolling sample rooms come in various sizes, but the most popular is the large or medium-sized trailer attached to the salesman's car. It is usually fifteen to twenty-five feet long and may carry up to a 2,500-pound load. The latest trend is to devote part of the trailer to sales demonstrations and the remainder for sleeping accommodations for the salesman.

Miniature Models

The miniature model ranks next to the actual product in effectiveness in a sales presentation. Models are constructed to scale and are often working models. Salesmen of engineered specialties use a cutaway model to show construction and a working model to demonstrate engineering principles and benefits. A model can be transported and displayed where the actual product could not because of its size.

Demonstration Kits

A *demonstration* kit may be a briefcase, an attaché case, a small suitcase, or a specially constructed container. It may contain miniature models, exhibits, specimens, the actual product, graphs, charts, booklets, and any other aids needed to help sell the product or service.

Demonstration kits are good devices for highlighting sales presentations. The variety of materials provided helps to retain the prospect's attention. Some kits include a humorous "gimmick" to amuse the prospect. Kits are among the oldest sales aid devices and also among the most effective.

Kits should be kept in good order with everything carefully arranged and displayed to the best advantage. Items should be easily removed for handling, sampling, and testing.

POWER POINTS

A dramatic presentation of proof of benefits through visual aids saves time, helps avoid misunderstandings and disagreements, and adds effectiveness to the sales talk. While selling by sight is more effective than selling by sound, visual materials and devices must be carefully chosen, with thought given to their timing as well as to the specific points to be stressed for each buyer. When a salesman explains his sales proposal clearly to a qualified buyer, supporting his presentation with oral and visual proof of benefits, he will be on his way to overcoming obstructions to the close of a successful sale.

DISCUSSION QUESTIONS AND PROBLEMS

1. a. Distinguish between the content of a *presentation book*, a *scrapbook*, and a *portfolio*.
   b. Describe the technique you would employ when using each of them during a presentation.

2. Scrapbooks are often useful as sales aids.
   a. Explain why and when they may be of greatest value.
   b. Describe how you would use them.

3. Some salesmen find uses for company posters, manuals, booklets, advertising tear sheets, and brochures. *How* would you use these materials and *why* might they be of aid to a salesperson?

4. Films of various kinds, as well as overhead projectors and transviewers, are useful aids for some salesmen. What kind of salesman and what products or services would be aided by these visual devices?

5. When might it be desirable to take a prospect on a tour of the salesman's plant or home office? Do you believe that a plant tour is really a visual sales aid? Why?

6. Describe a situation in which a disc or tape recording would prove to be a valuable sales aid.

7. Imagine yourself as the salesman for a company selling a cleaning compound used in hotels, restaurants, institutions, and industry. Would you *demonstrate* this product or would you use visual sales aids? Tell how you would use or employ the method you choose.

8. How would you arrange and organize your own file of proof materials or evidence for efficiency and accuracy during your presentation?

9. A salesman for a manufacturer of welding and cutting equipment sells his product to metal manufacturers, junk dealers, garages, trucking companies, earth-moving operators, and many other concerns. His products are technical and intricate in construction.

    a. Should he use visual aids to help his presentation? Why?

    b. Should he demonstrate his products while he talks? Why?

    c. Should he use both? Why?

10. You are a salesman for a company which manufactures and distributes projectors. To assist you in your sales presentation, you have been given a sound-slide projector and appropriate film about your products.

    a. Is this device likely to be an effective sales aid for your purpose? Why?

11. One of the most effective visual aids of all is the physical appearance of the salesman himself. The salesman's facial expression, mannerisms, bearing, and grooming are often the deciding factors in a sale.

    a. Why might these physical attributes be considered good visual aids?

    b. When might they be considered liabilities as compared to visual aids?

12. Think of three visual aids which might help you if you were selling canned fruit and preserves for a large food cannery.

    a. After deciding on the three visuals, which would be best for this kind of selling?

    b. Would product demonstrations be more effective?

    c. In either case, explain why you selected visuals or the demonstration and explain *how* you would use the aid, or aids, you selected.

SELLING PROBLEMS AND PROJECTS

---

1. Merryweather Plastic Company Case

John Merryweather is the owner, production manager, and sales manager of a small plastic manufacturing concern that specializes in extrusion items such as toys, tableware, advertising novelties, containers, bottle caps, and similar small products.

He has three salesmen who regard themselves as plastic engineers rather than salesmen. These men call on manufacturers, wholesalers, jobbers, agents, and specialty houses. Since much of their work involves figures and planning, all have college degrees. They are intelligent, speak well, and make an excellent appearance. They regard themselves as members of a high echelon in the sales field. Because of their education and morale, they do not want to carry samples nor do they want to demonstrate. They feel that such activities would imply that they were peddlers or identify them as belonging to a lower level of salesmanship.

Their sales are only fair. Mr. Merryweather is not making much money but he is not losing any. He feels, however, that his operation is close to the breaking point and that he must increase sales volume to have a financially safe operation. The only method that he can think of that might increase sales is to have his salesmen show samples and demonstrate the actual products to supplement their oral presentations.

Since Mr. Merryweather cannot afford to spend much money on a visual presentation, he would like his salesmen to compile their own books of facts, containing photographs and charted information concerning their large products. He would also like them to carry kits containing the full line of small items. He thinks his salesmen would give more effective sales presentations and increase their sales volume with the use of presentation books and sample items.

Questions

1. What is the problem in this case?

2. What should Mr. Merryweather do about the problems?

3. Do you believe that, since the expense of visuals is important, presentation books and the actual products will be sufficient for demonstration purposes?

4. Do you believe that these devices would help his salesmen to increase sales?

5. What other visuals can you suggest which might help close more sales?

2. Planchard L. Whiskum Case

My name is Planchard L. Whiskum, and at one time I was sales manager for a large food processing company, which, in addition to a standard line of foodstuffs, sold a special strawberry preserve. I tried without success for many months to get my men to push this excellent product. My salesmen insisted that it was too high-priced, that their customers were carrying a large inventory of competing brands, and that buyers would not stock a new line.

However, I had one salesman in Illinois who suddenly started to send in orders for strawberry jam. Soon he was selling more strawberry jam than all the other salesmen combined. So, I went out to Peoria to find out what this salesman had on the ball.

I soon found the reason and began to urge my other salesmen to adopt this man's method. The other salesmen at once raised the objection: "That's a good idea, but who is going to carry around a batch of gooey, sticky strawberry jam to feed customers?"

Questions

1. What is the basic lesson to be learned from this case?
2. How did the Peoria salesman increase his sales?
3. How would you put together a demonstration of this product?
4. Do you know of anything that cannot be demonstrated?

CHAPTER 15

Overcoming
Objections and Excuses

Through practice and training a skillful salesperson establishes a
pattern of behavior so ingrained that he is able to discuss and explain
his product without conscious thought, hesitancy, or concentration.
Even though he cannot take time to consider all factors, the professional salesman reacts fast and in language understandable and
pleasing to the buyer. He knows that his presentation will not be
successful when he backtracks, fumbles, or corrects himself. Therefore,
before he even attempts to sell, he organizes his presentation in an
idea sequence.

When a salesman uses the *idea-sequence* presentation, he is
organized so thoroughly that he not only knows what he will say
and what benefits he will emphasize, but also in what order he will
present them. The idea-sequence presentation technique was discussed
in Chapter 9.

A GOOD PRESENTATION OVERCOMES OBSTACLES

The presentation should be so firmly established in the salesman's
mind that he will react without conscious thought. Because he has
an idea-sequence, he will be able to pick up his presentation at any
point. Thus, when a prospective buyer interrupts his presentation
with an abrupt question such as "How much does it cost?" the salesman with a carefully planned idea-sequence will not be sidetracked.
With his mind free of other details, he is able to detect questions
before they are asked and is prepared with an automatic answer.

This ready reply will also help to deter the buyer's questions about prices until their proper place at the end of the interview. The sales presentation is retained as a unit in the mind of the professional salesman. His primary purpose is to be prepared to make his presentation in its entirety and in the most effective way. Because he is habituated to present and react according to a definite pattern and because he employs the idea-sequence to present the benefits, he neglects nothing and is able to use his ingenuity and resourcefulness in a way most becoming to a professional salesman. In other words, he is able to overcome with relative ease any obstacle to a successful sale.

Obstacles may also be handled in such a way that they work for the salesman instead of against him. The experienced salesman makes a thorough study of his prospective customer. He analyzes his needs, studies his behavior traits, interests, plans, and problems. In this way he is able to present relevant points and thereby avoid confusion and needless discussions which so often reflect the presentation of an untrained salesman.

When salesmen analyze objections, they find that new ones seldom occur. Sometimes objections may be expressed in a different way, but basically they are simply recurrences of frequently heard objections. Also, further analysis of objections has revealed that whenever a prospect objects to anything, he is inclined to defend his objection. Then, having committed himself to a negative attitude, the prospect's pride prevents him from reversing himself, and he will continue to object to everything the salesman says.

Reasoning from that premise, one of the major tasks of a salesman is to anticipate obstacles. Therefore, the alert salesman presents convincing proof of his claims before the buyer thinks of anything negative to say. The right idea planted in a buyer's mind is the most effective antidote to the objections and other obstructions.

It is advisable for the salesman to make a list of all the obstacles he might possibly meet and then ask himself what kind of behavior pattern the prospect showed, or what kind of mental dodging or negative remarks influenced his attitudes. He could then write out a plan for dealing with each behavior pattern (see Chapter 14).

When interesting benefit facts are worked into a strong, convincing presentation, most prospects will be too interested to raise barriers to further progress. They will be too concerned about the benefits to raise impediments. Also, this kind of skillful selling will give the salesman a new eagerness for his job and he will no longer be afraid of negative, discourteous, and hard-boiled prospects.

OBSTACLES

Many of the obstacles which impede successful salesmen have already been explained in Chapter 12. However, there are other obstacles and they are commonly known as requests for information, objections, resistance, obstructions, rejections, and impediments.

Requests for Information

One of the most common obstacles to the sale is the request for more information from prospects who want answers to their questions and problems. Fortunately for the salesman, this is merely a small obstacle and need not worry him, providing he applies the procedure suggested here.

- He should aim to win the prospect's liking and respect.
- Replies should be made in such a way that they indicate respect for the prospect's attitude and viewpoint.
- The salesman should answer the prospect's questions with a short review of the major benefits.
- Success stories from satisfied users are always impressive.
- Questions should be asked by the salesman as each benefit is mentioned, to gain acceptance as he goes along.
- The salesman should ask for the order.

The prospect usually raises sincere questions and problems when he does not fully understand or is skeptical because what the salesman says sounds too good to be true. When a salesman encounters something that is difficult to explain, what should he do? There is a simple method of coping with situations such as these; it is relax, listen, understand the prospect, use assurances.

First, the salesman should relax, emotionally and physically, but not mentally. He should never hesitate to make explanations. He should recognize that questions are signals that the prospect has certain doubts and wants the salesman to make him feel that they are groundless.

Second, he should listen to the question so that he understands what is on the prospect's mind. The prospect wants to be understood. He does not want an argument. The salesman should let him know that he believes his thought is worth careful listening. The prospect should be encouraged to express himself. The salesman should know by his attitude that he respects the stand the prospect has taken.

Third, he should understand the prospect's viewpoint. He should respond to the prospect's questions by providing the information asked for clearly, completely, and with an understanding of his viewpoint. Keep this rule in mind in handling explanations: Answer to the prospect's complete satisfaction and with an understanding of his viewpoint. When the prospect has a receptive mind, the salesman can provide the information he wants. In providing that information, one thing should be remembered: No prospect resists being turned into a customer when he feels certain that he will benefit.

The only time a prospect resists is when he feels that something is being taken away from him. He resists when he feels that he is giving something without getting back an equal or a greater value from the seller. Anyone would feel this way under similar conditions. A prospect does not want a salesman's goods or services. He wants what they will do for him. If the prospect is made to concentrate on what he will receive rather than on what he is giving, the salesman is more likely to be successful. Likewise, when the salesman answers questions, he must remember to add benefit point to benefit point, each one more closely related to the prospect's primary motive of gain.

The fourth thing a salesman should do is use assurances such as: "Mr. Jones, I can understand why you feel that way. In fact, several of our most satisfied customers felt exactly as you feel. But now that they have seen the extra profits that they are making from their purchase, they are very happy about their decision to buy."

When these assurances are used with explanations, the salesman shows that he understands the prospect's problems. He shows that he sympathizes with the prospect's position, although he may not necessarily agree with him. He reopens his mind for further selling while figuring out a solution for the prospect's questions.

Finally, the salesman must recall what Charles Schwab once said, "Winning an argument never put a dollar in my bank account." In other words, discretion is the wisest course to follow.

Knowing Answers

Giving an explanation, and answering questions to the prospect's entire satisfaction, implies that the salesman knows the answers. Certainly, he should know the *why, where, when, what, who*, and *how* of his product and his competitive products. Certainly, he should know about his company, its personnel, its policies, and other details if he hopes to overcome the question and problem obstruction.

When a salesman does not know the answers, he should say so. If the question is technical and he does not know the answer, he should never hedge or bluff. It is not always possible to anticipate all questions, nor is it possible to know all the answers. If you do not know the answer to a question, admit it and say that you will get the answer. The prospect's confidence is often increased if the salesman says, "Well, Mr. Jones, that's a new one on me. Frankly, I do not know. However, I will look into it and get the answer for you just as soon as I can."

Objections

When a salesman starts with a qualified prospect, he can offer things that are so important and beneficial to him that the prospective buyer would be foolish to offer insincere excuses. When the salesman shows a qualified prospect the facts and figures, the prospect's questions and objections are greatly decreased.

Advantages of Objections

Salesmen should not entirely believe the old saying, "Salesmen should welcome objections." Salesmen know, or at least suspect, that some objections can lead toward lost sales. And they also know that skillful handling of objections identifies a professional salesman.

Objections cause some salesmen to become confused and nervous. They lose confidence in their ability to answer and they become flustered.

Successful salesmen know that objections offer them the chance to:

- Clarify their sales presentation points.
- Review benefits and advantages.
- Offer more information.
- Discover the real objections or real needs of the prospect.
- Meet competition.
- Gain a favorable buying decision.

When to Answer

Prospects can interject objections at any time in a demonstration or presentation. Often these objections are unrelated to whatever the salesman is presenting. In this case, the salesman can stop at once and dispose of the objection, or he can ask the prospect's permission to hold it in abeyance until he can answer it completely.

Generally, it is better not to answer an objection until a complete presentation has been made. Meanwhile, the salesman can classify the objection as one of need, product, company, price, or when to buy. He can fit his answer into the most suitable place in his presentation. A delayed answer gives him time to give a more realistic and more acceptable reply to the prospect.

When answering any objection the salesman must guard against being too fast with his replies. When an answer is given too quickly, the prospect may receive the impression that he is being rushed into making a decision. The "yes-but" method, as explained later, is a good way to pace the reply.

How to Answer Objections

It would be impossible to list absolute, foolproof answers to all objections for specific products or services. Only the salesman, his sales manager, and other company officers can offer the product and background knowledge to do that. But the following basic outline, or method, can be profitably used to present explanations which will suit many prospects.

1. Learn the real objection and why it is an objection.
2. Restate the objection, then answer it completely and concisely.
3. Do not evade or minimize objections.
4. Avoid arguments.
5. Discuss objections positively.
6. Use the "yes-but" technique.
7. Use the objection as a reason for buying.
8. Do not let the objection deflect the main issues.

Undoubtedly, there are other techniques, but these eight represent the methods used by professional salespeople.

Asking Questions and Listening

If the salesman has the ability and willingness to ask questions himself, he will find that dealing with objections is not difficult.

The salesman will need to know how to ask questions to test the objection; in this way seller and buyer reach agreement and speak the same language. Sometimes this process is not necessary; for example, when a prospect says, "But your product is not well built," the salesman knows that the prospect is making a product objection. On the other hand, a prospect may say, "I just do not know how I can use it right now." Does a salesman know what he means? The salesman can find out only by asking the prospect a question to clarify the statement.

The salesman must listen carefully and learn to pick up phrases that tell the prospect's hidden interests or motivations. For example, a prospect might tell a salesman that the new company cafeteria is saving employees time, trouble, and money. The salesman might think his prospect is motivated by convenience, unless he also heard him say, "It cost us plenty to install it!" The salesman would then realize that the prospect is really commenting about the high construction cost.

Restating Method

When a buyer voices an objection, the salesman can often restate it and feed it back to him in the form of a question. This technique not only places the prospect slightly on the defensive but it also gives the salesman extra time to think how he will phrase his answers. The technique is simple but effective. The objections and questions occur somewhat like this:

BUYER (objection): Your price is too high. The product we use costs 10 percent less than yours.

SALESMAN (question): Then you are wondering why you should pay 10 percent more for a similar product? Is that your question, Mr. Jones?"

BUYER: That's the question, all right.

SALESMAN: Well, I can answer that in a few words. Competitive products appear the same, but in this case there is a difference. Research tests show that our product lasts longer. Note this demonstration. See how it works. You try it. Our customers say you'll save on labor costs with our product. Next, you can reduce your inventory because our warehouse is in this city. These add up to logical answers to your questions, don't they, Mr. Jones?

"Yes-but" Method

Whenever most objections come up, the "yes-but" method can almost always be used to good advantage. It is one of the strongest methods in salesmanship and the nearest thing to being scientific. The "yes-but" method overcomes either real or insincere objections. If a sales-man thinks of the "yes-but" method every time his prospect raises an objection, he cannot go wrong and he will close more sales.

When the customer says, "Your product costs too much," all the salesman need do is say, "Yes, I know just how you must feel, Mr. Customer. No one likes to pay more money for anything than it's worth. You can buy a lower priced product, that is true. But . . . let me tell you about the built-in economy and comfort values of this. . . ." Then the salesman should continue to tell the prospect why his prod-uct offers the best investment in service, safety, comfort, and economy that he could make.

Analyzing the statement above, it is seen that the salesman first agreed that price is important; then he gave the prospect all the reasons that his product is fairly priced and an excellent investment. This is how the yes-but method can be applied in solving real and imagined objections.

Suppose the prospect says, "Most of my driving is around town. I think a less expensive tire would serve my purpose."

The salesman should try answering with something like this: "Yes, you're right. I can understand how it would appear that way. But have you ever stopped to think of it this way?" Then he retells the bene-fits—protection against skidding, safety from blow-outs in fast traffic—stressing the great importance of these features in driving in city traffic and along high-speed highways.

The fact that the yes-but method is very useful does not mean that the words "yes" and "but" must appear in a sales talk. To use the method, the salesman (1) acknowledges that he recognizes the position of the prospect in making the objection; and (2) goes on to show the prospect why he did not have enough adequate information. For instance, if the prospect said, "I prefer the XYZ brand," the sales-man could reply, "I know that you want the safest and most econom-ical product. That is why I feel so confident in urging you to depend on our product which your engineers have determined will give you greater performance than the next best." Here, as in most cases, the words "yes" and "but" are not actually used.

Although the yes-but technique will apply in most instances, there are a few exceptions. Suppose the prospect says, "The only time I ever used one of your products, it gave me such poor service that I swore I would never buy another." His trouble could likely have been caused by poor use or care of the product. Therefore, the salesman can handle this situation by encouraging the prospect to tell all about this experience and perhaps feel better about it.

There is another situation where yes-but does not apply. For example, a prospect interrupts a presentation with the statement, "I don't need a product as good as that one. I never had trouble with the one I use." Very often the best solution to this problem is to say absolutely nothing. To give a serious answer would possibly provoke an argument. But a smile from the salesman will probably result in the prospect having a higher opinion of the salesman's common sense.

Sometimes an ordinary explanation will not work and a genuine objection will have to be answered. Naturally, no salesman can hope to overcome all objections, but if he can develop his overall skill he can increase his sales.

Doubt-creating Method

The doubt-creating method is useful when dealing with someone who cannot make up his mind. The following illustrates how this kind of person acts and what the salesman can do to turn them into good customers.

Suppose, for example, an automobile dealer has shown his prospect a number of cars and one particular style seemed to please him. However, the prospect says, "I believe I'll look around and if I don't find something better, I'll be back."

A professional salesman will recognize the uselessness of trying to get an outright reversal from this prospect, so he will employ a time-tested technique and reply somewhat as follows: "That is a wise decision. When you buy a car, you want one that will give you pleasure when you drive it."

"Now when you look at other cars, note carefully if they have these features." (The salesman then touches each item and points out each feature as he talks.) "Is it economical to operate? Is it a comfortable car? Is it a quality product? Is it the right size for your family, as this one is? Is it well constructed for long life? Does it have the conveniences this one has? Is it a well-known car? Note whether it has an adjustable seat, convenient arm rests, ample leg room, fine upholstery, sure-catch door handles. Be sure to ask about the services offered. Finally, ask about guarantees and warranties."

This salesman did not push the customer into buying, nor did he use "scaremanship." He did, however, fix in the prospect's mind the outstanding features of *his* car. If this prospect does go into a competitor's showroom to look at other cars—and he probably will not—he will wonder, "Is this as good as the one that nice person at Blank's showed me? Is it economical to operate? Is it easy to drive? Will it suit my family? Is it worth the price?"

The prospect will, in most cases, come back and buy from the first salesman. The "looker" and the "staller" are interested in benefits, and when the salesman has the proper facts and figures he will be able to convince the looker (or staller) that he will gain if he buys.

Questions for Favorable Reactions

Good questions from the salesman can be used to stimulate favorable reactions. The best salesman can "roll with the punches" whenever obstacles arise. They never lose control of a situation. For conditions that seem to be impossible they use a three-point formula:

1. Relax completely.
2. Concede points when advisable, that is, when the customer is right.
3. Ask questions to clarify the issue.

The salesman who takes pains to become expert in asking questions which tactfully and skillfully develop this technique makes it difficult for prospects to become annoyed or angry. These salesmen rarely lose sales because of stubbornness by the prospective customer.

Questions for the Skeptic

Sometimes a prospect will put off a decision to buy because the salesman has used too much *expertise!*

A flawless presentation may render the prospect skeptical. He may think, "What's the catch?" The salesman can convince the prospect by feeding him an objection in the form of a question. He could say something like this: "You seem to be bothered about something, Mr. Jones. Could it be this [product benefit]?"

This kind of question often brings a denial, followed by a genuine objection from the prospect. It may get to the hidden objection that may be holding up the sales decision. When out in the open, the hidden objection can be further examined and answered to the prospect's satisfaction.

"Why" Questions

One of the most useful little words to use in dealing with objections is the inquisitive "Why?" There will be many situations where use of this word will reveal what reasons a customer has for hesitating or objecting.

PROSPECT: Well, I just don't know. I think the Acme refrigerator would be better for us.

SALESMAN: Why, Mr. Roundtree?

PROSPECT: Well, it just seems to be a better buy.

SALESMAN: I hope you'll pardon me for asking again, but why do you feel it will be a better buy?

PROSPECT: Well, it boils down to roominess. It seems to me that you can store more large bottles in the Acme.

SALESMAN: I see. Well, I guess I owe you an apology, Mr. Roundtree. I didn't explain that fully enough. I believe that I can show you how our refrigerator can afford you even more space for tall bottles than the Acme.

Asking "why" is usually a good method for handling the opinionated, positive person. For example, a customer is looking at a living-room chair and says, "I know this fabric won't wear well." The salesperson could counter with, "You evidently know a great deal about furniture, Mrs. Gray, and I'm interested in learning your opinion. Would you mind telling me why the fabric won't wear well?"

At this point the customer usually begins to express positive opinions, and before she knows it, she has talked herself out of the objection and the salesperson gets another chance to prove that the item is of very good quality.

This method is effective because it flatters the customer; it makes her feel that her opinion is important.

Sidetrack Questions

The principle use of the sidetrack question is to guide the prospect's mind away from objections and toward an analysis of his statements. The sidetrack question also may be used to control resistance because of its value as a retort or retaliation.

When the client states, "I'm not interested," the salesman can often guide and control the interview if he replies with "Wouldn't you be interested if I could show you how to make $1,000 next week?"

If the client says, "There is no demand for your goods," the salesman counters with "Is every item on your shelves in demand now?" In this way, sidetrack questions can be devised to guide and counteract any objections the prospect may make, as well as to discover his real needs.

Turnaround Questions

Turnaround questions probe for a prospect's needs and make his objections a reason for buying. For example:

OBJECTION: I'm too busy to talk to you now.

ANSWER: Are you too busy to learn about something which will take away most of your worries?

OBJECTION: I wouldn't pay that much for a dress shoe.

ANSWER: But you want to look your best, don't you?

OBJECTION: I can't afford a car that costs that much.

ANSWER: Honestly now, can you afford to be seen in a low-priced car?

OBJECTION: I am satisfied with my present source of supply.

ANSWER: May I explain to you why satisfied customers are joining our ranks every day?

OBJECTION: I'm not interested.

ANSWER: Are you interested in getting lower operating costs?

OBJECTION: I don't want anything to do with your company.

ANSWER: That's why I'm here. Are you interested in a new business-building merchandise plan?

OBJECTION: I'm satisfied with the product I am already using.

ANSWER: We, too, have many satisfied customers; would you be interested in learning how my product can earn you a lot of money?

Handling Specific Objections

Before he goes out to call on prospects, the salesman knows well that he will encounter obstacles in the form of different objections. Since objections are inevitable, he should be ready to deal with them. Analyses of constantly recurring objections indicate there are six categories which embody practically all objections. The prospect's thinking goes something like this: "I'll not buy unless you convince me that—

1. It will pay me to give you an interview.
2. I need the benefits you offer.
3. Your proposition is better than that of your competitors.
4. Your company has prestige.
5. Your price and terms are right.
6. Now is the time for me to buy."

"I Don't Want an Interview"

How may a prospect be convinced that his time will not be wasted in an interview? The answer is that everything depends upon the prospect's first impression. If the salesman's appearance is poor, if his approach is awkward, if the idea is conveyed that the prospect's time will be wasted, his excuse of being too busy is actually a legitimate objection. It is always important that the salesman convince the prospect that he has something of real value to offer.

The excuse of being too busy when uttered by an insincere buyer should not be confused with the honest, polite objection of a person who is truly busy. One is a flat dismissal; the other can be an honest invitation to return. In the latter case, all that is needed is an agreement on when it will be mutually convenient for an interview. To explain more fully the methods of dealing with interview objections, the following examples are presented.

OBJECTION: *I'm too busy to talk to you now.*

ANSWER: I certainly do not want to take up your time when you are busy. When is the most convenient time for you? Would next _____ be convenient?
(Make appointment.)

OBJECTION: *I'll let you know when I'm ready to buy.*

ANSWER: Eventually, why not now? (Find out the reason in back of this objection.) If I can save you time and money eventually, why not start now to get these advantages? Let us make an analysis. What are you using now?

OBJECTION: *I want to think this over before I place the order.*

ANSWER: Certainly, you want to be convinced that it is to your interest before you buy. Perhaps I have not made certain points clear to you. If you will let me know what your questions are on these points, I can answer them while I am here today. If you wait to think it over while I am not here, you might forget some points important to your advantage. (If it must be delayed, make an appointment for the answer.)

OBJECTION: *Not interested.*

ANSWER: At first glance, Mr. Jones, I don't blame you for not being interested, knowing the great number of brands that are on the market. Here, I'll demonstrate to you exactly how this compound will save you dollars each month you use it.

OBJECTION: *I'll phone you when I'm ready to buy.*

ANSWER: Thank you very much, Mr. Black, but you are a very busy man, with so many things to think of besides my product, that I cannot reasonably expect you to keep me in mind. Suppose I call back and see you tomorrow.

OBJECTION: *Send me a sample.*

ANSWER: I have a sample here, and I'll be very glad to show it to you, or give it to you. Please remember, however, that a sample is not always sufficient to give you any idea of its value. I could come in with the worst product in the world and put on a good demonstration, because you might not use it right. In either event, you would have no way of knowing whether or not your employees could use the product, week-in-week-out.

"I Don't Need Your Product"

In this case the client is asking to be convinced that he has a real need for the product. He wants to know about the benefits he will receive. If, at the start of the interview, when the prospect knows only the salesman's name, he says, "I don't need any today," he is making an excuse. The salesman should recognize this statement as an excuse and try to go ahead with his presentation.

However, if the salesman has presented his facts and then meets this objection, he knows that something is defective in his technique. The prospect may have a genuine reason for not buying. Either the salesman has failed to qualify the prospect, or he has talked about product features rather than benefits. Therefore, additional evidence may be needed to convince the prospect that he really needs the product.

Convincing proof of need and benefits may be done in many ways. For example,

a survey, personal inspection, or inventory can be made by the salesman of the prospect's plant, business, or situation. Or success stories and testimonials can be told or shown of people similar to the prospect who are already enjoying benefits from the product or service. Or a frank discussion can be held with the prospect regarding his needs. Usually, a purchase results when a prospect admits he has a need for the product.

"I'm Satisfied with the One I Have"

If the prospect says at the outset of the interview that he is satisfied with the product he is presently using, he is often giving an excuse. He may be prejudiced, cantankerous, or just too lazy to want to improve his situation.

If the statement is made after hearing the salesman's story, either the proposition offered was no better than the one he had, or the salesman failed to convince him that he had superior benefits, values, or advantages.

The salesman can prepare himself in advance to meet this basic objection by listing the needs, desires, and problems that his product or service can satisfy. This list should then be checked against a list of similar needs and benefits for other prospects so that no important factors will be overlooked.

This listing may be made by (1) writing down all the things the product and the related service can do for the customer and (2) naming all the benefits that the customer can reasonably expect to derive from his purchase. Having fortified himself with such facts, the salesman can confidently answer the retort, "I don't like the quality," with a reply such as, "What exactly don't you like about the quality?" This would place the prospect slightly on the defensive, reveal the objection, and thereby allow both individuals to examine it and arrive at a satisfactory conclusion.

Remember that claims should never be made to convince a prospect unless substantiated with acceptable proof in the form of a demonstration, a test report, photos of the product in action, statistics and illustrations, testimonial letters, written guarantees, and perhaps other sales aids.

Sample illustrations of the methodology employed to deal with this kind of objection follow:

OBJECTION: *Your product is wasteful and inefficient.*

ANSWER: So are paper towels, paper drinking cups, paper wrappers, and other onetime products. The biggest cost of any operation is labor, and the main reason for using my product is because it saves labor.

OBJECTION: *We have gotten along without it for years; I can't see any reason for changing now.*

ANSWER: That is quite true. Years ago all business got along without telephones, cash registers, and other time-savers. You have to modernize, why shouldn't you use the best?

OBJECTION: *That's a good product for a big company, but we don't need it.*

ANSWER: Every business has the same fundamental key operations. The differences are only minor. The great majority of our orders come from relatively small concerns. (Show samples.) Perhaps we can take the good features and incorporate them into a product tailored to your needs.

OBJECTION: *We tried that years ago and it didn't work.*

ANSWER: That is interesting to know. Perhaps there was some good reason why it did not work. Perhaps it was not planned and installed properly. Maybe a different product or a few changes would make it work. (Here is an opportunity to analyze and suggest new ideas.)

OBJECTION: *Your stuff is a racket.*

ANSWER (The salesman becomes a little angry; he lets the prospect know that he is not a mere peddler.): "Mr. Schackenpoofer, my company is no more a racket than yours. Here, let me show you what others have said about it. You see, they're making money and their worries have stopped. Does that read as if a racket is being operated? Now, as I was saying...."

"I Don't Like Your Company"

Here, the salesman must alleviate doubts which the prospect has expressed about the company policy, service, the salesman's part in rendering the service, and the reciprocity problem.

When the prospect says, at or near the start of the interview, that he is satisfied with his present source of supply, he may believe that he is really satisfied, or he may not even have given it thought. He is, perhaps, not interested in the interview.

If, after the prospect has seriously considered the facts presented, he says that he would prefer to continue with his present source, the salesman can again resort to his question technique and say, "Why do you believe that, Mr. Jones? How can your present supplier give more advantages than we are able to give?" The salesman then cites more benefits and repeats others. The salesman enhances his position when he asks honest, frank questions, with the obvious intention of helping the prospect reach a wise decision. He can also ask questions to bring out attitudes, facts, and viewpoints which reveal what is going on in the prospect's mind. Finally, questions free the salesman from the necessity of shadow boxing, a costly waste of time and effort.

Whatever a salesman says about his company is of vital importance: size of the company; age of the company; company personnel; company sales promotion; company methods and policies of conducting the business. Nevertheless, these are similar to product *features* and they mean nothing to a prospect unless they are expressed in terms of *benefits,* such as better deliveries, fair treatment, prompt adjustments, promotional aids, profits, and fast turnover. There is probably no stronger force for building prospect confidence than the enthusiasm of a salesman who is thoroughly "sold" on his own company.

"I Usually Buy from Another Company" (Reciprocity)

The reciprocity problem is increasing, and for many salesmen it presents a serious problem. However, the problem can be solved if the following simple, time-tested method is employed. The reciprocity obstacle may start something like this:

"Sorry, I cannot buy from you because the Blank Company spends approximately $10,000 with us every year and we naturally feel we should buy from them exclusively." Although this is a difficult obstacle to overcome, the salesman may reply somewhat as follows:

> ANSWER: I understand how you feel. However, if we can show you a product which the Blank Company does not manufacture and which will do a better job for you, will you buy it? As for local buying, was your automobile, your washing machine, or your cash register made in this city? We have an office here, too, and we also spend money. I spend my money here, too . . .
>
> ANALYSIS: This salesman used an assurance statement to begin. Then he used the yes-but technique. He also indicated that benefits were possible from the purchase of his product. He suggested that few items were made locally and that the wise buyer obtains his merchandise from the best sources.

The reciprocity *switch method* may also often bring success. For example, a salesman could say:

> ANSWER: You are indeed fortunate to have such a good customer. We do not solicit business from a reciprocity standpoint, and I cannot, therefore, offer you any of our business. However, is it not true that your business would suffer materially if you lost this one big account? And is it not true that you are banking rather heavily on their business? And is it not true that you have no assurance of its continuance? Under these circumstances, it might be well not to keep all of your eggs in one basket. Why don't you go on record with my company by purchasing at least a portion of your requirements from us, and then when your salesman calls on our purchasing department, he is more likely to receive favorable consideration.
>
> ANALYSIS: This reply may switch the customer's attention from the company's failure to give him an order to his failure to place himself in a position to get it. This twists the situation in favor of the salesman. While the salesman makes it clear that he cannot promise anything, he plants the seed of hope in the customer's mind and indicates that reciprocity is a two-way street.

Some other frequently heard reciprocal objections, together with answers, are the following:

OBJECTION: *We've always bought from the Blank Company.*

ANSWER: I admire your loyalty. However, we make the broadest line of products in our industry, and therefore we are without prejudice concerning these products. Perhaps you should be using something that he does not have. Our business is founded on ideas. If I can suggest an idea that will save you money, would you buy from me?

OBJECTION: *You require too much time for delivery.*

ANSWER: If you mean we do not play favorites with our customers, you are right. Have you ever seen our line of stock products for immediate delivery? The fact that we have a backlog of orders indicates that many people like to do business with us. Our quality, service, and price must be right.

OBJECTION: *I don't want to change companies; we're doing all right now.*

ANSWER: You do not necessarily need to change your system. Perhaps I have ideas on design and construction to save you time and money and make your present production even better.

"I Don't Need It Right Now"

When the time arrives for the prospect to make a decision the presentation has progressed to its climax. Presumably all obstacles have been overcome and the *time to decide* has arrived.

If the prospect states that he is not ready to buy, or that he wants to think it over or talk to an associate, the salesman may make one of two assumptions. Either the prospect has indicated politely that the interview is over and the sale has not been made, or he is revealing that he would like to buy if he could.

Making a decision to buy is very difficult for most people. Therefore, the professional salesman rarely pays any attention to delay or postponed decisions. He knows that the prospect has received enough reasons to make an intelligent decision, so he avoids being side-tracked. If he has observed that the prospect has an urge to buy, he attempts a trial close. If the prospect repeats his objection, "I want to talk it over with my boss," the salesman should say, "If the general manager gives his consent, you'll sign the order, is that our understanding?"

If the prospect answers yes, the salesman acts immediately on that agreement and arranges for a meeting. If the prospect hesitates about the meeting, the salesman knows the prospect is not completely convinced. But the salesman does have a clear pattern for checking on the uncompleted part of the sales talk. He knows that, when the prospect is satisfied on all six of the buying conditions previously outlined, he will say yes and mean it.

He may also ask the prospect, "Is there any question in your mind, Mr. Prospect, or any problem that I may clarify?" If the prospect reveals that he is doubtful about his reply to this question, the salesman knows that he must do more selling on that point. The prospect's needs must be analyzed, explained, and proved until he fully appreciates his need and agrees to it. This may satisfy the prospect and, if so, the way is open for another attempt for a close. If the prospect still hesitates, the salesman moves on to the product. He says something like, "You are fully satisfied, aren't you, that our product will do an effective job for you and give you the results you need?"

If the prospect wants to delay further, the salesman can summarize the advantages of buying now and the disadvantages of further delay. When he can show the results in actual dollars and cents gained or lost, he has a particularly strong leverage for obtaining an immediate order, or at least in arranging a three-way conference for a final decision.

Additional factors and methods for dealing with the postponement will be found in the discussion of procrastination in Chapter 14. However, there are so many variations of this obstacle that descriptions of several of them should clarify the topic and render the salesman better able to cope with it.

> OBJECTION: *I can't afford to change all at one time and I have never bought anything on the installment plan.*
>
> ANSWER: Mr. Customer, if you prefer, replace your machines one at a time, but actually buying on installment is about the same as signing a lease for a building. You sign for the full amount of the year's rent, but pay in monthly installments, letting each month's business carry its share of the rent. Further, the savings you make with the new equipment help pay the installments. Some of our largest accounts, who normally discount their bills, take advantage of our easy-payment plan because they like the idea of letting the equipment help pay for itself.
>
> OBJECTION: *I'll have to talk that over with my manager.*
>
> ANSWER: An excellent idea. However, he might have some questions that I have not covered. Might I suggest that we both see him together? Could we see him now? He will probably have some more questions and I'll be there to answer them.
>
> OBJECTION: *I will buy this outfit later on, but not now.*
>
> ANSWER: There is only one reason why you will ever buy this outfit and that is to make a profit. If it is an expense, you do not

want it now, next week, or next month, not ever. If you want a profit, you want it now because it starts making money for you the day you put it in. When do you want it installed?

OBJECTION: *Business is not good enough to warrant spending the money.*

ANSWER: Is it bad enough to warrant studying possible economy of operation? When things are slow is the time to make a thorough checkup.

OBJECTION: *We are making some changes right now; see me later.*

ANSWER: Perhaps I can be of assistance in helping you plan the new changes. I make my living suggesting products to do the job my customers want done. All this experience is at your disposal. Shall we start now?"

OBJECTION: *We have a large supply on hand. We'll talk it over when we are ready to order.*

ANSWER: So much the better if you have a large supply on hand. That gives us plenty of time to look over your stock for possible improvement in design or construction. We can submit ideas and sketches. It is much better to do it thoroughly than wait until the last minute when there will be no time to consider changes. (Mention time needed for delivery.)

OBJECTION: *We have a contract.*

ANSWER: I can show you that you would save money through the use of my product, even though you may only use small quantities. You could easily do this, and at the same time, continue to use up your other product on this contract. When would you like to start?

OBJECTION: *The boss has a friend in the same business.*

ANSWER: Isn't it possible that it is costing your boss money to keep that friendship? If that is the case, I might as well leave and not waste time. However, I'd like to compare my product with the other product and I can positively show you how much more it is actually costing you to buy that other product. If the other product is as good as mine, I would not blame you for buying from a friend. Is that fair?

OBJECTION: *All buying is done at the main office.*

ANSWER: Mr. Jones, your statement is true, for I know your company buys that way. But I have looked your place over and you know that if you want anything very badly you could buy it. If you buy this product, your manager will credit you with sharp buying, because you will save your company a lot of money.

POWER POINTS

Sometimes an interview starts with the salesman telling the prospect all about his proposition. Because the prospect was interested, he listened attentively. He watched the salesman's demonstrations and visual aids, because they were important to him. Then, like a flash, he thought of an objection. If he was like many prospects, he said something like this: "Your product is more expensive than others."

From the moment he voiced that objection, he wanted an answer. If the salesman tried to pass over his objection and go on to another part of the presentation, he would probably leave his prospect behind. The prospect will continue to think of that objection and he will eventually want an answer to it.

Quality is the keynote usually used to combat price objections. The quality answer really means that the salesman must give proof of value; proof that his price is right in terms of the benefits he will receive. Since he must convince the prospect that he will benefit, he must be well prepared to offer proof of value before he can guide his prospect to a positive decision.

The salesman may say to himself, "That old price objection again! How shall I answer him?" First, he must recall that he does not want to argue with the prospect. However, the salesman does want him to feel that he has raised an honest objection that deserves an honest answer.

There are many ways to answer the price objection. What the prospect has said is possibly the result of a misunderstanding. When he says, "Your product costs too much," a good salesman would not say, "Ah, you don't know what you are talking about." Nor would the salesman ask, "Are you crazy?" A salesman may be able to tell a prospect what he thinks of him, but the customer can refuse to buy. The salesman may win the argument, but lose the sale.

The man who spends money wants to feel he is important. When he says, "Your product or service is more expensive than others," he is really asking to be convinced that the salesman's product or service will benefit him more than others. His statement is not meant to be insulting. It actually means he is challenging the salesman to convince him about its worth, value or benefit to him. The prepared salesman can easily meet his challenge!

No matter how the seller thinks his prospect feels, the salesman should always assume that the customer does not understand the point he has tried to make. The salesman may also assume that the prospect does not agree with the way the salesman has tried to make it. Maybe he still is not completely convinced that what the salesman said was right. The salesman must constantly visualize his target. He is not trying to fight the prospect; he is trying to make a sale.

DISCUSSION QUESTIONS AND PROBLEMS

---

1. Explain why the idea-sequence presentation helps salesmen to overcome obstacles to favorable buying decisions.

2. State and explain the procedures for answering objections described in this chapter and explain how you would use them in actual practice.

3. What is the general procedure for answering valid questions, as explained in this chapter?

4. Explain the value of asking questions and listening to the answers as a useful method for handling objections.

5. You have read that the yes-but method for handling objections is one of the strongest in salesmanship. Do you agree? Why?

6. What are some of the variations in the use of the yes-but method?

7. When should the yes-but method not be used?

8. What categories embody practically all objections?

9. Describe and state how you would deal with objections to interviews.

10. Describe and state how you would deal with prospects who say they do not need your product.

11. The following are a number of resistance phrases. Based on your reading and experience, which are excuses, vacillations, or honest resistance? Give your reasons.

a. Too busy to talk.	g. Same supplier for years.
b. You sell to everybody.	h. No call for your product.
c. Not interested.	i. We're overstocked.
d. I'll think it over.	j. Too many suppliers now.
e. See me later.	k. Not buying today.
f. Let me sleep on it.	

12. When a procrastinating buyer is at a loss for an honest answer, he often will say, "Your price is a little out of line, I'll have to think it over." Exactly how would you handle this situation?

SELLING PROBLEMS AND PROJECTS

1. Herman Bozarth, Space Salesman

Herman Bozarth is an advertising space salesman for a group of magazines published by a New York firm. He is successful in his field and makes a comfortable living.

Occasionally, his clients threaten to discontinue their space advertisements in the magazines. The objections are essentially one of these two: (1) they don't need to buy advertising when business is booming, for people come to them to buy when a seller's market comes along; and (2) they claim that when business is poor, there is no reason to advertise, for that would be a waste of money.

Questions

1. Do you believe that these objections are legitimate? Explain.

2. Would you treat this kind of objection seriously? Explain.

3. How would you deal with this kind of objection?

2. Add Up Appeals

Fred Freund sold for one of the plastic drinking cup manufacturers. His job was to call on restaurant owners and convince them that it would pay them to use the new cups. One of his prospects, Chris Charos, wouldn't buy from him. Chris had been in the restaurant business for 30 years, and he preferred heavy chinaware cups. After listening to Fred for a few minutes, this is what Chris said:

> "That four-for-a-penny stuff sounds fine, Fred, until the costs are added up. With all the customers I serve every day, I can just imagine my plastic cup bill. No thanks!"

Fred had heard this objection before and this is what he replied:

> "I know how you feel, Mr. Charos (sincerely, courteously), and you're perfectly right. That cup bill certainly will add up (pause). But then, so will your dollar volume (enthusiastically). That is only natural because a faster service will help you serve more people than ever before.

To the increased sales from faster service, you'll get a profit, then you add the savings of labor, towels, soap, brushes, savings from dishwashing, and I know that you'll agree that plastic cups, far from being expensive, are really a profitable investment. You can begin this very week to collect dividends that plastic cups will pay you. Our cup trucks are in your neighborhood Tuesday and Thursday. Which day would be most convenient for you, Mr. Charos?"

Questions

1. What method did Fred use to handle his customer's resistance?

2. What affect do you believe add-up appeals would have on the prospect's thinking?

3. How were the prospect's objections turned into sales points?

4. How did Fred employ repetition?

5. What suggestion did Fred make to close the sale?

6. How did Fred try to close on a minor point?

CHAPTER 16

Coping with
Price Resistance

PRICE FACTORS

More than one hundred years ago John Ruskin wrote, "It's unwise to pay too much, but it's worse to pay too little. When you pay too much you usually lose only a little money. When you pay too little you sometimes lose everything because the thing you bought fails to serve its function. It is impossible to pay a little and get a lot. The law of business prevents it."

All salesmen believe one can't get something for nothing, because it is common sense. However, very few salesmen agree with the equally sensical statement: Price selling is the penalty a buyer demands for a salesman's mistakes and inefficient selling methods. Failure to accept this statement occurs even when salesmen realize it is a factual statement. But they refuse to admit it.

The price problem presents a hurdle which many would-be salesmen are unable to get over. These types of salespeople are unfortunate; they are mere order-takers. They are the kind who call on customers with the sterile inquiry, "How many cases can I book you for?" Or, "How many can you use if I give you a good price?" Or, "I can give you a low price if you buy today." These men sell price; they do not sell benefits, values, advantages, and exclusives.

Professional salesmen agree that price is not the most important deterrent in selling. Obviously, price is important to every buyer, but it is not all-important. A great many salesmen overemphasize price.

Usually they have difficulty in discussing prices and therefore complain about how troublesome prices are. A price-conscious salesman should ask himself these questions and give himself honest answers:

- Do I understand pricing?
- Do I like to negotiate prices?
- Do I take orders rather than sell?
- Do I believe a product is bought, not sold?
- Do I use selling points other than price? For example, do I discuss product advantages and values?

Price Is Secondary

Price is not the most important element in selling, but there are those who argue that sales are a direct result of pricing policy. They will point to the fact that department store sales always attract more buyers.

They are, in fact, talking about price appeal, not selling. Salesmanship is not necessary if merchandise is given away at something less than its real value. Profitable sales cannot be closed by selling on a price basis.

A professional salesman will not sell his product on the basis of price alone. He will skillfully spotlight benefits, values, advantages, services, house policies, and the like. He will prepare himself to meet the price problem. He will take it for granted that prospects and customers are going to bring up price and he will plan all of his interviews to meet and solve this problem.

A salesman should actually believe his prospects when they say his price is too high. They may be correct, for they are comparing the salesman's price with their estimate of the value. If the prospect's estimated value is lower than the price asked, the salesman usually has not made a good presentation.

Price Determination

A hundred or even fifty years ago, prices were settled by the law of supply and demand. Today, instead of the exclusive use of the law of supply and demand to determine price, the industrial executive approaches his pricing problem in at least two different ways. First, to determine price, he adds up the cost of materials, labor, machinery, and distribution, plus an equitable amount of profit. If goods do not sell at the set price, then management intensifies promotional activity or curtails production. Business that does not pay its own way is refused. However, this kind of refusal is primarily intended to protect capital, not to price and sell.

Second, there is another type of price setting, a more dynamic one. Instead of adding costs together to arrive at a price, executives start with the needs of the buyer and his ability to buy, and then find a way to satisfy those needs at a price the buyer can afford to pay. In other words, the modern way to determine price is to start with the marketing-management concept rather than with a supply, demand, or cost-accounting concept.

One part of the marketing-management philosophy that carries major significance for salesmen, as well as for management, is the growth of profit-conscious volume. This concept is giving way to an increasing awareness of the importance of profitable volume. More and more, management is teaching the salesmen that volume is meaningless unless it is accompanied by a corresponding increase in profit.

Of course, the actual price policy followed by a particular firm may be a combination of many pricing considerations. Some items in the line, for example, may be priced on the basis of underselling competition, while others may be promoted by heavy advertising and priced high in proportion to their production costs. An item can be given a relatively low price and be heavily advertised in order to move a larger volume at a comparatively low unit profit margin. Notice that marketing-management philosophy does not state that it is necessary to reduce the earnings of a company to get an order.

Nonprice Competition

Business firms often attempt to stress some factor other than price in their marketing program. In price competition, the seller attempts to influence demand by changing the price; in nonprice competition, the seller attempts to influence the demand by product differentiation, promotional activities, and other devices. For example, if the seller decides to differentiate his product, he may improve its quality, change its design, or alter the ingredients in the product. In promotional activities, the seller may embark upon an aggressive personal selling campaign or an intensive advertising program designed to acquaint prospective buyers with the merits of the product. Other devices could include the use of trading stamps or the introduction of a lucky-number contest. Both are designed to stir up action on the sale of the product without changing the price.

Among the major factors contributing to greater use of nonprice competition are:

1. General tendencies toward price uniformity within industries.
2. Proven ways of holding satisfied customers.
3. Successful nonprice firms imitated by less successful firms.
4. Adoption of the marketing concept and better trained salesmen.

Among the minor factors affecting nonprice competition are these:

1. More advertising to promote sales and price acceptance.
2. Increased knowledge of customer motivation.
3. Growing doubt in many industries that price cutting will increase sales.
4. Growth of service and related sales promotion devices.
5. The benefits of quality and service as compared to price alone.

There is an increasing use of nonprice competition in marketing. When a seller employs the strategy of nonprice competition, he does not lose his advantageous position when a competitor undercuts him in price. The reason is that customer loyalty for the product has been established. That is, customers believe that the product possesses other virtues that more than offset a higher price. They will not change to another product merely because it costs less.

Benefits of Nonprice Competition

1. Eliminates constantly readjusting prices to meet competitors.
2. Promotes better understanding and goodwill with prospects, customers, and even competition.
3. Leads to greater stability in production.
4. Earns a better net profit for each competitor.

Regardless of the specific factors which influence the establishment of a price, and regardless of the care and study which goes into its determination, price is always on trial in the marketplace. No matter how logical the price may seem, if it attracts an insufficient number of customers, or if it loses money for the company, it is the wrong price. Unrestrained "price selling" is always considered to be the wrong price policy.

Competition and Price

During periods of merchandise shortages, price obstacles rarely occur, for in such abnormal periods cost becomes secondary although still an important consideration.

In a normal market, however, competition grows more keen, and price becomes more of a factor for salesmen to consider. Salesmen hear such statements as:

"I want a better discount."
"Your price is too high."
"You're out of line on price."
"It costs too much."
"My customers won't pay that much."

These statements are certain to occur and the alert salesman anticipates them by preparing to meet them.

The salesman has little or no control over the prices of the things he sells. Nevertheless, he should know how and why the prices are what they are and why they are justified. When he has this information, there is probably no need for hesitation or errors in explaining prices. There is always a reason for a price. A prepared salesman can use the reason effectively to turn price obstacles into a reason for buying.

Listing and Analyzing Price Impediments

The prospect may phrase his objection in many different ways. The salesman will need to know how to deal with each one. By making a list of all the price obstacles he encounters and then proceeding to analyze them, the salesman will find that they are basically the same and each one can be successfully handled with its own appropriate method.

Planning Interviews

The salesman should take for granted that customers and prospects will say, "Your price is too high." Then he should plan all his interviews to meet this objection. When a buyer says the price is too high, he may be right. On the basis of what the salesman has told him, the buyer places a value on the product. If the prospect maintains that the value is lower than the price, it is usually the salesman's fault. He has not made a good presentation. The value and quality of the product should be stressed so that the price seems lower by comparison. If a salesman wants to succeed and close successful sales, he will spend a great many hours planning answers to questions about price. That is the best way to prevent trouble. To overcome obstacles, a successful salesman will look at his product or service through the eyes of every prospect he expects to contact. He will know the benefits of that product or service from the prospect's viewpoint and his business needs. He will know the claims his competitors make about their product, and its price.

Timing

There is a definite time to introduce the subject of price. The time is near the end of the sales talk, after the product has been fully discussed. When the subject of price arises too early in the presentation, too much emphasis is placed on it. The entire purpose of a sales presentation is to build desire in the mind of the prospect to the point where he wants the product regardless of the price.

Price should never be treated as an obstacle until the salesman discovers that it is a genuine obstacle. How does he find that out? Usually when the prospect says something like, "I can't afford it." The salesman must decide how qualified his prospect is as to his need and his ability to pay for the product or service. If he qualifies, cost cannot be a genuine objection and the salesman should continue to prove to the prospect that he cannot do without his product or service.

The technique of rebuttal to this obstacle is one in which the salesman should get considerable practice. The basis of the rebuttal is to stress the product's quality, durability, and satisfactory performance.

When the price becomes an obstacle, it will generally be at one of these three times:

1. At the very beginning of a salesman's contact with the prospect, usually as one of the prospect's opening remarks.
2. During the presentation when the prospect begins to have the feeling that the proposition has more value than he can afford.
3. At the end of the presentation at which time the prospect feels he cannot afford the price at this time or he can buy a comparable product for less money.

When the subject of price arises during a demonstration, there are usually three reasons why: (1) the salesman does not know the prospect's needs and desires; (2) the salesman has not pointed out the benefits and usefulness of his product; (3) the prospect may be ready to buy and it is now time for the salesman to ask for the order.

When price is mentioned at the beginning of an interview, the salesman can sometimes postpone his answer. For example, if the prospect immediately asks the price, the salesman might put off the issue by quickly asking a question such as:

"Wouldn't it be better if you knew all the facts before we discuss price?"

Such a reply will not only temporarily put aside the question of price, but it will also give the salesman a better idea of what to say and do next. The salesman should then be in a favorable position to appeal to the prospect's curiosity and interest.

If the prospect becomes suspicious that the salesman is attempting to avoid the subject of price, he will become even more price-conscious and will likely hear nothing more until he is told the price. Postponing and setting aside the price issue requires tact and diplomacy on the part of the salesman.

In any event, when the prospect asks the price, the salesman should use the question as a signal. It is then up to the salesman to use the price issue to his advantage and to discuss it at the time when it will do him the most good.

REMOVING THE PRICE OBSTACLE

There are several methods of handling the problem of price in the course of a presentation. These methods include discussing benefits instead of price, taking the initiative by introducing the subject of price, the savings method, and the cost breakdown method.

Selling-Benefits Method

In approaching any client, the salesman should ask himself what benefits this client would be interested in, what quality of product would he want, and what price would he be willing to pay.

A professional salesman knows that if his prospects were willing to buy only on a price basis, they could buy directly from the manufacturer or a mail-order house. They do not always buy directly because they want the salesman to help them decide the problems of how, when, where, and why a product or a service can benefit them. Advertising cannot supply this information and, obviously, merely quoting a low price does not help.

Creative salesmen should realize that the responsibilities and opportunities of their jobs are to sell people what they should have. This can be accomplished by convincing a client that he could benefit greatly from buying the product.

Salesmen do not make sales because their prices are lower or because they are smarter than a prospect. They do not obtain orders by outwitting or overpowering a prospect. Instead, they demonstrate, explain, and prove to a prospect that what they are selling will fulfill his needs.

Strike-First Method

There are some buyers who think only of price. Since a number of prospects feel this way, it will often pay the salesman to work out a short sales presentation such as the following:

Bring up price
Figure up price
Play up price

These nine words constitute the strike-first approach to meeting the problem of price. The strike-first method is employed somewhat as follows:

Bring Up Price

"I suppose your product is all right, but it is priced too high" is a remark which is very familiar to everyone who sells. Usually it comes toward the end of the conversation and it prompts the salesman to justify his price. Too often he settles for a trial order or doesn't conclude the sale. Fortunately, a salesman can anticipate the price obstacle and bring up the price himself very early in the presentation. For example, "Chances are, Mr. Smith, you buy the product that will do the job and cost you the least money, isn't that right?"

It should be noted that the suggestion question was asked as soon as possible. The important thing to remember is that if the salesman brings up price before the prospect does, he gains the initiative. When the salesman promptly brings up price, he is off to a good start toward a favorable decision from his prospect.

Figure Up Price

When the salesman initiates the topic of price, he must be prepared to quickly and accurately determine what the price is in each sales situation. It must be done quickly because the prospect expects the salesman to know his prices. It must be done accurately because the estimate may greatly influence whether or not a sale is made.

On the other hand, any price estimates must be considered as estimates, not irrevocable commitments. Too many other things can affect the price. Differences in freight charges, market changes, and unforeseen events can cause the estimated prices to be revised.

The important point is that when the salesman initiates a discussion of price, he should relate his discussion to the advantage of his product.

Play Up Price

Once the salesman introduces the issue of price, he should disclose the total price of the product or service. He can then use this as a selling point in his presentation. For example, when the prospect states that he thinks the price is too high, the salesman can point out what the prospect will receive for that price.

Savings Method

For those clients who are price-minded, the salesman should stress the savings which would be realized by the client if he took the product. Here, for example, is a typical case.

PROSPECT: I'd like to do business with you, Mr. Salesman, but $12,000 just seems too big an outlay of funds for us to consider at this time. I feel that the firm should continue buying our chairs and desks from outside sources.

SALESMAN: I can understand your reluctance to take on an additional debt at this time, Mr. Jackson. This was the same way Mr. Patton felt. You know Mr. Patton, General Manager for the Uptown Desk Co.?

PROSPECT: Oh yes, I've heard of him. They have a very successful operation. Did Mr. Patton actually feel that way?

SALESMAN: He certainly did, and he was faced with the same kind of a problem that you are faced with today.

PROSPECT: What's that?

SALESMAN: Namely, what to do about more intense competition and price increases at a time when production costs and especially factory wage levels are increasing.

PROSPECT: How did you handle it?

SALESMAN: Well, we worked out a cost analysis of Uptown's old method and then compared a projected five-year cost breakdown using two new AD101 machines. Do you know what we came up with?

PROSPECT: No, what?

SALESMAN: A savings of 16 percent a month in the cost of milling and finishing legs and rails alone, even after you take into consideration the amortized cost of the new equipment. This put Uptown back on a competitive basis again. That savings meant that the equipment paid for itself in six years.

PROSPECT: Do you think you could achieve the same results for us?

SALESMAN: Sure, why not? Let me propose this. Let's figure it out the same way I did for Uptown. If my figuring shows you save money even after you deduct the cost of the new equipment, I get the order; if I can't prove that I save you money, I don't.

PROSPECT: Let's get to work.

Cost Breakdown Method

Another good method for dealing with the price obstacle is to give the cost of the item per day over its normal period of life. For example, under this method, the price of a $500 item would be a mere 14 cents a day—less than half the price of a pack of cigarettes—certainly a very small and reasonable amount from the buyer's viewpoint. In this way the cost is made to appear inconsequential.

BUYER'S TECHNIQUE

Studying methods of how to deal with the obstacle of price is not enough. It is as important to understand some of the processes which may go on in the buyer's mind. It is also important to know that purchasing agents study the psychology of buying at least as much as salesmen study the psychology of selling.

Pressure Tactics

Shrewd purchasing agents prefer to use pressure tactics to obtain a lower price. One tactic, for example, occurs when the buyer tells the salesman that everything is fine, that his product is just what they want. The buyer will say that placing the order is a routine matter; that in a week or two the order will be written up.

A salesman might feel that the sale could possibly be lost if this happened to him. He might become a little anxious, and this anxiety might put him in exactly the frame of mind the buyer wants.

A week later the salesman may be asked to call. At the meeting he finds two or more new men in the office of the buyer, and they insist on going over the specifications again. Then, at the last moment, one of them suddenly says that he would like very much to do business, but the price makes it impossible and must be revised downward.

Now the salesman is on the spot. His desire for the order has been deliberately stimulated. He was certain that the order was secure. Suddenly, he finds the whole sale is apparently in jeopardy.

When a salesman recognizes this strategy and refuses to budge, he will more often than not have a good chance of getting the order.

If he weakly or foolishly cuts the price or refers it to his company, he admits that his quotation was elastic and can be reduced still lower. Professional salesmen never permit themselves to succumb to this buying tactic.

Big-welcome Technique

Another clever buying method is to make the salesman very welcome and to flatter his ego. The salesman might be told how much the buyer wants to do business with him if it were not for one little obstacle. The buyer is almost ashamed to mention it, but it is too bad that the salesman's price is five dollars more than his competitor's.

If the salesman succumbs to this proposal, he may get one order, or perhaps two, but in the long run he will lose out, as will his company. This kind of buyer cannot possibly be a reliable, steady customer.

Quantity-order Technique

A third common buying technique is for the buyer to start an argument about proportionate prices on different quantities of the same product. "Yes," says the buyer, "your price is fine, but not on the quantity I want to order."

Then, to back up his demand for a lower price, he will refer to a few technical facts and figures about the product and speak with such assurance about the ratio of price to quantity that he may be believed. This is likely to happen if the salesman is ill informed on product knowledge and buyer strategy.

The salesman may begin to feel that he had better recheck his estimates, that his company has made a mistake. But the very minute he begins to recheck, he reveals his lack of confidence in his company. He shows that his prices may be flexible and elastic and that he can be influenced to make price concessions.

Appropriation Technique

A fourth buying technique might be called the *appropriation dodge*. The buyer tells the salesman, "The product or service is fine and the price is reasonable, but if we accept it, we will be forced to exceed our appropriation for the item in question. We would like to buy it, but if we did we would throw our appropriation out of balance. How about trimming the price?"

The salesman will be subjected to tactics such as the appropriation technique and the three described above. He must learn how to handle these tactics forcefully. He will command greater respect from the buyer and make more sales if he does not yield to pressure from him.

POWER POINTS

Most customers buy only when they think they are getting the most value for their money. No matter what you are selling, you can never take it for granted that the customer will recognize the full value of your product. Be sure to describe what the product will do for him. Let him translate the facts in your sales talk into terms of his own intended use of the product. In this way, just by emphasizing significant sales factors, the salesman actually creates value for his product in the eyes of his customer. When the value is lower than the price, the customer ignores the merchandise. When the value is equal to the price, the customer recognizes that he is getting a fair deal. However, when the salesman has pointed out sales facts that inflate the value of the product until it is higher than the actual price in the customer's opinion, then the customer feels he is getting a bargain.

Generalities don't sell quality; only specific sales facts can do that. If you put yourself in the customer's place and take his viewpoint, you know he wants to save money. He thinks he is saving money by buying a less-expensive product than yours. You can show him that he isn't. It is the essence of true salesmanship to be able to persuade the customer that he should buy a better product—even at a higher price —if it will serve him better and longer and give him full value for his money.

Keep the quality points about your products or services readily available for instant use. To make selling easier and more pleasant, know why your product or service is of better quality. You then have a basis for more sales to dealers and consumers.

Much of the true value of products and services is hidden. To induce the customer to buy quality products, the salesperson must point out these hidden values and show the prospect what these values mean to him.

Many persons buy low-priced merchandise because they have no comprehension of a product's true value to them. Others do not have the money to buy anything else. However, there are always customers who will react to the quality appeal if it is properly presented in terms of serviceability and durability.

Customers are justifiably confused when two items of merchandise look alike yet have a wide variation in price. An alert salesperson can find the hidden values which account for the difference in price. Sales value is value only if the customer is able to see it.

After he has delivered his sales talk thoroughly, listened, questioned, motivated, and coped with all problems, the successful salesman is ready to start his decision-making activities. If he has performed well up to this point, he will have none of the nervous reaction so often experienced by novices. He is ready to try for a favorable decision from his prospective buyer.

There is no magic formula for closing sales. Obtaining a favorable buying decision from a prospect is the natural reaction to the proper approach and presentation. The time to ask for a buying decision is often so obvious that it is sometimes overlooked. The methods of asking for the order are equally obvious and simple. Learn and practice them.

DISCUSSION QUESTIONS AND PROBLEMS

---

1. Explain the statement, "Price selling is the penalty buyers demand for a salesman's mistakes and inefficiency."

2. How would you distinguish between genuine *selling* and *price appeals?*

3. What is the modern method for determining price?

4. What is the basis for price consciousness?

5. When may a price obstacle arise?

6. Explain the various methods employed to establish market price. Which is preferable? Why?

7. What are the major factors affecting nonprice competition? What are the advantages of nonprice competition?

8. What advantages can a salesman realize from listing and analyzing price obstacles that occur in his daily selling activities?

9. In relation to the price problem, what is the importance of *timing* in presenting a proposition to a buyer? Explain each point in your answer.

10. Explain and demonstrate the *strike-first* method for handling price.

11. Select a representative specialty item such as a deep freeze, a vacuum cleaner, an automobile, or a similar product. Common objections to these products are listed below. Explain how you would counter each objection.

   a. I won't pay the highest price for anything.

   b. When your article is priced right I may buy, but not until then.

   c. I can't afford to buy now.

   d. If you could just cut the price to meet my budget, I may be interested.

12. "Your competition beats you on both quality and price" is a comment frequently heard by salesmen. How would you reply to this *obstacle?* How would you handle this comment if it were an *excuse?*

13. Describe and explain the following strategies employed by many professional buyers:

   a. Pressure tactic.

   b. Big welcome technique.

   c. Quantity order technique.

   d. Appropriation technique.

SELLING PROBLEMS AND PROJECTS

---

1. Dick Lafflin Case

Paul Spade discussed his company's line of tractors with Dick Lafflin, and all seemed to be going well until Dick objected to the price.

   DICK: This thing costs a lot of money. I can buy the Dwyer line for $1,500.

   PAUL: Sure you can, Dick. It is a lot of money. But the difference in price between our equipment and the Dwyer line will be returned to you in time saved alone. In addition, we can offer our parts and service facilities. You realize how important efficient service facilities are in case of a breakdown, don't you, Dick?

   DICK: Yeah, I guess so.

Questions

1. Would you start closing the sale at this point?
2. Do you think Paul is trying to close the sale now?
3. What method is he using?

The conversation continues:

PAUL: They certainly are. Don't you think the added power, the added speed, and the advantages of Touch Control are the answers to your problem?

DICK: Yeah, I guess you're right. I hate to part with my old tractor, though.

PAUL: Well, you'll forget the old one as soon as you get this new model. There's no reason why you shouldn't start using it today, is there?

Question

4. What closing method is Paul using?

DICK: I can think of 1,695 reasons—dollars, that is.

PAUL: Don't let that worry you. I'll write the order now and take the old tractor and cultivator as a down payment. We'll arrange your payments to match your income. Does that sound fair enough, Dick?

DICK: That's OK, but what will you give me for the old tractor?

PAUL: Remember, Dick, we've already agreed that $400 was a fair allowance for the cultivator and tractor.

DICK: Yeah, I guess we did.

PAUL: Now, let's see, that's one new tractor at $1,486 and one cultivator at $209, minus $400 for your old trator and cultivator, leaving a balance of $1,295. Let's figure out the balance of the down payment and work out the payments to match your income.

Question

5. Does Dick have any further objection?
6. What closing method does Spade use here?

2. Lew Llewellyn Case

Lew Llewellyn has a thriving little business selling refrigerators, deep-freeze units, and other electric appliances. Lew has made three calls on the Johnson family and has interested them in a deep-freeze unit. Lew is now about to try to close the sale when Mr. Johnson, his prospect, makes an objection. Mr. Johnson says:

MR. JOHNSON: $399.95! That's an awful lot of money. We just can't afford to spend that much.

LEW: Tell me, Mr. Johnson, is there any other reason why you shouldn't begin to enjoy this freezer other than the fact that you feel you can't spend that much money right now?

MR. JOHNSON: No, I don't think so, but that's reason enough.

Questions

1. What kind of objection is this?
2. What method is Lew using?

Let's see what Lew does now. Lew says:

LEW: You like the freezer, don't you, Mrs. Johnson?

MRS. JOHNSON: Yes, very much. Maybe later on we can buy one, but not at this time.

LEW: But you should really be taking advantage of it right now. Fruits and vegetables are in season. You can freeze the vegetables from your garden, and prices are much lower on the vegetables you'll want to buy than they'll be next winter. You should fill your freezer at this time while prices are low and quality high. With this freezer you can eliminate that hot job of canning. If you invest in this freezer it will be one of the best investments you'll ever make. If you let this freezer work for you, it will more than pay for itself. Wouldn't you like to start those savings right now?

MR. JOHNSON: Yes, but we just can't dig up that much money right now.

LEW: Tell you what, Mr. Johnson, so you won't have to pay for this freezer all at once, we can arrange it so you can make a small down payment and you can go right on using it and the savings on your food bill will help you to make the monthly payments. What do you say?

Question

3. What method is he using now to handle the price objection?

As we interrupted, Lew was saying:

LEW: What do you say?

MR. JOHNSON: How much of a down payment would be necessary?

LEW: You can pay as little as 10 percent down. The balance can be arranged in easy monthly payments.

MRS. JOHNSON: Ten percent! That's about $38. About how much would the payments come to?

Agreement

Agreement is indicated by approval of what the salesman says and does. The buyer agrees that the proposition is appealing and has a lot to offer him. He asks for complete details, figures, and statistics.

Attention

It is easy to tell whether a client is attentive. If he is, he follows the salesman's presentation with interest. He asks questions, makes complimentary remarks and responses to the presentation. If he is bored, it will be obvious from his facial expression.

Operation

When a prospect asks questions about the operation of a product, he probably wants to be told that he is not too ignorant or non-mechanically minded to understand it. When these questions are asked, the prospect should be given full assurances and instructions. Then the salesman should attempt to obtain a decision. If the prospect picks up the item again and redemonstrates it to himself, the salesman is justified in assuming that the customer is in the process of making a decision. For example, clothing salespeople agree that a customer who tries on a coat or a dress for the second time is signaling his (or her) interest in buying.

Terms

Questions and remarks about terms reveal that a prospect has begun to consider how the purchase can be financed. It usually indicates that the prospect is satisfied with the benefits, values, and advantages of a product or service. After answering the queries, the salesman should ask for the order.

Guarantee

Questions about guarantees or warranties indicate that the prospect is satisfied with all other aspects of the product and only needs assurance that it has a long life, or that it will be replaced, if necessary. When a salesman hears the word "guarantee" or "warranty," he is receiving strong signals that the prospect wants to buy. It is time to start moving toward the close of the sale.

Service

The service inquiry is closely related to guarantee and warranty questions. It indicates that the buyer is thinking of the product as already purchased and in his possession. He is ready to discuss service facilities.

Summing Up

In most selling situations, as soon as there is a clear indication of interest in buying, the salesman should start to sum up the important points of his presentation.

The summary is a way of making as sure as possible that, when the salesman actually asks for the order, the prospect will say yes. It is his way of being sure that the prospect remembers and understands all the reasons for replying affirmatively.

So the prospect should be given a quick, clear review of the benefits that seemed to interest him most. The sales talk should be made in terms of "you and yours," and the prospect should be carefully watched to see how he reacts as each benefit is mentioned. Does he show approval? Does he seem to understand thoroughly? If the salesman is not sure he should ask a test question, "Have I made that perfectly clear?" or "So doesn't it seem logical that this should get you new customers?" This method helps to bring out any fears which may be in the back of the prospect's mind, and gives the salesman a chance to explain them away.

When salesmen have obtained agreements on every point, why shouldn't the prospect buy? It is only natural when a professional presentation has been made.

ASKING FOR THE ORDER

It has been said that more sales are lost because salesmen fail to ask for the order than for any other single reason. Although this seems ridiculous, it is quite true.

Ask for the order. This should be done without prompting. Why else do salespeople make their presentations? Professional buyers are shocked at the small number of salesmen who ask for the order.

There is an old example which illustrates this point rather well. It's about the salesman who worked hard at telling the story of his product. For over an hour he had told the prospect the entire story about his proposition. For more than an hour he had gone over it, point by point. Finally, in desperation, because he could sense he was not going to get the order, he yelled, "Why in the heck don't you buy my product?"

"Why in the heck don't you ask me?" replied the prospect. "I was ready to buy forty minutes ago."

Probing Questions

Leading the buyer to make a commitment may also come in the form of probing questions. These are usually direct questions which check, explore, or probe into the prospect's mind to determine if he is willing to buy. Probing questions are also called test or "feeler" questions. At any point in his presentation, but particularly after making each benefit statement, the salesman can ask probing questions to find out if the buyer is ready to make a decision.

Answers to probing questions inform the salesman: (1) if he is on the right track; (2) if the prospect understands; (3) if the prospect agrees with the salesman. Sample probing questions are:

"Will you OK this order now so that I can make delivery as soon as possible?"

"Is there any good reason why you should not have this just as soon as possible?"

"Would you mind okaying this order so we can take care of the installation?"

It is not always necessary to smother a prospect with facts, figures, and demonstrations before asking for his business. The prospect knows why the salesman is there. He knows that he is supposed to be asked for an order. He may even be waiting to be asked for the order. Valuable time can be saved when the order is asked for as soon as possible.

METHODS OF CLOSING

Pro-and-con Method

Many salesmen summarize their presentation and start their decision-making activities by writing out a list of the reasons for or against the proposition. For example, in one column they might include all of the prospect's reasons for wanting a later delivery. In another column they might itemize all of the reasons why the prospect will benefit from an immediate delivery. The salesman then asks the prospect to compare the two, in order to help him make the right decision. Then he asks for the order. This is sometimes called the close-by-contrast method because the salesman helps the buyer make a decision by contrasting the advantages with the disadvantages.[1]

For the prospect who wants to postpone his decision, this method is usually effective. First, it is businesslike. Second, it is convincing to the prospect. Any salesman can think of more reasons for buying now than the prospect can think of reasons for buying later.

When competition must be met, this same technique can be used. In one column, the salesman lists all of the benefits, qualities, and advantages of his own product. In the other column, he lists all of the features which the prospect likes about a competitor's product. Again, the salesman asks the prospect to compare them, item by item, and decide for himself which has more advantages.

When the prospect cannot make up his mind this technique is effective, especially when the salesman's list is longer. When the prospect compares the lists before him and the salesman reviews each item, the advantages of the other product become less significant. Here's how a salesman selling a kitchen modernization plan might do it:

SALESMAN: That about completes the story, Mrs. Miller. In view of the many benefits you will get from our new Happy House Kitchen, may I have your OK to go ahead now?

PROSPECT: Mmmm—I don't know. I think I'd like to hold off for a while.

SALESMAN: Just why do you feel you would like to hold off, Mrs. Miller?

PROSPECT: Well, I think it might work better if we remodeled a small portion at a time. Then it won't cost so much.

SALESMAN: This is a big decision for you, Mrs. Miller, and I know you want to get the most for your money. I'd like to help you make the right decision. So, why don't we think it over together. Let's list the pros and cons of doing a complete remodeling job against doing it piecemeal. Let's start with the piecemeal method first, OK? Just what big advantage can you think of in doing it this way?

PROSPECT: Well, I wouldn't have to pay as much.

SALESMAN: Are you sure about that, Mrs. Miller? Isn't it possible that you might be paying more over a period of time?

PROSPECT: Yes, that might be true. What I mean is that I wouldn't be spending a large amount of money at one time.

1. John W. Ernest and Richard D. Ashmun, *Salesmanship Fundamentals,* 4th ed. (New York: Gregg Division/McGraw-Hill Book Co., 1973), pp. 295–296.

SALESMAN: But under our convenient budget financing plan you also wouldn't have to pay a large amount at one time. However, I'll write it down as an advantage of doing your remodeling over a period of time. (Salesman writes "no large debt contracted all at once.") Are there any other advantages, Mrs. Miller?

PROSPECT: Well, as I mentioned before, when I remodel a little at a time I can take advantage of new developments as they come.

SALESMAN: Yes, you are right, but I don't think that there will be any significant new developments in kitchen appliances in the next few years, Mrs. Miller. However, let's write that down as a point also.

Now, can you think of any other advantages of remodeling a little bit at a time?

PROSPECT: No, that's about it.

SALESMAN: Fine. Now let's consider some of the advantages of doing a complete remodeling installation all at one time. First, you get a completely new and attractive kitchen with all the new and modern appliances you want right now, not years later. Isn't that important to you, Mrs. Miller? (As prospect agrees, salesman writes it down on the advantage side for complete, all-at-once remodeling).

Second, you have the services of a kitchen-planning expert and a skilled interior decorator to insure that you will get a style-coordinated kitchen. Don't you think this is a big advantage over doing it piecemeal, Mrs. Miller?

PROSPECT: Indeed I do. (Salesman then writes it down as an advantage.)

The salesman then proceeds to bring out other important advantages such as an accurate, all-inclusive estimate of cost, written guarantee, convenient financing, the immediate increase in resale value of the house, the ease of selecting the kitchen built-ins all at once, the comfort and convenience of being able to get the entire job done in only a week. When he has finished, he has a list of advantages for his proposition over five times as long as that against his proposition. He asks the prospect to review the list saying, "Now, as you look at these lists, Mrs. Miller, which proposition offers you the biggest net total of advantages?"

Minor-point Method

To discover whether or not a prospect is ready to decide in favor of a proposal, a salesman may ask the prospect for a decision on a minor point. He takes for granted that the prospect is going to buy. At a favorable moment, the salesman seeks a commitment on a minor point instead of immediately asking the prospect to make a major decision.

This method is frequently used in retail selling. The salesman asks the prospect, for instance, whether he prefers a certain jacket in blue or brown. If the question is asked in a quiet, normal manner, and with a seeming desire to be helpful, the prospect will make his color choice and move one step closer to his buying decision.

Minor decisions may be of little consequence, but when a prospect has made several of them, the salesman has conclusive evidence of his readiness to buy. If the salesman does not obtain a favorable response on a minor point, he has not lost the way to a sale. He simply continues his presentation by offering additional reasons for the prospect to buy and continues to ask for the order at frequent intervals. Other examples of minor-point questions are:

Do you wish to pay cash, or is this a charge?

Would you wish this installed in the kitchen or service porch?

Do you wish this in mahogany or walnut?

Order-form Method

The order-form method (also known as the physical action technique) is a standard method. It is based on the principle known to every stage manager that there is something almost hypnotic in the well-timed motion of actors on the stage, even when no lines are being spoken. The salesman who, during the closing phase of his presentation, calmly and unhurriedly fills out his order form, is using this principle. The prospect knows that he is well aware that the sales order is being written up if he does not stop the salesman's physical action, but the suggestion to continue is so powerful that he usually finds it very difficult to resist.

When using this method, some salesmen offer the pen to the prospect and place the partially filled-in order form in front of him, and suggest he place his signature at the bottom. Other salesmen have found it effective to ask the buyer to fill in those portions of the order form which are directly above the signature line, thus making it easy for the prospect to add his name.

Some authorities also recommend using an order book in which many orders have been recorded. This may suggest to the prospect that many others have purchased and that he too will benefit if he decides to buy.

This method of closing a sale must be tactfully employed. Many prospects who are ready to buy will be upset if the order blank is suddenly brought into view. The professional salesman keeps his order form in sight during the whole presentation, so the prospect will become accustomed to it. When the time comes, the seller fills out the order form and presents it to the prospect for his decision.

Most prospects do not like to be asked to sign the order or contract. Instead, the salesman should request the prospect to approve or okay it.

Naturally, to use the order-blank method effectively, the salesman must be aware of his prices, specifications, and other details. He can then write up the order very quickly. He also will avoid looking up or figuring the price in the presence of the prospect. Either may confuse him and cause him to delay his decision.

Name-spelling Method

The name-spelling method is a variation of the order-form method. When a salesman feels that his prospect is about ready to place an order, he should start to write the order. After the customer has become conditioned to the order blank, the salesman says: "Let's see, Mr. Smith, are your initials "E.W.""?

If the prospect answers, "No, they are W.E.," the salesman replies, "Oh, that's right." Then, he quickly follows this up with "Your address here is, ah . . ." Then, if the prospect gives him the address, the salesman hands the order blank to him and says, "Mr. Smith, would you just OK the order on this line?"

Mr. Smith is completely aware that the salesman is writing an order. If he has not decided to buy, he has to stop the salesman. But the act of writing the order helps the prospect come to a decision. Relatively few people will actually stop this kind of closing procedure.

Reversed-position Method

Sophisticated buyers who think that they know how to combat the appeals of salesmen can often be won over by the reversed-position technique. When using this method, the salesman pretends to give up the sale as lost. The prospect then feels that he can relax. Then, the salesman quickly begins a new sales appeal before the prospect has a chance to develop new resistance.

In this way the prospect is forced to reflect. If the salesman follows up his lead energetically, the prospect's mind may be diverted from resistance to a consideration of the benefits that he will derive from the proposition.

In some selling situations, this method may be quite effective. For example, when a prospect wants the salesman to leave, the salesman may act as if he wants to leave and make preparations for leaving such as picking up his hat, gathering papers together, and reaching for his briefcase. Having thus conditioned the prospect to expect a certain action, the salesman suddenly reverses himself and surprises the buyer with the exact opposite action. He does this by abruptly stopping his preparations for leaving and introducing an apparently sudden thought, such as, "Mr. Prospect, it just occurred to me that one important factor has been overlooked . . ."

The prospect is not prepared for this change of method and is off guard. This is exactly what the salesman wants. A moment before, the prospect was confident that he had dismissed the salesman. He knew exactly what he was doing and he was sure that the interview would be terminated at once.

Now the prospect is not so sure of himself, because a new situation has developed which cannot be handled effectively in his usual manner. The reversed-position method is often successful because it reverses the situation and places the prospect on the defensive.

Transfer Method

Life insurance salesmen, after building up the sale to a climax, often use the following technique: "In case anything happened to you," they tell a prospect, "can you transfer to your wife the responsibility for providing for your family? Do you really want to place that tremendous responsibility on her?"

A refusal to buy compels a "yes" to these questions — an almost impossible answer for the prospect to give. He must say "yes" to mean "no" to the order, and a "no" would mean "yes" to the order. This method also places the prospect on the defensive. It also makes his objection appear to be somewhat ridiculous.

The same technique may also be used to change the meaning of words. When a prospect tells a salesman that he is already buying the product from a friend, the salesman could reply, "That is fine. Everyone would rather do business with friends, and nowadays we're all looking for business friends. The purpose of my visit with you is to establish your company and my company on that basis."

Since the prospect wants to do business with a friend, the salesman immediately puts himself in that classification and tries to qualify as a very good friend. In this way, the obstacle may often be pushed aside and the salesman continues to assist the prospect toward making a favorable decision.

Last-chance Method

Another useful method for closing a sale is based on the principle that people often want what they cannot get. Their inability to gain what they want may be due to their inability to pay or to the limited supply of the product or service.

When appropriately used, the last-chance method is often advisable. It should certainly never be used, however, in a dishonest manner.

An example of this method is furnished by the earth-moving equipment salesman who tells his prospect about another buyer who wanted the equipment very much but was unable to make the purchase due to short supply. Thus the prospect realizes the inability of some people to purchase the item and this intensifies his desire to be among the successful applicants.

Another example is furnished by the salesman who says to a merchant, "It may be impossible to fill orders after today, since the demand for this item has been sensational and the stock is very low." Limited editions of books, limited bond issues, limited styles, limited time, limited sizes—all of these claims illustrate the use of the last-chance method.

Such limitations boost the value of the product or service, intensify the desire of many prospects, and help to crystallize desire into decisive action. It must be emphasized, however, that all statements regarding limited supply should be truthful. Professional salesmen know that it does not pay to use dishonest methods to make sales.

Focusing-attention Method

Many products and services have been sold on the value of one benefit or one feature. Often the resourceful salesman will sense, during the demonstration, that the prospect is very interested in one particular aspect of the product. When the time comes to close the sale, the salesman stresses the importance of that feature and emphasizes the benefits and values to be gained through its use. Then the salesman simply proceeds to use the direct or double question to complete the sale.

Sometimes it is difficult to determine the prospect's principal interest. If the salesman has completed his presentation, yet has received no positive response from the prospect, he could probe for the buyer's main interest and, having found it, pursue the closing of the sale with this valuable piece of information. For example:

SALESMAN: Mr. Allen, during the last hour we've gone over a number of excellent features which our roofing installation will provide you. But, for the life of me, I can't figure out what you consider the most important. Is it the neat attractive appearance of our asphalt shingles?

PROSPECT: No, they're the same as your competitors'. They're all attractive.

SALESMAN: I see. Well, is it the careful and thorough installation?

PROSPECT: Well, that's important, but I'm not particularly worried about it. I know you would do a good job.

SALESMAN: Well, then, how about the low-maintenance feature we talked about? No need for oiling or tarring and no replacement for years to come. In fact, you just forget about roof care after installation.

PROSPECT: Yes, that's what interests me. If I could just be sure that I don't have to put up with any fuss or bother maintaining this roof, I think we could work out a deal.

SALESMAN: O.K. Let's concentrate on this point, Mr. Allen. Right here in my briefcase, I have a number of case histories of customers who specifically mention how satisfied they are over the easy maintenance on our roofs. Here's a letter, for instance, from Ronald Jones, right in the next block. Do you know him?

PROSPECT: Oh sure. I know him well. Great guy.

In this example, the salesman probed for the key issue in the prospect's mind and finally found that it was the low-maintenance feature. The buyer's interest was immediately re-engaged. Now, the salesman has only to prove that the benefit does indeed exist; he intends to offer proof by using testimonial letters from satisfied users. If he handles this stage well, the decision to buy should be easy to obtain.

Implied-ownership Method

A very common selling device used by many successful salesmen assumes that the prospect has already made up his mind to buy. During the explanation the salesman makes such statements as these:

"Mr. Prospect, when this service is installed, you will find it will be a great time saver."

"You will be proud to tell your management that you can effect such a savings for them, won't you?"

"Your family will be delighted with this, won't they?"

"This would be a good location for the new_____, don't you think, Mr. Prospect?"

The salesman then goes on with a direct or double question close to bring about the prospect's decision.

Referral-to-authority Method

Salesman may find that, with all their powers of persuasion, they cannot persuade the prospect to arrive at a favorable decision. There are some prospects who will deal only with the sales managers or some other authority. These prospects feel that by doing so they are getting the best possible terms. It may be that they want a word of assurance from someone in authority. At such times, it is well to enlist the services of the sales manager, or perhaps a company officer, to help in closing the order. Frequently this note of assurance is all that is needed to obtain the prospect's signature.

Another form of this technique is to have the senior salesman or sales manager act as a consultant to determine whether, in his opinion, the proper item has been recommended. While some prospects may dislike this method, many others desire it.

Assuming-a-close Method[2]

For many salesmen, the assuming-a-close technique is the best of all. The salesman assumes, even before he faces his prospect, that a sale is certain. He feels this confidence because he thinks of his proposition in terms of service and benefits. He knows that he would not be making the call if the prospect did not qualify and if he did not have something of value to offer. He maintains this positive, buoyant attitude through every phase of his presentation. Then, after summarizing the benefits, he asks a double question. A dialogue similar to the following ensues:

SALESMAN: Do you want this shipped by rail or by express?

PROSPECT: Wait a minute, I have not bought it yet.

SALESMAN: I realize that, Mr. Brown. I was just wondering if you would be in a hurry and if we could give you good service.

2. *Salesmanship Fundamentals,* p. 297.

Now there are a few points that I am sure I have not made clear . . .

Actually, assuming the order and asking for it is not high-pressure salesmanship. If the prospect is not completely convinced of his need for the product, he will tell the salesman so, and he will also commit himself by telling the salesman why he is not ready to buy. It may be because a point was omitted from the sales talk or because something was not made clear in the buyer's mind. If necessary, the salesman should go back and emphasize again the particular points on which the prospect has not been sold.

When the salesman has done this, he once more asks for a decision, assuming that he has agreement. In most cases, the salesman will conclude a successful sale.

Doubt-elimination Method

If the salesman is not sure that the prospect is ready to buy, he should ask a test question: "Have I made that perfectly clear?" or "So does it not seem logical that this should solve your problems?" This method helps the salesman to discover any obstacles or fears which may be in the back of the prospect's mind. When he has obtained agreement on every point, there is no reason why the prospect should not buy. The only requirement at this stage of the sale is for the salesman to ask for the order.

Free-trial Method

Sometimes the salesman arranges for the prospect to sample or use the product and to demonstrate it to himself. "Take it home and try it," says the appliance salesman. "Take it out on the highway and get the feel of it," says the auto salesman. In many areas of selling the free trial method is being employed more often. Automobiles, motorboats, typewriters, newspaper subscriptions, electric appliances, and many other items are being sold by the free-trial decision-making technique. This method is based on two principles: (1) the prospect will be too thrilled with the product to return it. (2) the prospect engages in a high degree of participation and actually sells himself.

Objection Method

Nine times out of ten an objection from a prospect is really a request for more information. When a salesman gives the information and explains the benefits to the prospect, it is time to try for a close. Note in the following example how an objection is turned into a sale.

JONES: I don't know; I am not sure whether I like that one particular feature.

SALESMAN: Well, Mr. Jones, that is a very important point. But, before my company builds any product, it researches for months, even years, to be sure that it knows just what is most desirable to most people.

According to an extensive survey on the feature you mentioned, most customers have actually preferred the item because . . . (Here the salesman retells his benefits, values and advantages.) I am sure you will be very happy with this product because of these benefits. That is really important, isn't it, Mr. Jones?

JONES: I never thought of it in just that way.

SALESMAN: That is understandable, Mr. Jones, and I am glad I have been able to clear that up for you. Would you want us to deliver this week or will next week be soon enough?

If at this point Jones says, "The price is too high," the salesman could answer, "I don't blame you for thinking so because a lot of my other customers felt this way until they used it and found out that . . ." Then the salesman tells more benefits and success stories. Then again he asks for the order, probably using a subtle question.

If the prospect tells the salesman he wants to think it over, he probably expects the salesman to give him a lot of reasons for buying now. This is a good time for the salesman to use the yes-but technique and say, "Naturally, you should be sure that you are right. Now, bear in mind, while you are considering it, that this product . . ." Then the salesman is back in his sales story again with more benefits and more success stories. Another opportunity has been created to ask for a favorable decision.

Similarly, if the prospect says, "I think I will stick to the Rainbow brand because that is what my customers want," the salesman should use his yes-but technique again: "I am glad you brought that up, Mr. Brown, because lots of people feel that way and it is important. We experimented with a similar product but we feel that our product has these advantages. We find that people like a balanced product . . ." This method offers the salesman still another chance to ask for the order.

This method of helping the prospect toward a favorable decision is considered good salesmanship and it illustrates how objections can be turned into real decision-making opportunities.

Showdown Method

The showdown closing method has its values when used with the procrastinating, the lazy, and the fearful prospects. It is effective with those who repeatedly tell the salesman "see me next trip," and those who say one thing but mean another.

The showdown close is a salesman's last resort. Everything else has been tried, and still he gets no order. He forces the showdown by confronting the prospect with: "Mr. Prospect, my proposition either fits your company or it doesn't. If it doesn't, please tell me and I won't take up any more of your time. If it fits, here is the order form which I would appreciate your okaying." Better than 50 percent of prospects will probably buy. The other people are probably mere *suspects* who weren't qualified prospects in the first place. The salesman was only wasting his time. The showdown close takes courage, but often it helps to close successful sales.

Other Methods

There are other and somewhat special decision-making devices that can be used. However, enough has been written to indicate the range of possible decision-making methods. The salesman may vary his methods and even experiment a little to make sure that he is using the methods best suited to his personality, his prospects, and his product or service.

Because there are such wide ranges of personalities and behavior patterns among both salesmen and prospects, it is impossible to state that there is one method suited for everyone. The techniques which professional salesmen find most profitable for their use vary according to the particular prospect, the product or service being sold, and many other factors. *Even the best salesmen do not win favorable decisions from every prospect, but they never allow themselves to be discouraged.* They profit from their errors and gradually develop the techniques which work best for them.

WHAT TO DO AFTER

Salesmen have been told for years, "When you get the order, leave. Don't stick around and talk yourself out of the order." Undoubtedly there is some truth in the statement. Still, wide misinterpretation has caused many, many returns and cancellations.

Suppose, for example, you have approached a prospect and said,

"This product will last as long as two of the ordinary kind. Let me show you," then you demonstrate. The demonstration appeals to the prospect, he is in somewhat of a hurry, he gives you an order and you leave.

Now let's see what is liable to happen. . . . He may say to himself later, "I wonder if I didn't act too quickly in ordering that product. It certainly looked too good to be true—I wonder if there isn't a catch in it some place. Maybe it needs a lot of servicing. Perhaps I can buy it elsewhere for less."

Perhaps a competitive salesman calls on the client and is told that he has already ordered your product. So the competitor says, "Well, they are a good company, but that's a new product and I'm wondering whether it will do everything they say. It looks OK, but will it do the job you want?" His boss or his partner may say to him, "Why did you buy that stuff just on the strength of a short demonstration? Why didn't you ask him to send one to test before you ordered? It may not wear, it may break down easily."

In any of these cases, the customer is liable to cancel his order. Why? Because he has been disenchanted by the very selling points which you could have used but didn't! Wouldn't it have been wiser, after the order was written up, to have said, "Mr. Jones, I just want to say that you have bought a good product. Your employees will like it. It will do the job better than anything I know." Such after-sale assurances will keep the sale final.

Praise the Client's Judgment

No prospect will ever object to a compliment expressed about his judgment. The salesman is talking about the prospect's product, not his product. The prospect is being told what a wise buyer he is and when he accepts that kind of statement he will be very unlikely to complain later.

After the sale the salesman may touch upon some of the important selling features that were left unsaid because the sale was completed before the salesman had a chance to bring them out. One important aspect to go over with the buyer after the sale is care of the product. For example:

SALESMAN: Mr. Buyer, you have made a good decision. You will get a great deal of enjoyment and satisfaction from this new Moncata Impala motorcycle.

BUYER: I sure hope so.

SALESMAN: It will provide you with a lot of fun. Here are a few pointers on how to take care of this fine bike. First, always make sure you put the kick bar down when you are parked, this will . . .

POWER POINTS

Fear, the sensation of extreme nervousness that almost mows down many salespeople, is natural. It is similar to stage fright and, if mastered, is no deterrent to good salesmanship.

There is another type of fear that is not so easily subdued. It is the fear of asking for the order—fear of the close. A surprising number of sales managers state that many men who score high on almost every other phase of selling fall down on this part.

The enthusiastic beginner may wonder why it is necessary to lay so much emphasis on this point. Asking for the order seems the easiest and most natural act in the world. But after a few barrages of objections, excuses, and many uncompromising "no's," the question of how and when to close assumes a very different coloration.

As with most selling problems, the studious salesperson discovers the answers through trial and error. But he can at least compile a few pointers which will ease his way. Important among the pointers which have been offered in this chapter are these: *when* to close and *how* to close.

It may be proper to apply pressure when seeking an order, but never high pressure.

The order should be asked for when buying signals are flying, before the prospect shows signs of becoming cold.

If one opportunity to close is lost, or fails, another can be made. Opportunity knocks more than once in every selling situation. Opinions vary as to the number of times a close should be attempted. Some say three, some four, some more.

The greater the number of objections answered in the course of the presentation, the more likely there will be a favorable close.

If persistence antagonizes a prospect, try to make an appointment to discuss the matter again. Have a different approach for each call if possible.

Every "no!" leaves the way wide open for your competitor to reap where you have sowed.

Take pride in completing a finished job. The coping stone of a sales presentation is the order, the close.

Make sure that everything has been said and done to justify asking for the order.

When the close has been successful, the order signed and checked, a "thank-you" offered, and the customer complimented, it is time to stop and leave.

DISCUSSION QUESTIONS AND PROBLEMS

1. When should a salesman begin to close his sale?

2. What are the three forms of buying signals that a prospect gives to the salesman? Provide examples of each.

3. How do successful salesmen push for action?

4. Explain the pro-and-con method for closing sales.

5. Is it possible to achieve satisfactory results in a sale by an early close?

6. The customer is always right. Is this statement true or false?

7. Describe the minor-point method of closing. Furnish examples for closing a sale on a color television, Honda motorcycle, and an electric toothbrush.

8. How should a salesman treat the order blank in a sales situation?

9. In what way is the name-spelling method similar to the order-form method? Explain how, why, and when you would use the name-spelling method.

10. Explain how the reversed-position method of closing is used on sophisticated buyers.

11. The transfer method is used to answer objections from the prospect and then guide his decision-making. Explain how this is done. In your own words, tell how you would use the transfer method to sell a product or service with which you are familiar.

12. When properly used, the last-chance method is often advisable. Give an example of how you would use this method.

13. Briefly explain how the salesman would use the focusing-attention method of closing the sale.

14. Explain and describe how you would use the implied ownership method.

15. What should a salesman do after the sale?

16. How can a salesman handle procrastination in a sales presentation?

17. Study the following closing statements. Which statements would you consider acceptable? Which unacceptable? Why?

   a. Will you please purchase this set of books? I am working my way through college.

   b. I am sure that, if you do not purchase this lot, I can easily sell it to your competitor.

   c. How soon would you want delivery?

   d. And remember, we will be glad to service your machine absolutely without charge for the next three months.

   e. I am glad you decided to take this shirt. But do you know that the style of tie you are wearing doesn't suit you?

   f. Even if the color does not suit you, you are saving quite a lot by purchasing it.

SELLING PROBLEMS AND PROJECTS

1. Joe G. Childs Case

Day in and day out, I meet only a few different objections that delay my closing of sales. The first barrier is caused by the hesitant buyer. The second is caused by the procrastinating buyer. Here are the ways in which I close sales when I encounter these prospects:

   a. *Hesitant prospect.* He is sold but is naturally cautious, hesitant. Such prospects need a little extra push, an additional urge. To him I say: "There is only one way you will be able to enjoy the extra dollar volume that my product will give you and that is to start it working for you immediately."

   b. *Procrastinating prospect.* He wants to put it off, think it over. The job here is to get over the value, the reward of immediate action, the loss in putting it off. Here's the usual pitch. "Mr. Prospect, you've seen for yourself how our product can speed up your service and help you to serve more people than you do now. An increase of just 10 percent means 100 more people a day. As a businessman, can you afford to lose the profits this extra volume will give you between now and the time you suggest I call back? Can you afford to continue paying a premium on your operations? Don't you agree that it woud be a good idea to plug these profit leaks right now?"

Then I try to isolate the one point that usually stands in the way of the order. Next, I review the chief benefits of my product. I, then, assume that he is sold and give him a choice. For example, a choice of delivery dates, of terms, of quantities, of colors. If the prospect remains hesitant I give him a strong personal close. Here, I build up the prestige and reputation of my company and the personal reliability of myself as reasons for the prospect accepting my recommendations. I say, "Mr. Buyer, I have been calling on you for years and our company has been doing business in this area for years, and we expect to keep on doing business not only with you but also your neighbors. We wouldn't think of recommending a single proposal to you that wasn't sound, because we value your goodwill and our past business relations too highly."

Questions

1. Do most salesmen meet only two different objections? State your reasons.

2. What do you think of the devices for closing used by this salesman?

3. Do you think his closing statement results in sales?

4. Is it good practice to isolate the one point that may cause the procrastination? Why?

5. Are these closing devices used in a logical manner?

6. Will these closing devices be successful in every sales situation?

2. Bill Dewlap Case

Bill Dewlap was hot under the collar the other day when he exploded, "Too much bunk has been written decrying the 'psychological moment' and the 'sixth sense' of knowing when to close.

"Every successful salesman knows there is a 'psychological moment' and that he must have a 'sixth sense.' I've been selling for 25 years and I know that much, at least, about selling.

"There comes a time in a sales talk when a prospect's desire has been raised to such a pitch that it sticks out all over him. That's the 'psychological moment' and your 'sixth sense' tells you it's time to close the deal.

"Trial closes? Hooey! I don't need to fiddle faddle with double questions or any kind of Mickey Mouse stunts. I know when my sales talk is appealing and sound; I know all about shipping details, credit, popular styles, sizes, and prices. For my money the easiest sale is when the buyer buys as the result of a good 'hard sell.'

"This is not to say that the closing devices of other salesmen are not good. Maybe they are, but I am dubious. I claim that the closing has to come naturally from the prospect. When he wants what you have to sell, he'll buy! That's the 'psychological moment' and a good salesman has enough 'sixth sense' to know that the time to get out the order pad has come."

Questions

1. Is there a "psychological moment" in a sale? Explain.
2. Is there a "sixth" sense? Explain.
3. Are trial closes necessary? Explain.
4. Do people buy voluntarily or are they sold?

CHAPTER 18

Successful Suggestion Selling

Suggestion is a process of responding directly to a thought stimulus without the intervening thought processes which normally would occur. Salesmen interpret this definition to mean "hint, insinuate, imply, or indirectly insert into the prospective buyer's mind an uncritically accepted idea having no proof or evidence of reliability."

For a salesman, the chief difference between a reliable fact and a suggestion is that the former appeals to an individual's logic and reasoning, while the latter appeals to his emotions. In many cases, the individual's mind does not respond readily and easily to logic and reasoning even when it is overwhelmed with proof, pressure, and push. Actually, too much *proof* causes many prospective buyers to become suspicious and to erect a mental and emotional barrier against the marketeer's claims. Therefore, *suggestion selling* is very effective because it makes no claims and thereby tends to disarm any suspicions and safeguards which the buyer's past experience might have caused him to retain.

THE POWER OF SUGGESTION

The following episode illustrates the power of suggestion: A professor displayed before his class an important-looking piece of apparatus, and told them that, when he opened a valve, a peculiar-smelling gas would pour into the room. He wished to see how long it would take each student, as soon as he detected it, to raise his hand. The professor then opened the valve. Hands in the front row began to go up, then those in the next row, and soon nearly all hands in the room had been raised. Then he explained to the class that there had been no gas and no odor.

The chances are that the students who were fooled by the professor would be suspicious of any later experiments he might conduct. Whether their future reactions were associated with pleasure, pain, frustration, fear, suspicion, or any other attribute would not matter, however. Their reactions under other circumstances and with other individuals would be quite different, depending on the power of new suggestions and the apperceptive base of the individuals involved. This is explained by the conditioned reflex activity.

CONDITIONED REFLEX

There is nothing mysterious about suggestion—nothing that cannot be explained by the conditioned-reflex theory. For example, if a child is badly frightened by a barking dog, he thereafter shows fear at the very sight of a dog. This new connection in the child's nervous system is called a conditioned reflex. Pavlov, in his classic experiments with dogs as subjects, tried to separate the conditioned reflex from all other reactions he observed under laboratory conditions. From these experiments, indoctrination and orientation procedures have been developed—particularly the brainwashing techniques employed during recent years by the totalitarian governments.

Many professional purchasers of industrial items have learned to condition their own reflexes. Because some salesmen have deceived them, these men have learned *not* to respond to statements about a proposition's merits until they have first investigated the product for themselves.

The story of the old army veteran walking down the street with his arms full of bundles illustrates the importance of conditioned reflexes. When someone jokingly called "Attention!" he immediately dropped the bundles and assumed the proper military posture. He had responded to a stimulus. Suggestion selling has the same effect.

Suggested Response

There are marketing people who make claims about their propositions and offer little or no reliable proof or evidence of value. This does not mean that claims are of no value in selling critical thinkers, because they are effective with them, too, when suggestion is used as part of the claims. Everybody is influenced by the emotions aroused by suggestion. However, suggestion is much more effective when the prospect is a weak reasoner who wants to feel that he is not buying on impulse or on insufficient grounds. For example:

SALESMAN: The leader in any field cannot afford to produce anything but the best. We are the leader in our field and have a reputation to maintain. Therefore, you can be certain that our products are superior and that you will benefit by buying them.

Notice that the first sentence in this claim is one that is considered true by the prospective customer. Most suggestion selling begins with an assertion to which the prospective client agrees. The tendency is then for his mind to travel with the salesman without resistance to the desired conclusion.

Other examples of employing suggestion to short-cut critical reasoning are revealed in the following statements made by many marketing men:

A manufacturer cannot grow unless he has satisfied dealers. Our company has grown every year since it was organized. Therefore you may be confident that you will be absolutely satisfied if you join our ranks.

Everyone knows that people don't continue buying a branded article year after year in greater quantities unless that article is giving satisfaction. XYZ is selling better than ever before; therefore it is bound to give you satisfaction.

"The cheapest is the most expensive" is a common expression which could cause the buyer to challenge a reliable fact, start an argument, and induce him to think critically. It is so much simpler to bypass logic and reasoning with a suggestion such as, "You, no doubt, have often found it to be true that the cheapest item is often the most expensive."

"Ten or twelve tons should handle your requirements" is much more suggestive than the blunt statement, "You should have twelve tons to carry you."

"You want economy and low gas bills, don't you, Mr. Jones? You save on these with a compact car." This, too, is much more suggestive than the flat statement, "You save money with a compact car."

Such suggestions have almost universal appeal, since they cause a positive response without mental blocks to hinder them. Universal appeals may be considered as necessary in a marketing man's repertoire as hammers and saws in a carpenter's kit.

The following caution at this point may serve a good purpose: Suggestion words should not be confused with such hackneyed generalities as "best," "finest," "largest," "safest," and similar adjectives. Nor should they be confused with the half-truths implied in such superlatives as "stunning," "tremendous," "gorgeous," "fantastic," "breathtaking," "spectacular," and other exaggerations.

PERSONALITY AND SUGGESTION

The buyer's personality and the seller's suggestion stimulus will largely determine whether the seller's remarks are accepted. The seller must be respected by the buyer, and for this reason suggestion is most successfully practiced by a person of mature years, because people will much more readily believe and trust the ethics of such a person. Suggestibility is sometimes said to be "the emulation of ideas and attitudes." Buyers, therefore, are prone to think as the seller thinks, but usually only when they regard the latter with favor.

Even unsupported statements and claims are effective if the prospective buyer looks up to the seller. When the salesman's voice rings with sincerity and conviction, when his presentation is sprinkled with similes and metaphors, when he reveals confidence and enthusiasm, the buyer will usually feel that reliable proof is unnecessary. In fact, unsupported statements are even used at times with professional purchasers when the seller can suggest buying action through his personality.

Situations vary in their suggestive power, and persons vary in their suggestibility. Some suggestions will succeed with nearly everyone; others will get the suggested response from only the most suggestible, and the remainder will be critical, resistant, and scornful at the unsuccessful attempt to fool and deceive them.

Suggestible Conditions

Among conditions that render most persons more suggestible than usual are alcoholic intoxication, fatigue, monotonous and rhythmical stimuli, and a submissive attitude toward the source of suggestion.

Submissive attitude toward the source of the suggestion deserves an explanation. Both men and women fall into this category, but there are more submissive women than men. Women lack product knowledge and are therefore forced to submit to sales presentations. It is a rare woman, for example, who understands the mechanical construction of refrigerators, automobiles, washing machines, or power lawn mowers. Women probably know comparatively little about shelter items, and even less about certain economic principles such as finance. Therefore, since the intrinsic merits of these and many other items are very difficult for women to logically evaluate, they base the bulk of their purchasing on emotion, imagination, rationalization, and suggestions from the marketing men.

THE CRITICAL BUYER AND SUGGESTIBILITY

A salesperson who uses only generalities, similes, metaphors, and claims without proof arouses suspicion in the mind of the analytical buyer. Imagine the intelligent, reasoning individual who goes to an automobile showroom with the intent of buying a new car. After waiting several minutes for a salesman to greet him, one of them finally appeared and said, "Yes, Sir! Good car. She's a dandy, and I can give you a good price." The salesman forgot to mention benefits, hidden values, and status symbol.

The car buyer asked him the size of the tires, and he had to kneel and read the figures before he could answer. He also failed to answer practically all the buyer's questions about the product he was selling.

Under the circumstances the prospective buyer could only question everything the salesman said and did. After this performance, even the most complete proof of value and the finest kind of suggestions would have failed to convince the prospective buyer.

SUGGESTIBILITY OF QUESTIONS

Successful salespeople often use questions to suggest ideas in an indirect way. Questions that can be answered yes or no are not effective for suggesting ideas. They are called "closed-end" questions because, when they are answered, the topic is closed. The alert marketing man uses open-end questions to keep the prospect thinking uncritically. If the salesman asks, "Do you want brown shoes?" he would have asked a closed-end question, and a "no" answer would have ended the transaction. On the other hand, an open-end question would have kept the prospect talking, stimulated his desire and avoided the possibility of his asking critical questions and requesting explanations.

Questions can also be used in other ways to suggest many things. The following table illustrates how questions may be used to suggest the desired response.

Table 18-1

SUGGESTIONS	QUESTIONS
To suggest friendly attitude and common interests to a prospective buyer:	"You were in business with your brother for a few years, weren't you?"
To suggest a person who is a satisfied user of the seller's product or service:	"You know Bill Brown, the owner of Bill's Market, don't you? He's a good manager, isn't he?"
To suggest the prospect's response to the seller's reply to an objection:	"When you evaluate the savings this product offers, as well as the service, the price is relatively unimportant, don't you agree?"
To use a "trial close" suggestion to buy:	"Mr. Brown, you seem to approve of everything about this model. When would you like to have it delivered—this week, or would next week be soon enough?"
To suggest that quality is more important than price:	"But you realize, do you not, Mrs. Brown, that we carry only quality merchandise?"
To build customer confidence:	"Mrs. Jones, I'm glad you had enough confidence in our store to come in to see us. I just want to ask you one question. Did the other item have three coats of varnish?"

SUGGESTIBILITY OF SIMILES AND METAPHORS

Similes and metaphors are vivid forms of imaginative comparison that arouse interest and furnish a certain amount of convincing evidence because the prospective buyer easily understands and believes them.

The simile is a figure of speech, introduced by "like" or "as," comparing two unlike objects. Note how the following examples of similes, through their suggestiveness, offer a certain kind of proof:

"The cloth will wear like iron."
"These mutual funds are as sound as a dollar."
"This motor is as quiet as a gentle summer breeze."
". . . as solid as concrete."

The metaphor, in contrast, identifies one object with another and ascribes to one the qualities of the other without the use of "like" or "as." Samples of metaphors which possess rather high suggestibility and offer proof and evidence follow:

"These brakes are the guardian of your safety."

"This refrigerator is a penny pincher on electricity."

"This life insurance policy is the security of your future."

"This safety belt is your assurance of safety."

EFFECTIVE WORD CHOICE

As has been stated, words are one of the vehicles for transmitting ideas from one mind to another. If the word-vehicle is efficient, it quickly transmits ideas from the salesman's mind to the customer's. If it is overused, it breaks down and fails to convey the desired ideas. Actually, ineffective words are the reverse of suggestive, since they detract from the value of what is being said.

Since words are part of the marketing man's tools, they should be carefully selected and properly used in order to interest, offer proof, and convince the prospect through suggestion, with a minimum of effort. Shopworn words should be avoided. For example, in a ladies' apparel store, a saleswoman used the word "smart" thirteen times. "Smart" suggests and proves nothing. And the dictionary reveals that there are many equivalent words—lovely, clever, attractive, piquant, becoming, desirable, unusual, delightful, stylish, fashionable, distinctive.

The salesperson can find effective substitutes for many shopworn words. Instead of the word "cheap," for example, the salesperson can use "inexpensive," "moderately priced," "good value," "reasonably priced" or "excellent value." Instead of referring to a lady's purse as "nice," which is an old and uninteresting expression, he could choose stronger suggestive adjectives, like "attractive," "pleasing," "desirable," "dainty," "stylish," and "chic."

It is evident that professional salesmen analyze the features of their propositions and then select words which will effectively suggest hidden values, freshness, and exclusive qualities to the prospect's mind, and transmit them in an interesting, convincing manner.

SLOGANS

Slogans are short messages designed to be frequently repeated word for word. Slogans have high suggestibility and can be used in toto or adjusted to suit the salesman's personality and the situation. The following represent some of the best-known slogans. Note their high suggestibility.

"You can be sure . . . if it's Westinghouse."

"Cleans your breath while it cleans your teeth."

"A diamond is forever."

"A woman never forgets the man who remembers."

"The pause that refreshes."

"Get a good education."

RATIONALIZATION

Rationalization is a plausible explanation that a person gives to himself or to others to account for his own behavior or beliefs, though it may be based on motives not apparent to the rationalizer. The salesman knows, then, that prospective buyers may pretend to act for rational and creditable motives, but do not analyze their true motives. When rationalizing, the prospect acts on the basis of wish or habit, but explains his activity in logical, reasonable terms.

Quite often people who reason about their purchases want things because of a certain urge or desire, but they do not act because their critical minds fail to find a logical reason for purchasing. When that occurs, the marketing man may want to use suggestion to help the buyer rationalize. He does this by presenting a logical reason for buying which will satisfy the reasoning part of the buyer's mind. For example: a person may buy an expensive automobile to gratify his pride, but explains his act by saying that the impression of prosperity that it creates helps his business. Or, a person may want to take a trip for the pure pleasure it affords him and his family, but he justifies the expenditure on the ground that it will benefit his health.

Practical Examples of Rationalization

How does suggesting by rationalization apply to individual sales-people? Suppose that, by appealing to the buyer's pride, a salesperson had developed a situation where the buyer would like to do business with him. The buyer likes the salesperson and believes that his future business relations with him will be enjoyable; he is friendly, sociable, and respectful. Yet his logical, reasoning mind warns against making a decision on the basis the salesman presents. The salesperson would have to satisfy his critical mind by offering him proof of benefits showing conclusively that his products are superior and why it would be to his advantage to buy them instead of similar competing products. His logical, reasoning mind now satisfied, he would approve the order. Nevertheless, the primary reason for the purchase would be the prospect's desire to do business with the salesperson because he likes him, and he likes him because the salesman has appealed to his pride.

Other examples of rationalization may be found in a great many advertisements—particularly in the slogans used. For example, a well-known insurance company makes the blunt, positive suggestion that it "has the strength of Gibraltar." Many people are convinced by the boldness of this suggestion and seek no proof or evidence in the form of a certified financial statement or other facts which appeal to logic or reasoning. Using the same method, a securities salesman says, "Why work hard all your life? Make your money work for you." How many people buy stocks every year because of the assurance with which a salesman makes this kind of rationalization?

Some stores sell a limited number of prominent brands of merchandise at lower prices than their competitors. The subtle but positive suggestion is thereby made that all their merchandise must be lower priced, which may be far from the truth, but the prospective customer is nevertheless given a good start toward rationalizing. The same situation is created and the same rationalization starts when a store paints "greatest discounts" on its building or repeats the words in advertising. Without a semblance of logic or reasoning, this claim causes the typical retail buyer to rationalize himself into believing that he will save money. Actually, he rarely does.

A radio salesman suggests repeatedly and effectively throughout his sales talk, "It's the tone quality you want." An automobile salesman repeats the suggestion, "Supreme comfort and safety costs no more." A real estate salesman obtains results with the suggestion, "What good is life if you don't live?"

People also rationalize from what they have repeatedly heard suggested to them through advertising, from associates, from those whom they believe to be recognized authorities, as well as from marketing people. For example, "The flavor of Spearmint gum lasts"; "Buy now and save"; "Chesterfields satisfy"; "Ivory soap is 99-44/100 percent pure"; "This is imported and therefore has a certain rare quality." These suggested rationalizations may or may not be true. However, prospective buyers accept them as truths because of repetition, because people want to believe, because most people do not want to employ logic or reasoning before they commit themselves.

POWER POINTS

This chapter has emphasized that—under ordinary circumstances— additional statements of facts, even when presented logically and reasonably and accompanied by adequate proof, are ordinarily not enough to convince a prospect. The additional ingredient of suggestion selling is needed to complete the sale.

The power of suggestion in selling is frequently underestimated, while the power of reason and logic is often overestimated. When salesmen recognize that, through suggestion, they can deflect much critical thinking as well as awaken emotional responses, they acquire a clearer concept of the possibilities of this approach. The salesman whose product or service is merely superior does not sell as much as he could if he used more suggestion.

Suggestion selling as a method may be carried to an extreme, used where logic or thought should be employed. Nevertheless, a suggestion may be the most effective means to induce action and to remove obstructions at the conclusion of a sales presentation.

Suggestion should seldom be used to the complete exclusion of reason, just as reason should probably never be used without suggestion. Ordinarily, however, the suggestion selling method could be used by many more marketing men.

DISCUSSION QUESTIONS AND PROBLEMS

1. Define the meaning of *suggestion* as it is used in personal salesmanship.

2. Why is suggestion said to be extremely effective?

3. How does the suggestion episode about the professor and his experiment apply to a personal selling situation?

4. Give a practical example of an actual selling situation and show how the conditioned reflex enters into it.

5. Explain the principle or principles of personality and how it applies to suggestion selling.

6. Explain in detail the impact of suggestion selling on the critical buyer. How does he respond? How does the methodology employed with the critical buyer differ from that used with ordinary prospects?

7. Explain how questions may be used to suggest ideas and evoke appropriate responses. Make a list of questions which you would use to sell a product of your choice.

8. Assemble a list of descriptive words that would be effective in selling. Opposite each word write equivalent words which you believe

would be more effective for suggesting values and advantages to a prospect.

9.   What is meant by *rationalization?* Give several examples of how it is used by marketing men to influence people to buy.

10. Do you believe that suggestion selling may take unfair advantage of buyers? Why? Can suggestion selling be carried to an extreme? Why? Could suggestion selling be practiced by more salesmen? How?

SELLING PROBLEMS AND PROJECTS

---

1.   A Typical Sale

The following sale is typical for a retail salesperson. It is presented in dialogue form so that you may see and analyze each step of an excellent retail selling procedure—including suggestion selling.

The salesperson notices a customer examining a feature end display of a 32-piece dinner set and approaches the customer saying, "Good morning. That is one of our featured Cambridge dinnerware patterns."

Question:

1.   What kind of suggestion selling is used in the following narrative?

CUSTOMER: It really is beautiful, but I'm afraid it is too expensive for me.

SALESPERSON: Maybe not. You see, this dinnerware comes directly to us from the manufacturer, eliminating the dealer and jobber profits. Furthermore, all expensive advertising has been eliminated; therefore, we are in a position to save you from 25 to 40 percent on better dinnerware.

CUSTOMER: I often wondered how you could sell for less. I was always under the impression that your merchandise was of cheaper quality.

SALESPERSON: All of our dinnerware is of first quality. We only accept the best. To insure this high standard, our dinnerware must pass rigid inspections. Experts made sure that all pieces are shaped evenly, without chips, glazed smoothly, and evenly, and that patterns are uniform in both color and application.

CUSTOMER: That certainly sounds good, but tell me, is this china, or . . . how can I tell the difference?

SALESPERSON: This is Cambridge—a special semi-porcelainware, 25 percent lighter in weight than ordinary semi-porcelain.

CUSTOMER: But it looks so fragile—I'd be afraid to use it.

SALESPERSON: Yes, it does look fragile, and that is one feature that makes it so appealing. However, it is actually stronger and more resistant to chipping and cracking than similar dinnerware. Cambridge contains tremolite, a mineral ingredient which gives it the lightness and strength usually associated only with expensive china.

Question

2. What kind of suggestion selling is used in the following narration?

CUSTOMER: I really didn't know there was so much difference in dinnerware. You see, I'm planning to be married shortly and thought I'd look at chinaware.

SALESPERSON: You are certainly more than welcome to look around in my department but I do believe you have your heart set on this Cambridge dinnerware. Will you be using these dishes for company, or were you planning to use them everyday, too?

CUSTOMER: Well, quite frankly, I'm pretty sure I am getting a luncheon set and one of those bright-colored sets as gifts. Intended to use those for everyday and buy a new set for my best dishes.

SALESPERSON: Since these are mostly for special use, you'll want something nice—something you would be proud to use when entertaining your friends. (Here the salesperson goes into a little more detail about pattern and styling.)

CUSTOMER: Yes, I'm sure this is the pattern I want.

Question

3. What kind of suggestion selling is being used in the following narration?

SALESPERSON: Of course, you'll want the 95-piece set with complete service for twelve.

CUSTOMER: Oh, I'm sure I'd not be having more than eight guests at one time. I think the fifty-three piece set that serves eight will be all right:

SALESPERSON: The larger set is complete, including two-handled soup cups and square plates. You may not use the entire service for twelve, but the extra pieces are good reserve stock—if you break a piece you'll have the replacement on hand. Considering how much more you get for your money, don't you think you should take the larger set?

CUSTOMER: I would want complete service—but I hadn't intended to spend so much for dishes. In fact, I don't have that much with me.

SALESPERSON: Perhaps you would like to use our budget payment plan. You could get the whole set now and pay for it a little at a time. You will probably want glassware, too.

CUSTOMER: Well, I could do that. There are a lot of things I will need and it would be easier than paying for all of them at once.

SALESPERSON: Let me show you some of the goblets we just received. They would really look good with your dinnerware. (The salesperson brings a goblet, a sherbet glass, and a plate to match and arranges a single place, adding a 24-piece set of glassware to the 95-piece dinnerware order.)

Question

4. What kind of suggestion selling is used below?

SALESPERSON (after closing the sale): Please come in again. I will be only too glad to help you select the kitchen utensils that you will need.

CUSTOMER: Thank you, you've been very nice. I certainly will come to you for whatever I need.

SALESPERSON: You might walk through our furniture and drapery department—we have some beautiful things there, too. I am sure you will find whatever you need at our store, and I know you will be well pleased with the merchandise.

2. Ruby Shoe Company Case

A Ruby Shoe Company salesman checked into his hotel, arranged his samples in a showroom, and then went to Main Street to call on dealers to whom he had sold shoes on his previous visit. The first dealer on whom he called was busy, so the salesman waited in his outer office for about thirty minutes. Finally, however, the dealer's business slowed down long enough for the salesman to invite him over to the hotel to look over the shoes he had on display.

DEALER: I really can't make it today. We're terribly busy and I'm short two shoe-fitters. I just don't see how I can leave even for a few minutes.

SALESMAN: But you should see my line, the best buys I've had for years.

DEALER: Well . . . bring your samples over here and I'll look them over. 'Bye for the moment—I've got two customers over there waiting for me.

SALESMAN: But for heaven's sake, man, you can't expect me to bring all that merchandise over here . . . trunks full of samples . . . can't you drop over after closing up?

DEALER: No, not today or tonight. I'm slated for a business meeting after closing here. This is my busy season, you know.

SALESMAN: Sure, it's my busy season, too. I'm leaving town tomorrow, and you don't get a chance to see merchandise such as mine very often. I just can't bring all those shoes over here. If you want to buy right, you'll have to come over to the hotel.

DEALER: I told you once I couldn't come. (Getting hot under the collar.) And don't bother me about it any more. Good-bye. I've got to take care of my customers.

SALESMAN: Well . . . it's your loss if you don't want to see the best merchandise that's come to town for months.

Questions

1.   In the light of what you have learned about suggestion selling, what do you think of the behavior of this salesperson? His attitude? His perception? His sympathy?

2.   How would you have handled this buyer? Why?

CHAPTER 19

Closing on
Call-backs

In general, there are two types of call-backs: (1) those on prospects who have failed to buy on previous calls and (2) those on customers the salesman wishes to retain and develop into better customers.

Although a sale may not be closed on the first call, the salesman should not assume that no sale will ever be made with that client. Many sales cannot be made in one call, and this simply necessitates another interview. Quite often the inability to bring a sale to a successful close occurs because the prospect must consult with other persons (partner, top management) before a decision may be reached. If a salesperson has reason to believe that eventually he will obtain results, he should follow up by trying to arrange a definite time and place for another interview.

TIMING OF FOLLOW-UP CALLS

The timing of the follow-up call should be planned. If a call is tried before the prospect has finished his consideration of the proposition, it could have the effect of delaying the decision. When such a situation develops, the nature of the call should be changed to a summary of the presentation, or a review of a particular advantage of the product. The salesman should not attempt to close the sale at that time.

A call summarizing the points of the presentation should be followed by additional short calls to inquire if the client has come to a decision. When the client gives a positive signal of his intention to purchase the product, an attempt to complete the sale should be made. If he does not buy, then more calls may be necessary. The salesman should remember that the cumulative effect of many calls is more decisive than the minor effect of a single call, providing that the calls are at short intervals so that the prospect is able to remember previous presentations.

Follow-up calls should be well timed. The effectiveness of the first call can be lost if the second call is made past the time when the prospect remembers the presentation. Timing calls will depend on the product being sold, the strength of the impression made in the previous call, and the prospect's recall power. While it is not possible to state the length of time which should elapse between calls, it is safe to state that calls made too frequently will not be effective and can possibly annoy a client. Conversely, if a long interval were to occur, it would be necessary to conduct the interview as though no previous call had been made. The right time to call is determined by examining the results of calls at different periods of time, until a pattern is discernible.

In the interval between calls, the presentation can be reviewed in the light of experience with the prospect. In this way the salesperson can determine where his sales talk was ineffective and where it was effective, and at what point he had gained the prospect's interest and how his product benefits might solve the prospect's problems. This advance preparation should enable him to capitalize on the facts gained during his initial call, and use them as aids in future calls.

Methods for Follow-up Calls

Nothing should be taken for granted on follow-up calls. Between calls the salesman should assume that the prospect has usually forgotten the salesman, his company, and everything that he has said. The prospect has seen many other people since the last interview and he has had many problems to solve. Therefore, the salesman should reiterate as much sales information as he would offer a new prospect.

The methods to be used in follow-up calls are practically the same as those used for the first call on a prospect. The salesman approaches and greets the prospect first, and then proceeds to build up interest, desire, and conviction in the prospect's mind as a preliminary to the decision to buy.

Often, too much is taken for granted when making repeat calls, a natural reaction but it can be a pitfall. On every call, new or repeat, a creative sales job must be done. At least one important benefit must be offered the prospect and the salesperson must be prepared to go through each step of the sale. The benefit must consist of a new product, or idea, that will help both prospect and salesman earn more money. The job is not only to sell a product or service, but also to help the prospect make a success of his business.

Questions

In follow-up calls, if the salesman uses a question to which the prospect can easily answer no, he is unnecessarily handicapping himself. It is better to start a follow-up presentation by saying, "Last time I talked with you, your problem was one of price. Is that still so, Mr. Brown?"

The prospect must say yes. By presenting the customer's difficulty in the form of a question, the salesman has avoided a negative beginning in the follow-up.

Meeting an Obstacle

When the salesman knows that he is going to meet an obstacle on a follow-up call, he should bring it up himself before the prospect has a chance to get it out in the open and create a difficult situation. This approach is often useful for dealing with the price-minded buyer.

For example, the salesman can say, "I have been thinking about the price and I wonder if we should not look at it from this angle." Then the salesman makes a different and more interesting presentation based on the topic of price. He also may mention new benefits to the prospect and thereby re-create his interest. Most important of all, the salesman does not have a "no" to surmount before he launches into his presentation.

Typed-order Method

Salesmen often use the typed order form on a follow-up when they have been unsuccessful in closing the order on a previous call. It may be that the prospect has put off the salesman by saying something like: "See me tomorrow"; or "See me next week"; or "I'm too busy now."

A neatly typed order has a compelling effect on many prospects because it indicates a confident attitude on the salesman's part. Even more important, it saves the prospect from making a decision; the typed order form has done it for him. However, the typed order method, when used by young and inexperienced salesmen, is a dangerous one. Many purchasing agents are extremely independent and resent this type of approach. Consequently, this approach should be used only after the salesman has acquired the finesse and judgment that is accompanied by experience.

New-approach Method

The new-approach close can frequently be used on a follow-up call when the salesman has been unsuccessful previously. If he has failed to obtain the order, he should review again the needs of the prospect and tell him how the product or service can fulfill those needs. Many orders may be obtained from an apparently hopeless situation by presenting a new approach: "Mr. Prospect, in presenting our product to you the other day, there is one point which I entirely overlooked and I feel that this feature should be explained to you more thoroughly."

It is usually best to concentrate on one feature when using the new-approach close. If the salesman finds that this is not successful, it is easy to extend his explanation to other benefits of the product or service. And he always remembers to ask for the order before leaving!

Repeat Calls on Regular Customers

In calling back on regular customers, the salesman should be eager to continue his development of friendship, but on a business basis only. He knows that personal friendships lead to familiarity and familiarity may lead to trouble.

Only a few minutes at the start of the interview are necessary for reestablishment of the respectful relationship built up during previous calls. The procedure may vary, but after the friendly greeting, the salesman may offer suggestions about a new development in the prospect's industry, or a new merchandising or display idea which he has observed during his travels. Attention to such things may distinguish the professional from the mediocre salesman.

In this area of thought, the importance of trifles should not be overlooked. Perhaps the salesman has certain *mannerisms,* such as nervously beating a finger on the prospect's desk or slouching in his chair, that may irritate the buyer. The salesman should guard against them and other unconscious mannerisms; business relationships are quite fragile, easily damaged or destroyed.

Persistency of Purpose

There may be times when the repeat call has served its full purpose, because the salesman has reestablished his friendship with the customer. He makes what is known as a courtesy call and in some instances, unwilling to trespass on the time of a busy man, the salesman departs without an order. Generally, this situation is not typical, because the salesman usually wants an affirmative decision regarding a new promotion, the ordering of new merchandise, or additional items.

Persistency of purpose means that the salesman never loses sight of the fact that he is there to sell. In call-backs on regular customers, the temptation is strong for the salesman to say to himself, "Oh, I've told this man my story before; I've told it ten times today and I'm tired of it." The best cure for this attitude is for the salesman to remind himself that a number of competitive salesmen have interviewed the customer since he last saw him. Also, he should be aware that memory is short and that very few customers remember more than a fraction of what they are told on any one call. It is essential in every repeat call to establish again the prime reason for the call. A good salesman realizes that what may be old to him may be new and interesting to the prospect.

Refractory Phase

According to the *refractory-phase principle,* there will be times when less sales effort will be needed than usual. At other times the prospect will buy if a little more sales effort is applied. This is known as the *relative refractory phase.* At other times, no amount of selling effort will induce a prospect to buy. This kind of buyer would be in an absolute *refractory phase.*

For example, if a person has just purchased a new Cadillac and he is thoroughly satisfied with it, the salesman may assume that he is in an absolutely refractory phase. It is probable that no amount of persuasive appeals will, for a time, make him buy a new car. However, as the months and years of usage accumulate, the car owner's attitude changes and, although he really does not need to buy a new car, the time will arrive when he will buy if a good salesman persuades him. A good trade-in, a new model, or some other incentive may cause him to buy when otherwise he would not even listen to a sales talk.

The auto owner, for example, is in an *absolute* refractory phase when his car is brand new; he refuses to think of purchasing a new car until he has used it for not less than one year. Even if great persuasive pressure is applied during this time, the salesman will ordinarily not close a sale. When new models appear, his attitude may change a bit. During this time the buyer would be in a *relative* refractory phase. However, immediately after he has paid to have the car repaired or repainted he would probably resolve to make the car last for another year or more. When he is in this frame of mind, he may again be in an *absolute* refractory phase and therefore need greater persuasive pressure to induce him to buy.

How much persuasion, how much pressure to apply will depend on a consideration of the *refractory principle*. It should be realized that sometimes no amount of persuasive sales effort will be successful, while at other points differing degrees of persuasion will be needed. When the salesman has properly assessed the prospect, he will know how much persuasion to apply. The amount of persuasiveness to use will be dependent on the fact that the salesman is the middle man between his employer and the prospect. He cannot employ so much forceful persuasion that he becomes obnoxious to the prospect and thereby prejudices future calls; he cannot sell at a loss to his employer; and he cannot waste his time on prospects who are not ready to purchase.

METHOD BETWEEN CALLS

Keeping prospects interested between calls is every bit as important as keeping prospects alert during a sales talk. Experience has taught salesmen that they must use the method of communicating that is most suitable to the individual client. Sometimes a letter is most appropriate, sometimes a telephone call, and occasionally a telegram is the best method. Salesmen learn to pace the attention they give to customers; some customers deserve more between-call attention than others. Remember that customers, like all people, appreciate attention and being acknowledged. It is dangerously easy for an aggressive competitor to wean away customers in the period between the salesman's calls.

Letters are possibly the first and most obvious method of recalling a salesman to the customer's mind. A note may merely acknowledge a courtesy or express thanks for an order. A letter that includes something other than routine matters is most appreciated—for example, outline the way your product can be adapted to the customer's problem, or enclose a clipping about an industry trend, or describe an outstanding sales promotion or a window display that could be applied to the customer's own business.

Company sales aids, such as direct mail and point-of-sale handouts, are also appropriate at this time. This material can often be enclosed with an effective personal letter, not with the idea that literature can close a sale, but to remind the customer that the salesman is thinking about him. Usually it is advisable to direct the reader's attention to items of special interest.

Greeting cards for holidays and for a personal or business birthday or anniversary are effective methods of contact between calls. It is well to keep a carbon copy file on such mailings so they may be reviewed in connection with other records in advance of the next call-back.

The occasional friendly telephone call should include a worthwhile message, to justify using the prospect's time. The customer should be asked if he is free to talk. Otherwise, the salesman may unwittingly intrude when the prospect is tied up with something and in no mood to chat.

Promises

Probably the most important factor about these interim contacts is to be constantly alert to fulfill the most trivial promises. A promise made to a customer should be kept. If, during the interview, a promise was made to send the customer a quotation on price, for example, a written note of the commitment should be made and the promise kept as soon as possible. Nothing contributes more to the deterioration of business confidence than a history of unkept promises.

It should not be understood that anything in the foregoing paragraph implies that a salesman should be sycophantic, for that is not the way to build esteem. However, a good salesman never forgets his role as problem-solver and counselor. The customer-salesman relationship must rest on a sturdy foundation.

RECORDS

The heart of a salesman's work is *systematization*. Throughout this text the need for systematic review of personal attributes, of territory organization, and of selling time has been stressed. In the same way, the successful salesman recognizes that he cannot keep in mind an encyclopedic index of information about a host of customers, so he gives constant attention to the records on which repeat calls are based.

Many records come to him at regular intervals from his company. They are indispensable, because they show such items as past purchases and credit ratings. Equally important are his own records, which relate to many details of no direct concern to management. The salesman's aim should be to make every customer record card a complete history of all his contacts with the customer, both in person and by mail. Immediately following each personal contact with a customer, the salesman should record the nature of the interview, and include not only the transaction completed but also the customer's personality, habits, motivations, hobbies, new business possibilities, new objections, when to follow up, and many other factual details.

SELF-ANALYSIS

Customer record cards may contain evidence of self-analysis on the part of the salesman. They might show answers to such questions as:

- Where was I strong during the interview?
- Where was I weak?
- Did I contribute anything toward helping the customer with his problems?
- Was my presentation complete? If not, what was overlooked?
- Did I work toward a favorable decision or am I softening up with this customer because of personal friendship?

COMMON COMPLAINTS

Credit refusal by the home office is a common complaint. For example, "Last year your company refused to grant me credit; my honesty was questioned; my financial standing was damaged. Why should I give you an order and be insulted again?" It is possible that this complaint was justified. The credit reference may have been handled as a routine affair and the refusal may have been due to carelessness or oversight on the part of a credit department clerk. The basis for handling a complaint like this is to assure the complainant that a company credit policy and procedure is not a personal affair and that it is never used to insult a prospect or customer. The customer should also be assured that the situation will receive his personal attention and be corrected if possible.

Poor service is another common complaint. "Your service is terrible" has been heard by practically every salesman. Service embraces every phase of a business operation; therefore, the salesman must discover what was "terrible." Was it delivery, refunds, allowances, exchanges, or an overcharge? What is the real cause of the complaint?

If the buyer has mistaken ideas about the company's policies and services, the salesman should explain *why* they were adopted. He should promise to forward the facts to the home office, to follow up and try to have the situation corrected. Service complaints should be taken seriously and the prospect given the understanding that the salesman is taking a genuine interest in his problem.

Refund and allowance complaints are not only serious; they also represent wasted effort and they are costly. Nearly always these complaints arise as the result of poor sales techniques and it is usually safe to imply that they occur because of the salesman's lack of skill.

These are only three of the common complaints, but they should serve as examples heard every day by salesmen. Furthermore, the technique for handling complaints can be reduced to something resembling a formula.

HUMAN RELATIONS FORMULA

Practically all complaints and grievances can be handled through the human relations formula. Professional salesmen say that they have to give attention to the all-important factors of *human relations,* particularly when dealing with complaint situations. These salesmen know that complaint handling is an important part of their work. If there were no complaints, much of their work would be unnecessary and it would be difficult to justify their employment.

Professional salesmen know that they will never succeed in handling all complaints, but they know that they will have a 90 percent better chance of succeeding if they base their procedure on the following human relations formula:

- Relax emotionally and physically—but not mentally.
- Listen to the complaint.
- Protect the buyer's pride.
- Show sympathy.
- Use assurance words and phrases.

Relaxation

Prospects and customers usually complain because they resent inconveniences and loss of money; also, they fear that the salesman will not make a just settlement. When the salesman relaxes emotionally and physically, it is contagious. When prospects observe his relaxed manner, they too will relax and lose much of their skepticism and fear. The salesman should then have little difficulty in making a good presentation.

Listening

A professional salesman listens when a customer or a prospect wants to air a grievance. The salesman lets the prospect do the talking because he can usually siphon off most of his steam. Salesmen can almost see customers deflate like a balloon, while they listen. Actually, some salesmen even encourage a customer to get everything off his chest by asking questions and then listening sympathetically to his answers.

Usually, a prospect's grievance or complaint is exaggerated. The salesman often finds that it is imaginary. He may recieve many complaints, only to find out that it was another salesman's product or service that had given the trouble. Quite often it is the way the customer used the salesman's product or service that created the complaint. Relaxed listening allows the customer to air his grievances and clarifies the atmosphere so that the salesman can again start to close a successful sale.

Protecting Buyer's Pride

Most people dislike to admit that they are wrong. Once they have taken a position, it is hard for them to retreat; their pride is at stake. A professional salesman will never try to prove anyone wrong, particularly to a customer, or a prospect for his product or service.

If the salesman tries to prove that a customer's attitude is unusual or silly, he does the one thing that will certainly encourage the complainer to maintain it. But if the salesman shows that he respects the complainer's position and understands why and how he happened to get that way, he makes it easy for the complainer to come down to earth and agree with him.

All salesmen must be careful to protect the other person's pride. Even after the complaint is satisfactorily solved, they must guard against any impression that might reflect against the prospect's good opinion of himself. When a complaint is handled in this way, the customer feels that he was the smart one who had all the answers and the salesman nearly always turns such a complainer into an enthusiastic booster for himself, his product, and his company.

Sympathy

People crave sympathy. When a salesman has a sympathetic, understanding attitude, he can take the complainer off the offensive. A professional salesman shows by his attitude that the customer is worth listening to. He always listens attentively and when the complainer has unloaded his mind, he gives the salesman a chance to come in with his explanation and close a successful sale.

The following solutions for complaints are always used by professional salespeople and they seldom fail. First, when things go wrong—when the customer is in trouble—come through with super-service; right then is the time to smother trouble. A professional sales-man will jump into his car and rush over to see the customer because he knows that the troubleshooter can build real friends. When the salesman himself is in a predicament—in real trouble—he likes the person who will "be right over." Any salesperson likes to be treated this way and so do his customers.

The professional salesman gets to the trouble and stays with it while it is hot. He knows that someone will be burned and it may be him! A complaint, properly handled, can tip the scales in favor of the salesman and turn the resenter into a booster.

Experience has shown that in ninety-nine complaints out of a hundred, the product or service is not to blame. Most complaints are caused by misunderstandings rather than any failures of the product or service. Therefore, a professional salesman would offer a solution for a complaint, and then sell his solution in the same way as he did the first sale to the customer. Finally, the professional would never have an "I-told-you-so" attitude when dealing with a customer.

Using Assurances

In explaining away complaints, questions, excuses, alibis, and delays, the good salesman tries to use assurances. He uses assurances that suit his personality. He is never afraid of repeating his assurances. And he is sure that they are said naturally and expressed with quiet confidence. To dispel complaints, to banish suspicion and fear, many successful salesmen use assurances like these before they give a direct answer:

"That is a perfectly natural thought . . ."

"I can understand your viewpoint . . ."

"Yes, I see your position . . ."

"I am glad you brought that up . . ."

HOLDING CUSTOMERS

Salesmen can often keep a sale merely by using a little common sense and good human relations. One of America's top sales managers used to say, "Make the presentation stay presented." What he meant was that many an order that is written up is never delivered because the customer changes his mind. This would not happen if the customer had been thoroughly sold.

For years sales managers have told their salesmen, "When you get the order, leave — do not stick around and talk yourself out of the order." Granting that there is some truth in the statement, still it has been widely misinterpreted and has been the cause of many, many returns and cancellations. Successful salesmen know that a sale is not really closed until the customer knows how to use the product, or how to sell it to his trade. When a salesman tells his whole story his commissions increase because he will then have his customers working for him and his follow-ups and cancellations will drop almost to zero.

POWER POINTS

It usually pays to call back on both customers and prospects. Call-back is also spelled "repetition" and repitition is generally thought of as dull and unimaginative. However, repetition is imperative if you want your message to stick. There are some thought-provoking facts about repeat calls and call-backs. These facts were part of a study made of a group of people by Walter Dill Scott of Northwestern University and several psychologists. They discovered that:

1. 25 percent of all people forget an impression in one day.
2. 50 percent of all people forget an impression in two days.
3. 85 percent of all people forget an impression in three days.
4. 97 percent of all people forget an impression in four days.

What implications do these facts have for salespeople? Salespeople, for example, will have to make a great many more callbacks to counteract this human tendency to forget. Speak your piece at least three times, but with a different approach each time. That will make the message stick.

Plan it so that you will be expected and welcome when you call back. It is better for you to be able to say to a receptionist, "Mr. Chillicothee told me to come by to see him on my next trip to Pittsburgh. I phoned yesterday to arrange for a brief interview at about this time. Is he free yet?" Otherwise you might have to sell yourself all over again, even to get past the receptionist. Orders established through strong call-backs can develop into a salesperson's strongest accounts for the close of one sale can be the start of another.

If something has gone wrong, don't waste time with alibis, even if it is not your fault. To the customer you *are* your company; so go to bat for your customer. Listen to his complaints as carefully and attentively as if they were sales objections. Hear him out, don't interrupt. Then, decide on the proper adjustment procedure for his case.

Most people are honest and most complaints are genuine. However, when you do get a chronic complainer, defend your company. That kind of customer is not likely to buy from you again anyway. Actually, while a sale is a sale, one like this can be too costly in time, energy, and damaged reputation. Settle the claim fairly, then write him off the books. You don't need him!

DISCUSSION QUESTIONS AND PROBLEMS

1. What are the essential differences between *follow-up* and *repeat calls* on prospective customers?

2. Describe each of the following decision-making techniques and tell how they are used with call-back and complaint activities:

    a.   Typed order

    b.   Referral to authority

    c.   New approach

3. What is the relation of the refractory-phase principle to call-backs on customers?

4. Explain how the "idea-sequence" is related to call-backs.

5. What is meant by persistency of purpose and how is the concept used in call-back activities?

6. Explain how you would use each of the five items in the human relations formula.

7. Why should the salesman introduce potential obstacles early in the follow-up or repeat call? Should a repeat call be handled like a completely new presentation? Why?

8. How are assurances used to relax prospects and win them over to the salesman's side?

9. During the first few minutes of repeat calls on established accounts, how would you keep the interview on the track, and eliminate any possibility of the buyer thinking, "I have heard your story before. Why tell it to me again?"

10. What methods might be effective for "keeping customers hot" or warmed up between calls?

SELLING PROBLEMS AND PROJECTS

---

1.   The Perturbed Salesman Case

It was easy to see that this mild-looking gentleman was perturbed. He was raving mad, as a matter of fact — a thing no salesman, whose life is involved in being pleasing to others, should ever be.

I calmed him down, and asked him to tell me what was bothering him. It was routine — an old customer had become a "quit."

When the salesman had called earlier in the afternoon, for what he expected would be an easy order — what is called in selling a "wrap-up" — he received, instead, the information that the customer had just placed the order with a competing firm.

"I've had that fellow for ten years," the salesman told me. "He was my best customer. I did my best to keep him. No one ever gave a man better service. And now that's all the thanks I get out of it."

He was bitter toward the duplicity of his best customer. "The idea that a guy I've treated like a brother would cross me up like that!"

I pointed out that losing customers is no sin. All salesmen lose customers.

"But there's one sin in connection with losing a customer that I hope you never commit," I told him.

"What's that?"

"The sin of not going back and inviting the customer to be your customer once more."

"Do you mean I should go back and ask that heel to buy from me again?" he demanded. "What do you think I am? I wouldn't go back to call on him again if he were the only customer on earth."

"And if you persist in having that attitude," I told him, "pretty soon there won't be any customer on earth — for you, anyway."

Then I told him the philosophy of the really topflight men in selling. It boils down to this:

There isn't anything more important that a salesman can do than to hold a customer once he gets him. If a customer, for any reason at all, or for no reason at all, decides to quit, it's the salesman's duty to go to him — at once — and ask him to come back, no matter how humble he must be, how much saying the words stings his throat.

After all, a salesman is a professional manufacturer of customers. Every time he loses one it is a black mark on his shield.

Questions

1.   What is the basic thought in this case?
2.   How would you deal with this kind of customer? Why?

2.   John Perrins and Sam De Ventas Case

John Perrins sold stationery supplies to retail store managers. He was easily influenced by prospects who'd say, "See me some other time" or "Come back later." John would give up quickly and leave.

Although John had more than the average number of call-backs to make, he did not discourage easily. Many of his prospects simply repeated their suggestion that he call again. Others strongly objected at the time, but did not exactly discourage a call-back.

Nevertheless, John continued to fail on his call-backs. He finally asked Sam De Ventas to give him some advice. De Ventas found that John would start out by saying, "Well, Mr. Prospect, have you changed your mind?" He also found out that many of John's prospects would sit back, smile, and reply, "No. I haven't changed my mind yet."

So, John would leave, saying something like, "Well, someday you will, and when you do, be sure to think of my proposition. Here's my card again." De Ventas remarked that many of the prospects possibly took the card, laughed to themselves and thought, "That guy is never going to sell anything."

Questions

1.   What is John's most obvious mistake in his call-back method?

2.   What should John have done first and how should he have done it?

3.   What could John say that would tend to lead the prospect toward an agreement to buy?

PART

FOUR

SPECIAL
SALES
SITUATIONS

CHAPTER 20

Creative
Retail Selling

Much of a retail salesperson's effectiveness will depend on how he starts his presentation of the merchandise. In this respect, there are three broad rules to observe:

1. *Cleanliness.* This means not only personal cleanliness, but also a neat counter, orderly stock, and attractive displays.
2. *Promptness.* Every customer should be approached and greeted promptly as soon as he or she enters a store or a department. Nothing irritates a prospective customer more than to be ignored while the salespeople engage in conversation, housekeeping, or bookwork.
3. *Showmanship.* This begins with a greeting which can range from "Good morning, Mrs. Doe" to "May I help you?" or even to a pointed reference to a product that has caught the customer's eye.

PRESENTING THE PRODUCT

After the greeting, the salesperson shows the merchandise. For example, if the salesperson happens to be selling furniture, he can determine what the customer is interested in by saying something like, "May I show you some of our new easy chairs, Madame?" If the customer does not want easy chairs, she will usually tell the salesperson why she came in. The primary reason for the question is to discover if there is a specific product that the customer is looking for.

If she indicates that she is just browsing, the salesperson can say, "Fine, we are glad to have people look. I will be glad to answer any questions." The customer's attention may also be directed to a nearby display or item of merchandise.

The salesperson may ask the customer if she is interested in fine chairs and may receive only a nondescriptive answer in reply, such as "chairs" or "tables." More questions will then be necessary to pin down the type of chairs or tables that the customer wants. However, the salesperson should not ask bluntly, "What kind of chairs?" Instead, he should ask, "Something for your living room?" If this draws a "yes" reply, he can then find out whether the customer wants a pull-up chair, a lounge chair, a rocker, or an occasional chair.

As soon as the customer indicates the type of merchandise he wants, he should be led directly to it. The merchandise that the salesperson believes the customer may like should then be selected and the sales presentation started.

What Does the Customer Want?

The first merchandise shown by the salesperson is usually to explore or probe the customer's preference. Few customers will have decided in advance exactly what they want. They may know only how much they can spend, but be open minded on style, design, color, and utility. Or color or style may be the determining factor, and price a lesser consideration.

In any case, the salesperson will have to find out what is in the customer's mind. Probably the easiest way for the salesperson to do this is to pick one piece of merchandise he thinks the customer may want and then begin his sales talk. The salesperson can soon tell what is uppermost in the customer's mind from the customer's questions and reactions to his presentation. If no interest is shown in a particular item, it is generally advisable for the salesperson to direct the customer's attention to another piece of merchandise.

The Starting Price

Suppose a customer wants merchandise that comes in several price ranges. Which should be shown first? The safest plan is to show merchandise in the middle-price range. The salesperson can then work up or down the price scale according to the customer's preference and ability to pay.

If the salesperson begins with his lowest-priced merchandise, he may lose the chance of selling better merchandise at a higher price.

It is very difficult to switch a customer from the lowest price to the very highest price. Also, a sensitive customer may be offended if the salesperson immediately shows him the lowest-priced merchandise he has in stock. Finally, the difference in price between the lowest- and the highest-priced merchandise may create an artificial barrier to a successful sale. The reason for this is that the customer is suspicious that he will be paying too much or getting a low-quality product.

On the other hand, if the salesperson begins with his most expensive goods, he may discourage the customer, especially if the goods are beyond the price that the customer is willing to pay, and lose the sale. Or he may make his "economy" line appear cheap in comparison, forcing the customer to go elsewhere.

Beginning with goods in the middle-price bracket is usually the most sensible. If the customer indicates an interest in something better, the salesperson can easily switch to higher-priced goods. If something less expensive is wanted, the customer will not be as hesitant about going to the lower price range as he would be in jumping from the highest to the lowest.

Consequently, if it develops that the customer wants something definite in color or style, it is easier to satisfy these qualifications if the salesperson can offer something that costs a few dollars more or less than the original price the salesman suggested.

THE RETAIL SALES TALK

Many businesses, such as house-to-house selling concerns, use a "canned" sales talk, that is, a sales talk that is memorized. Because a retail salesperson may sell many varied items, a canned talk may not work for him. Like the outside salesman, the retail salesperson must apply selling techniques to suit the customer and the merchandise.

It usually pays the retail salesperson, however, to develop a general pattern which can be adapted to fit the individual sale. In this way, he is sure of covering his entire selling presentation.

A good retail salesperson should make it a rule to cover all his sales points in a way that represents the viewpoint of the customer. The following sales points cover the major interests of the customer, even though motives for buying may vary with the merchandise.

Enjoyment—Because many items are bought chiefly for enjoyment, the salesperson may want to concentrate on the ways in which the product can be enjoyed if it applies to his merchandise.

Appearance—Appearance is very important to the customer who is proud of his or her personal appearance or home, and should be employed in the sales presentation when applicable.

Convenience—Convenience is an important motive for many women customers and should therefore be stressed when selling merchandise such as furniture, appliances, hardware, and similar items.

Quality—The salesperson may also talk about the quality of the product. Since this is an important factor with careful buyers, the salesperson should stress the manufacturer's reputation, the store's guarantee, and the durability, appearance, style, and other attributes of the item. Most better grade merchandise is sold on the basis of quality.

Price—Price should not be discussed until the last, unless the customer lets the salesperson know at the beginning that the price is of utmost importance. The customer's desire for the goods should be developed, and if the goods are wanted badly enough, price usually is a secondary consideration. It should be recalled that price is justified only on the basis of quality. Therefore, the salesperson must be ready to show where the value lies. If the customer demands to know the price, the salesperson should tell him and not evade the issue. If he thinks the price is too high, the salesperson can say, "Yes, but let me show you why it is worth it." The customer's attention can also be directed to a lower-priced item.

A customer should be given all of the facts available on a product, with emphasis on its benefits. Usually, one of the points mentioned above will appeal to him. As soon as the salesperson notes which benefits seem to impress the customer most, he should concentrate on those particular benefits. Stressing only one or two points about a product can result in a favorable buying decision.

SHOWING AND DEMONSTRATING

Very few important products are sold by merely looking at or hearing about them. In nine cases out of ten, showing and demonstrating influence the customer to buy. A customer will be induced to buy costume jewelry if the jewelry is demonstrated or if she tries it on and sees how much it improves her appearance. She is persuaded to buy an easy chair because it is comfortable when she sits in it. She is inclined to buy an appliance after she tries it out.

No matter what the product is it can be sold more easily when it is shown or demonstrated. A man should not only be told that he would look good in a blue suit but also that he should try it on and find out for himself. In buying an automobile, the customer should be encouraged to test-drive the car to experience the ease of handling and quick acceleration.

How to Demonstrate

While the salesperson is talking, he should let the customer share in the demonstration of a product. This will provide an opportunity for injecting many questions that bring affirmative answers and lead to a decision to buy. Also, the customer gets a feeling of ownership from trying out the items. He sees the benefits that the merchandise has to offer.

Whenever a salesperson talks about his merchandise, he should handle it at the same time. The customer should also be encouraged to touch, feel, smell, or try the merchandise. For example, if the item has a pleasant odor, like soap or perfume, the salesperson should persuade the customer to smell it. The salesman should always handle the merchandise carefully and knowledgeably.

When the retail salesperson is showing or demonstrating an item, he should stand behind or beside the product and talk toward the customer. The customer can then see him and the merchandise at the same time. Also, the salesperson can see the customer's reactions to each sales point that he has offered.

SUGGESTION SELLING

The salesperson often gains command of the sale from the start by using suggestion selling in a greeting. He may say to an approaching customer, "Good morning, this is an unusual item. You'll be interested in seeing how it works. Would you like to examine it?" In this way he can arouse the customer's interest in using the merchandise. This technique is always productive when the salesperson suggests that the customer examine the article or when he suggests that the customer watch the operation of a mechanical item. Suggestions in a greeting help make sales. Good salespeople use them constantly.

"Trading Up" Through Suggestion

Customers often ask to see a low-priced item when what they really want is one of very good quality. They do this because they fear that the price of the quality product will be prohibitive.

The way to approach this is to show an item from a better quality selection as soon as possible. This method is called trading up. When he has aroused the customer's interest, he will point out that the higher-priced item is usually the better buy because of its additional features and better construction.

The following example shows how this idea works when stoves are being sold. The customer appears to be interested in the least-expensive model.

SALESMAN: You certainly couldn't go wrong on that stove, but I suppose your wife likes to keep her salt and pepper handy when she's cooking. This model over here has its own condiment set and a light that illuminates the entire top. Most of my customers who have bought this type say they wouldn't be without that light for anything.

Another thing you'll notice is that there is a better type of regulator on this model. It provides more accurate heat control. With the less-expensive kinds your regulator may say 250, for example, but your actual oven heat may vary 10 degrees either way. With the better type, 250 degrees means 250 degrees—right on the nose. It means that you won't have to do any experimenting with the oven to find out how to regulate it.

Suggesting Related Items

Once the sale is made, the salesman may suggest further items to purchase. Many experienced salesmen can take what started to be a modest sale and, by logical suggestion, triple the amount in just a few minutes. The number of items related to other items is almost unlimited. For example, a can of paint suggests a brush, turpentine, cleaner, and varnish remover. Shoes suggest polish and laces. Wallpaper suggests paste or a kit of wallpaper tools. Skirts suggest blouses and jackets. In fact, nearly every item sold in a retail department suggests something else.

Suggestion selling after the close is appreciated by three out of four customers. It is actually a reminder to a customer about something she may have forgotten.

Suggesting Alternates

The phrase "suggesting alternates" means to mention a similar item when the exact one the customer asks for is not stocked. The word "alternate" is preferred to "substitute." Too many times retail salespeople are content to say "I'm sorry" when the customer asks them for merchandise they do not have.

But consider these points. The customer is in front of the salesperson and she has expressed a willingness to buy. In fact, she would rather buy from this particular salesperson than spend the time and energy looking elsewhere. Therefore, the alert salesperson will take advantage of the circumstances to interest the customer in something similar to the article she originally requested. For example, the salesperson might say, "I'm sorry, we're all out of that item just now, but here are some new designs that will be very popular this fall. Would you like to look them over? I'm sure you'll see something you'll like."

Narrowing the Choice

When a salesperson offers the customer a large selection from which to choose, he should try to narrow the customer's choice. It is easier for a customer to make a selection between two items than to make a selection from many. The salesperson can narrow the choice by determining the preferences (color, style, price) of the customer, but he should do this without reflecting on the quality of the merchandise that has been eliminated.

SALES RESISTANCE

The retail salesperson has to overcome the same kind of sales resistance that salesmen everywhere encounter. All the methods described in Chapter 15 can be used by the retail salesman. But when a customer comes into a store, the salesperson needs to be alert to certain obstacles that salesmen everywhere do not meet in the same form. And the good retail salesperson often turns these obstacles into a sale.

Excuses

Probably the most common form of resistance is when a customer says, "I am just looking." This is usually a defensive action to discourage the salesman. But the salesperson can be assured that the customer would not be in his department if there were not some interest. The best way to meet this type of resistance is by prevention instead of cure. The greeting "May I help you?" invites the answer, "I am just looking." But when something is said about the merchandise in the salesman's opening statement, the customer's response is different.

Price Objections

The best way to handle the retail price objection is by meeting it fairly and squarely. The price may be justified, for example, in terms of service, comfort, convenience, or durability. The salesperson who can convince the customer of the basic quality of the merchandise will have less trouble when it is time to talk price.

Another way to overcome price resistance is by talking about the easy payment plan, if the store has one.

> CUSTOMER: But we had not planned to spend $398 on floor covering.
>
> SALESMAN: That sounds like a lot, I know, but look at it this way. This is well-made, beautiful carpeting. You will be proud to have it in your home, and it will give you years of good service. Now, on our special plan, you pay us only X dollars down and the rest in small payments every week (or month). You pay for it in a way that doesn't hurt and you have the rug right in your home where you can use it while you are paying for it.

If the store does not have a time-payment plan and the customer has a charge account, it may be possible to arrange for payment over a period of sixty or ninety days, with a portion of the sale price being billed each month.

A customer was looking for an item in a furniture store, where she had been a regular patron for several years. She liked the item but finally told the salesman that she would look around before she made up her mind.

She went to another store where she saw what looked like an identical item for 20 percent less. Very much annoyed, she hurried back to the first store and overwhelmed the salesman with these words:

> CUSTOMER: I am astonished that a store of your reputation would attempt to rob customers who have faithfully purchased from you for years.
>
> SALESMAN: Mrs. Jones, I am glad you had enough confidence in our store to come back and see us. I just want to ask you one question. Did the other item have three coats of varnish?
>
> CUSTOMER: (with a certain degree of indecision): I don't know about that . . .
>
> SALESMAN: Ours has. Let me show you, and also some other important features.

The customer finally bought the item, and neither the salesman nor the customer knew whether or not the furniture at the rival store had three coats of varnish—and neither really cared.

This salesman had sense enough to build up the value of his merchandise in the customer's mind, rather than to attempt to sell on price alone. The inefficient salesman always sells on price in the hope of increasing his volume, while the intelligent salesman attempts to increase the customer's appreciation of his merchandise until the customer's appraisal of its value equals or exceeds the price.

This example illustrates how the question method of closing can be used effectively to put the customer on the defensive, as well as how to take care of the price issue.

RETAIL CUSTOMER BEHAVIOR

If a salesperson wishes to be technical, he can list almost as many kinds of sales resistance caused by customer behavior as there are customers. There is no foolproof way of dealing with the different kinds of resistance. Retail customers can be identified, however, by certain outstanding behavioral traits that can be used as guides by the retail salesperson.

The Looker. The looker is a common type of retail prospect. Perhaps she came into the store to escape the rain, or because the store's displays are attractive, or because she likes to browse. But she should not be dismissed casually. She is a potential buyer, if not an immediate buyer. She will continue to remember the merchandise that caught her attention and come back later when she needs it. Or she will tell friends that she saw "a darling hat" at Blank's and maybe the friend will buy it. The salesperson should try to sell her something, but if she is not interested she should be treated courteously and perhaps invited to browse around.

The Shopper. The shopper usually knows what she wants and continues to look until she finds it. Because the purchase is important to her, she will shop in two or three stores before making up her mind. She will then buy from the store she likes best, or from the one that has the most suitable merchandise.

This customer merits a salesperson's most careful attention. She is the one who tests salesmanship skills because a salesperson in one store will have to do a better job of selling than the salesperson in the store down the street to get her business. She may not buy today —but if she is sold on the merchandise, she will return.

The Bargain Hunter. Salespeople see price-minded customers whenever a store has an advertised special, a season sale, or a bargain day. She will buy almost anything if it is priced right. She should be sold a special, or, if possible, she may be interested in a better buy.

For this type of buyer, however, price is usually the only consideration and she must be handled accordingly.

The Dubious Customer. Every person who comes in the door represents a potential sale. He should not be classified at first glance by the salesperson as to whether or not it is worth while to wait on him. There is no way of determining a customer's buying power accurately. Many wealthy people dress plainly or even carelessly. Many timid-appearing people have stubborn minds. Sometimes a person who looks like a fugitive from a rag bag will buy expensive merchandise because it represents a good value. The safest plan is to treat everyone as a potential buyer. It is also wise to recall that many well-dressed customers are poor credit risks.

The Irritating Customer. Occasionally a salesperson will have a customer who is obstinate and difficult. He does not like anything. He is sarcastic in his comments. He argues every point with the salesman. He may be hypercritical of the merchandise. He may be belligerent, overbearing, or even dictatorial in attitude. But whatever the provocation, the salesperson can never afford to lose his temper.

Many times an irritated customer is not angry with the salesperson or the store. Something else may have put him in a bad humor and he may try to take it out on the salesperson because he is the nearest at hand. But one of the penalties of serving the public is that one must be tolerant of the customer's moods. Meeting disagreeableness with courtesy and pleasantness can usually clear the atmosphere and often end in a harmonious transaction. Meeting like with like, on the other hand, will make an enemy for the salesperson and a "knocker" for the store. A salesperson cannot afford to risk such a situation.

Instead, the irritable customer should be met with good humor and understanding. He needs something or he would not have come in. If the salesperson refuses to be upset by comments or attitudes, he may obtain a sale. And instead of making an enemy, the salesperson may make a friend and a permanent customer.

The Complainer. A customer with grievances, whether real or imaginary, is seldom tactful. He may burst into the store airing a complaint in a loud voice and create a lot of damage to the store's prestige. The best way to handle a complainer is to calm him. The salesperson should talk in a low voice, be courteous, and show a readiness to listen. If necessary, the customer should be shown into a private office where other customers cannot eavesdrop. Then the salesperson should learn what the trouble is and adjust the matter if it is at all possible. Otherwise, the salesperson should call someone who will be able to make the proper adjustment.

USE OF ORAL TESTIMONY

Most salespeople are familiar with the use of testimonials in newspapers and magazines and on radio and television. This form of advertising must be very effective in influencing people or large corporations would not spend so much money on it.

Testimonials can also be used to combat retail sales resistance. A casual mention that "Mr. Smith has purchased a television set (a rug, a living room suite, or any other product) just like this one" can be the statement that clinches the deal for the salesperson. Most customers have confidence in what Mr. Smith or other well-known, prominent local persons buy and use. Names of a customer's friends and neighbors who have bought similar merchandise from a salesperson may also break down certain types of resistance. A woman, however, may not care to buy a hat or dress like Mrs. Astorbilt's, but she will buy the same type of furniture, car, or house, in the belief that Mrs. Astorbilt's judgment in buying is sound.

Endorsements of nationally known testing bureaus, seals of approval, and Underwriters' Laboratory tags on electrical merchandise, as well as other informative labels, are all testimonials of quality that are used by successful salespeople.

SUCCESSFUL CLOSINGS

A decision to buy may start with the buyer's original idea of making a purchase or with the salesperson convincing a customer to buy. Thus, the decision-making process could have begun when a salesperson prepared himself before approaching a customer, and continued as the salesperson presented and demonstrated the merchandise, successfully countered sales resistance, won customer confidence, and obtained a commitment to buy.

The time a salesperson should attempt to work toward obtaining the commitment to buy can be determined from the buying signals displayed by the customer.

Buying Signals

If the customer has looked at several articles and returns to one which she has already inspected, this usually indicates a genuine interest in the article. It shows that she has compared values, and assured herself that the article is what she wants. The salesman would be correct in assuming the customer intends to buy the product.

If the customer holds a garment in front of a mirror or tries it on, this action may indicate that she is interested enough to buy. If a customer manipulates an appliance or tries it out, this may also be a buying signal.

When a person asks about the wearing qualities of a dress, whether or not it will shrink or fade, how to clean it, whether the fabric is guaranteed, or whether she may return it, these questions are definite buying signals. They prove that the customer is thinking of the merchandise in terms of her own needs and is probably ready to buy.

When a customer is accompanied by a friend or a relative, the customer will turn to the friend or relative and say, "How do you like this?" The salesperson should listen carefully to the other person's reply. If the reply is favorable, he should ask for the order. If the reply is unfavorable, he should bring out more merchandise and direct his attention to winning the friend's or relative's approval. Although retail salespeople can become very discouraged with friends or relatives who interfere with sales, it is a mistake to disregard them.

When there is no positive response on the part of the customer, the salesperson has to help the customer decide. He probes for buying cues by asking questions; he finds out why the customer hesitates. Then he explains why the purchase will satisfy the motives behind the customer's interest in the merchandise.

Attention Focusing

The salesperson should concentrate on the items that interest the customer. After the customer has narrowed the choice to a few articles, the salesperson should put away the merchandise that has not appealed to the customer. This focuses the customer's attention on the favored merchandise and helps him or her reach a decision more quickly. It also allows the salesperson a better opportunity to concentrate his selling points on fewer items. The salesperson must be sure, however, that the items he removes are definitely not wanted by the customer, and must employ tact to avoid creating an impression of being impatient or in a hurry to do something else.

Minor Points

The salesperson leads the customer to make a number of minor decisions that result in a sale. He does this by asking questions and listening to the answers. He tries to obtain affirmative responses from the customer at frequent intervals. For example:

SALESPERSON: First of all, Mr. Black, you want an appliance that will last, don't you?

CUSTOMER: That's right.

SALESPERSON: Then, you want a device that will not require constant attention—something that will work easily for you?

CUSTOMER: That would certainly be an advantage.

SALESPERSON: And on top of that, you want an appliance that has beauty and style, comfort and usefulness.

CUSTOMER: Naturally.

SALESPERSON: Then this is the appliance you want. It's made of the finest-quality chromium-plated steel, and has given hundreds of our customers long and satisfactory wear. Furthermore, it is automatic; you don't need to watch it. You press down this knob, and the appliance does the rest: less waste and easier operation. And notice the design and highly polished finish. You certainly would enjoy this in your home, wouldn't you?

Obtaining a number of favorable minor decisions goes hand-in-hand with putting the customer in the receptive frame of mind. For example:

"Do you prefer the large or the small model?"

"Would you prefer the deluxe model or the standard model?"

"When you consider all these features, don't you think this is the model that best suits your needs?"

"The use that you will get from this appliance will save you money in the long run. That is important, isn't it?"

These minor decisions and agreements—when taken together—are definite indications of a desire to buy. When the customer has responded favorably to several statements involving a minor decision, it is easier to persuade him to make a major decision to buy.

Summarizing

Agreement to buy may often be obtained by reviewing the main selling points at the end of the presentation. For example: "Now, let's go back over these points, Mrs. Customer. Here's what this product offers you. First. . . ."

If agreement is not obtained by this technique, the salesperson can at least determine the customer's objections and then try to overcome them by using new and different appeals. Agreement is often brought about by impressing the customer with the feeling of ownership. For example: "Think of the beauty and comfort that will be obtained from having this furniture in your home. Just watch the family go for this when you bring it home."

When a salesperson is ready to close the sale, he should stop talking, showing, and demonstrating. Many sales have been lost because the salesperson simply didn't know when to stop talking. The successful salesperson knows exactly when to stop talking and reach for his sales book. At the same time, he can ask for the order through a direct or double question. These have also been discussed in earlier chapters, but are reiterated here.

Questions to Close

Some of the direct questions that can be used to close the sale:

"Which do you prefer?"
"When could we start?"
"Shall we deliver it?"
"When would you like to have it delivered?"

The customer may also be induced to buy by the salesperson asking double questions, both favorable to the sale. For example:

"Do you prefer this one or that one?"
"Do you wish to open an account or pay cash?"
"Shall I have it shipped express or parcel post?"
"Do you want one black and one red?"

While the closing questions are being asked, the salesperson can assume that the customer has reached a decision and have the sales book ready and pencil poised to write the customer's name. Here again, tact and judgment must be exercised to avoid the impression of high-handed tactics. For example:

SALESPERSON (writing out order): I'm sure that you'll get a lot of satisfaction in using this appliance.

The salesperson, using this "assumption method," must be absolutely sure that any doubts the customer had have been fully answered and that he or she is convinced of the desirability of the article.

SPECIAL INDUCEMENTS

Price

The salesperson may tell the customer that the article is a special and will not be available later at the same reasonable price. A special discount for quantity purchases may also be offered as a buying stimulus where company policy authorizes it. However, price inducements should be used only where other methods have failed. Special price inducements should be handled with extreme tact to prevent the feeling that high-pressure selling is being used.

Terms and Special Services

The use of terms and special services to help retail decision-making are shown in the following example:

SALESPERSON: If you don't wish to make a cash payment at this time, may I suggest that you open an account? I am sure that our credit department will welcome your order.

SALESPERSON: With this beautiful appliance, you get lifetime service. If you ever get even a little scratch on it, just call us up and we'll have our serviceman come out to give you free repairs.

Guarantee or Refund Policy

How to use the guarantee or refund policy to obtain a decision to buy is shown by the following example:

SALESPERSON: Why not let us deliver this desk, Mrs. Snodgrass? After using it a few days, I'm sure that you will come to like it. If I'm wrong, then you can give the factory a ring and we'll come out and pick it up. Your complete purchase price will be refunded.

This method is particularly effective with prospects who cannot make up their minds as to whether the merchandise is of the quality or kind they want. This can be a dangerous method to use, however, since it might encourage the salesman to rely upon the guarantee or the company's refund policy, rather than on his sales ability.

POWER POINTS

When attempting to obtain a decision, the salesperson should not rush the customer. No attempt should be made to obtain a decision before all sales resistance has been overcome. It will always lead to suspicion on the part of the customer. Rushing the customer is often said to be high-pressure selling. The decision to buy should be allowed to develop in the customer's mind in a natural manner.

A salesperson must not stand around with an indifferent look on his face. A sales talk must not be weakened with words such as "if" and "provided." Successful salespeople assume that the customer will buy and they convey to the customer their confidence in the merchandise. They use a positive approach, saying something like this:

"I know you will enjoy having this, Mrs. Jones, because . . . When you get this in your home, you will always enjoy its utility."

The salesperson should avoid just hoping for the sale. For example, he should avoid saying: "I wish you would give this a try, Mrs. Jones," or "I was hoping you would let me give you a demonstration, Mrs. Black."

Customer sales resistance is a natural part of any sale. It is usually the customer's way of obtaining more information or reassurance about the quality, quantity, or price of the merchandise. For example, a customer may speculate that a color will fade when in reality she wants to be shown or to be reassured that it will not fade.

A customer must never be left in a state of indecision. Customers must be helped in their decision-making. Salespeople should not say, "It's up to you, sir" or "Well, I think all three of these are desirable." If the customer lacks decision, the salesperson should supply reasons that will help the customer reach a decision. For example: "Either of these dishwashers is desirable, but I feel that this would be more suitable because . . ."

A salesperson should not review the wrong selling points. Early in the discussion he should discover just what the customer's needs are and then fit his sales presentation to those needs. He should select the selling points that answer the customer's needs or those in which the customer has shown a strong interest, and keep stressing them throughout the sale.

It rarely pays to try to force the customer to buy. It is always better in the long run to retain the customer's confidence and goodwill rather than to make an unsatisfactory sale.

An effective salesperson does not continue talking about the sale after the customer is ready to buy, because the customer is already sold. The salesperson can, however, talk about the terms and the care of the merchandise or suggest additional merchandise and make other pertinent remarks to conclude the transaction.

A mature salesperson does not show dissatisfaction if the customer does not buy. He lets a customer know that he is ready to help whenever the customer comes back to him. He is courteous and puts aside his disappointments. He leaves his customer in a pleasant frame of mind. A customer should never have reason to say, "I dislike trading at Blank's because they look so angry if you do not buy." It is good business to say, "It has been a pleasure to show you our merchandise. Come in again, please."

When the customer is ready to buy, the salesperson should stop presenting and demonstrating a product. Many sales have been lost because a salesperson literally talked himself out of them. The experienced salesperson usually senses when the sale can be made and starts reaching for his order pad and pencil while he asks a single or a double question.

There are intangibles in salesmanship which go far deeper than glibness, knowing the right answers, persuasiveness, and the technique of asking for the order. These things may be subtle and difficult for many salesmen to apply. They have the magic, however, not only to make the individual grow in sales ability and personal depth but also to make his customer like him, trust him, and depend on him.

DISCUSSION QUESTIONS AND PROBLEMS

1. What are the three rules to observe when showing merchandise?

2. What would you *say* and *do* to discover what merchandise is of interest to a customer?

3. Why are questions by the salesperson important at the start of a retail sale?

4. How would you place sales *suggestions* in your greeting of a client?

5. Why should a salesperson begin with medium-priced goods?

6. How would you proceed to *trade up* your merchandise through suggestion?

7. Exactly how would you handle price in a retail sale?

8. Why are *hidden values* important? Give several examples of how to sell hidden values.

9. Why should the salesperson get the customer to demonstrate, test, or use the product?

10. Select an item which you believe you would like to sell. Then, show how you would present and demonstrate the item according to the instructions in this chapter.

11. What is meant by suggesting *alternates?* What would you say and do to suggest alternates?

12. When should a salesperson stop talking and reach for the sales book?

13. What are the main reasons for customer complaints and how can they be settled?

14. How may oral testimony be used to combat retail sales resistance? Give several examples.

15. How would you handle the excuse, "I want to look around"? Write a dialogue between a customer and salesperson, illustrating exactly what you would say.

SELLING PROBLEMS AND PROJECTS

---

1.   Mrs. Edwards Case

Not long ago, I saw an advertisement which described a sale of bedspreads in a local department store.

At the store I found hundreds of spreads piled high on tables. A salesgirl was nearby. I approached her, described the color of the rug and walls in my bedroom, and asked if she had something suitable in a bedspread. She said sweetly, "Everything we have is on the tables. You may find something there." I looked and found something I liked. I returned to the salesgirl and handed her the one I picked out, saying, "Here's a sale for you." She smiled and said, "These are not returnable. Are you sure you want them? Chartreuse doesn't blend with everything." I hesitated and then said, "Perhaps you're right. Although these spreads appear to be unusual bargains, they aren't bargains if I can't use them in my home."

Questions

1.   Analyze the conduct of this salesperson.

2.   What would you do to improve this salesperson's selling technique?

2. **Suggestion Selling Project**

   Explain how you would improve the following sales situations.

   a. A customer asks for a certain brand of paint. The salesman says, "We carry that brand, but let me show you our own brand. It's much cheaper."

   b. A customer purchases a shirt. The salesperson says, "Do you need any ties?"

   c. A customer asks to see a tire advertised at $14.95. The service station attendant says, "Those tires are not very good; let me show you our $21 tire."

   d. A customer has just purchased a pair of women's slacks. The salesperson says, "You don't need a handbag, do you?"

   e. The customer enters a drugstore and asks for a roll of film. The salesperson replies, "Yes, ma'am, here it is. How about some toothpaste, lipstick, hand lotion, hairpins, hair spray?"

CHAPTER 21

Creative
Industrial Selling

Industrial selling is often specialized; usually requires more product knowledge than selling skill; requires patience and ability to explain details; demands creative thinking and promotional acumen. Not everyone can meet these requirements, but for those who qualify there are many rewards—financial and personal.

NATURE OF INDUSTRIAL PRODUCTS

Industrial products are classified as raw materials, fabricating materials and parts, installations, accessory equipment and services, operating supplies and services, and finished products for resale. To successfully sell such products and services a salesman must be a specialist such as a technician, scientist, or engineer, in addition to being a skilled salesman.

Both products and services are sold in the industrial market. The product may be *heavy equipment* such as computers, earthmovers, lathes, and locomotives. *Light equipment* might include fork-lift trucks, hand tools, cash registers, display fixtures, duplicators, and automobiles. The product may be a complete *plant,* a warehouse, a mill, a factory. The product could also be *raw material.* Timber, chemicals, minerals, oil, gas, wheat, cotton, tobacco are *raw* materials. *Fabricating materials* are products such as nuts, bolts, buttons, batteries, and packages. *Processed materials* include items such as flour, steel, brick, and aluminum. *Operating supplies* are products, too, and include such things as fuel, soap, paper clips, stationery, lubricants, and paper towels.

Services include such intangibles as insurance, transportation, advertising, banking, laundry, janitorial service, police protection, and so forth.

Sources for Industrial Purchasers

Purchasers of industrial products and services are usually found in governmental units, business organizations, or institutions. Governmental buying is done at the city, town, county, state, and federal levels. Business organizations include manufacturers, public utilities, processors, and sellers of services. Institutions include hospitals, hotels, schools, and churches.

Wholesalers and retailers may buy industrial products for resale. They may also buy products for their own use which are industrial in nature, such as delivery trucks, cash registers, display counters, and computers. When making this kind of purchase, wholesalers and retailers are considered to be industrial buyers.

THE INDUSTRIAL SALESMAN

The industrial salesman is in reality a *manufacturer's representative.* He is an employee and works for a company. He calls on other manufacturers, wholesalers, dealers, and distributors.

In addition to his duties as a salesman, he may also serve as a contact and promotion man, advertising supervisor, sales manager, complaint handler, adjuster, and goodwill ambassador. In short, *he is the company* more than any other type of salesman.

He must be a topflight man of considerable selling experience. He must be imaginative, aggressive, emotionally well adjusted, able to manage his time, and capable of making fast decisions. He must know all about his products; their use and application; company policies and prices; and how his products will benefit prospects. He must be able to make an intelligent presentation to a buyer about a new product, a dealership, or a franchise.

He must be well educated and versed in business operations so that he can offer advice and counsel to his buyers. He sometimes calls on established businesses, or he may make his own outlets by setting up new distributorships and dealerships in new areas. If the product is already established, the manufacturer's representative will enlarge and increase the number of products handled, as well as the sales volume.

The industrial salesman travels extensively. He may cover an area as large as a 500-mile radius, or a region, or the nation. He lives out of his suitcase more than other salesmen.

He must be able to train others to sell his product on the retail level, to hold meetings, to give lectures, to teach salespeople how to overcome customer objections and how to close profitable sales. He must be able to inspire and enthuse others to sell more.

Sometimes this salesman turns over his sales to the wholesaler, jobber, or distributor, since he receives credit at any level. He must keep his manufacturer informed at all times about every aspect of the product and territory; refer customer complaints to the proper person; offer suggestions related to advertising and sales promotion in general. He actually conducts his activities as though he owned the company in his territory.

A great many topnotch salesmen prefer this kind of selling, since it offers them an opportunity to earn larger salaries, as well as to be their own boss. Compensation may be on a base-salary and commission basis, but more often these salesmen will be paid a straight commission.

The manufacturer's representative is not to be confused with the *manufacturer's agent*. The difference between the two positions is that the agent is in business for himself, whereas the representative works for an employer. The agent needs the same qualifications as the representative, however, and his responsibilities are approximately the same.

Problem-solving Attitude

The vital element in industrial selling is the ability of the salesman to understand and appreciate the buyer's needs and wants. The salesman's chief job is to know how his proposition will satisfy those needs and wants and at the same time possess the selling skill to motivate the buyer to make a purchase.

Industrial salesmen must be able to solve the problems of prospective buyers and customers. This ability has an important incidental advantage in that it smooths the path of the presentation, because the buyer finds it difficult to be unpleasant or unresponsive to a salesman who wants to be helpful.

In turn, the concept of anticipatory problem-solving automatically encourages the salesman to pay careful attention to the buyers' needs. It is also valuable even before the salesman comes face-to-face with the buyer, because it stimulates him to accumulate all possible information about the buyer's personality, responsibilities, needs, and motives. The salesman must always keep in mind that the professional buyer tries to avoid buying on whim; he strives to base his decisions on facts.

Personality of Purchasers

It is commonplace to hear salesmen refer to the purchaser as "the enemy." These salesmen seem to think that purchasing agents, in particular, are cold, skeptical, unsympathetic individuals who try to operate completely objectively and on the basis of hard facts, without any regard for warm personal relations.

It is true that purchasing agents usually buy on the basis of specification; that they try to buy as advantageously as possible; that products, prices, and services offered to them by other salesmen are practically standardized and identical. How, then, does the purchasing agent choose his vendor? The conclusion can only be that he places his orders with the salesman with the pleasant, outgoing personal traits which have been emphasized throughout this textbook.

Emotions *do* influence the most hardened, logical purchasing agent. Therefore, professional, career salesmen always try to build a purchasing agent's self-esteem; they try to make him feel important; they employ assurance words and phrases; they maintain a professional atmosphere; they *listen* to the prospect; they enter the purchasing agent's office with a carefully planned presentation. These things outweigh anything their competition may be able to offer, and prove the point that purchasing agents are *human,* too.

PREPARING TO SELL PROFESSIONAL BUYERS

The act of selling industrial purchasing agents and other professional buyers requires, as we have stated, salesmen who possess poise, urbanity, technical knowledge, and great selling ability. It is not strange, therefore, to find that industrial selling requires a considerable amount of careful preparation.

Buyers Like Planned Presentations

A professional salesman emulates the professional speaker, the actor, or the lawyer by leaving nothing to chance. What can the good salesman do to remove the chance of errors from his oral presentation?

What is the best way of presenting a proposition? What words and phrases should be used? To what motives should he appeal and in what order should he appeal to them? How can he prove that the prospect will benefit if he buys? How can he avoid making off-the-cuff sales talks? The good salesman will answer these questions for himself by preparing a well-constructed, interesting sales presentation.

Professional buyers like the kind of planned sales presentation which was made recently by a young salesman of industrial specialties who knew how to organize himself. He knew the name of the buyer, the average production of the factory, the type of product manufactured, the approximate amount of supplies that were used, and other vital facts about the business.

When he entered the buying office and introduced himself, there was a businesslike air about him which instantly appealed to the buyer. His sales presentation was so brief, so complete, and so well constructed that it gave the buyer a pleasant surprise. He did not force himself upon the buyer; he let his benefit facts speak for themselves. He demonstrated and even suggested that the buyer test the product before he asked for the order.

It required considerable time to prepare a presentation of this kind, but it had its rewards. He closed many sales and he did it swiftly and profitably. His sales talk was very different from that of the salesmen who have the happened-to-be-going-by-and-just-thought-I'd-drop-in attitude, which makes it so easy for professional buyers to turn them down.

How to Organize a Sales Presentation

As previously noted, an organized sales talk usually starts with a written outline. The first outline from which the salesman is to practice his talk should consist of complete statements, not simply words and phrases. This is essential, for it is in this phase that the salesman forces himself to organize and clarify his ideas and to delete unclear and meaningless words.

When the industrial salesman has organized his outline, he writes it out on small note cards. He then rehearses his presentation, referring to the cards whenever necessary. Each time he practices the talk —and fewer than ten rehearsals is not adequate—he varies the way in which he words it. The chief value of this method is that it forces the salesman to think on his feet and prevents him from hardening the talk into parrotlike repetition.

Once he has become sufficiently familiar with his material and has practiced saying it aloud many times in slightly different ways, the salesman substitutes a single card containing the key words or phrases and speaks from that. Finally, he throws the card away. Thereafter, it is a matter of developing and refining his technique and of analyzing and judging the suitability of his examples and other supporting materials.

The Ideal Sales Call

Professional buyers have their own ideas of how salesmen should sell, and they have suggested the ingredients that should be used in the creation of an *ideal sales call,* as well as the order in which they should be mixed. Harry T. Flynn, an executive of the Grand Union Company, describes his idea of the ideal sales call as follows:

1. Whenever feasible, the salesman should telephone in advance to make an appointment.
2. When the salesman arrives at the buyer's office, he should be prepared to make the buyer aware of his company's background. He should be able to do this clearly, briefly, and thoroughly.
3. The salesman should be prepared to describe his product and its purpose. A sample of the product should be shown at this time, or visual representation of it.
4. Next, the salesman should state briefly the need his product is going to fill for the buyer.
5. The salesman should then be prepared to tell the buyer what his product might replace in the buyer's present inventory.
6. The salesman should be able to give the buyer a price comparison, comparing his own product with those of competitors. While price may not be a determining factor in completing a sale, it helps if the price is a realistic one.
7. The salesman should be prepared to give a brief description of his company's promotion plans for the product. He should be ready to sketch the upcoming advertising campaign; have samples of the art work or proof of ads which will be used in the promotion effort.

In the ideal sales call the salesman usually makes an oral presentation based on the foregoing factors, then leaves his written presentation, or survey. The buyer then analyzes the material the salesman has left. If the salesman has made a good presentation in terms of buyer benefits, the proposition may then be sent to a buying committee. If the committee accepts the proposition, a purchase order is either mailed or phoned to the salesman's company.

Once the product is in the stockroom, many professional buyers want the salesman to keep them informed about such things as price changes, allowances, additional advertising, new facts about the product, what competitors are doing, and other details which might affect future purchases.

Preparation of Surveys

The professional salesman of industrial products considers himself a problem-solver. This concept includes surveys of the prospect's situation. In this regard, the definition of survey is *to look over thoroughly*.

This means that instead of merely trying to deliver a sales talk, the industrial salesman examines the prospect's needs so that he may recommend the best product or service to satisfy those needs.

Buyers and purchasing agents like the survey idea and generally appreciate the efforts of the salesmen who use them. The survey may consist of only a few minutes' conversation to ascertain a few simple facts, or it may consist of a detailed study of the prospect's needs in many different departments over a long period of time.

The results of a short and simple survey might be communicated verbally or explained by a simple design or sketch. On the other hand, the results of a long, detailed survey should be given to the prospect as a neatly typed presentation folio. Such a presentation folio, complete with all the necessary supporting data and illustrations, serves not only to impress the prospect with the thoroughness of the survey, but also carries a fairly complete sales story for the prospect who must, in turn, often convince other members of his organization of the desirability of the proposition.

The survey offers these advantages to the industrial salesman:

1. Since the prospect is getting professional advice without charge, the proposition is lifted out of the price-commodity class. This very often eliminates competition.
2. The survey method encourages the salesman to seek help and advice from his sales manager, fellow salesmen, or his home office before he makes his final preparation and recommendation. This assistance helps to eliminate possible errors and weaknesses in his presentation.
3. Such tailor-made surveys and presentations make for the smoothest and easiest kind of presentation.

4. Prospects and buyers like the survey idea and generally appreciate the efforts of salesmen who use them.

Purchaser's Value Analysis

A purchaser's value analysis is a form of survey used by many professional buyers and purchasing agents when *they* evaluate a product or service. The questions are phrased so as to cover all of the major points concerning the product's usefulness.

1. Does the item's use contribute value to the end product?
2. Is the cost proportionate to its usefulness?
3. Does it need all its features?
4. Is there another product which would better fulfill the intended use?
5. Can a usable substitute be made at a lower cost?
6. Can a standard item be made to do the job?
7. Is it made with the use of proper tooling?
8. Do material, labor, overhead, and profit charges justify the purchase price?
9. Will another dependable supplier provide it for a lower price?
10. Has anyone else bought it for a lower price?

The questions in the purchaser's value analysis are studied, analyzed, and specific answers are prepared by the salesman before the interview. This is a realistic and accurate way to explain to the purchasing agent what the product can do for him. It would certainly provide the background for a more convincing and dynamic presentation than the usual sales talk.

Group Audience Approach

Industrial salesmen often find it necessary to sell to a purchasing committee instead of a single buyer. This is particularly true in the food field, in which as much as 80 percent of all food volume moves through committee buying. Committee buying is expected to reach a volume of 90 to 95 percent in the immediate future.

This shift from the traditional method of buying has come about in recent years largely because of the growth of large business units and the decline of small ones. The purchase of thousands of different items in great volume by one business organization could not be performed through a simple seller-to-buyer relationship. The movement away from person-to-person selling in many businesses has caused the men who sell to substantial accounts to employ a more formal *group audience* approach.

As in all good salesmanship, the group audience approach requires adequate preparation by the industrial sales representative. Before the meeting, the salesman may try to talk with each committee member to influence a favorable attitude toward his proposition, as well as to learn something about each individual's interests, attitudes, behavior pattern, experience, and education. He may attempt to discover their individual opinions of his product or service. If he cannot meet with everyone on the committee, the salesman may try to discover the strongest personality in the group and talk to him. He may also find it advantageous, when possible, to have an advance talk with the member who usually raises the most objections. The salesman should also study a prospect's current purchases or use of competitive products or services. He should try to discover the strong and weak points of his competition and what complaints the prospect may have about the competing product or service.

An important part of the salesman's preparation should be to plan an *agenda* of the major points to be presented. This might be in the form of a schedule, showing the time limits for each part of the presentation.

The next step in the salesman's preparation should be the making of a *specification sheet*, which should state clearly and briefly the product's chief advantages, benefits, values, services, conditions, and other necessary details which might interest the committee. A copy of the specification sheet should be given to each member of the buying group at the start of the meeting.

Finally, a rehearsal is needed—a rehearsal that simulates the committee presentation. Perfecting the presentation demands practice and more practice on the salesman's part. If a mechanical product is being presented, a cast of characters may be needed for practice, corresponding to the personnel of the buying committee—engineers, finance men, accountants, and researchers. The rehearsal should be as authentic as possible, so that he can make a good presentation before an actual committee.

Buying Sequence

Recognizing a *need* is the first step toward an industrial purchase. The recognition may start with a requisition from a department to the purchasing office. Or the need may arise because management realizes that the factory needs expansion, or someone puts in a request for new equipment to replace the obsolete. However, most sales do not result from felt needs of management. At least 50 percent of purchases are made because a salesman created a need in the mind of the prospective buyer.

Having recognized the need, the next step is a decision as to the type of product which will satisfy the need. Quite often the prospective buyer will draw up specifications for the item he wants to buy. Then the purchasing officer will select or investigate one or more possible selling sources and write or telephone them for bids, or give the specifications directly to one or more salesmen.

The next step is to decide on the source of supply, negotiate the transaction, and issue a purchase order to complete the transaction.

The final step is to receive the product, inspect it for quality, quantity, and completeness, and then check it into the inventory or warehouse. After the vendor's invoice has been verified and found acceptable, payment is authorized and made. The transaction has been completed, except for personal follow-up by the salesman.

Market Channels

Marketing of industrial products often takes the channel of manufacturer-to-user, which is known as direct selling. In this case, purchasing agents for business firms, institutions, and government buy directly from the manufacturer. Middlemen are sometimes eliminated because products must be tailored to the purchaser's specified needs.

Often the purchaser needs technical advice which can only be supplied by the maker of the product. Also, since large sums of money are involved in many industrial purchases, direct transactions become the most practical way to buy.

Some industrial products are sold through indirect channels if the product is low in price, standardized, or widely used by small business purchasers in distant areas. In these cases the middlemen may be merchant middlemen, such as wholesalers and mill supply houses or agent middlemen, such as broker's or manufacturer's agents and selling agents. In short, the industrial salesman may sell for a manufacturer, a merchant middleman, or agent middleman.

DIFFERENCES IN SELLING

Industrial selling is almost the opposite of one-time selling. First, there is usually a long time between a salesman's first call on an industrial purchaser and his first sale to that purchaser. Quite often the salesman must wait for approval to make a survey of the prospect's business operation, and then he may find the survey quite time-consuming. Next, the salesman may need to cooperate with his company engineers in an analysis of the findings and in the drafting of a proposal. This takes time. Finally, either before or after delivering the proposal, the salesman may find it necessary to demonstrate his product, that is, actually setting it up for practical use, and then follow up the sale.

And, in the meantime, the salesman must continue to emphasize the benefits to the purchaser and to offer assurances that the supply will be steady, that satisfactory service will be available, that the price is right, and many other possible details.

COMPANY POLICY

Every business organization has operating policies, or *company rules*. Many of these rules affect individual salesmen or sources from whom purchases are made.

A common kind of company policy related to sources is *reciprocity*. This has been mentioned earlier, and simply means "You buy from me and I'll buy from you." This is a satisfactory policy when each company sells something the other needs, for each can then grant the other advantages such as lower prices and longer terms. Sometimes these arrangements violate federal antitrust laws because they restrict competition. However, such agreements do not have long lives because pressure from competitors tends to disrupt them.

Many companies have a policy of *preference* for more than one source. It often pays them to split the order, even when all competition is equal and they could obtain all their needs from one source. They believe that by keeping several lines open, they insure themselves against a possible loss of supply due to the failure of a single source.

SELLING INDUSTRIAL ITEMS TO DEALERS

It is helpful to students to study an actual job analysis of the duties and responsibilities of an industrial salesman. In the example which follows, the salesmen "sell industrial items to dealers." However, the job analysis would apply to practically any industrial salesman in any marketing channel.

Pittsburgh Corning Glass Company*

Specific Duties and Responsibilities. The specific duties and responsibilities of the representative are to increase the use of his products. To fulfill this requirement he must:

1. Establish and maintain a desirable relationship with distributors in his area.

    a. Act as their advisor in their merchandising of his products; participate helpfully in their sales meetings and other related activities.

    b. Increase their knowledge of his products.

    c. Educate them as to possible markets for his products.

    d. Inform them of potential sales and encourage their active follow-up.

    e. Point out to them, wherever possible, opportunities to profitably substitute his products for those specified.

    f. Stimulate their enthusiasm and aggressiveness in soliciting business by working with them in the field and by keeping them informed of his own promotional activities in their behalf.

    g. Encourage them to maintain adequate stocks of products at all times.

    h. Encourage them to maintain sufficient supplies of up-to-date samples, literature, and other promotional aids and assist them in making efficient use thereof.

    i. Maintain an atmosphere of goodwill and friendly cooperation between the distributor and his company.

    j. Maintain a strict impartiality where two or more distributors may be in competition.

    k. Bear in mind at all times that our distributors constitute our most important customers and warrant treatment as such.

2. Promote the specification and use of his products by architects, engineers, owners, occupants, installers, and original equipment manufacturers. He must:

    a. Maintain regular contact with these groups.

    b. Provide samples, current literature, and information of a pertinent nature to these contacts as the occasion arises.

*Courtesy: W. J. Reily, *Field Sales Representative,* Pittsburgh Corning Glass Company. From: *Job Description, Field Sales Representative,* 1960.

    c.   Make systematic repeat contacts to encourage reliance upon him as a dependable advisor.

    d.   Vary presentation to build and maintain interest and avoid boring repetition.

    e.   Establish several contacts in each office, remembering that the junior man today may be the key man tomorrow.

    f.   Determine current attitudes towards his products and competitive materials, and relay this information to management.

    g.   Obtain information on current and future projects, and use it to guide his promotional efforts.

    h.   Strive to change negative attitudes by informational and imaginative presentations.

    i.   Be accurate in recommendations for use of [company] and related products.

    j.   Follow through with on-the-job service calls.

    k.   Engender goodwill with these groups by service and consultant advice and help on customer problems.

    l.   Participate in company authorized trade or technical meetings and shows, as assigned, in order to promote his products and acquire useful competitive and other data.

    m.   Provide complete follow through, where required, from assisting in writing of specifications, insuring proper bidding, expediting placing of order, to supervision of field installation.

3.   Work his territory efficiently. To do this he must:

    a.   Familiarize himself with key people in important firms, governmental agencies, and trade associations of all kinds.

    b.   Maintain complete and up-to-date records of all regular contacts, including names, addresses, telephone numbers, and other pertinent data.

    c.   Stay abreast of day-to-day developments in fields that affect or influence his business and report significant information.

    d.   Plan a program of calls, initially and continuously, that insures the most comprehensive coverage of potential users; review and revise this program periodically.

e. Utilize all available publications and reports that reflect construction activity.

f. Develop authoritative sources of information among his contacts.

g. Maintain and use a follow-up system on potential jobs, and also on completed installations which can be used as local references.

h. Know who his competitors are and what their tactics are.

4. Know his company's products, specifications, and literature.

a. Be completely and thoroughly conversant with the background of his company.

b. Be familiar with the physical characteristics, proprietary superiorities, and particularly advantageous applications of [company] products, as well as their practical limitations.

c. Know company standard specifications to the extent that reference to literature or outside assistance is minimized.

d. Develop a sound working knowledge of related materials and approved accessories.

e. Learn the practical problems of handling and installing his products, the common objections deriving therefrom, and the means of overcoming them.

f. Be thoroughly familiar with all price lists and their proper use.

g. Develop a sound working knowledge of the approximate in-place costs of his products in their various applications in his territory.

h. Seek new applications and/or new markets for [company] products.

5. Be familiar with competitive materials:

a. Advantages and disadvantages relative to his products.

b. Limitations.

c. Installations techniques.

d. Expected performance.

e. Material prices and approximate in-place costs relative to those of his products.

f. Be alert to new competitive products and developments which may affect the business, and report same promptly.

6. *Communication.* The field sales representative should keep management (and other interested parties) informed of his activities by use of the following:

   a. Weekly Itinerary Forecasts

   b. Weekly Summary of Calls

   c. Daily Call Reports

   d. Weekly Expense Reports, including auto expense reports

   e. Informal reports on market conditions, business trends, competitive pricing or product changes, and other information of interest to management and other personnel

   f. Special reports, surveys, or forecasts as required by management

7. *Supplies.* Each company representative is equipped initially to begin operations. Thereafter he must assume responsibility for requisitioning and maintaining an adequate supply of literature, prices, technical material, samples, sales aids, report forms, stationery and business cards to cover his needs in connection with his routine operation.

8. *Personal Salesmanship.* The sales representative must strive to merit the confidence and develop personal goodwill of his contacts so that insofar as possible they will prefer to deal with him rather than with his competitors. Towards this end he should:

   a. Present a neat and well-groomed appearance at all times.

   b. Conduct himself in a friendly but dignified manner.

   c. Be considerate of his contacts, their moods, and their likes and dislikes.

   d. Abide by their local rules in the plant or office.

POWER POINTS

Industrial sales of any consequence are said to be more the result of preparation than of selling techniques. The buyer's office is no place to plan; it's the place to carry out preplanning which ends in successful sales.

Knowledge of product benefits, features, characteristics, performance, advantages, and uses, as well as of competitive differences, is the salesman's ammunition. He must have all of this knowledge stored in his memory for use collectively or by individual items. This specialized field often requires more product knowledge than selling skills.

The nature of industrial selling varies with the emphasis of the business. If the industrial firm manufactures supplies, the salesman is primarily concerned with servicing the account. In many respects he follows a procedure similar to that of the salesman who sells to the retailer. He may place special emphasis on obtaining the account and then make periodic calls to present new items, but not with the specific objective of writing an order. Often the salesman for this kind of firm is called upon to suggest products suitable for specific uses. There are also occasions when the industrial salesman may have engineers formulate and arrange special materials to help him meet the needs of particular customers.

Industrial selling can be very involved; for example, in the sale of heavy machinery or production equipment. Such sales may be initiated in two ways: A salesman may follow up a lead and persuade a prospect to consider using the equipment, or a potential purchaser may send letters of inquiry to several manufacturers of the desired machinery. In the first instance the salesman may suggest that he or his company's engineers undertake a survey of the prospect's manufacturing or other operations to learn if a need exists for the equipment the salesman would like to sell.

Once the prospect's need is determined, the salesman must demonstrate the desirability of accepting his recommendations, and finally obtain a signed order or contract. This phase of selling can become quite complicated, and some orders may take months to close.

In general, the primary responsibilities of an industrial salesman are: (1) to contact leads provided by the company; (2) to develop leads by canvassing prospects; (3) to arrange for customer surveys; (4) to prepare proposals; (5) to make a personal presentation of the proposal; (6) to keep an up-to-date list of prospective accounts; and (7) to follow up proposals to obtain signed contracts.

The industrial salesman's secondary responsibilities are: (1) to study changes made by the company in the products manufactured; (2) to learn about new uses for company products; (3) to learn about probable changes in customer products or production processes; (4) to learn about competitive activities in his territory; (5) to learn about activities of customer firm personnel who have influence in buying or specifying company products; and (6) to study types of equipment owned by the company's prospective customers.

Because he is the only company representative in the field, and because he usually has the technical training necessary to locate the cause, the industrial salesman often handles complaints related to equipment malfunctions. Sometimes the underlying problem is the customer's lack of ability to operate mechanical equipment properly.

It then becomes necessary for the industrial salesman to teach the customer or his employees the correct use of the equipment.

DISCUSSION QUESTIONS AND PROBLEMS

---

1. What are the main categories of industrial products?

2. What are some of the principal sources for purchasers of industrial products?

3. What is meant by *problem-solving attitude*?

4. Why does industrial selling require more detailed preparation?

5. What are the primary elements of the ideal sales talk?

6. What are the advantages of a survey to an industrial salesman?

7. What are the advantages of a purchaser's value analysis to a salesman of industrial products?

8. Briefly describe a buying sequence.

9. Through what marketing channels do industrial products move?

10. How does industrial selling differ from other kinds of selling?

SELLING PROBLEMS AND PROJECTS

---

1. The Joe Sikspak Case

Joe Sikspak was a rugged old Vermonter, an old-time salesman who had been selling to major industrial purchasing agents for more than thirty years. Joe had many good old-fashioned stories about his days "on the road." Here's one he told me in the lobby of the Tavern Hotel in Montpelier.

"When I sold those big shots I always appealed to profit and prestige more than anything else. I claim that profit and prestige, in that order, are the universal motivators. I discovered very early in my career that a salesman selling to industrial purchasers knows that not far beneath the skin of every one of them is a deep desire to earn more money or to save more money. And hardly one layer of his epidermis below that is the desire to be recognized as an important person, to have other people admire him."

"I wouldn't venture to tell you how to run your business," Joe would say to a hard-nosed prospect, "but one of my other customers tried my product and it raised production 5 percent in one of his plants, and between 10 and 15 percent in another, over a period of six months. But it probably wouldn't apply to your organization. You're pretty efficient already."

Joe Sikspak claimed that his casual remarks made the purchasing agents' ears prick up. Joe said he could almost see the buyer determining what that extra 5 to 15 percent would mean on his profit and loss statement.

Question

1. Do you agree with Joe Sikspak that profit and prestige are all a salesman has to appeal to? What selling elements would you add to or subtract from his statements? Why?

2. Denny Spear Case

Denny Spear's company and another firm were locked in a tug-of-war to sell a computer system to one of the largest shoe manufacturers in New England. When Denny, who was sales manager for his company, was called in to help his district manager, the prospect company's purchasing agent—an engineer—was on the verge of signing up with the other firm.

Denny and the district sales manager went to the city where the shoe company was located. There, they met the local salesman and began to prepare to meet the prospect. They stopped at a local hotel and proceeded to thrash the problem over carefully and thoroughly. Unless he knew precisely what the problem was, Spear reasoned, he would have very little opportunity for solving it when the right moment in the interview came. In short, Denny began to gather the facts necessary to orient himself to the prospect's point of view, as well as to become familiar with his problems.

At the prospect's factory the next day, Spear entered a large general office in which about twenty-five people were at work. He saw the purchasing agent, his target, sitting at a corner desk bent over his papers. He was a big man, partly bald, with his shirt collar open and his sleeves rolled up, and he was perspiring profusely. The purchasing agent beckoned Spear over and indicated he should sit down. He tiredly asked to be excused for a minute so he could finish an important bit of work. Obviously, he thought he was in for another session of high-pressure salesmanship such as he had been going through with other salesmen.

Finally, the purchasing agent finished his paper work and opened the transaction by saying, "I've just about made up my mind, but I'm willing to listen to what you have to say."

Instead of launching into a glowing and possibly disastrous talk about the virtues of his firm's equipment, Spear opened by explaining that he wasn't an engineer or a computer expert, but he would appreciate it if the purchasing agent would describe the operation for which the computer was being considered.

The purchasing agent—an engineer—started talking about the operation of his factory, obviously his pride and joy. Within a few minutes he became quite enthusiastic and began calling to his secretary for charts and blueprints to show how he wanted the new operation to function. The tone of the meeting began mellowing considerably. More important than that, additional facts about the factory's operation and the need for a computer system began to appear.

As a result, when the purchasing agent raised the question of servicing and the fact that Spear's electronic computer system was too delicate for an ordinary workman to repair or adjust, Spear, who had been listening carefully, was able to answer him intelligently. He was able to point out several places in which his computer would actually be easier to repair than a conventional system.

Although the purchasing agent seemed to be impressed, Spear kept remembering that he would have to justify his decision to his superiors. So Spear gave him facts that would enable the purchasing agent to support a recommendation to buy it—how it had been tested, tried, and rebought by some of the largest computer users in the country; how it could save much more than its 30 percent greater cost over the computer systems of Spear's competitors.

Significantly, Spear finally clinched the sale by keeping the prospect's viewpoint in mind. Knowing that the purchasing agent was not trying to select a batch of equipment, but looking for a means of running his plant more efficiently, Spear emphasized the reliable, quick expert service which would be available on a continuing basis. "You've made a deal," the purchasing agent said, and after settlement of the details the contract was signed.

Questions

1. What is the important factor in this case?

2. After consulting with the district manager and the salesman, Spear conducted the interview alone. Why do you think he did that?

3. What would you have done differently in this situation. Explain *why* and *how* you differ in any respect with the way Spear handled this sale.

CHAPTER 22

Selling at Conventions and Trade Shows

Conventions and trade shows are not new, but they are currently being emphasized more than ever. The difference between conventions and trade shows is slight. The primary function of a convention is to present speakers and discussions, with exhibits playing a secondary role. A trade show is primarily exhibits, with less emphasis on the speakers and discussions. A teacher's convention, for example, would have exhibits, but would emphasize speeches, workshops, and discussions. A trade show featuring household appliances would be likely to consist exclusively of exhibits.

Another difference between conventions and trade shows is that conventions are structured to attract *potential* customers rather than to obtain immediate orders. Convention exhibits are intended to attract attention and interest, but they are not primarily aimed at customers with checkbooks in hand.

Trade shows, on the other hand, are specifically structured to appeal to qualified prospects and customers. People attend them primarily to buy and only incidentally to listen to a luncheon or dinner speaker. Many trade shows are designed to encourage and solicit on-the-spot orders and do not admit the general public. For example, at the Chicago Furniture Mart retailers from all over the nation buy merchandise to be sold in their stores. Although the furniture association sponsors several speakers, the primary business of the show is select and order new furniture stock.

WHY TRADE SHOWS AND CONVENTIONS ARE HELD

There are two primary reasons for trade shows and conventions: First, visitors, customers, and prospective purchasers are there to *obtain* ideas, information, and products; second, the participating companies are there to *offer* ideas and products to these customers and prospective purchasers. Both sellers and buyers enjoy benefits, and that makes the affair worthwhile. Also, in modern marketing, trade shows and conventions are part of a total media approach. Since one medium alone seldom suffices, the best promotion plan utilizes all possible media and coordinates them toward a common objective. Trade shows and conventions have a vital place in this total promotion program for many products and services.

Visitors to trade shows and conventions have an opportunity to shop and compare products, and no better way has been found to do so than at these affairs. Within a day or two, the prospective buyer can look at and examine a dozen different items, compare prices, quality, service, and terms, make his decision about buying, and, if advisable, he can place an order.

Trade shows and conventions enable vendors to bring their propositions to the buyers, and both save time and much of the expense of the marketing process. Industrial buyers save time when they attend trade shows, because they can usually find everything they need under one roof. They do not, therefore, need to visit the manufacturers at their place of business. In the same way, the salesmen are saved much valuable time, because many of their prospect calls can be eliminated when buyers are attracted to a show or convention. As we've said, the buyers can easily compare product features and benefits, make fast decisions, and place their orders without a time lag or wasted effort.

There are specialty trade shows designed for the general public, such as auto, cattle, boat, and hobby shows. These specialty trade shows permit the consumer to examine and compare the items on exhibit. Many of these shows do not take orders for their items, because they sell through middlemen such as dealers, distributors, and retail stores. These exhibits do, however, satisfy the curiosity of those who are interested in the specialty.

A product is often featured in many other kinds of promotional media, but manufacturers believe that exhibits make up the *final* media approach. This approach gives prospective buyers their first chance to examine products about which they have heard or read.

ATTENDANCE

Trade shows and conventions offer participating companies four advantages:

- To display their products.
- To show their company images.
- To make customer contacts through salesmen.
- To evaluate competitive products.

People who attend trade shows and conventions are there so that they may learn about the products on display, meet old friends, have fun, and perhaps purchase something. To the company representative this interested prospect is "hot." When he stops to look at an exhibit, he is much more receptive to hearing how the product might benefit him. He wants to know! The sales representative is primarily there to explain and demonstrate the product. In many cases, the phases of the usual sales presentation are shortened because the prospect is mentally and emotionally ready to forego the introductory talk and immediately asks for *explanations*. Quite often, the buyer can be brought to the point of ordering by the time he leaves the exhibit or booth.

A convention or trade show offers excellent opportunities to exhibit new products, a variety of products, and complex or intangible products. A major advantage is that a wide selection of products, far greater than a salesman can carry, can be displayed at an exhibit. Large and complex items that cannot be carried into a prospect's office can be fully exhibited. Intangibles are often graphically shown through visual sales aids and demonstrations that would be impossible or impractical in a prospect's office.

PLANNING THE PROMOTION

Long before the trade show or convention is scheduled to open, the sales management staff must work out a timetable and arrange for personnel participation. The time schedules, the sequence of events, the dates and hours of the exhibit, meetings, hospitality hour, and duties of exhibit representatives must be planned. The purpose of planning is to assure that everything will be ready at the right time and that representatives know what they are to do. After the show opens it is too late to add new equipment and new exhibits, or to train sales representatives. Obviously, any errors or shortages cost the company money—sometimes a great sum of money, for these affairs are very costly.

Much of the advance planning involves the activities of the sales representative. Salesmen are notified in detail about the purpose of the trade show or convention, and they are expected to relay the product and service information to their customers and prospects. The salesman's home office often mails printed announcements directly to prospects and customers. Advertisements in trade journals and articles in company house organs carry news items, stories, and a full schedule of events. All suitable promotional media may be used, including radio, television, and newspapers, or any other device that will attract the attention of prospective buyers.

Booths and exhibits can be quite profitable to the sponsors when they are well planned and properly staffed. The exhibit staff is considered to be the most important element in showing, demonstrating, and selling products and services.

EXHIBIT SALES PROMOTIONS

Exhibit Staff

Staffing an exhibit booth is one of the most difficult problems in sales promotion. First, the question arises whether the exhibit personnel should consist of local or regional salesmen, or specialists from the home office who are perhaps more knowledgeable, or both salesmen and specialists. Companies selling technical products or services may rely more heavily on professional or technical men to handle their exhibit.

Many companies believe that an exhibit is a good place to familiarize trainees and younger salesmen with company policies and to let them work under fairly close supervision, so that they can perfect their sales presentations and receive remedial instruction on the job. An exhibit also gives the trainee and younger salesman an opportunity to ask questions, to experience another form of sales work, and to understand the sales organization.

There is one point, however, which must not be forgotten. If the convention site has been well selected, as in a teachers' convention, the audience will consist of the largest group of potential buyers for the products presented, in the most competitive situation possible. Therefore, to gain the most from the exhibit, the company's objective cannot be left solely to the trainee or junior salesman. Competent, seasoned salesmen must be used to make the major presentation, for they are the people who have the ability and experience to make and develop the contacts and to do each in a minimum of time, thereby obtaining maximum results.

The *technical staff* at an exhibit may consist of product development specialists and other professional or technical experts in any phase of the company's research, manufacturing, or distribution procedures. It does not include service or repair personnel engaged in product or other maintenance at the exhibit.

When a company participates as a secondary exhibitor—in other words, in a show that is not primarily in the same industry as the exhibitor, but in which the exhibitor knows he has a good market potential—it is always advisable to have available in the booth a man with technical knowledge who is able to answer questions or to consult with prospects on technical problems. The importance of the presence of a technical man in this situation is often overlooked. For example, a manufacturer of photographic supplies and equipment who has an exhibit at a chemical industry convention should have a chemist on its exhibit staff, to answer those questions which are too technically complicated for the sales representative. For example, many chemical problems are involved in the manufacture of photographic materials and supplies, even though such companies are not considered chemical manufacturers, since many of their major problems are also optical and mechanical. One of these companies exhibiting at a show for the chemical industry would be certain that its own chemists, thoroughly familiar with their own products and their applications in chemical companies, would be present.

Staff Indoctrination

Prior to the exhibit, a meeting for the exhibit staff is often held, in which the purpose and reasons why the company is exhibiting are outlined. In this meeting the staff also gets a complete rundown of what is expected of them.

First, the staff is indoctrinated with the importance of the method of their presentations, their manners and appearance, and any other factors common to good human relations. If these things are not clearly understood, there is the possibility that the staff will spend its time doing little, or only those things *they* prefer to do, or those things *they* believe to be most helpful, and in the manner *they* believe to be best. A knowledge of the purpose and a review of *exhibit selling* principles for their company will pinpoint their part in the effort and enable them to further the company's objectives.

Management knows that, no matter how attractive and carefully planned, an exhibit can be completely ineffective if its staff is not properly trained and supervised. These are company representatives and they are cautioned to know their product and service benefits so well that their presentations will attract attention, create interest, and arouse at least a certain measure of desire. Naturally, these representatives are not averse to closing successful sales whenever possible.

Staff members are also cautioned to be alert for every opportunity to be of service. They are told, "People come to the exhibit to see what you have to offer. Indicate in some way that they are welcome and that you want to talk with them about their problems and interests. While they are on neutral ground, being neither in their office nor yours, they are likely to be more receptive to a proposition. Each visitor should be given equal opportunity to ask questions and receive answers. This is not the time or place to qualify prospects, or to be selective, for no one can tell who is an immediate prospect or a future one. Furthermore, these visitors are not all mere 'lookers' and you never know who are 'hot' prospects and who will need to be slowly developed."

Staff personnel should rarely be seated during the hours they are assigned to work in the exhibit area. This may seem to be a bit rough, but schedules are usually arranged to give frequent rest periods. Standing up for one's company and its products or services makes a good impression on attendees. If possible, the salesman should not encourage a visitor to sit while he is showing or demonstrating. If he does, the visitor may just rest and not really listen nor see anything. If it seems to be advisable to be seated with him at a later time and it cannot be arranged away from the booth, the salesman should be sure not to take advantage of this time to rest himself.

Something should be going on in the exhibit area at all times. If there is a demonstration it should be continuous. This will not only let attendees know the salesman is there; it will also let them know that he is active and anxious to meet them.

As a major promotional effort, exhibiting merits a review from the salesman's management and occasional reports by the salesman, who should do his part in collecting and passing along information. Most important, the salesman must make sure that his leads are written up fully and accurately.

The salesman should be alert and enthusiastic up to the last minute of the exhibit's last day. This isn't always easy to do when one is getting anxious to close up and is tired from a successful exhibit or discouraged because it has been disappointing. Nevertheless, important prospects are as likely as not to come late to the show when they find it more convenient, and the salesman should expect this to happen.

Making appointments with his family or friends, or using his booth as a meeting place, is not recommended. This is the surest way to drive away prospects, for nothing creates a worse impression than a display jammed with persons obviously not connected with the show or the product the salesman is to demonstrate and sell.

Staff personnel should dress conservatively and act with dignity. Prospects are looking for substance and quality in a company's personnel as well as in its product. Salespeople must live up to that expectation and by continuous good grooming give that impression at all times.

Exhibit staff members are placed in one of their company's most highly competitive selling situations. These salesmen are among their company's best men, and this is their opportunity to prove it. If a trainee has been assigned to the exhibit staff, responsibility should not be passed to him; he is there to gain experience and to assist, not to earn a full-time salesman's salary.

If the salesman's company permits and if he must entertain, particularly on an emergency basis, he should be certain someone else is available to take his place on the floor.

MEETINGS

Many salesmen will have occasion to hold meetings with attendees at conventions and trade shows. In preparation for such meetings, they are trained not only in the specifics of their product or service but also in the techniques of speaking to adults. They are trained to communicate with adult groups in a learning situation, and they are supplied with everything they need in the way of training aids and materials.

These sessions can only be worthwhile when appropriate topics are selected and the meeting carefully planned. The chief topics of interest to both wholesaler's salesman and retail store manager, for example, are increased sales, volume, and net profits. Therefore, if the wholesaler's salesman arranges training sessions around the following topics, he will have interested and receptive audiences.

Customers: How to attract new customers; how to hold customers; how to build up accounts; how to handle small orders; how to resurrect dying or dormant accounts.

Products: How to demonstrate merchandise; how to introduce a new product; the manufacturer's promotion and support plans; the advantages of stocking the salesman's line.

Salesmanship: How to interest customers; how to prove claims; how to handle obstructions; how to build up the benefits from the merchandise; how to close successful sales.

Preparing the Meeting

Publicity about the meeting must never be omitted. Everyone even remotely interested should be made aware of the time and place of the meeting as well as the topics to be considered.

When the meeting is to occur during the operating hours of a trade show or a convention, it must be fitted into the overall time schedule. If the exhibit schedule and the salesman's meetings are not coordinated before the meeting, the salesman may have postponements, absenteeism of people who were to have had important parts in the program, and, quite often, partial or complete failure.

Even though a salesman has an excellent memory and exhibit plans have been carefully prepared by his home office, nevertheless he must be sure that he has a fresh schedule showing the specific place, day, and hour of his meeting. The written outline should state the topics to be treated, time for each topic, and aids to be used. The salesman who writes out in advance his opening remarks, tentative questions for discussion, closing remarks, and a bit of appropriate humor will be relaxed rather than nervous and will therefore be much more effective. Reading from notes is not a part of a good training method, however. It is better to miss some particular point than to bore an audience by reading from a manuscript.

Company Programs

Many companies sponsor meetings during trade shows and conventions. These are usually breakfast and luncheon affairs held for invited guests. Obviously, these occasions are intended to build goodwill for company products. There is usually light entertainment; perhaps a good speaker; good food; perhaps a brief, unobtrusive sales talk; and of greatest importance, a gathering of friendly people. These affairs have become so popular in certain industries that attendees eagerly seek invitations to participate in them.

Company personnel usually provide the speaking talent, but not always. Sometimes management will obtain a very well-known speaker who commands a large fee. Naturally, the identification of the speaker with the company is intended to impress the audience.

As in any training session, there are rules to follow if these sponsored programs are to be a success. These rules approximate those for any meeting, but there are three additions: a menu must be chosen, the entertainment must be carefully selected, and an appropriate speaker must be employed. Follow-up of the program by management follows the same routine as for any other training endeavor.

THE HOSPITALITY ROOM

Duty in the hospitality room is at least as demanding as that at the exhibit. Sometimes there may be less confusion than on the exhibit floor. On the other hand, it may be very confused and raucous and fatiguing for the salesman. He has the same responsibility to greet guests as they arrive; to see that each guest receives the refreshment he wants; to answer questions; and to act as host when needed. The reason for this activity is to build his company's reputation and to establish a mutual feeling of goodwill.

Hospitality can go too far if the salesman forgets that a convention or trade show is a place for sales work. The hospitality room usually, but not always, is held only after the more formal part of the convention day has closed, so many salesmen find themselves working far beyond their normal hours. Some hospitality room salesmen may be tempted to be their own best bar guests, and this must be guarded against. They must remember that their jobs and alcohol do not mix well—their image as salesmen may suffer, they may lose sales, they may hurt their company's reputation.

Setting up the Hospitality Room

How much floor space will be needed in the hospitality room? This is one of the first questions the company must consider. How many people will visit? How many comfortable chairs and sofas, tables and telephones will be needed? What refreshments should be on hand? Coffee, sweet rolls, sandwiches, soft drinks, liquor?

The next consideration is to determine who to invite. Should the hospitality room be open to all attendees at the show, convention, or exhibit? Or should it be open only to those invited, probably customers, prospects, acquaintances, or friends? Some companies give printed invitations, or their business cards, to selected visitors; some invite them by word of mouth; a few have signs in their exhibits which invite anyone who cares to do so to visit the hospitality room.

Should the hospitality room be opened only after lunch, after five o'clock, after dinner, or later in the evening?

Should the hospitality room be used to exhibit products or services? Should there be demonstration equipment or visual sales aids available? Is it advisable to have company literature in conspicuous spots? The answer varies with each company, the product, or the service, and the facilities in general. Some companies maintain a hospitality room only as a place to relax, meet friends, talk, and enjoy oneself. Products, sales aids, and literature may be readily available if someone wants to see them, but usually the hospitality room should not appear to be an exhibit booth.

MANAGEMENT WANTS TO KNOW

Follow-up

With exhibits there is always a lurking suspicion that the event was not worth the investment. On the other hand, there might be evidence that it was a success as a clientele builder. What was right and what was wrong are two things management always wants to know about their exhibit. For example, management wants to know: How much business did we book? Did we attract a sufficient number of prospective buyers? Did we get our quota of visitors? Did our booth exhibit attract as much attention as the competition's? Who had the best exhibit? Who had the poorest? What was the rank of ours? What improvements should be made next year? What seemed to impress visitors most about our exhibit? Did we run over our budget?

The answers to the first three questions are the most important. If the exhibit helped close sales, fine. If not, the other questions should provide the answers as to whether the exhibit should be continued, discontinued, or improved.

It is believed by most companies that when exhibits are properly planned, staffed, analyzed, and followed up by salesmen, they are a good investment in terms of the number of sales produced.

DISPLAYING PRODUCTS ABROAD[1]

Trade Fairs

International trade fairs are of great help to manufacturers who want to introduce new products to foreign customers. About six hundred

1. Lawrence C. McQuade, December 1970. Mr. McQuade is Assistant Secretary of Commerce, U.S. Department of Commerce.

fairs for specific industries are held around the world each year. Any firm in the particular industry is eligible to take space at the exhibit.

Before exhibiting at an international trade fair, a U.S. firm will usually conduct market research to determine whether there is potential for selling the product line in the area. In recent years the number of U.S. firms exhibiting at foreign trade fairs has increased markedly —almost to the point that U.S. exhibitions outnumber all other exhibits.

Trade Centers

U.S. Trade Centers are permanent showcases located in central marketing areas overseas. Every year each Center holds about eight major product exhibitions. Exhibitions are built around specific products or themes selected for sales potential. Moscow has a Trade Center showing exhibits from the United States. It is anticipated that a similar exhibit will soon be housed in Peking.

Technical meetings, in conjunction with appropriate exhibitions, help increase interest. Between major shows, Trade Center space is available for meetings held by individual firms or their agents.

At U.S. Trade Centers in Milan, Stockholm, Tokyo, London, Frankfurt, and Bangkok, the exhibitor pays a nominal sum for space and hospitality. Costs vary, depending on location, size, and scope. The exhibitor also agrees to ship exhibit products to the foreign port of entry and to staff his display.

The U.S. Department of Commerce will help with exhibit design, fabrication, transportation details, market promotion, and locating agents. The department also assumes the cost of returning the exhibitor's unsold products to the United States.

Sample Display Centers

If a U.S. firm wants overseas sales agents, it can recruit them by showing product samples and literature for thirty days in sample display centers in cities such as Beirut, Nairobi, and Bagdad. Recruiters may be sent with the display, but if this is not practical, the commercial officer at the U.S. Embassy will make certain the samples are seen by prospective agents, distributors, or licensees.

The office will forward names of prospective sales representatives. Company management can then negotiate with them directly. There is no charge for exhibit space and related services.

Mobile Trade Fairs

Fairs are also carried by plane, ship, or motor transport to two or more foreign markets. Mobile fairs are often combined with a trade mission.

Selling Overseas

In addition to assistance with trade fairs, trade centers, sample display centers, and mobile fairs, the U.S. Department of Commerce offers much more help to individual and small business exhibitors. This assistance is especially valuable for those with limited resources who want to sell overseas for the first time, or for expanding export business or licensing products in other nations.

POWER POINTS

Conventions and trade shows are time-tested methods of bringing buyers and sellers together under mutually beneficial conditions. Conventions emphasize discussion groups and workshops and are directed primarily at *potential* customers; while exhibits and booths are featured at trade shows, which are designed to attract *immediate* prospects.

Visitors to these affairs have an opportunity to examine, compare, and learn about new products, market movements, new sources, and competition. These shows are usually designed for special interest groups, but specialty trade shows, such as boat shows, are aimed at the general public.

People who attend these affairs are deeply interested and inquisitive about the latest trends in the particular field. Therefore, when the exhibits are well publicized, managed, and staffed, they result in increased sales volume for the exhibitors. Exhibit staffing is considered to be the most important element in these shows and conventions.

Choosing the right staff and providing training and indoctrination for them is the most important factor in an exhibit. Management knows that poor staffing and training can completely negate even the most excellent display. When the product or service is highly technical, the availability of a technically knowledgeable *expert* to answer technical questions is particularly important.

There should always be a person in charge and everyone concerned should be sure who he is. All exhibit salesmen should be informed of their company's objective, either by advance bulletin or in a pre-exhibit meeting. At the pre-exhibit meeting the whole group should go over the details of the presentation and the method to use in filling out prospective buyer cards. Each one on booth duty should know exactly what is expected of him and then see that he follows these instructions:

1. Keep the booth adequately staffed at all times.
2. Know the products and the other members of the exhibit staff.
3. Make the attendee (prospect) feel welcome and invited.
4. Keep the exhibit neat and orderly.
5. Fill in the inquiry forms accurately and immediately.

The booth personnel are there to promote and sell. There should be an adequate number of exhibit staff members to keep the working shifts reasonable, so that all attendants on duty at the show will be fresh and alert. A responsible person should be in charge of the general exhibit, leaving demonstrators free to concentrate on their presentations.

In addition to exhibit and demonstration work, salesmen may be asked to operate special meetings, sessions, or workshops. The important thing for the salesman to remember is that the participants are adults and the methodology described in this text for preparing any meeting should be employed. Company-sponsored breakfasts or luncheons require somewhat different treatment such as arranging for the menu, entertainment, and featured speaker.

The *hospitality room* requires at least as much selling expertise as any other aspect of the convention or trade show. It, too, is a place for serious sales work, even though it is work of a public relations type. As in any other kind of exhibit and convention promotion, there are rules to be followed for successful hospitality sessions. It should be kept in mind that this is a place to meet friends, talk, and enjoy oneself, and should not appear to be another exhibit booth.

To determine if the event was worth the investment, there must be a *follow-up*. Management will want to know how much business was signed or promised, how many visitors called at the booth, and how the exhibit can be improved.

Overseas Trade Shows and Exhibitions

The principles of selling and displaying at exhibits are the same overseas as in the United States. There are only a few minor exceptions, primarily having to do with manners and courtesies in the countries involved.

Although overseas selling has traditionally been done by individual enterprising merchants, they no longer need to "go it alone" unless they wish to do so. Today, the U.S. Department of Commerce stands ready to assist businessmen to exhibit and sell in overesas markets all over the world. For example, the department can help with international trade fairs and centers, sample display centers, and mobile trade fairs.

Supplementary Readings

The following readings emphasize adult education methods with special reference to the conduct of meetings, exhibits, trade shows, conventions, and hospitality:

1. Haas, Kenneth B. *How to Develop Successful Salesmen.* New York: McGraw-Hill, 1957.
2. Lang, Rudolf. *Win, Place, and Show.* New York: Oceana Publications, 1959.

DISCUSSION QUESTIONS AND PROBLEMS

---

1. What is the difference between a *trade show* and a *convention?*

2. What are the primary purposes of trade shows and conventions?

3. What is the most difficult problem in trade-show planning?

4. Why is it recommended that an exhibit staff have at least one individual who is technically knowledgeable concerning the product line?

5. What should a salesman know about how to conduct a meeting or a training session during a trade show or convention?

6. Of what value is a hospitality room?

7. Why do exhibits offer a good place to train beginning salesmen?

8. What is the most important element in an exhibit or display booth?

9. What good and bad points can you think of regarding exhibiting at international trade fairs and overseas trade centers?

10. Discuss the importance of following up what is accomplished at an exhibit.

SELLING PROBLEMS AND PROJECTS

---

1.   Joe Daniels Case

Joe Daniels had labored long and diligently in the company exhibit booth at a trade show. The exhibit was modest but interesting, and kept within the budget. Joe believed that his salesmanship ability was above average. As sales aids Joe had business cards, product brochures, reprints of company advertisements, but no materials with which to demonstrate and no hospitality room.

Question

1.   What suggestions do you have to help Joe foster more interest in his exhibit and product at future shows?

2.   Spike Drumbang Case

Spike Drumbang, after many years of experimentation, had perfected a crystallized, freeze-dried orange juice. A tablespoon of the crystals mixed in a glass of water made a delightful drink which tasted almost like fresh orange juice.

The crystals could be produced in California or Florida and transported at a fraction of the cost of fresh oranges or orange juice. Spike knew that there were foreign countries, especially in Europe, where fresh oranges were seasonal and extremely expensive, which naturally limited their sale. Spike felt that this vast market must be reached. He was sure that someone, or some organization, could help him market his product, but he wasn't sure how to go about it.

Question

1.   How could Spike Drumbang determine if there was a potential market for his product overseas?

2.   How could he successfully reach that overseas market?

3.   Dick Dyke Case

Dick Dyke is a salesman for a firm which manufactures and sells automatic control systems. He knows exactly how his prospective buyers could benefit from the use of his product.

Dick is a good salesman, but his product is quite complicated, very bulky, high-priced, and his prospects are widely scattered around the eastern seaboard. Obviously, he could not call on his prospects as often as he wished. The result has been that Dick's sales were not as great as he expected. His company advertising is above average in specific trade journals, booklets, and reprints, but it does not seem to help his sales very much. Dick thought a trade show exhibit might raise sales, so he wrote a memo to his management in which he presented his reasoning.

Question

1. If you were Dick, what reasons would you give for exhibiting at a trade show?

CHAPTER 23

Establishing
a Clientele

Much of a salesman's success in his efforts to increase his list of clients depends on his own attitude toward his business. If he is enthusiastic about his company policies and services, and if he believes in what he is selling, his confidence will be contagious and will carry over to his customers. The salesman who really believes in his proposition simply cannot prevent others from believing in him. Establishing a clientele is an individualized activity, and when and how it is done depends largely on the salesman himself.

Cold Canvass

Quite often the only effective way to build a clientele is to use the cold-canvass method. This kind of clientele building calls for much ambition, initiative, and selling skill, but it can be effective for those who understand its use.

Referrals

A most important source of new business, and a source which is usually ignored, is the customer who knows a salesman and his product and is often pleased to supply the names of friends and acquaintances who would buy what the salesman has to sell. The salesman should not be timid in asking his customers for the names of possible new buyers. It has always been true that nothing gives a person greater pleasure than doing a favor for a friend. The following are the important ways in which satisfied customers can help to build a bigger clientele:

1. They can pave the way for an interview with friends, acquaintances, or relatives by phoning them, writing a letter of introduction, or by personal introduction.
2. They can write testimonials giving proof of satisfaction with the product or service.
3. They can give names of their acquaintances and important information about them.
4. They can provide experiences that point out how badly they needed the product or service and the benefits they received since buying it.

It has been said that a salesperson's *users*, or his customers, are the lifeblood of his business. In a sense, they sign his paycheck. A continual job of prospecting among satisfied users and customers is a vital part of a salesperson's job. In other words, sell them but never forget them!

Goodwill

A clientele is built slowly through the years and is based on the customer's understanding, sentiments, and beliefs about the salesman and his company, in other words, on goodwill.

Goodwill is the advantage in trade which a business has acquired beyond the mere value of what it sells. It can also mean friendly or kindly feeling.

If goodwill exists, it is not always necessary to have a better product or service for the price than a competitor. It is not even necessary that a product or service be as good as a competitor's if goodwill makes up for the difference in value between the two.

In this book, emphasis has been placed on what is believed to be superior sales skills and procedures. However, there is no denying the fact that superior products, services, skills, and procedures are usually not enough. To build a faithful clientele, it is necessary to have the additional value of goodwill as well as superior products and superior sales methods.

There are generally three ways to build a faithful clientele: through company effort, through the product and service, and through the personal efforts of the salesman.

Using the Company Effort

Reliable companies continuously build a faithful clientele through the following activities:

1. Years of satisfactory service, resulting in recognition of dependability and ethical principles.
2. Advertising—educational in character and building buyer acceptance through consumer appeals and repetition.
3. Quality of product or services.
4. Fair dealing with customers.

The company's quality standards in making the product, in servicing accounts, in policy-making, in advertising, and other managerial functions are beyond the salesman's control. A professional salesman knows, however, that these elements make up the goodwill of his company and that it is one of his most valuable assets. He makes the most of his company goodwill by constantly explaining his company's policies, objectives, and services to his customers. He realizes that the continuing goodwill his customers hold for his company depends very largely upon himself, for to customers the salesman is the company.

A salesman, for example, can build goodwill by showing tear sheets, reprints, or photographs of his company's merchandise to his prospects, together with facts about how many consumers they reach and the potential sales increase which may follow. He should be prepared to indicate the increased number of readers who will be influenced in favor of his merchandise. He should try to expand the interest produced by the advertising into desire and action, or its effect will be nil. He must use his advertising to the fullest extent or it ceases to be an advantage. When good advertising and good selling are teamed together, they may form an unbeatable combination.

Without these assets, a salesman cannot continue to sell his merchandise profitably. Mere statements designed to sell his company's record, experience, and prestige are not sufficient.

The Salesman's Personal Efforts

The alert salesman realizes that his efforts to build a clientele depend in a large measure on himself. When they think of his company, prospects do not think of the sales manager or the president; they think of their direct personal contact, the salesman. They think of his appearance, speech, and manner; his knowledge of his products; how he helped solve their problems; they think of his knowledge of modern marketing services. All of these have a bearing on clientele building. When cordial relations are established with prospects, salesmen can cement goodwill and make themselves sure, profitable clients.

Many companies are constantly improving their products through experiments, tests, and research. They also create and develop industrial and efficiency reports, merchandising plans, cost control systems, and many other services for customers. These goodwill devices may not be appreciated, however, unless the salesman tells his prospects about them and motivates them to buy.

On the other hand, when the salesman misrepresents, ridicules complaints, resorts to unfair practices, and fails to provide service and aids, the goodwill which the company has built up over many years at great expense is destroyed or lost.

Little interest is aroused, for example, when a prospect is told that the salesman's company has been in business for twenty years. However, success stories from satisfied users over the years will influence their buying decisions. Company exclusives or "firsts" are also impressive, as well as written testimonials and other tangible evidence. Tear sheets of company advertisements and references to radio and television shows sponsored by the salesman's company are also impressive to customers and prospects.

In addition, the salesman's personality is quite important. The people he is trying to sell have natural human attitudes, reactions, prejudices, and individual behavior traits. When the buyer likes and respects the salesman, a fine start has been made toward building acceptance and goodwill.

Empathy

Since friendship and goodwill are so closely related, clientele building is aided when a salesman likes his customers. Each individual has good and bad points, and the good traits almost always outweigh by far the bad ones. The salesman should look for the good traits in a prospect and remind himself to like everyone. Everybody will like him in return. A friendly, cordial attitude can work wonders in influencing clients.

Presentation manner—The manner in which a presentation is made can affect clientele building. A supercilious, know-it-all, unenthusiastic manner can never gain clients. These things will never convey the idea of benefits to prospective customers.

The benefit story may become "old stuff" to a salesperson, but it is always fresh and interesting to his listeners. Repetition of the benefits of products or service is nearly always worthwhile and will usually serve to counteract the impressions other salespeople may have made between his calls.

Courtesy with objectors—When handling objections, it is quite easy to incur a prospect's displeasure, particularly if his views are slighted or an argument is permitted to arise. On the other hand, clientele building is most easily accomplished by handling objections with tact.

Follow-up—After each sales effort, whether successful or unsuccessful, the prospect should be left with the idea that the salesman will be back again for an order. He should leave the prospect with the happy feeling that it will be a pleasure to call on him again, that the prospect will look forward to future calls because of his personality, thoughtfulness, and fairness.

Goodwill is also built when a sale is followed up to determine if a product or service is living up to promises or to offer the buyer advice and help in using or caring for it. Buyers like repeat calls, provided they are offered helpful suggestions, advice, and assistance.

Customers are pleased when they are not forgotten or overlooked. The alert salesman tries to keep in touch with them through telephone calls, courtesy letters, remembrance cards on birthdays and anniversaries, and congratulatory cards for special occasions.

When call-backs are made to build a clientele, they should be kept on a strictly business basis. They are not social visits; they are business calls, and something worthwhile should be done at each call. The salesman often has to do considerable advance thinking to find helpful suggestions for the prospects on his call-backs.

Services

The salesman who hopes to enjoy the benefits that come from a faithful clientele must be willing to put something extra into his relationships. He must prepare himself to help his customers. He must give them new ideas for increasing their business, suggest different ways for moving their merchandise, inform them about new products and new uses for old products, mention new promotional methods and profitable applications of new ideas.

An alert salesman will be able to estimate the local market, to secure facts about it, evaluate them, and report to his customers. He should be able to report those facts in an inspirational, yet logical, manner. If he sells to dealers, he should be able to advise them about every phase of their business: finance, record keeping, departmentalization, displays, training, sales techniques, and many other things that will help him to build a strong clientele.

Other services that can be offered as a part of clientele building may include such things as expediting deliveries, notifying customers when they may expect deliveries, checking on delivery dates, and being on hand at delivery time to help install or operate the product or service. These services not only build goodwill; they also enable the salesman to correct errors and complaints which may destroy goodwill.

Company services may also be used to build goodwill—services such as laboratory tests, engineering assistance, and the solution of a prospect's production or distribution problems. In brief, an alert salesman knows the buyer's problems and helps to solve them.

Many salesmen hesistate to offer company services because they are looking for something extraordinary—something outstanding that will enhance their personal importance. Although an accumulation of small services over a period of time may be less evident, it generally will produce better results than a single "big" service.

As part of his preparation for personal service, a successful salesman frequently asks himself, "What will my proposition do for the prospect and what can I do to help my customers?"

To answer this question in part, one salesman who sells to retailers has a photographic collection of window and counter displays that have been unusually successful in stores of other cities. These visual aids aroused considerable interest on the part of customers.

An office equipment salesman who subscribes to several business magazines and trade journals may lend them to his customers. He also keeps up with the new books that are written on salesmanship, merchandising, and advertising, and should be glad to lend these to customers.

Some salesmen carry newspaper clippings, bank bulletins and charts, and analyses of business conditions which are effectively used with certain prospects who would probably not have enough free time to see such materials.

These are all potential methods of producing goodwill. A salesman who uses these methods makes himself and his company distinctive, because the average salesman will not go to the bother of helping the customer by bringing him new and profitable ideas.

The word "service" is somewhat shopworn, but the willingness to serve in order to give complete satisfaction helps build a clientele. Service can be expressed only in deeds, not in words. Successful salesmen build up a reputation for *giving* service, not merely for just talking about it.

Learning from Errors

Another part of clientele building is an analysis of the results of every call, whether or not it led to a sale. It is important for the salesperson to discover the reason behind every "yes" and "no." The clientele builder will never overlook the value of analyzing his major mistakes and of developing an attitude of self-evaluation. The following listing may be of assistance to the client-conscious salesperson in his efforts to discover why his efforts were sometimes unsuccessful.

1. Entered interview without necessary information and the prospect did not buy.
2. Worried by competitor's advertising and started a comparison of the two products instead of discussing the merits of his own merchandise.
3. Failed to have reserve selling points and additional information to gain a favorable buying decision.
4. Engaged in an argument and lost the goodwill of the prospect.
5. Neglected the prospect, who was sold by a competitor.
6. Did not present and demonstrate properly, and the prospect lost interest.

UNDERSTANDING CREDIT

Few salespeople like to concern themselves with credit and collection duties. Nearly all are inclined to remark, "This is not for me. It's my job to sell. It's up to the credit department to establish credits and to collect money for goods sold."

It is true that nearly all companies give the bulk of this responsibility to a credit manager. It is also true that the majority of business enterprises do not expect their salespeople to pass on credit references or to make collections. Nevertheless, the credit department cannot do all the work and the competent salesperson knows that when he makes a sale, he should at least be aware of the importance of credits and collection and be willing to assist in dealing with them.

While many salespeople do not at first understand and appreciate the importance of credit and collection activities, they do so when the facts are explained to them and they then fully agree.

1. No order can be profitable until it has been paid for in full by the purchaser.

2. A good reason exists for company credit and collection policies.

3. There is a need for cooperation in this field between salesmen and management, with the salesman collecting credit data and reporting them to the credit manager.

Credit Responsibilities of the Salesman

A salesman should acquire a perfect understanding of his company's credit policies. His best source of information on this topic is the company credit manager. The credit manager will probably be delighted to outline the assistance the salesperson can furnish which will be helpful in determining the credit to be allowed the prospects in the salesman's territory. The reason that the credit manager will be delighted is that the salesman has the opportunity to observe conditions at first hand. He can see and hear many things which have a bearing on the character, capacity, and capital of the prospect or customer, things that ordinarily do not appear in credit ratings supplied by such organizations as Dun and Bradstreet. The salesperson can make a personal appraisal of the prospect's properties, plant, and equipment. If the prospect handles merchandise for resale, the salesman can gain much information from observing the stock and its condition. He can tell whether it is fresh or shopworn; whether the dealer is overstocked or in short supply and whether the stock is of good quality or not. He can also see whether the store is in a good location for attracting trade.

Appraising a prospect or customer in this way requires diligence, care, and keen judgment. To obtain valid facts and make reliable judgments, the salesman should question the local banker, insurance man, the prospect's competitors, and other miscellaneous sources before he formulates a report to be passed on to his credit manager. Such intelligent and conscientious reportings on the things he sees and hears—things which affect a customer's ability to pay—will benefit the salesperson in many ways.

Benefits to the Salesman

That the salesman profits when his company profits should need no further clarification. However, an intelligent understanding of the relationship that exists between sales and credits may prove beneficial to a salesman in these ways: (a) his ability to intelligently discuss and interpret credits and collections will gain him the goodwill of his customers and thereby assure him future business; (b) it brings to him the realization that he should spend his time only on those prospects who can pay for his products or service easily and quickly. The competitive salesman educates his customers to pay promptly. The salesman should be alert to any signs of financial deterioration in an account. In a frank discussion with the customer, the salesman can obtain the true economic status of the account. He can sustain a weakened account or help make special arrangements for payment to tide a customer over. This can prevent loss of the account and gain the goodwill of a customer. A customer whose accounts are in arrears may well begin looking elsewhere for his stock and become "open territory" for competition. The account may then be lost and the company invoices remain unpaid; both the company and the salesperson will lose out. But when a credit reputation is not damaged during a difficult period, everybody gains.

A salesperson who understands his customer's financial situation is in a position to know how much debt the customer can handle. The amount a prospect could safely buy may differ from month to month or from year to year, depending on such factors as increasing competition, economic conditions, and customer selectivity.

New Accounts

When competitive selling is in full force, salespeople in all fields are asked to locate new customers for a wider distribution of the products they sell. The new outlets, however, must be good credit risks or the new sales will never be consummated. More than 300,000 new businesses are established each year in the United States, and many of these new businesses are not given credit ratings by reporting agencies. The salesperson, in his search for new customers, trains himself to recognize the probable credit rating of a prospective customer. In this way he can judge whether it is worth his time to pursue this client or to seek more promising clients.

Reviving Accounts

Good credit judgment will prompt the alert salesman to revive customer accounts that have been rejected because of poor credit ratings or slow collections. These companies may have made bad starts or encountered lean years and yet have overcome their difficulties through capable management and become good credit risks. Bringing old accounts back into the fold may be difficult, and require tactful handling, but it can be an effort well spent.

Special Terms

A good company representative always adheres to the credit policy of his house. There are occasions which may justify special arrangements and concessions, but such action should be undertaken only with the understanding and approval of the credit manager. Under ordinary circumstances, special credit terms are regarded as an indication of poor financial conditions that frequently lead to difficulties.

Credit Terminology

For the man in business, legal knowledge is a valuable asset. Although no one expects a salesperson to be able to pass a bar examination, the salesperson stands to gain if he knows how to analyze financial statements, understands the meaning of current assets and current liabilities, can recognize a valid contract, and is aware of the legal aspects of credit and collections. The effort to acquire such facts will be amply rewarded.

If the salesman feels that giving so much time to observing credits and collections in his territory is limiting his selling time, he is regarding the situation from the wrong angle. What he is actually doing in this effort is laying the foundation for *selective selling*.

By reviewing the prospective customer's credit position through a careful study of the general market, business reports and news items and an intelligent estimate of local conditions, it is possible to judge accurately how much a customer can buy and how rapidly he can turn over his stock. Such analyses make it possible to have maximum sales with profit; a decrease in losses due to poor credit and additional profits for all.

Collections

In most businesses, salesmen are not required to make collections. However, those who acquire basic knowledge of credits and collections can be of great assistance to their credit managers.

Whenever a company has to pressure a customer for payment, it nullifies the goodwill which has been so carefully built. Also, it becomes difficult to obtain a friendly acceptance on later calls. On the other hand, tactfully following an account on collections will often enable a salesperson to obtain additional business.

Irritations can be forestalled by planting the importance of prompt payments in each customer's mind. As each customer is presented with sales aids, materials, ideas, and suggestions that will help him turn his stock more quickly, the salesman contributes to a more satisfactory credit and collection situation. This kind of selling is one of the best aids to prompt collections.

Frequent conferences with the credit manager can help to solve collection problems. The credit manager can restate the company policies and methods, so that even if he has had no part in actually collecting, the salesperson can serve as a kind of business counselor to his customers, and in this way avoid misunderstandings and ill will. The credit manager can also explain the conditions under which longer credit terms are permissible.

OBSERVING SALES ETHICS

The observation of high ethical principles is a very important aspect of clientele building. Ethics has been defined as "a set of values; moral principles, or rules of conduct in accord with socially acceptable standards of behavior and a professionally accepted code of conduct."

Personal Ethics

Personal ethics may or may not be the same as the ethics of business in which a salesman is employed. Some individuals may see no conflict in *praying* all day Sunday and *preying* the other six days of the week. Some individuals have been brought up in a family which believes that the answer to any ethical situation is only yes or no. Other individuals adjust accepted ethical principles to suit their avaricious desires, regardless of the rights of others. Some individuals believe that ethical codes are expendable, to be used as a pretense, so that buyers can be lured to their disadvantage.

Integrity

A vast majority of salespeople do observe the rules of accepted social and business conduct, as well as legislative rules and regulations. These salesmen have *integrity;* they have an uncompromising adherence to their occupation's moral code. They have sincerity, honesty, and candor. They are the salesmen who avoid deception, expediency, artificiality, and shallowness of any kind.

A group of sales managers was asked to list, in order of importance, the qualifications necessary for successful selling. *Integrity* was placed first. With faith in himself, his product, and his company, the salesman with integrity does not need to sell by subterfuge. This kind of salesman scorns fake enthusiasm, phony friendships, misleading presentations, and meaningless promises. When he is wrong he admits it; when he is right he sticks to his facts with *pleasing persistence.*

"What I like best about my two leading salesmen," said one sales manager, "is their integrity, their honesty toward their work. They don't consider their job a 'racket.' "

"If you're going to make persuading people your life's work, you've got to have integrity" was the comment of a second sales manager.

Some salesmen have what the Pennsylvania Dutch call "the knack of jollying along" or of wheedling people into buying from them. However, the successful salesman knows that this kind of selling soon causes prospect indifference, if not actual dislike and distrust.

Salesman and Employer

A salesman is an agent of his company, a role that requires a high degree of *loyalty* to his employer. In return for his income, the salesman owes his employer his working hours and his continual effort. His loyalty and integrity to his company are presumably unquestioned. If he violates these commitments, his conduct is considered unethical, because when he accepts employment he also accepts the rules, policies, and code of his management.

When a person is hired for a selling position, he is told what is expected of him, and a salary or commission, or both, is agreed upon. Quite often his management spends thousands of dollars to train him before he makes his first sale. Under these conditions, the salesman owes his employer his complete effort and any refusal to adhere to his agreement or contract violates this trust. If the salesman feels that he is not paid enough, he should openly and honestly settle the difference with his employer and not continue to shirk his responsibilities.

Expense accounts. Too many salesmen regard an expense account as a fringe benefit. As a result, they do not hesitate to overcharge for meals, tips, entertainment, auto mileage, and other expenses which the home office cannot always verify. Although the practice of "padding" an expense account is widespread and commonly acknowledged to be so, it is nonetheless dishonest. The expense account is a privilege with *responsibility.* In completing reports of expense, the salesman should include only those expenditures which were incurred in the performance of his work for the company.

Moonlighting. Many salesmen hold two jobs, one during regular hours and another during the evening or night hours. For example, a salesman may feel he needs extra income and work eight hours a day for his "regular" employer and six hours pumping gasoline in a service station. Some may applaud such employment as indicating an ambitious individual. Actually, this fellow cheats one employer or the other, for he cannot do an effective job for both. Dishonest? Yes!

Switching accounts. Predictably, salesmen attempt to carry old accounts with them when they leave one employer for another. Their reasons for doing this are that they established the accounts, developed them, made friends of them, helped them grow—therefore, those accounts belong to them. There is some degree of truth in this, but such conduct is actually dishonest, since it betrays management's faith in their salesmen and ignores the costs involved in carrying the accounts, sometimes for many years.

Separation notice. A salesperson's management is placed in a very difficult situation when he gives no notice, or an unreasonably short notice, that he is seeking work elsewhere. Obviously, an ethical salesperson will follow the custom of his business line and thoughtfully determine how much notice of his leaving he should give his management.

Salesmen, Prospects, and Customers

There are salespeople who do not fully understand the details of unethical conduct, but they owe it to themselves to at least be able to recognize it whenever it is likely to occur. Dubious ethical behavior might pay immediate rewards, but in the long run it does not pay and those involved will discover that they have cheated only themselves.

Misrepresentation. Salesmen cannot be condemned for slight exaggerations in speech, nor for exhibiting unusual enthusiasm for their proposition. They can and should be condemned for either outright lying or misrepresenting facts. Both are unethical and fraudulent.

In addition to the importance of the principle of ethical behavior, salesmen should practice honesty, because, from a practical standpoint, it generates reciprocal behavior from their customers. Honesty begets honesty, and that quality attracts prospective customers, creates a good reputation, and helps to build a clientele.

Graft or bribes. An ethical salesman will be very reluctant to offer sums of money, free gifts, kickbacks, or free goods. This does not mean that the salesman should never offer price and quantity discounts, trial selling period, and free samples.

On the other hand, prospects or customers should never seek such graft or bribes. When prospects do, the honest salesman should politely refuse to accede to such requests or offers. Otherwise, the reputation of both the salesman and his company may suffer, competitors would probably offer more and better bribes, and the particular line or type of business would be seriously disrupted. Sometimes illegal activities have grown out of bribing situations, and the end result has been very unpleasant and unprofitable.

Entertainment. Entertainment often has a valid part to play in salesmanship. If the salesman and his prospect or customer are genuine friends, then it may be ethical. This is especially true if it is the practice in the salesman's line of business to entertain while arranging a business deal. However, it should be recognized that entertainment is only a substitute for salesmanship.

At the same time, it is unethical for buyers to expect to have money spent on them for entertainment. Even when entertaining is an accepted, normal part of a certain kind of business, there is always a suspicion that everything is not aboveboard. There is no doubt that excessive wining and dining and expensive gifts are forms of business solicitation that are dishonest and eventually compromise the salesman or the client.

Price buyers. Some prospects will attempt to buy strictly on price, and some salesmen will meet him by shipping him poor quality, short weight, or items which are not suited to his needs. This kind of selling goes on every day and it is unethical. In addition, the salesman should realize that he cannot sell on price alone, for it is the full benefit received for the price paid that concludes a successful sale.

Downgrading competitors. It is not considered ethical to criticize competitors, but there are many temptations to belittle them, even when the salesman knows that it is not the smart thing to do. The salesman's job is to illustrate how his products will solve problems and satisfy needs. Prospects cannot be motivated and persuaded by statements knocking the product they already have, or may be considering. Such comments are usually considered unethical and certainly unprofessional.

Fictitious prices. Salesmen are often encouraged by management to inflate prices in the belief that the buyer is a swindler who will want to buy at a lower price. The buyer, too, often claims he can only buy at a lower price. Both parties are dishonest, and salesmen should not succumb to the practice. However, there are certain marketing situations where demand or supply is severely limited and a basis for determining prices does not exist. Sellers of highly seasonal or perishable products, such as livestock and eggs, often charge an artificially high price to determine buyer response. If response is slow, the price is adjusted downward.

Reciprocity. As already stated, reciprocity refers to the practice of doing business with the salesman if he does business with the prospect. It is a common practice in many businesses, and it is acceptable so long as it does not prevent the right of each party to choose other suppliers. Reciprocity must be based on reasonable prices, values, and services. Unfortunately, reciprocity is somewhat less than desirable in most cases and should not be encouraged.

Service. Frequently the buyer purchases service with the product and the seller is obligated to provide it after the sale is made. Usually, only the conscience of the vendor determines how much service will be given, but quality of service may be stated in a contract of sale. In either case, it would be unethical to provide anything less in the way of service either implied or stated.

Returns. Upon delivery, products or service may not have the quality provided in the oral or written contract. In that event, the buyer should have the option to return his purchase because the product or service does not suit his needs. By accepting returns, the seller is also protecting his reputation.

However, too many prospects try to return worn-out items or items they have abused, or try to claim defects in products when none existed when purchased—all of these actions, of course, are unethical.

Legislative Ethics

In addition to ethical relationships with prospects, customers, and management, there is clearly defined municipal, federal, and state legislation related to commercial transactions.

Federal, state, and municipal laws govern many business activities. Since they are law, they are not subject to a salesman's personal interpretation, and they are therefore clearer guides to his ethical conduct. Failure to obey the law may not only be a breach of ethical conduct; it may also be a punishable crime. A majority of commercial laws, especially those related to advertising, product control, and manufacturing, are primarily for the control of management, but salesmen should at least understand them.

Laws concerning contracts, customer orders, and certain selling methods must be understood and obeyed by salesmen. The ethical and legal principles involved in these situations must not be violated.

THE CONSUMER MOVEMENT

In Relation to Management

Concern for the consumer's protection and welfare is age-old. The Romans said, "Caveat emptor." The Chinese said, "The buyer needs a thousand eyes; the seller but one." In 1202, King John of England issued a food law prohibiting adulteration of bread with ground peas or beans. In 1784, Massachusetts enacted the first American food law. In 1872, Congress enacted the Criminal Fraud Statute. In the freewheeling late nineteenth century, confrontations between a business tycoon and a vocal minority resulted in the memorable out-of-context quote, "The public be damned."

It became clear, however, that the public did not intend to be "damned." In the years before and after the turn of the century, the pressure of public resentment led to the enactment of new laws designed to curb business abuses.

World War I and World War II slowed the spread of the consumer movement. However, the need for governmental controls of certain phases of business became even more apparent in the early 1960s, and there was a momentous legislative program by Congress in the consumer sphere because of President Kennedy's four-point program: the right to *safety*, the right to be *informed*, the right to *choose*, and the right to be *heard*.

In January 1969, Congress began to make up for lost time by passing additional consumer-minded legislation and regulations. Many state and municipal governments simultaneously hurriedly enacted consumer laws, but industry's attitude continued to remain a mixture of confrontation, lamentation, and pious posturing. The marketing fraternity, especially, was virtually united in its opposition.

E. B. Weiss,[1] a vice-president of the advertising firm of Doyle Dane Bernbach, Inc., has warned: "This is the road to a quasi-utility status for marketing. I do not predict that corporate marketing departments will be supervised in the minute way that railroads or power companies are. But I do foresee a future in which, rightly or wrongly, marketing will be regulated by law far more than it has ever been before. Most marketing leaders have only themselves to blame if they do not like the prospect."

Weiss, a veteran marketing and advertising agency man, is far too involved to write a blanket indictment of business. On the contrary, he concedes that at the top-management level "consumerism is

1. E. B. Weiss, *Harvard Business Review,* July–August, 1968.

tending to be accepted as part of the new concept of corporate responsibility." He cites specific business efforts to anticipate Washington in promoting safety and product quality; for example, the power mower manufacturers' campaign to acquaint the public with the hazards and proper use of motor-driven equipment and the American Gas Association's two laboratories where appliances and equipment are given exhaustive tests. However, Weiss clearly implies that these are exceptions.

There are indeed exceptions, and before further commitment let us realize that the predators among marketing men are not really aware that they are predatory. They are not immoral, nor are they unethical, nor without consciences. They simply do not know the meaning of these words. They are absolutely *amoral*. They are, therefore, individually innocent of wrongdoing.

The list of consumer legislation, ranging from auto safety laws and product warranties to meat controls and truth-in-lending regulations, is obviously a serious indictment of the failure of marketing to regulate itself. So are the dozens of fair practice codes voluntarily drawn up by industry under Federal Trade Commission supervision.

Today's better educated and far more skeptical and sophisticated shoppers are beginning to rebel. It is believed that "politicians are paying heed; marketers are not." Here is a summary of recent warnings:

Additional consumer legislation is inevitable for years to come. For example, all used car dealers are due to be subjected to a truth-in-lending law. Under this legislation, any buyer of a used car would be able to discover the car's entire history, including recalls, repairs, inspection records, and accidents.

Technological progress alone will require marketing men to provide more guidance to consumers. As it is, even for the better-than-average educated shopper, the market is a bewildering maze of prices, packaging, sizes, models, brands, colors, and so forth.

The young corporate executive today and tomorrow will insist on higher levels of marketing integrity. It has been suggested that companies establish a new position of Vice-President—Consumerism. This executive would have the responsibility of insuring more consideration of ethical issues and collaborating with governments in drafting appropriate laws and rules related to consumerism.

It is possible that momentous consumer legislation will be developed and enforced and that a turning point in the marketing executive's attitude toward consumerism has begun to take place. "It is none too soon," according to many authorities. "The time is already late."

In Relation to the Salesman

What has consumerism to do with the salesman? First, the salesman should take to heart what has been said in this book, as well as a multitude of others, regarding his conscience, morality, ethical principles, and honesty. He should practice personal integrity as far as his awareness and his management permits. Second, he should continue his readings about the consumer movement and its philosophy, so that he will be aware of the trend in social and individual thinking related to integrity, ethics, and honesty in marketing.

Third, salesmen will need to sustain higher ethical standards and to collaborate fully with their managements on industry trends and the rules and regulations of municipal, state, and federal legislation.

Legal Aspects of Selling

Sales-related legislation has three major objectives: (1) to encourage free competition by discouraging restraints to trade, (2) to limit competitive actions by directly outlawing tactics and practices which may be detrimental to public interests, and (3) to provide some competitive advantages to certain groups of manufacturers, middlemen, and retail outlets.

Major laws regulating competition are the Sherman Antitrust Act, the Clayton Act, the Federal Trade Commission Act, and the Robinson-Patman Act. All of these laws were designed to foster competition in the interests of the customer and to protect him from the consequences of sub rosa agreements to maintain prices at a higher level than they would be if competition were allowed to operate freely.

Laws designed to protect the buyer in the quality of goods offered to him include the Wheeler-Lea Act and the Pure Food and Drug Laws and regulations.

The Miller-Tydings Act and the McGuire Act operate to eliminate so-called price discrimination and also to promote freedom to compete in the marketplace.

Besides these federal laws, many states and municipalities have legislation designed to regulate advertising, pricing, and other elements of the sales code. Therefore, salesmen who are not disposed to establish and live up to a good code of ethics voluntarily may have some legal motivation to do so.

POWER POINTS

Clientele building is an individual activity, and where and how it is done depends largely on the salesman himself. He builds his clientele through referrals from users of his product or service; through cold canvass; through empathy; through courtesy with objections and complainers; through faithful service; through judicious use of his company's advertising and promotional material.

While many salesmen do not at first understand credits and collections, they soon learn that no order can be profitable until it has been paid for by the purchaser, and that good reasons exist for company credit and collection policies. The salesman also learns that there is a need for cooperation in this activity between salesman and management, and the latter, in turn, keeps the salesman informed.

The salesman benefits from his credit activities. First, it gives him the ability to intelligently interpret and discuss credit policies with his prospects. Second, credit work brings the salesman a better realization of why he should spend his selling time with good accounts rather than weak ones. Third, he can often help delinquent debtors get on their financial feet and make paying customers of them. Fourth, he learns to identify good credit risks, so that he will spend little or no time with dubious prospects and more time with those who are on a sound financial footing.

The observation of high standards of integrity, honesty, and forthrightness may be a slow way to build a clientele, but it surely works to the advantage of both salesman and management in the long run. People like to deal with salesmen who reveal candor, sincerity, and faith in their moral principles.

A salesman is an agent of the company, and in return for his salary the salesman owes his employer a full day's work and his loyalty. A violation of these commitments is unethical, because when a salesman accepts employment he also accepts the rules, policies, and code of his management.

Laws concerning contracts, customer orders, and certain selling methods should be understood and followed by today's salesmen. Ethical and legal principles are frequently involved and they must not be breached, or the salesman and his management may find themselves in legal difficulties.

DISCUSSION QUESTIONS AND PROBLEMS

1. What are three ways to build goodwill?
2. How can product and service help to build a clientele?

3. How can personal service help to build a clientele?

4. In what ways can a salesman cooperate with his credit manager?

5. What factors should be considered in a personal credit appraisal made by a salesman?

6. How does the salesman benefit from knowledge and appreciation of good credit rules?

7. Why has the subject of business ethics become more important during the past few years?

8. What are five salesman-employer situations in which ethical principles are important?

9. What are the most important ethical principles affecting salesmen and their prospects and customers?

10. Why has recent legislation involving the consumer been necessary?

11. How may the consumer movement affect personal salesmanship?

12. Tommy Thompson sold silverware for the Easterling Company. His clientele was young working girls, usually age 18–19 years, and elderly people with grandchildren. Tommy drove a Chrysler Imperial, with all of the available extras. When calling on prospects he parked it as near to their home as possible, so it would be seen. Tommy was challenged about his conspicuous display, his critics saying that people would think his merchandise was overpriced, so he could pay for his luxurious car. Here is Tommy's reply:

> "My prospects like to buy from salesmen who appear successful. They like to buy from me because I travel in a high-priced car, look prosperous, and happy with myself. I once drove a beat-up jalopy and dressed very badly. I did it because I thought as you think about too much prosperity spoiling sales. But I found that people did not like to deal with me when I appeared to be unsuccessful. They wanted to feel proud of doing business with a successful person.
>
> a. Is Tommy Thompson right or wrong?

SELLING PROBLEMS AND PROJECTS

1. Lester B. Colby Case

"We want you to go out," said the memorandum from Colby's head-quarters, "and ask a group of management men what they think of gift giving and entertaining as part of routine sales operation.

"Let names be off the record. We want honest opinion. We want to know if common sense is coming back in style after the expense account bonanza so many firms have indulged in.

"We realize that most company policies probably lie in the middle ground between no entertainment at all and free spending at the salesman's discretion. So we're trying to distinguish between the kind of entertainment (or the sort of gift) that is a casual courtesy and the kind that is too lavish, in questionable taste, and of highly debatable business value."

One opinion was as follows:

"If you are going to court the friendship of anyone, go after the solid buyer. He's the man who is anxious for goods that will turn over fast or ideas that will speed the turnover.

"Out of our experience we have developed a 'no-entertaining' policy. Instead of entertaining, we tell them to take sales ideas to our customers and their buyers."

Questions

1. Do you believe that entertaining prospects helps build a clientele?
2. When does a friendly gesture become a danger to building a clientele?

2. The Hillside Auto Sales Case

Boy, was he proud! My next-door neighbor recently drove his new car home, beautiful and shiny. The entire family piled in and drove around for the neighbors and friends to see.

Was the salesman happy? I'll say he was, just as much as the owner. There is no greater fulfillment in selling than to sell a product that the owners want to show to all the world.

And that's why this salesman took a little extra time and effort to turn the car over to his customer bright and spotless. He was not only proud of it, but realized the value of first impressions.

But a few weeks later, my neighbor returned the car to the garage for some slight adjustments. This time, though, a mechanic got some grease smears on the upholstery and apparently made little or no attempt to remove them.

Questions

1. Which part of this transaction would build a clientele?
2. Which part would tend to destroy a clientele? Why?

Unimportant? Well, perhaps so, but I've heard this new owner remark, "I wish those guys would give their customers the same treatment *after* they buy as *before* they buy."

The customer not only bought a car but also service for it. True, he got the car, which he is immensely proud and pleased to drive, and he got the service he bought but not the friendly, accurate service he expected.

At first glance this may seem trivial, yet it meant an owner satisfied with the product but dissatisfied with the dealer's service.

Question

3. How would you feel if you received this treatment?

What customers think of you is based almost entirely upon the treatment they receive from you, even long after the sale has been made. Customers rightly expect the prompt installation and demonstration of their new purchase. They expect prompt and courteous service, should the purchase require adjustment.

Question

4. Do you agree or disagree with these statements? Why?

3. Don Ramsey Case

Don Ramsey has been selling industrial chemicals for many years. He has dealt with many small manufacturers whose credit often becomes important in doing business. Don learned a long time ago how to separate the sheep from the goats in the matter of finding prospects whose credit standing was questionable. Don would watch these people, and if their credit improved, he would try to sell them. Otherwise, he would pass them by.

Sometimes he would encounter a prospect who used Don's credit policy as an excuse for not buying. They would say that Don's employer's terms were "too tough." Then Don would say, "Mr. Prospect, our terms are standard in the industry. However, if you will tell me just what terms you feel would be satisfactory to you, I'm sure I can prevail upon my company to accept any reasonable proposition."

Questions

1. Do you believe that Don's policy of refusing to sell dubious credit risks is a good one? Why?

2. What is your opinion of the way Don handles the prospects who use their credit standing as an excuse for not buying?

4. The Passamaquody Case

John Gilbert was a salesman for the Passamaquody Company, distributors of gasoline-station equipment. Gilbert sold to the first customer he called on the first day he tried to sell. His customer was the owner of a theatre, who planned to use an adjacent lot for parking cars. This customer was a glib talker and a man free with promises. He greatly impressed Gilbert with his anecdotes and allusions to substantial capital.

He planned to install a complete service station on the lot and to sell gasoline, oil, washing and repair service. He used superlatives, but his claims were so infectious that Gilbert soon found himself agreeing with the prospect on the profit possibilities of the parking lot and several other proposed schemes.

Gilbert took a chance that his credit was good, without a check-up, and entered into a contract to supply the equipment. However, after the equipment was installed, the customer could not pay the bill.

Questions

1. What is the basic lesson in this case?

2. Would it have been advisable to make the contract subject to the approval of the credit office?

3. How would you have dealt with this situation after the sale had presumably been made?

5. Cold-canvass Calls

Charlie Ross had a tough time last year with three young college graduates he was trying to train as salesmen. He gave them good territories, set low requirements, and thought they would therefore become happy with their jobs and fairly successful salesmen.

They disliked part of their job—the part Ross insisted on most: They had to spend a certain number of hours each week cold canvassing. Each time Ross had them in his office the young fellows would say, "Give us more inquiries and leads and we'll sell more volume. The company needs to advertise more."

After several weeks of these excuses, Charlie Ross lost his patience with them and told them that each man had to make at least five cold-canvass calls each day or get off the payroll. The young men squawked, but stayed on the job and went to work.

From the first day of cold-canvass calls, their sales volume shot up. All three found that it was the cold canvassing that did it. Charlie Ross maintains there is no salesman who can afford not to make some cold-canvass calls each day.

Question

1. Charlie Ross had four reasons for insisting that these young men must make cold-canvass calls. How many can you think of?

CHAPTER 24

Time and
Territory Management

Sir Isaac Pitman is reported to have said that "well-arranged time is the surest mark of a well-arranged man."

Well-arranged time is one of the salesperson's greatest assets. It enables him to conserve not only his own valuable time and effort but also that of his clients and prospects.

Suppose a stranger driving from Manhattan to Newark, New Jersey, found himself stranded in Jersey City. He would see nothing but a maze of buildings and unrecognized streets. He might ask directions of eight or nine people before reaching his destination, get misdirected half the time, and finally arrive in Newark three hours later, only to discover that the main highway was only three blocks away. This is a simple example of what can happen when a salesman is so buried in problems and so far behind on his original plans that he can't see for the life of him how he will ever finish his work. It may require three days to accomplish what could have been done in one day with planning.

If the same salesman could, on the other hand, ride in an airplane over the Hudson River, he would see Newark just across the Jersey Meadows, he would see the main highway across the Pulaski Bridge, and he would see that the highway was near his starting point. That airplane view, that vision from a few thousand feet up, represents the essence of maximum use of time for selling.

When a salesman obtains an overall view of his job, he will not be confused and he can proceed directly to accomplish the end he has set for himself. In his daily work the salesman can choose the most important duties, arrange them in order of importance, work at one duty at a time, and end the day without having to put in a great deal of overtime or feeling a great deal of pressure, because he will be getting maximum use of his selling time.

PREPARATION FOR SELLING

In any discussion of the effective use of time by salesmen, it has been traditional to emphasize the few hours of each working day that the average salesperson spends in the presence of customers and prospects. The professional salesperson thinks of every hour of his working day as *action time*. He is definitely time-conscious and spends a great many hours, in addition to his regular hours, preparing to sell. From this person's viewpoint, even the time spent in getting a good night's sleep and in seeking recreation and social activity are considered to be preparation for his hours of action.

Time Spent with Buyers

One survey has indicated that the average salesman spends approximately three hours each day in the presence of prospective buyers. Another investigation of an industrial specialty business revealed that their salesmen spent approximately two hours and thirty minutes each day in the presence of buyers. The exact figures may not apply in all cases, but they do indicate the limited action time available to salesmen. For example, the salesmen for National Cylinder and Gas Corporation are reported to have spent their working hours like this:

Travel	30 percent
Waiting	25 percent
Reports, etc.	20 percent
Nonbusiness conversation	5 percent
Action time	20 percent
	100 percent

According to these figures, this company's salespeople spent only 20 percent of their work time in the presence of prospective buyers. Much of the 80 percent was wasted because of poor planning, according to the sales trainer of this company. Many sales managers believe that approximately 50 percent of a salesman's time could be spent in the presence of prospects if he really tried to increase his action time through just a little planning, analysis, and self-organization.

Time-and-duty Study

Another picture of how salesmen spend their day was revealed in a time-and-duty study conducted by *Salesweek*.[1] This was a study of 255 salesmen in nineteen different fields of work. Their average 9.3-hour working day was divided in the following way: getting ready to sell (including planning work, gathering information, and prospecting)—19 percent of time; activities between interview (including travel, waiting, and lunch)—45 percent; actual selling—36 percent.

In a time-and-duty study made by Atlantic Refining Company, the average salesman's day was divided this way:

Selling to customer	17 percent
Selling new business	1 percent
Related sales activities	27 percent
Waiting for customers	5 percent
Nondirect selling talk	11 percent
Travel between calls	37 percent
Time unaccounted for	2 percent
	100 percent

As a result of this time-and-duty survey, Atlantic Refining Company corrected certain poor practices and achieved a reduction in the base selling cost of 38 percent in one area, with an increase in new business of more than 15 percent—all in a period of six months.

Daily and Monthly Plans

Assuming that sales volume and personal income are roughly in proportion to the time spent in the presence of prospects, the salesman who plans on adding one or two hours each day to his action time will attain a proportional increase in his sales total and personal income.

Route cards should be inspected every month to note the gaps in service and the customers who should receive calls. Those who are most important should be identified and listed for an early call. Prospects who should be called on at some time during the month may also be listed.

When all of the above calls are accounted for, the salesman has an overall picture of the number of calls to be made in a month of

1. Special Management Report, "Cure for High Sales Cost: Better Time Usage," *Salesweek*, December 12, 1960, p. 13.

planned effort. The difference between this total and the total number of calls he can make represents the number of calls the individual should consider and organize.

However, no monthly plan is worth much without daily work plans to supplement it. Each night, the salesman should plan for the next selling day, deciding not only where to make his first call of the day but also where to go every minute during his working hours.

Getting Ready for the Next Day

Each evening, the salesman must spend some time preparing his schedule, or itinerary, for the following day. The hour or so that is devoted to this important task might be called the planning hour. The object of the planning hour is to maximize the effectiveness of the selling time available in the following working day. In this hour the salesman should list the names and locations of the clients to be called on, arrange the order of calls to make the most use of his time, and note all relevant facts relating to these businesses, which might be helpful in the sales interview.

When his daily schedule is brief, he can memorize it. If many calls are to be made, however, the schedule should be written down with adequate regard to balance between active accounts and desirable prospective accounts. A salesperson has the right to decide whether he will increase his efficiency or ignore it altogether. He alone is the one who can increase his income and personal satisfaction. Actually, very few people will ignore the idea of increasing their efficiency, but many unconsciously dislike the idea of planning and therefore avoid it.

Suppose, for example, that a salesman unexpectedly has a major presentation scheduled early in the morning. Without a daily work plan, he would probably not have a clear idea of what else he had intended to do that day. So he will devote all of his time to the major sales presentation and let other things slide.

There may be times when a daily plan should be abandoned, but when the salesman has a carefully developed daily plan that directs him to be at the best places at the best time, he is in a position to make a decision based on the facts and not on wishful thinking. A particularly shaky account or one in which a particularly serious situation exists and cannot be solved at a later time might call for a decision to abandon the day's plan. However, this decision is then based on facts and considered judgment, not on guesses.

A *clean-up day* might be set for the middle of the week in certain kinds of selling. Emergency phone calls, requests from the office to make a collection, miscellaneous requests for advice or assistance, follow-up promises, and similar matters should all be cared for on this day. This day would be used to clear up all unfinished business. In this connection, the salesman should not view calls from customers for immediate service as emergencies that require him to stop everything else and make a headlong rush to the customer's door. When a call comes in for fast service or a prospect demands that the salesman "drive over here right away," it should be remembered that the customer has probably known of his difficulties for quite a while, but just decided to do something about them.

Clustered Calls

If a salesman has averaged too few interviews in past months, he can be sure that it was caused by a lack of personal management and insufficient time spent in prospecting. One solution to this problem is to organize and cluster calls in the same locale.

In planning a day's work, the calls should be clustered so that the minute the salesman finds the buyer is out, he can go to the next office and then come back again. He should not just arrange calls by route, but should also include in the plan the time he expects to be at each call. When he knows he will have a long call, he should arrange the other calls of the day around the long call.

Advance Appointments

If the nature of the salesperson's business and daily routine permits, he should not overlook the importance of making advance appointments with potential buyers. This will, in many cases, eliminate time wasted in reception rooms as well as time spent in fruitless travel. While advance appointments may not always be possible, they can add 25 to 45 minutes each day to the salesman's selling time.

Seeing the Right Buyer

Whether he is selling to a regular customer or to a prospect, the alert salesman sees the man who has the authority to place the order. It may require some detective work to discover who the man with the final say about buying is. It will also help if the salesman can discover whether the prospect makes his own decisions or relies on the opinions of others, perhaps a shop foreman or another executive. There is no sense wasting five minutes on the man who has no authority to buy or who has no influence with the person who does. Courteous attention directed toward the wrong man will not help you make a sale.

Spending Selling Hours Wisely

Another time-waster is the failure of many salesmen to apportion their time according to a buyer's potential purchasing power. It simply does not make sense for a person to spend an exorbitant amount of time with small account buyers if, as a result, he spends only a few minutes later in the day with a buyer of substantial amounts. The salesman must learn to apportion his time in direct relation to the expected return.

The large account is a challenge to the professional person because it is usually more difficult to sell. To the person who is well prepared, however, the challenge is welcomed with confidence.

Oral Presentation

A good oral presentation will assist in providing additional selling time because nothing saves time better than to be quickly and favorably understood. A salesman improves his presentation if he:

1. Analyzes his sales talks and learns to use the best choice of words.
2. Practices answering common objections before asked.
3. Learns to think on his feet.
4. Learns to use visual sales aids and devices.
5. Learns effective closing techniques.

Observance of these fundamentals will:

1. Help to decrease lost motion in the salesman's daily procedure.
2. Increase his ability to react more promptly.
3. Help him keep his presentation to the point and thereby eliminate extraneous matters and time-involving discussions.
4. Help reduce complaints and call-backs and thereby save the time of the salesman and the customer.

An excellent method for adding to selling time is to have the sales talk so well in mind that the presentation can be made with dispatch. A skilled salesman covers the essentials but does not linger. He terminates the interview himself, feeling it to be a psychological advantage over the prospect. Buyers like planned presentations because streamlined sales talks with accurate facts and a comprehensive review of buyer benefits are welcomed as time-savers by purchasers.

Visual Sales Aids

The selling time itself can often be cut in half when visual sales aids are used. What buyers see attracts their attention almost nine times more than what they feel, touch, smell, or hear. Visual sales aids also help buyers remember a product or service about 65 percent longer. A recent survey revealed that 82 percent of purchasing agents questioned like salespeople to use visual sales aids. Sales managers also like salespeople to use visual sales aids because they are known to have increased sales 15 percent the first month they were used. Sales aids, therefore, enable salesmen to decrease wasted time and to increase selling time.

The Right Start

Getting off to a good start each selling day doesn't just happen. The first call of the day is most important and must be carefully chosen. In case the first choice is not in, a nearby alternative call may be kept in mind so that little time will be lost.

A salesman cannot even approach the professional level if he does not exercise personal management. A plan gives a salesman the supervision he needs to start a successful day.

One of the secrets of the professionals is to plan and finish a definite number of calls by noon. This type of planning leaves the afternoon open for several service, emergency, or prospecting calls.

Early Morning and Saturday Calls

A professional salesman is careful not to make his early morning calls on prospects who insist on going through the morning's mail and planning their daily routine before talking to salesmen. This salesman knows which companies and prospects restrict interviews to certain hours of the day or even certain days of the week. Early morning calls are possible, however, in practically every community if the salesman restricts them to buyers whose daily schedule makes such interviews possible.

However, the salesman should not assume that all prospects are tied up at the start of a business day and on Saturday. He can always start the day with a call on a customer or prospect he is reasonably sure he can see or with whom he has made a definite appointment. There are, likewise, many buyers who have no objections to interviewing salesmen on Saturdays, and the salesman should welcome the opportunity because the buyer will probably be able to give him more time, be more relaxed, and be in a more favorable mood.

Off-hours Calls

Some buyers must see as many as twenty or thirty salespeople a day during certain days of the week. They cannot possibly give each salesperson more than a limited amount of time. Many sales are lost because the salesperson is pressed for time in his presentation. By observation, inquiry, prearranged appointments, or casual approach, the unapproachable buyer can sometimes be reached during off-hours. The salesperson is then able to obtain undivided attention and successfully hold the prospect's interest until he wants to buy.

Ending the Interview

Having started his selling day with an early morning call, a good salesman does not spoil his daily schedule by not knowing when to bring an interview to a close. He does not drag out interviews or talk himself out of sales. He does not yield to the temptation of letting hard-hitting presentations degenerate into mere social hours. He knows that minutes can be saved daily, and hours saved every week, by concluding his presentation when the reason for the call has been accomplished.

Turning Social Time into Sales Time

It is usually proper to take a good prospect or customer to lunch. When kept on a business basis, luncheons can accomplish much that might be impossible on a regular call. Likewise, by taking a buyer to dinner after business hours, a salesman can frequently accomplish the same objective as he could on a call during the day. This is one more way to add that profitable extra hour each day.

Much time can be saved by avoiding long lunch hours and an irresistible urge to sneak in a little nap, a recess for golf, a ball game, or a movie in the name of goodwill. A salesman is his own boss when he is out selling and sometimes stern self-discipline is necessary to resist the siren call of these distractions.

Out Tuesday, Back Friday Complex

The "out Tuesday, back Friday" complex unfortunately affects many salesmen who cover a territory outside a metropolitan city. These men offer many reasons why they must work at home or in the office on Monday and Saturday. However, the bee that gets the honey doesn't hang around the hive, and those salesmen who have an "out Tuesday, back Friday" complex are simply deluding themselves. They are trying to rationalize their laziness by claiming the need for paperwork or for plant contacts or other excuses. A great part of these two days can usually be turned into action time for the salesman.

Personal Records

A successful salesperson keeps records on himself to assist him in his planning. They indicate his past performance and enable him to plan for better future performance. They enable him to establish a goal.

He keeps actual time sheets or records of his calls, travel time in between, waiting time, even planning and record-keeping time, as well as time for correspondence and seeking new prospects.

In addition, at each day's close, many individuals find it advantageous to compare the planned-in-advance schedule with the day's actual accomplishment. This gives them a means of discovering shortcomings, of figuring out where time is being lost, and provides a basis for determining how such losses can be eliminated in the days ahead.

Exception to Planning Rule

Although the necessity of a carefully worked-out daily plan has been stressed, there are times where it should be laid aside. This is because every salesman has moments when he hits the crest of a selling wave. These times are apt to occur when the salesman unexpectedly obtains a big order from a particularly rough buyer. At that particular time the salesman often reaches his selling peak and believes that *all* prospects are easy to sell to. Therefore, he wants to do something about it. He wants to see quickly the biggest and toughest buyer in the city and make his presentation while he is "hot." He does not want to cool down and he cannot afford to do so. He should abandon the plans he has made for the day and call on the big and tough buyers just as fast as he can get to them. He would be quite foolish if he did not take advantage of this selling momentum.

POWER POINTS

The following are principles observed by creative sales people because they guarantee maximum use of selling time.

Balance your calls. If your day's schedule is a brief one, you may carry it in your head. If many calls are to be made, commit your schedule to paper, with due regard for balance between active accounts and good prospective accounts.

Cluster calls. In planning a day's work, cluster calls so that the minute you find one buyer is out you can call almost next door and find another who is in and then come back. Schedule longer calls ahead for less important hours and then plan to follow the schedule.

Plan the route. It is known that a half hour each day spent on planning the route will often save one day each week. The salesman who plans his route will usually sell more quantity to more quality buyers and do both in less time.

Advance appointments. Advance appointments will eliminate time wasted in reception rooms as well as in fruitless travel.

Visual sales aids. Action time itself can often be cut in half when visual sales aids are used. What buyers see attracts their attention almost nine times more than what they perceive through the other four senses combined. Visual sales aids also help buyers remember a proposition about 65 percent longer than they would without them.

Oral presentations. A mastery of the skills necessary for a good presentation will help to provide more action time because nothing will speed up a call more than to be understood quickly and favorably.

The early bird gets the worm. Have you considered early morning calls? Have you tried to make Saturday calls? Both are possible in almost every locality.

"Terminal facilities." Don't drag out the interview—don't talk yourself into and out of a sale, just because you have mislaid your "terminal facilities." Don't let a hard-hitting presentation degenerate into a gabfest. Reach for your hat when the reason for your call has been accomplished.

Spend most time with paying accounts. It does not make sense to spend an exorbitant amount of time with minor buyers if it results in spending only a few minutes later in the day with a buyer of substantial amounts.

Turn social time into action time. When kept on a business basis, luncheons can accomplish much that might be impossible on a regular call. Likewise, by taking a buyer to dinner after business hours, you can frequently accomplish the same objective as a call made during the day.

Out Tuesday, back Friday. Those salesmen who have an "out Tuesday, back Friday" complex are trying to rationalize their laziness by claiming the need for extra time for paper work, for plant contacts, or for other questionable purposes. At least part of Mondays and Saturdays can be turned into action time.

Use basic sales methods. Greater knowledge and constant use of basic selling methods will shorten interviews, and thereby provide more action time with additional buyers.

Planned sales talks. Many authorities say that a planned sales talk is one of the very best ways to obtain maximum use of selling time. When presentations are delivered extemporaneously they are even better, according to professional salesmen. Good sales talks can create more action time than almost anything else.

Professional salesmen give to their sales talks the same interest and practice that they give to a sport they like. They know that good form is best, the same as in a sport, and good form only *seems* effortless. It is achieved at the cost of hard work, planning, and practice.

Some salesmen may say that these ideas are commonplace. But it is the commonplace, commonsense approach that is often passed up in favor of some quick, easy, "works like a charm" method. Common sense tells us that nothing works like a charm, but *work!* And that is what can create more action time.

DISCUSSION QUESTIONS AND PROBLEMS

1.   Why is personal management particularly important for a salesman?

2.   What is meant by *action time?*

3.   In relation to personal management, what basic elements should be included in planning?

4.   Read each of the following questions carefully before answering them.

   a. What value can you see in making sure you have a *planning hour?*

   b. What will a well-spent planning hour do for a salesman?

   c. What should the salesman do during the planning hour?

5.   What are the advantages of a *daily* and *monthly* plan? Should a plan ever be abandoned?

6.   How may sales aids increase time spent in selling?

7.   Would qualifying prospects increase selling time? Why?

8.   Would knowing where and how to locate prospects help increase action time? Why?

9.   It has been said that greater knowledge and use of basic selling methods will provide more action time. Discuss and explain.

10. a. Do you believe a review of a travel route at frequent intervals is necessary? Why?

b. Do you believe a salesman should be expected to plan his own route? Why?

c. Should the sales manager analyze the route and compel the salesman to follow it rigidly? Why?

11. Make an action-time plan for yourself as a salesman of a product or service of your choice. Include the following in your plan:

a. a time schedule showing the apportionment of your day;

b. a set of rules or guides that would give you the most direct and thorough coverage of your territory;

c. a series of record forms that you feel would provide the necessary information on your prospects and selling activities.

SELLING PROBLEMS AND PROJECTS

1.   Ronnie Jenne Case

Ronnie Jenne was just about to press the "Down" button for the elevator when he was surprised by a familiar voice. He turned, and there was Cliff Barton, an old friend.

"Hiya, Cliff. I stuck my head in your office, but you weren't around."

"Taking off, Ronnie?"

"Ready to go. I wrapped up my work here today."

"Oh, you've got a few minutes. Drop in my office and let's talk for a while."

Ronnie glanced once more at the elevator, then followed Cliff down the hall. After passing a pleasant forty-five minutes, Ronnie left the office. Back in his car he gave some thought to his next call. He had meant to drop in at the new processing plant on the south side of the city, but he wasn't too sure of its exact location nor how to get there.

About an hour later, Ronnie drove into the visitors' parking lot of the Harrod Processing plant. He opened his briefcase and took out a notebook in which were listed the names of the purchasing agents for his clients. Under "Harrod," there was a blank space. Then Ronnie recalled that although he was told the man's name by his sales manager, he had forgotten to write it down in his notebook and now he couldn't remember it.

Questions

1. Identify those times in which you think Ronnie exercised poor judgment or technique.

2. What suggestions would you make as to how Ronnie could improve his salesmanship?

2.   Pretzel Routing: C. H. Bietlerfield Case

The term *pretzel routing* simply means that some salesmen cover their territories by doubling back and forth, pretzel fashion. Better organized salesmen make their daily calls with a minimum amount of lost time and mileage between each call. The figure below shows the pretzel routing used by a salesman to make nine calls.

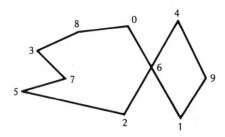

Questions

1. How would you plan these nine calls to save selling time and gasoline?

2. Do you believe a salesman should be expected to plan his own route?

3. Would it be advisable for the sales manager to take a hand in planning the sales routes of his salesmen, or, perhaps, to compel them to follow his routing plans?

3.   Telephone Presentation Project

Assume that you are selling burglary alarm systems to commercial firms and that you want to make an appointment with Mr. Miller, vice-president and general maanger of the Howard Grocery Company. Prepare, in written dialogue form, a telephone presentation that you feel will secure the appointment for you.

CHAPTER 25

Introduction to Sales Management

Sales management is concerned with the administration and management of the field sales force. If a salesman desires an administrative position in his company, the most logical place for him to seek it is in sales management.

The following is a list of the levels of positions within the sales area.

1. Sales Trainee
2. Junior salesman
3. Senior salesman
4. Sales supervisor
5. Product sales manager
6. Assistant to sales manager
7. Branch sales manager
8. District sales manager
9. Regional sales manager
10. General (national) sales manager
11. Marketing director
12. Vice-president of sales and marketing

Normally, a salesman may be promoted to branch manager, district or territorial manager, or regional manager. Opportunities, however, are not limited to the sales field. The entire field of distribution is open to the individual with a selling background. Departments that often need the practical experience of a salesman are sales training, advertising, sales promotion, merchandising, and market research. In addition, departments not related to selling, such as personnel or public and industrial relations, constantly need men who are adept at human relations and group psychology.

BECOMING A SALES MANAGER

It is generally true that any step up in a person's career brings the necessity for some adjustment of viewpoint, some change of focus.

The situation is the same when a student becomes a salesman or when the salesman moves up to sales manager.

Facing Facts

One of the most basic and most difficult of these adjustments, according to John G. McLean in the *Journal of Marketing,* is to adjust to "the responsibility for facing business facts in a hard-headed, realistic manner." This means the responsibility for establishing a method of collecting facts; for analyzing and interpreting the facts; for determining a plan of action; and then implementing the plan.

There is an important psychological transition which the salesman must make when he becomes a sales manager: He must face the facts and act on them whether they please him or not. And he must be prepared to make other adjustments as well, if he is to move up the organization ladder and assume an increasing number of broader responsibilities. In short, the sales manager must be a cold, hard realist.

To be successful, the modern sales manager must be able to think of all the elements and factors that go into a product or service from the time it is conceived until it is consumed. According to J. A. McIlnay, former president of Sales-Marketing Executives, International, "This concept requires a wholesome optimistic attitude toward three areas of company operations: (1) top management whose ideas the sales manager must translate into sales; (2) manufacturing and technical employees who must be taught the marketing concept; (3) sales department employees who rely on their sales manager for motivation and security."

Who Is Promoted to Sales Manager?

The beginning salesman may be surprised to learn that, with only a few exceptions, the practice of filling sales management positions with salesmen who have the highest sales records still prevails, regardless of their leadership or executive ability.

The rationale is that a successful salesman can transmit his selling ability to those under his supervision, and thereby step up sales in the entire unit. This rarely happens. In fact, the reverse is true. A look at statistics reveals that the best salesmen usually make the poorest sales managers. This is probably due to the fact that most sales managers insist upon molding those they supervise to their own preconceived pattern, instead of applying methods for building and developing individual salesmen. A top salesman normally has scant patience with anyone who has not developed his maximum sales skills. He may nag and bully his men and make them feel inferior at the exact time when they need encouragement and confidence.

The student of salesmanship and sales management will need to be aware of these liabilities and to guard against them. He should plan to develop patience and the ability to direct and work with others if he wishes to be a real leader.

The ambitious individual can develop these qualities so that he will be an above-average branch or division sales manager. The program for these goals can be elaborate or very simple as the need requires.

PERSONAL QUALITIES NEEDED

A recent study of 150 sales managers by the National Management Development Laboratory drew the following profile of the sales manager: "He comes from a relatively large family; lived at home until he was 21; was educated beyond high school; was self-supporting in his late teens; and has worked for only a few companies. He married in his middle twenties; is industrious; has above average intelligence; understands human relations techniques; possesses confidence, initiative, and integrity."

According to a recent American Management Association survey, the characteristics sought in a salesman who has potential for a management position are (in their order of preference):

- Management ability; the ability to assume responsibility, to plan and organize, to exercise judgment, to lead.
- "Drive," or willingness to work; initiative, imagination, aggressiveness.
- Ability to get along with people.
- Integrity, stability, balance, sincerity, and honesty.

The modern sales manager, as described by a group of psychologists, is above average in intelligence and possesses high verbal facility; he has broad interests, especially in persuasive activities; he possesses a high degree of realism, is congenial, and is extremely cooperative.

EDUCATIONAL REQUIREMENTS

The National Industrial Conference Board study of sales managers found that 77 percent of the firms they studied required a college education as prerequisite for sales managership. Sales and Marketing Executive International, Inc., found that only 10 percent of the sales managers polled did not have a college education and more than half had college degrees. A study by the editors of *Fortune* revealed that of the top executives interviewed who were under the age of 50, only 5 percent had not been to college, and that 84 percent had degrees. These statistics indicate that the sales manager of the future will have to possess a college degree if he wishes to ensure his success.

EXPERIENCE REQUIREMENTS

An adequate amount of selling experience is a requirement for sales management. However, the man need not be a top salesman. As mentioned above, the top salesman rarely makes the best sales manager. This does not mean that the prospective sales manager should be a

---

SALES QUESTIONNAIRE

Name _____ Age _____ Date _____

Address _____

Phone No. _____

1. Have you had any experience in selling?

2. Have you received any driving tickets in the last 12 months?

3. How many days have you been absent from work because of illness?

4. Do you agree to take our preemployment medical examination?

5. Have you had any previous experience in collection?

6. Have you ever been refused coverage by a bonding company?

7. List below all previous selling experience.

8. What year in the past ten did you have your highest earnings?
_____ Amount? _____

9. Which of the following types of sales work would you prefer to do if salary pay and special requirements were no object?

(Check Three Choices Only and Indicate by Numbers the Order of Your Preference)

☐ Take repeat orders.   ☐ Open new accounts.   ☐ Make collections.
☐ Check dealer's stock. ☐ Do display work.   ☐ Introduce new brands.
☐ Handle complaints.   ☐ Handle office detail. ☐ Make goodwill calls.
☐ Increase order size. ☐ Do "specialty" work. ☐ Plan promotion programs.

Figure 25-1. Sales Questionnaire

poor salesman, for he needs a background of successful selling experience. Such practical experience has several advantages. First, salesmen respect a sales manager with successful experience. They realize that he knows and understands their problems, and they have greater confidence in him because they trust his ability and judgment. Second, a sales manager with such experience can be more realistic in his control, evaluation, planning, and supervision activities. Third, his experiences with customers and prospects enables him to understand their needs and problems.

RECRUITMENT AND SELECTION OF SALESPEOPLE

Much of the future success of a sales manager depends upon the skill with which he recruits and selects his salespeople. First to be considered are the direct costs of poor selection; the direct cost and dissatisfaction of wasting time on people who are later revealed to be untrainable for selling; the direct cost of transferring, demoting, or discharging people who fail. In addition to direct costs, there is another potential dollar loss. If there is a great turnover in the sales force, prospects and customers begin to believe it is the company that is wrong and not the salesmen. Once buyers begin to think in that direction, it is a signal that some of them are going to change suppliers.

CONDUCTING A PERSONAL INTERVIEW

After the sales questionnaire is reviewed, ask the applicant to come in for a personal interview. The interview should be conducted with the following points in mind.

A
1 Appearance
2 Health and stamina
3 Speaking effectiveness

B
1 Personality
2 Intelligence
3 Experience
4 Achievement

C
1 Attitude
2 Persistence
3 Loyalty

Frequent replacement of sales personnel also has a bad effect on the morale of others in the sales force. Probably nothing else lowers morale faster than the feeling of insecurity caused by too many replacements. Also, competitors may be able to hire away more of the better men, a situation which no sales manager likes to contemplate.

Proper selection of personnel literally means giving salesmen a chance to produce. Few managerial responsibilities are more important than this one, yet few have been more often overlooked. Selecting the right job and the right man to train for that job is no less important than estimating sales potential, planning itineraries, holding meetings, and performing other managerial duties.

Recruitment

Little has been written about recruiting techniques, although this is an important part of the sales manager's job. For example, what should the sales manager use to attract the attention of college students: a high starting salary? job security? exceptional fringe benefits? In a recent study of 5,000 college students throughout the United States, Research Institute of America found that the sales manager who used those appeals would risk failure. Today's young men and women take for granted that they will have money and job security and, therefore, they rank the above-mentioned goals far down on the list of what they want in their new jobs. What would appeal to today's college students?

The survey revealed that incentives such as "opportunity for growth," "opportunity for challenge," a "chance to make a contribution to society," or a "chance to write your own job description" were what these students were looking for. Today's typical college student considers recognition as an individual to be more important than the size of his paycheck, or his seniority rights, or severance pay. Recognition is attained by being a member of a distinct group; the importance of the job; liking people enough to want to sway their behavior; the prospect of adventure and challenge; and freedom from routine. These career goals are far different than those of 25 years ago. Today's students have no concept of what it means to be penniless, or out of a job, and they simply do not put these things first at this time.

The message for today's recruiter of tomorrow's salespeople is: Do not be confused about student goals. Tomorrow's goals may again be for security, seniority, and severance pay. The sales manager must keep up to date on the reasons which attract new people into the sales force. These appeals have changed and they will continue to change in the future.

PROVIDING SELLING SKILLS

After recruiting and selecting has been done, there remains the task of reemphasizing where the new employees will work, what they will do, and how much they are expected to accomplish. Their learning rate may be slow and hesitant, they may lack basic knowledge and good planning habits, but they cannot be permitted to fumble and waste time. They must be taught the ability to sell, an ability that is the result of careful, conscientious, and planned training.

Product knowledge comes first because there is a close relationship between product benefits and features and the quantity and quality of a salesperson's efforts to sell them, and, of course, his success in obtaining orders.

Research in this area has also indicated that salesmen often avoid expending serious effort on products they have found difficult to sell. Usually, these are the products with which the salesmen are the least familiar. When salesmen are thoroughly trained in the benefits, characteristics, uses, and care of a product, their selling efforts and their successful closes increase.

Key Selling Factors

There are certain *key factors,* or practical methods, for selling specific products or services. These key factors can be established by traveling the territories with a number of good, average, and weak salesmen and observing their methods in detail. Then the methods observed are correlated with the orders obtained. Usually, the key factors would be found among the following:

1. The time expended for the interview.
2. Analysis of the prospect's needs.
3. The benefit appeals used in the presentation.
4. The salesmen's use of motivators.
5. Customer questions, salesmen's suggestions, and responses.
6. The use of samples, visual devices, and demonstrations.
7. The use of advertising and promotional materials.
8. The use of catalogs and price lists.
9. The use of questions and trial closes throughout the interview.
10. The degree and character of the effort spent on certain products.
11. The method of handling credits and collections, when this is done by the salesman.

12. The use of special influences, such as reciprocity, contractor relationships, and entertainment.

The key factor may be applied in two ways. First, a training program can be organized in which all salesmen are taught the key factors in obtaining more and larger orders. The success of such a program is sure, because practically every one of the important selling methods is neglected by most salesmen in a large proportion of their calls.

Second, the evaluation of the performance of individual salesmen may be made according to definite standards. This can be done by contrasting the sales techniques of weak salesmen with those of good salesmen, as revealed by the size of their respective orders. Sales managers may employ appropriate training methods to improve the performance of individual salesmen. Weak salesmen who do not respond satisfactorily to training or who do not follow the desired pattern are easily identified and proper action may be taken.

Motivation to Sell

Successful motivation depends largely on good managerial relations with the salesman. The salesman wants to know in *advance* about things that may affect him. He wants to be kept *informed* about company activities which may interest his prospects or about which his prospects may read in the newspapers. In this and many other ways, his stature with the trade is enhanced and his company's reputation is built.

The salesman's status as a part of the managerial team may often be enhanced. In this respect he should be given a feeling of responsibility for a profitable performance. This could be done by keeping a simple profit or loss statement for his territory. Sales margins on different products may be set up and gross profit may be calculated for his sales volume. From this figure, monthly or quarterly deductions may be made for his salary and expenses. The remainder would be the net selling profit or loss arising from his management of the territory.

This simple procedure will develop the salesman's judgment as a businessman and will give direction, meaning, and force to his performance, so that he will make effective use of time and key selling methods in exploiting the market and prospect potentials.

Moreover, the salesmen should have *psychological,* as well as monetary recognition for his superior selling. The sales manager recognizes his salesmen by praising them whenever it is justified and by reprimanding them whenever it is needed. They are *recognized* when managers correct them, without offending, in private. Recognition is given when the manager takes every opportunity to say and do those things which will make the salesman feel more necessary.

Every salesman likes to have his sales manager take an interest in his *personal problems,* his civic activities, or his hobbies. He likes good, honest advice and criticism, and he dislikes sarcasm or ridicule. He likes to have the sales manager listen when he has something to say, and he likes to know that the boss's door is always open to him. This is motivation at its best!

Probably the most important factor in the area of motivation is that the salesman must be made to feel that he is an important individual on an important team. He must have confidence in other team members, including his management. Enthusiastic, intelligent leadership, which motivates the salesman to make better use of his time, opportunities, and selling methods, will gain in response, increased selling effort, and greater sales volume. This kind of treatment is part of the salesman's psychological reward and provides an incentive which often outweighs his monetary incentives to produce.

Territorial Readjustment

Readjustment of territories is often necessary to make the opportunities of different salesmen more nearly equal. The potentials of different counties and cities within each territory are also important in establishing a salesman's headquarters and in helping him to distribute his effort. Salesmen often cover the cities in which their headquarters are located and neglect other cities because they do not know the sales opportunities in them, or because the territory is too large. When the sizes of territories are reduced, thus reducing travel time, and the number of salesmen is increased, then sales volume and gross profit will increase at a faster rate than sales expenses.

A general estimate of city and county purchasing power may be useful in measuring geographic potentials. However, in the case of industrial goods, such an estimate should usually be combined with other factors that affect the market for particular products.

Apportionment of Sales Effort

Apportionment of sales effort according to customer potentials should be made for economy and efficiency. It is characteristic of every industry, every group of wholesalers, and every kind of retailer that a large proportion of the business produces or handles a very small share of the sales volume. For example, one company producing industrial goods did not realize that 20 percent of its customers accounted for 90 percent of its sale volume, and that to obtain the additional 10 percent, four times as many customers had to be contacted and sold at a far greater unit sales cost.

The *uniform call routine* is often pursued by salesmen, with the approval of the sales managers, although this procedure may not be justified by the size and needs of their customers and prospects.

One sales manager, for example, found that 55 percent of his salesmen's calls were made on 80 percent of their customers and prospects and that they resulted in 3 percent of the sales volume. At the same time, practically no calls were made on a substantial number of major prospects, and the frequency of calls on all prospects was declining. A coal company found that 12 percent of its customers bought 88 percent of its volume, but these customers received only 8 percent of the salesmen's calls. This is a common situation in many companies.

Adequate adjustment of the call rates requires more than simple apportionment of calls to potential volume of customers and prospects. Profits and losses incurred in serving different sizes and types of customers must be considered. As previously explained, this requires that the costs of solicitation and service to each customer be determined and deducted from the gross earned sales to each of them. In this manner, the profitable and unprofitable sizes and types of customers can be determined, and the kind and amount of *effort* can be adjusted to make the accounts more profitable.

The sales manager must show his salesmen that the remedy for this situation is to shift their efforts to better opportunities and to find less expensive ways of soliciting business from the unprofitable trade. One of the first steps is to analyze every customer and prospect with the salesman, estimate the potential of each, and decide on the most profitable call frequency.

Subsequent steps may include: reduction in call frequency; use of junior salesmen who cost less for each call; use of mail orders; more frequent use of the telephone; customer pickup of small orders; use of a minimum-order rule, and the transfer of small customers to jobbers. Usually both volume and profits are increased by gearing salesmen's effort to their market and customer opportunities. This is one of the primary jobs of the sales manager and should be included in a consideration of action time.

Increasing the Salesman's Action Time

Action time is the time actually spent in the presence of a qualified prospect. There are indications that approximately half of the average salesman's time is spent with potential buyers. Much of the remaining 50 percent is wasted because of poor planning by both sales managers and salesmen. Increasing the number of calls a salesman can squeeze into one working day is perhaps the clearest and easiest way to reduce the high cost of selling. This requires giving close attention to time-saving measures such as these:

- More branch offices.
- Relieving salespeople of nonselling tasks.
- Reducing paper-work load.
- Improving sales-call planning.
- More selling by phone.
- Closer field supervision.
- Better use of waiting time.
- Conducting time study.
- Continuous sales training.

To impress the sales force with the importance of increasing action time, the sales manager might prepare a checklist such as the following. A copy should then be given to each salesperson and discussed with them individually, or in a group session.

TIME CHECKLIST

Time is your chief asset. Are you turning your TIME into money? Check yourself on your use of your most valuable asset. Are you guilty of:

- Late starts from the office?
- Neglecting those prospects who are in their offices before nine, after five, and on Saturdays and Sundays?
- Calls on friendly accounts that do little but bolster your ego?
- Excessive trips back to sales headquarters?
- Repeated call-backs on buyers who have little business potential to offer?
- Poor routing of sales calls, resulting in jumps from one side of the territory to the other?

- Failure to make appointments with prospects, resulting in excessive waiting time or no interview?
- Inadequate sales presentation, few sales aids, poor planning?
- Too much time spent in socializing with prospects and customers?
- Little or no planning or organizing of your selling time?
- Failure to stress the importance of more and better calls each day?
- Failure to discipline yourself?
- Failure to realize that time is your most important asset?

APPRAISAL AND DEVELOPMENT OF SALESPEOPLE

One of the most difficult tasks of a sales manager is to appraise the production of his salesmen, because business conditions vary, customers are different, and salesmen are distinct individuals. Although difficult, it is necessary to measure the production of salespeople, for the cost of selling is very high and sales managers must be sure that the company is getting its money's worth.

Sales managers often make errors in evaluating their people, and the first—and possibly the most vital—error is rating their personnel on sales volume alone. They evaluate on the number of sales calls made by each salesperson. They compare each salesperson's current sales calls with the same period last year or some other period of time.

Evaluating on sales volume by itself is wrong because it alone doesn't tell much about the profit or loss being made by each salesperson. Unless this fact is known, a salesperson can lose his company money and no one will know why. Some salespeople will concentrate on marginal accounts which may be so competitive that they have to cut the price to obtain the order.

Making calls is important, but only if they result in profitable sales. Of course, if salespeople are expected to service their accounts, then a standard routing of their calls may be necessary. However, paying salespeople to make friendly calls, to socialize, to do routine servicing, can be too expensive.

Sales managers who have had successful selling experience usually expect their salespeople to use the same techniques which succeeded for them and judge their sales force on that basis. This is natural, but it is often a mistake, for a selling method used successfully by one person might not work with another. Market conditions change, so the salesperson may face different problems, or he may have a radically different personality and approach than his sales manager.

The sales manager without selling experience faces even more difficult problems. He often gives his salespeople too much freedom because his knowledge of selling techniques may be very limited. He may simply not know what his salesmen should do.

One very common error is to compare a salesperson's current performance with the past. This can be very misleading. For example, some months have more working days than others; there are also changes in price and competition, and variations in territory and products which make this kind of comparison unreliable. It is better to appraise cumulative annual, semiannual, or quarterly programs toward the target objective.

Selling methods should also be appraised not only for salesmanship skills, but also to determine if the salesman follows company policies. However, if he is producing enough sales volume it may not be prudent to inquire into his selling methods, unless the sales manager wants to learn something from an expert salesperson.

Methods for Appraising

There are four very good yardsticks for appraising the performance of salespeople. These yardsticks enable the sales manager to base his appraisal on figures, and therefore provide him with concrete, factual information for his evaluation. These yardsticks are:

1. Volume in sales dollars.
2. Number of calls made on customers.
3. Number of new accounts opened.
4. Dollars spent in entertaining prospects and customers.

Other items can also affect a salesperson's performance and the sales manager will need to use his personal judgment in those areas. For example:

1. Amount of time spent in office.
2. Personal appearance.
3. Completeness and accuracy of sales orders.
4. Promptness in submitting reports.
5. Extent to which salesperson sells his company.
6. Accuracy in quoting prices and delivery dates to his customers.
7. Knowledge of his business.
8. Planning and routing his calls.

The sales manager has to make judgments in these areas, for they can affect a salesperson's performance. However, the sales manager should not allow his judgment on these items to outweigh the importance given the four items that can be measured in figures.

Appraising Profit Contribution

An important part of the performance appraisal involves what is known as *profit contribution,* or what is left of the sales dollar after direct costs and the salesperson's controllable expenses are subtracted.

Determining a salesman's contribution to profit involves markup. For example, imagine that a salesperson makes a $1,000 sale. If direct material and direct labor costs total $600, the salesperson would be given a credit for a $400 contribution. But if the salesperson lowers the price by $50 to close the sale, he would contribute only $350 profit toward overhead and selling expenses. Additional costs such as price cuts, nonreimbursed overtime or make-overs caused by him, claims or credits due to his errors, and expenses over his budget amount would also reduce his profit contribution.

Analyzing each sale this way will enable the sales manager to think in terms of the dollars his salespeople bring in to cover expense and profit. Salespeople must be urged to sell products with high profit margins, or if they sell low profit items, they must bring in a big sales volume.

The direct costs for each product or product line do not need to be totally accurate. Standard costs or annual estimates can be used so long as the salespeople know what figures or numbers their performance is based on. For example, product line A might have a profit contribution credit of 40 percent of the sales dollar; product line B, a contribution of 25 percent; and product line C, a contribution of 10 percent. This is aside from any salesperson's controllable costs.

Appraising Number of Calls

The number of calls a salesperson can make on his accounts depends largely on how he sells. One salesperson might average four calls a day, another six, another eight. Consider a person who averages six daily calls during 200 working days in a year. He then has 1,200 calls. He can apportion his calls among prospects in terms of the number of calls he feels he can afford to make on each for the sales volume he wants.

One method of determining each salesman's average number of calls is to have each turn in regular reports of calls made; another way is to have each record dates of calls on account cards. Many sales managers prefer the second method, because they do not have time to read all the reports every week. Furthermore, to discover what a salesperson is really doing would require an account-by-account personal review.

Weekly figures can be used if needed, but year-to-date figures average out the very good or the very bad periods and make it easier to determine the progress of each salesperson toward his annual objectives.

Using Appraisals to Correct

If the salesperson's record reveals that he is off target by 10 percent or more, corrective action is indicated. A review should be held of the number of calls he has made on each worthwhile account, as well as of whatever he feels are his accomplishments and problems.

Unless the salesperson is given a personal account of his weaknesses and strengths, nothing will be accomplished toward building and developing his sales ability. Simply telling him to improve without helping him is worthless. These are some of the important things a sales manager can do to help in the development of his people:

- Give each salesperson more day-to-day guidance and direction.
- Accompany him on calls to provide coaching.
- Have regular sales meetings on topics of interest to salespeople.
- Increase sales promotion activities.
- Transfer accounts to other salespeople if there is unsatisfactory effort or progress.
- Establish tighter control over price variations.
- Increase or reduce selling price.
- Add new products or services.
- Increase financial rewards and incentives.
- Transfer, replace, or discharge the salesperson.

Another important device is to obtain the salesperson's agreement on his goals for the next selling period—a full year, for example. The important points for agreement are:

- His total profit contribution in dollars.
- His profit contribution in dollars for each major product line; each territory; each of 20 to 30 new and additional customers.

- His agreement should also be obtained about the expense budgets within which he is to remain during the next year. These would include, for example, his total expense budget in dollars, and his budget in dollars for travel, customer entertainment, telephone, and miscellaneous expenses.

- The salesperson should also be helped to plan his itinerary and the number of calls he should make on both new and old accounts during the coming year or other period of time.

APPRAISING AND DEVELOPING SALES MANAGERS

How effective are sales managers? The obvious answer to this question is found in the sales production of the unit managed. However, constructive sales management does more for the business than merely produce sales, important as they might be. It also produces leadership. Therefore, something more than a sales total is needed to accurately measure the effectiveness of a sales management operation. Such a measure is found in a rating plan that serves top management in appraising and evaluating the work of those responsible for field management of salesmen. Managers are rated in this way on (1) leadership, (2) capacity for growth, (3) ability to develop men, and (4) executive capacity and skills.

The usual procedure in sales organizations where there are regional or divisional managers charged with the production of a group of branch sales units is to have these managers make the appraisals. Then they review the appraisals with the branch managers, after which they are forwarded to the general sales manager for evaluation and comparison with previous appraisals.

There are a variety of these appraisal forms in use. They vary according to which qualities a company considers to be most important. Thus, a distributing operation might require more emphasis on product knowledge, less on sales techniques. A specialty selling organization might attach greatest importance to knowledge of the prospect's needs and the application of the product to those needs. In any event, in making the evaluation the general sales manager weighs each qualification so as to arrive at an average rating which he may compare to the averages of previous appraisals.

The basic purpose of appraisals is to assist management in finding and correcting weaknesses in field managers and to increase the individual and group strength of the field management staff. It also serves to reveal training requirements and to locate promising individuals for replacements.

Among the most vital aspects of the sales manager's job are training and motivating his personnel. In this respect he must have the latest skills and techniques at his command, for there is no better way of influencing others than by setting a good example. When the sales manager can put the principles of good training into actual practice, the salesperson's confidence in this training ability will not only increase his selling skills, but also motivate him to perform to the best of his ability.

Although the salesperson's final success will largely be dependent on his innate abilities, drive, and desire for self-improvement, training remains sales management's greatest and most vital opportunity and the most valuable contribution to the continuing effectiveness of the entire selling profession.

POWER POINTS

Sales management is one of the broadest, the most demanding, the most comprehensive, and the most subtle of all professions.

As the reader now knows, the sales manager and his sales force hold a key position in today's economy. Although his role may change in the years ahead, the importance of the sales manager will increase rather than diminish. So far as human relationships and personal skills are concerned, selling will emerge as the most critical step in marketing goods and services in a highly sophisticated consumer economy.

It is important to note that the salesman who is promoted to sales manager has to adjust swiftly. He must learn to be pessimistic and dubious on occasion; to be critical, hardheaded, and ruthless when necessary. He must be a problem-solver and a decision-maker. He must learn to accept and utilize every new method and technique available. His responsibilities broaden. He must realize that he is no longer a salesman; he is part of the management team.

The sales manager is responsible for recruiting and selecting salesmen, and much of his future success is dependent upon how skillfully he performs this part of his job.

He must be able to discover the key factors or most practical methods for selling specific products or services. He must understand and know how to use purchaser's value analysis—for herein will be found the answers to most of the questions potential buyers will ask.

Motivation of his sales force, territorial adjustments, apportionment of sales effort, increasing the action time of salesmen (and himself), and handling appraisals are all part of the modern sales manager's job.

DISCUSSION QUESTIONS AND PROBLEMS

1. Define sales management.
2. What are the steps in the promotional ladder of sales management?
3. What types of salesmen are promoted to sales manager position?
4. Why may it be necessary for a salesman to adjust his attitudes after he becomes a sales manager?
5. Why is recruitment and selection of salespeople important?
6. What is meant by *key selling factors?*
7. What would you do to motivate salesmen?
8. Why is the appraisal of a salesman's work difficult?
9. What is meant by *appraising profit contribution?*
10. How would you use appraisals to correct your salespeople?
11. How would you make salespeople time-conscious?
12. What is the value of periodic appraisals of sales managers?

SELLING PROBLEMS AND PROJECTS

1. A Sales Manager Has Nothing to Do!

Nothing to do, that is, except:

*   To decide what needs to be done.
*   To tell somebody to do it.
*   To listen to reasons why it should not be done, why it should be done in a different way, or why it should be done by somebody else.
*   To prepare arguments in rebuttal that will be convincing and conclusive.
*   To follow up to see if the thing has been done.
*   To discover that it has not been done.
*   To inquire why it has not been done.
*   To listen to excuses from the person who should have done it.
*   To follow up a second time to see if the thing has been done.
*   To wonder if it is not again time to see if the thing has not been done.
*   To wonder if it is not time to discharge a person who does not do a thing, even when asked repeatedy.

- To reflect that the person in question has a wife and seven children, and that certainly no sales manager, except you, in the whole world would put up with him for another moment, and that in all probability any successor would be just as bad and probably worse.

Questions

1. What do you think is the basic thought in this project?

2. What would you add to this analysis of a sales manager's job which might improve his performance?

2. Ted Skrip

My name is Ted Skrip and I started to sell in 1930. It was a very bad year, since we were in the midst of a depression. In addition, no one told me much about selling, except one old-timer who said that enthusiasm made sales when it was combined with friendliness and the ability to make the customer feel important. The old-timer said that's all a good salesman needed to know.

My sales manager told me that enthusiasm was OK, but the law of averages was the real thing. He said, "Just keep on making calls and sooner or later someone will weaken and buy. Eventually you'll run into a weak-willed prospect." I worked very hard on that job, but there were not enough weak-willed prospects around and very few weakened and bought. I didn't earn enough to pay for shoe repairs.

Questions

1. What is wrong with that kind of sales training?

2. What kind of training would you give if you were sales manager?

CHAPTER 26

Selling Your Personal Services

This chapter was prepared for those who are about to enter the job market in search of a good selling job. We have tried to be factual and have limited the content to the actual skills and understandings needed to obtain a good job. We assume that you have already narrowed down your occupational choices, completed your preliminary education, taken stock of your potential abilities and now want to move on to the immediate goal of finding a job.

FACTS ABOUT POTENTIAL EMPLOYERS

Assuming that you have decided on the kind of job you want, your next step is to discover the potential job opportunities in your field and to investigate them in relation to ways in which they might match your qualifications.

Having decided on the company you want to investigate, your next step is to learn its correct full name and its address. Then, try to find the age of the company, where its plants, offices, or stores are located, what its products or services are, what its growth has been, and how its prospects look for the future.

These facts will give you something besides yourself to talk about during your interview, and provide the material to form the questions you should ask. It will help to protect your own interests also. A manufacturer of buggy whips might be recruiting for a new man, but you would want to know something about his potential market before choosing his field as your career. Do not forget to get the interviewer's full name and learn how to spell and pronounce it correctly.

Sources for Company Information

There are a number of publications which can help you research a company. Most of them can be found in any good college or public library. Among the most helpful are:

College Placement Annual, by the College Placement Publications Council.

Thomas' *Register of American Manufacturers.*

Moody's *Manuals.*

Fitch Corporation Manual.

Standard and Poor's *Corporation Records.*

McRae's *Bluebook.*

Pool's *Register of Directors and Executives.*

Dun and Bradstreet Reference Book.

Company annual reports.

Your school's placement office is an excellent source for booklets and other material prepared by various firms for recruiting purposes. You may find detailed information in the company's own literature that is unavailable in general registers.

A stock brokerage office may also be able to supply you with the information you want. If you use library texts, don't wait until the last minute to do your research. Someone else may have the book you need.

YOUR BACKGROUND

Personal Data Sheets

School placement offices may have a standard data sheet which you will be asked to fill out to show a résumé of your activities and work experience. Some companies may also ask you to fill out a similar sheet. In either case, be sure to do so accurately, fully, and neatly. Your data sheets will represent *you* to people who have never seen you. If it is untidy you will be judged accordingly.

Some schools, and a number of companies, prefer that the student develop his own résumé as a supplement to the personal interview.

The Job Résumé

A self-prepared résumé becomes increasingly important if you change jobs in the years after your schooling ends. It is almost indispensable in certain cases, such as application by letter, off-campus interviews, or an intensive job-hunting campaign.

Résumé of John A. Jones for a Sales Position

Age: 22 years
Height: 6' 2"
Weight: 185 pounds
Marital status: Single
Health: Excellent
Home address: 425 Wilson Avenue
                Henderson, Iowa
                Phone—766-1922

Job Objective: A position in sales with the eventual aim of a
                management position commensurate with my
                performance with your company.

Military Status: Member of the National Guard

Date of Availability: February 1, 19—

EDUCATION

Drake University—Des Moines, Iowa—September 19— to June 19—.
    Major—Retailing; Minor—General Business
    Grade point average—2. 65 (out of a possible 4. 0)
Henderson High School—Henderson, Iowa—September 19— to June 19—
    Graduated 28th out of a class of 264

WORK EXPERIENCE

Retailing apprentice—The Utica Department Store, Des Moines, Iowa
    September 19— - June 19—
    This retailing co-op program of Drake University gave me in-
    struction and actual experience in selling, receiving, credit,
    personnel, inventory, and merchandising.
College consultant and salesman—Martin Morris Company, Hender-
    son, Iowa — Summer of 19—
    Duties included planning my own advertising and displays and
    working with buyer on purchases.
Plant laborer—Henderson Corn Processing Company, Henderson,
    Iowa — Summers of 19— and 19—
    Employed with other college students as flying squadron for
    plant work.
Laborer—Nelson Lumber Company, Henderson, Iowa
    Summer of 19—
    Worked in construction and delivery.
Delivery boy—Smith and Johnson Company, Henderson, Iowa
    Summer of 19—
    Delivered furniture and appliances.

EXTRACURRICULAR ACTIVITIES

College: High School:
    President—Interfraternity Council   President—Senior class
    Delegate—Interfraternity Council   Track—4 years
    Vice President— Retailing Club   Football—3 years
    Sec.—Alpha Kappa Psi Frat. (prof.)   A Cappella Choir
    Member—Sigma Phi Epsilon Frat.   Debate Team
        (social)

REFERENCES

(Will be sent upon request.)

Figure 26-1

A good résumé will go a long way toward helping you make a good impression. A really bad résumé can seriously hurt the chances of an applicant who may seem desirable in every other way.

Contents and layout of résumés are as different as the individuals who hunt for jobs. Interviewers and companies also differ as to what they want to see on a résumé. The best guidelines, however, are to keep it simple and to keep it on one page.

Your résumé must be typed. Duplicate copies are acceptable if well done. Be sure to use good quality bond paper.

The résumé must be neat; careless erasures and misspelled words are inexcusable, and either may cost you a chance at a good job. Keep carbon copies to save yourself a rewriting job if the original is lost.

Your use of white space is most important in creating an impression of neatness and orderliness. Space can be used to isolate important points to which you want to draw attention, and sufficient spacing between all elements helps to create a clean, pleasing impression. Many elements crowded too close together result in an untidy appearance.

Your method of organizing the separate sections of your résumé is not as important as the fact that you show *some* kind of orderly, reasonable process. Unless you have proven that you have a better idea, it is wise to stick to a rather conventional, conservative layout with straight lines and ordinary paragraphing. "Gimmick" résumés have occasionally caught the interest of companies, but are best left to professionals, for they can backfire.

Since your major courses in school and your grades in those courses indicate your interests and abilities, you should cover that information in your résumé. Some statement of grades or class ranking is usually expected. Frankness is the wisest policy. Most companies do not limit themselves to seeking only students with high grades. Grades are an important part of the picture, but not the only part.

The student who has worked while attending school and attained good grades should include that information on his résumé. He should definitely state what percent of his college expenses were personally earned, and how many hours per week were usually devoted to working. Significant minor work experience, if it relates in any way to the job you are seeking, may help you, and should be included.

Extracurricular activities should be included. If you have been elected to an honorary, social, or professional group, list them; they indicate your ability to get along with people in a group. Further, if you participated in athletics, that, too, should be mentioned.

It is a fact that nearly everyone has something to offer if he will analyze his abilities, interests, and talents correctly and stress his strong points as they relate to the job he is seeking.

If you can do that successfully in your résumé, and if you follow through with it in your interviews, you need have little doubt that you will, sooner or later, find an organization that has been looking for you.

Rank of Résumé Items

Charles E. Peck, Professor of Business Administration, University of Washington, conducted a survey recently in which he sought to find what employers look for when they hire college graduates as salesmen, and how they evaluated résumés. Figure 26-2 reveals Dr. Peck's findings related to what personnel men of 106 firms considered the most important factors indicating sales potential.

FACTORS INDICATING SALES POTENTIAL*

	Very Important	Important	Little Value	Weighted† Total
Extracurricular Activities ...	54	44	8	410
Related Work Experience ...	49	46	9	392
College Courses	26	65	15	340
High Grades	10	80	16	306
Nonrelated Work Experience .	2	54	46	218

†Weighted total is determined as follows: very important, 5 points; important, 3 points; little value, 1 point. Multiplication of the numbers in the first three columns by the above weights gives the weighted total in the last column.

Source: Charles E. Peck, "Letters and Résumés," *Journal of College Placement,* February 1964, p. 126. Reprinted with permission.

Figure 26-2

DIRECT MAIL CAMPAIGN

There are several ways to arrange for a job interview: by personal investigation, through conversations with employees, friends, acquaintances, recruiters, and advertisements. But one of the very best methods for seeking a good job is through a personal direct mail campaign, because that method shows initiative and ingenuity. Employers like those qualities in an applicant for a sales job.

Initiative and Ingenuity

Regardless of business conditions, a prospective employer is always ready to listen to the person who proves by his method of seeking a job that he has initiative and ingenuity. A mere statement of personal experience and history will not help a job applicant very much. However, when initiative and ingenuity are demonstrated in an impressive way, the value of the applicant's potential service immediately rises in the estimation of an employer. When an applicant can show an employer how he may benefit through hiring him, he automatically raises himself above competing applicants. A direct mail campaign has proven to be highly successful in these respects.

The practice of advertising one's self and one's abilities in a direct mail campaign is a procedure which has produced remarkable results. A single firm in New York state located over 19,000 openings for clients this way in a five-year period. The reasons are obvious. When an employer realizes that the enterprising applicant has undertaken a personal promotion campaign of his own to locate a position, he reasons that the applicant is a man who believes in himself and his job— to the extent of paying money for the privilege of placing his merits before possible employers. The employer would rather deal with a person like this than with many of the men who answer his want ads.

An effective employment campaign frequently discloses a hidden market for the applicant's service. Not all selling vacancies are advertised in the newspaper or find their way to the card index of an employment agency. Many have not taken definite shape in an employer's mind. Thus, when an employer receives a carefully prepared application in which an applicant describes his ability and experiences in a way that recommends his services strongly, the employer is inclined to think he could use him and arrange an interview. Yet, before the job seeker's letter was seen, the vacancy was only an idea, not a fact.

Letter of Application

When the applicant is ready to write his letter, he should give some attention to its physical features. The first step in selling is to attract favorable attention. The successful salesman realizes how important his personal appearance is in accomplishing this purpose, and the same quality that helps him achieve selling results will help his sales letter receive consideration when it reaches the employer's desk.

A good grade of white bond paper, 8½ by 11 inches, should be used. A small quantity of such paper may be purchased with envelopes to match at almost any stationery store.

If possible, the stationery should be printed with the applicant's name, address, and telephone number. A neat letterhead increases prestige. If this is not possible, the applicant's name and address should be typed in the upper right-hand corner.

A businessman—through habit—reads typing more easily than handwriting, and gets a better business impression from a typed letter than from a handwritten one.

Multigraphed or mimeographed letters should not be used. Facsimile letters, regardless of how skillfully prepared and executed, are apt to be recognized for what they are by the observant employer. They will lead him to the conclusion that the applicant is too lazy to write a personal letter, or that he is searching for a job on a mass-production basis. Also, in a personally typed letter, the applicant can emphasize his reasons for desiring to work for the particular company and use the name of the employer several times throughout, such as, "When may I call and talk it over, Mr. _____?"

If an applicant cannot type, he should have a stenographer prepare his letter. The cost is nominal and the letter is likely to be much more acceptable to the reader.

The direct mail campaign is not necessarily expensive. On the contrary, it is much cheaper and often more effective than other methods commonly used, such as situation advertisements and employment agencies. Many people have successfully conducted mail campaigns for a total cost of less than fifty dollars.

Written Request for Interview

Personnel men do not want a complete autobiography. But they do want enough information in the letter to arouse their interest and to give the company assurance that the person's background is suitable for sales work. The recent college graduate can accomplish this in a one-page typewritten letter and a one- or two-page typewritten or reproduced résumé.

The applicant needs to give accurate information and he must demonstrate an ability to express himself clearly in writing. Personnel people react unfavorably to an applicant who sends a letter that reflects lack of care in preparation. As was mentioned in connection with résumés, inaccuracies in figures or spelling, grammatical errors, and a careless appearance indicate unfavorable evidence of the applicant's future job performance.

Other weaknesses to avoid in presentation of the written application include wordiness, poor organization, and an overly clever or insincere tone.

Letter Openings

How letters are started, or opened, is of great importance. Figure 26-3 illustrates the facts about opening statements that were discovered by Charles E. Peck in the survey previously mentioned.

HOW LETTER OPENINGS WERE RATED*

Openings	Good	Average	Poor	Weighted† Total
1. Please consider my application for a position in your sales department. My qualifications include 12 months of part-time selling, a college degree in business administration, and a sincere interest in selling.	63	28	10	409
2. I am deeply interested in the sales field and am seeking a position with a company, such as yours, which offers a chance to progress toward challenging positions of management responsibility. Please consider me an applicant for such a position.	49	28	22	351
3. Enclosed is a résumé of my background and qualifications. Will you please consider me an applicant for a sales position.	24	45	30	285
4. I would like to apply for a position with your sales force.	18	41	38	251
5. Mr. Alan McGregor (assume you know Mr. McGregor) suggested I send you my qualifications for a job in your sales department.	21	31	44	242
6. If you are looking for a salesman who has all-out desire, enthusiasm, and versatility, then I'd like to talk with you.	20	21	55	218

†Weighted total determined as follows: good, 5 points; average, 3 points; poor, 1 point. Multiplication of the numbers in the first three columns by the above weights gives the weighted total in the last column.

Source: Charles E. Peck, "Letters and Résumés," *Journal of College Placement*, February 1964, p. 126. Reprinted with permission.

Figure 26-3

A Successful Letter

The letter in Figure 26-4 was used by a student of one of the authors, with excellent results. With certain small adaptations this letter can be used by anyone with a good chance of success.

SAMPLE LETTER REQUESTING INTERVIEW

Heading

1800 Peters Gate
East Meadow, L.I.,
New York 10203
January 23, 1973

Inside Address

Mr. William J. Childs
Eutectic Molding Company
223 Canal Street
New York 10006, N.Y.

Salutation

Dear Mr. Childs:

You are always searching for prospective salesmen with potential—salesmen who have had experience in your kind of business, who have prepared themselves educationally, who understand your needs, and who want to work and succeed in your kind of business.

Body

For these reasons, you may want to give me an interview so that I may tell you in person why I would be a success in your organization.

A personal data sheet is enclosed with this letter. After you have examined it, would you write me at the above address, or call me at Pershing 9-1788.

Close

Thank you.

Very truly yours,

John M. Anchor

John M. Anchor

Signature

Enclosure

Figure 26-4

The Time to Mail the Letter

It is important to know the best time for a prospective employer to receive an application. Wednesday is the best day of the week; Thursday the next best. The businessman has less to occupy his mind on these days than at any other time during the week. The letter should arrive in the afternoon, if possible, because the mail is not so heavy then and there is less competition for the employer's time. It is advisable to avoid the first, fifteenth, and the last of the month; this is when bills arrive and the employer is ordinarily not in a favorable frame of mind to consider new proposals. Mailing letters directly before and directly after holidays should also be avoided.

Apply to the Person in Charge

It is usually a good idea to address an application letter to the attention of the sales supervisor or the manager of the division or department in which the work is sought. The application will then be presented to the person who can say yes or no in each case. If the executive's name cannot be found in the library, it would be worthwhile to telephone the company and get it from a secretary or from some other responsible person.

HANDLING THE INTERVIEW

Interviewers are continually amazed at the number of applicants who drift into job interviews without any apparent preparation, and with only a foggy idea of what they are going to say. Their manner says, "Well, here I am." And that's the end of it in more ways than one.

Others, although they do not intend to do so, create an impression of indifference by behaving as though they'd dropped in between dates. The young man who reports to an interview wearing moccasins and a sports coat, who leans back in his chair and lights up a cigarette, seems to be saying, "What can you do for me?" He is definitely making a bad impression.

Hard-to-hire Characters

Do you fit any one of these hard-to-hire categories? If so, you'd better reorient your thinking.[1]

1. Robert W. Wheeler, *Sales/Marketing Today,* July 1966, p. 23.

I-need-a-job character. This man makes no specific effort to sell his specific abilities. He invites the personnel director to analyze his talents and fit him wherever needed. Too vague an approach, says Bob Wheeler, talent scout for Goodyear Tire and Rubber Co. "He should first know his abilities, then present them with enthusiasm."

Inferior character. The inferior character's approach is a hat-in-hand approach, "I don't suppose you have a job for me, do you?" And he is right, Wheeler points out. Personnel usually doesn't.

Resentful character. The resentful job seeker is mad and it shows more clearly than he supposes. The only solution, says Wheeler, is to get rid of resentments, or leave them outside the door of the personnel office.

I-know-someone character. Perhaps he does, but it's far better to know *something* than someone. "Don't name-drop," Wheeler advises.

I'm-a-clam character. The "clam" presents a challenge to the interviewer, but he should make sure that when he does speak, his words are proverbial pearls of wisdom. "The prospect who impresses me most," Wheeler continues, "is the sincere man who presents himself in a straightforward way, with a smile.

"Grades are not the magna cum laude reason we hire a prospect. Here, it's a team operation. We look for a prospect with a well-balanced personality who has the desire to succeed. His fuse should be burning so strongly that you can smell the smoke. If he's properly motivated he's the kind of man we want."

Preparation for the Interview

When an applicant is selling his personal services, he should walk into an employer's office with a firm determination to work as hard and as intelligently to secure the job as he will to hold it. He must convince the prospective employer that he is the man being sought, that he will be a distinctly valuable asset to the business.

The applicant's appearance counts, too. The employer wants a certain kind of service, ability, and experience, but he wants it backed by certain personal qualities and character. The applicant's appearance and what he says and does are selling factors in the interview.

Therefore, as mentioned before, the applicant should check himself. His head should be carried erect. He should be well mannered throughout. He should not put his hat on the employer's desk, or do any of the things a well-bred person would not do. He should be natural, courteous, friendly, and firm. These are among the many details which influence a favorable impression, or a subconscious objection to an applicant.

The whole interview should be planned. It may be divided into four phases, just as you would divide a sales talk for a product: (1) Start; (2) Body of the interview; (3) Handling objections; (4) The close. The first few moments of the interview, his way of greeting the interviewer, and the manner in which he introduces his sales talk will largely determine the applicant's success.

Starting the Interview

The personal interview really begins with the applicant's arrival in the reception room. He should tell the receptionist, in a friendly and courteous way, that he has an appointment, and give his name. Making a good first impression on every firm member he meets is important in setting the mood for the actual interview.

You have learned that it is critical to use the right approach in those moments when you're seated across the desk from a man who does the hiring.

In this case, let's pretend it's B. M. Barrett, Personnel Manager, Montgomery Ward, Chicago, who has screened thousands of young men for jobs. The applicant may start like this:

APPLICANT (smiling): "Good morning, Mr. Barrett, I'm Joseph Brown. You suggested that I see you this morning about the position as sales trainee. I know you are a very busy man, Mr. Barrett, and I appreciate the time you have given me. So to save your time I have prepared a résumé and completed a sample application blank. Here they are."

Note what Joseph Brown did to get off to a fast start and a successful conclusion:

1. He pronounced the employer's name correctly.
2. He gave his name clearly.
3. He complimented the employer.
4. He was businesslike.
5. He demonstrated—showed—something.
6. He got down to business quickly.
7. He made the employer feel important.
8. He averted many questions by giving the employer prepared material.

Body of the Interview

After he has been introduced to a person with whom he has an appointment, it is up to the applicant to make a complete and convincing demonstration. In a few, well-chosen words he should summarize his experience, his training, his qualifications, why he is applying, and why he feels confident that he will be a successful salesman. He should try to adapt and fit his past experience and training to the requirements before him. He should forget the "I-am-looking-for-an-opportunity" approach. Statements of that nature are suspect, and the applicant's air and his manner will get the impression across far better than the spoken word. Besides, he knows that opportunity is there or he would not be applying, and the employer is interested only in what he hopes to receive from an applicant, not in what he can give him!

In summarizing his qualifications, it is important for the applicant to be completely familiar with his own personal history. The reason for preparing a résumé, or personal data sheet, is that it helps him to present his case easily, logically, naturally, and clearly, so that his facts have benefit value. Just as a salesman memorizes and rehearses his benefit sales points until he can give them naturally and convincingly, so it will pay an applicant to memorize his benefit points and to practice presenting them before a mirror until he can give a convincing sales talk to an interviewer.

It is the applicant's job during the interview to tell why he selected the employer's firm, why he thinks he would make a good salesperson for the company, and how his qualifications fit in with the employer's requirements. The employer often does not see how an applicant's training and experience actually enable him to perform adequately until he is told. The applicant should also be prepared for questions. Ordinarily, at the beginning of the interview, he will be asked to speak about himself; but, if he has a prepared personal data sheet, he can place a copy of it in the employer's hands immediately after the salutations are over and use it as his organized method of presentation.

Handling Obstacles

Unfortunately, many applicants are disqualified by an apparent lack of experience. When the employer tells an applicant that he has not had enough experience, it is either a challenge to him to prove his fitness, or it is a kind way of telling him that he is not qualified. Employers naturally want to know what the applicant can do. His experience—what he has already done—is to the employer the most obvious index of what the applicant can and will do for him.

The applicant's experience may be limited, but he has been studying many subjects and has probably worked part time after school and during vacations. The employer may look upon a person's training superficially until its value is explained as preparation for the given position. The applicant's experience may not have been exactly that of the job under consideration, but it may be the most useful preparation for that job. The job seeker must know *why*, and be able to tell the employer *why* he is a logical choice for the position.

An applicant who lacks experience nevertheless has his personality, his intelligence, his ability to talk interestingly and convincingly, and, perhaps, some sales training or related experience to offer as positive qualifications. If these assets fail to overcome the experience factor, he might back up his confidence with a "no result, no pay" offer.

Most employers will weigh an applicant's probable future to their organizations. They will consider him not only for what he is but also for what they think he will be. It is the applicant's business to present his qualifications so that these prospective values will be obvious. In this situation the applicant's training, ability, personality, and character count far more than his actual experience for the work.

Handling the Salary Problem

At one point or another in every interview that leads to employment, the salary question has to be settled. It is advisable for the applicant not to be overly anxious about the salary. He must use sales discretion, just as the employer uses his bargaining power. He must avoid the appearance of a flat or blunt demand, but if the employer asks, the applicant might suggest a figure that opens the way for negotiations and indicates the range for discussion.

The applicant may state that he wants a certain amount, but he will not ask to have it guaranteed until the employer knows what he is going to get for it. Sometimes it is a good idea for the applicant to say that he needs a certain income to take care of living expenses, or that he will start at a certain salary and work on a bonus arrangement by which it will be possible for him to earn the salary he originally had in mind. The skillful handling of this part of the interview is a very important step in securing the position and in getting started on a satisfactory salary basis.

When the employer asks, "What are your salary requirements?" or "What are your ideas of salary?" possibly the best reply an applicant can make is "Mr. Employer, it is obvious that I do not know the labor market. I really do not know what the going salary is for this kind of job. I respect your judgment and would much rather have you suggest the salary."

This reply places the salary problem where it belongs—with the employer. It places him a little bit on the defensive and the applicant retains at least partial command of the situation. The applicant is also in the position of not underbidding for the job and not overbidding. In either of those cases he would probably lose, but if he keeps the responsibility with the employer, he cannot lose.

How to Close the Interview

The minute the applicant feels that the interviewer is favorably impressed and that all important steps have been covered, he should stop selling himself. He should start settling the details. The applicant should not ask the employer if he wants to hire him. He should use the skills he has learned about the *assumption close*: He assumes that he is wanted and tactfully starts discussing his services just as if the employer had actually agreed to hire him. This method sells personal service as surely as it sells products.

The applicant should leave the interviewer with a good impression, so that he can follow up the interview if he wishes. After two or three weeks have elapsed, the applicant can telephone and inquire if his application is still being considered, or he might prefer to write a brief letter. In his letter he might express his continued interest in the position and ask the interviewer to indicate if he had reached a decision. Further follow-up is usually not necessary.

When a number of persons are being interviewed for a position, it is not always possible for the interviewer to indicate immediately whether an applicant is acceptable. The applicant should not be foolish enough, therefore, to demand an immediate answer. If he does demand such an answer, he will probably receive a negative reply. Neither should the applicant indicate that he questions the good faith of the prospective employer when the employer says, "I'll let you know." He should leave his résumé and a neat copy of his application with the employer, so that it may be referred to at any time. These will act somewhat as a silent salesman.

Postinterview Notes

When a person is applying for more than one position he will want to keep a record of each interview. Information something like the following should be written out soon after the interview. It will serve to refresh the memory.

Date and time:

Place:

Company:

Company address:

Interviewer's full name:

Age of company:

Growth of company:

Where would I be working?:

Notes:

Salary figure discussed:

Résumé left:

Further contacts indicated:

POWER POINTS

In these days of increasing competition, you must have certain skills to obtain any job. Good selling jobs are more and more difficult to find, but if you know how to get the job you want and how to advance in it, your future can be a happy, successful one.

Employers nearly always prefer to hire those graduates who did well in their school work. High scholarship and intelligence, however, are not the only requirements. Every aspect of an applicant's background and the impression he makes during the personal interview are all considered by an employer.

In spite of what we often hear, individuals are not "cut out" for some particular job or vocation. Every vocational test shows that any person with common sense can succeed in a great many jobs. Your question should not be "What am I cut out for?" but "What occupation can I train myself for?" Start your job hunting with a personal analysis of yourself, your capacities, your abilities, your interests. If you believe you need help with your analysis, ask experts. Practically every school has an occupational guidance expert to assist students. These people can tell you whether or not you belong in certain job fields. The particular job you want is up to you.

Sources for available job information are plentiful: friends, relatives, acquaintances, help-wanted advertisements, former employers, and instructors.

Many employers prefer a letter that asks for an interview. This letter must be carefully prepared, informative, businesslike, and brief.

It should defer to the prospective employer, be original, two or three paragraphs in length, have a neat appearance, and be accompanied by a personal data sheet, often called a *résumé*, which may be duplicated.

Some large companies require applicants to complete standardized application blanks. These blanks can usually be obtained from the company employment department and frequently require much detailed information and a photograph. The blank should be typewritten to receive preferred treatment, and every item should be neat and meticulous as to details.

Preparation for the personal interview should follow the principles already suggested for product presentations. First, you must present a well-groomed appearance; second, you should be able to reveal high ethical standards and a positive attitude; third, you should be well informed about the company; fourth, you should present orderly facts about yourself. Be sure to review your presentation before the interview.

Be prepared to answer the employer's questions about your work experience, your education, your attitudes, beliefs, opinions, and traits. Have replies for these specific questions:

"Why do you want to work for this company?"

"Why do you want this particular job?"

"Why do you believe you can be successful in this job?"

When the interview seems to be ending, don't prolong it. But before going, express appreciation and extend thanks to the interviewer for his time. Then leave quickly and quietly.

You may need to follow up the interview with a phone call or a letter, if you do not receive an answer within a reasonable time. The employer should not be rushed. If you get the job, fine; if you do not get the job, sit down and try to discover the flaw in your presentation, behavior, or appearance. Sooner, or later, you will be successful.

DISCUSSION QUESTIONS AND PROBLEMS

---

1. Review your school record. Study it in the light of what you have learned in this chapter. Assume that you are an employer seeking a new salesman. Would you employ a person with a similar record? Why or why not?

2.   Which four rating books would you study for information about a company for whom you might like to sell?

3.   If a sales manager asked you the following three *surprise* questions right at the start of an interview, how would you answer him?

   a. What can I do for you?

   b. What can you tell me about yourself?

   c. Why are you interested in this company?

4.   A few sales managers like to do most of the talking and judge applicants by their reactions—the interest, comprehension, and responses revealed. These are the toughest of all with whom to deal. Why do they prefer to do the talking?

5.   A favorite question asked of job applicants by sales managers is "What do you plan to be doing ten years from now?" A popular alternate question is "How much money do you expect to earn in ten years?" Why are these questions asked?

6.   The usual time allotment for an interview is between 20 and 30 minutes. What should you do and say when you feel the interview is ending?

7.   Many personnel men want applicants to send them a one-page sincere and personalized letter of application. What do they want in the content?

8.   When a personnel man studies a letter and a résumé, what part of the content does he consider most important?

9.   What is the most important item indicating potential ability according to Professor Peck's survey? Why do you suppose employers chose this item?

10. Review the wording of the best letter opening in Figure 26-2. Why is this opening outstanding?

11. To what do personnel men react most unfavorably in a letter of application for a selling job? Why?

12. Should an interview be followed up? Why?

SELLING PROBLEMS AND PROJECTS

1.   Vinnie Vincent Case

During an interview Vinnie was asked if he always got right into a school assignment and turned it in ahead of time. He answered, "I'm afraid I don't always get assignments turned in ahead of time. I sometimes have a tendency to put a thing off until the last minute. However, I have never turned in a term paper or major assignment after they were due. I was never late with them. And I am sure that the supervisors I've had on my last two jobs will be glad to tell you that my work for them was thorough and accurate, and both asked me to return to the job the following summer."

Questions

1.   Did this individual say too much? Did he impair his chances for employment?

2.   Is the plain, unembroidered truth always the best answer to a question?

3.   Is it possible that a frank admission such as this might be a disadvantage?

4.   How would you grade this applicant for his reply?

2.   Herman Hammerlocker, Recruiter

Herman Hammerlocker was speaking about job applicants and interviews. He said, "Be neat, wear a tie and jacket, be careful to keep your 'cool.' If you are argumentative you may give the impression that you cannot get along with people, much less customers. Don't get carried away with your own conversation. Let the interviewer ask the questions and make up his mind based on your replies.

"If you are nervous, admit it and your frankness will be appreciated. But don't stare out the window; give the interviewer your full attention. Don't bring up money. If you are considered favorably the interviewer will tell you how much to expect. Above all be on time for the interview.

"These may seem to be suggestions you do not need, but they are those of many employers who will hire the job seekers. The first impression you make may be the most important you will ever make."

Questions

1.   Should the interviewer ask all the questions? Doesn't the job seeker have any rights?

2.   Suppose the interviewer does not mention salary. Should you ask about it?

3.   In view of the statements in this case, is the method for starting the interview mentioned in the text advisable for everyone?

4.   Would you want to work for a sales manager who has the views expressed in this case?

INDEX